T0153853

John Paul II,
Islam and the Middle East

SOCIETAS
(Series)

BOGDAN SZLACHTA
(Editor)

37

Dorota Rudnicka-Kassem

John Paul II, Islam and the Middle East

The Pope's Spiritual Leadership in Developing
a Dialogical Path for the New History
of Christian-Muslim Relations

Reviewer:
Prof. dr hab. Krzysztof Kościelniak

Editor:
Adam Świątek

Cover design:
Judi Kassem

Graphic assistance:
Emilia Dajnowicz

Layout:
Małgorzata Manterys-Rachwał

This publication was subsidized
by the Department of International and Political Studies of the Jagiellonian University.

ISBN 978-83-7638-186-2

KSIĘGARNIA AKADEMICKA
6 św. Anny St., 31-008 Kraków
telephone/fax: 012 431-27-43, 012 663-11-67
e-mail: akademicka@akademicka.pl

Online bookstore:
www.akademicka.pl

To the memory of
my mother Maria and my father Bronisław

Table of Contents

Acknowledgments

The work on this book, including the research on John Paul II's documents and actions related to the issue of his dialogue with Islam and its followers, was for me a fascinating scholarly venture. While the narrative, analysis and all the assessments are entirely my responsibility, I have a great pleasure to express my thanks to those whose counsel, assistance and support made the work possible.

Special thanks go to the scholars from the Institute of Islamic Studies at McGill University in Montreal, among them professors Issa J. Boullata, A. Üner Turgay, Donald P. Little, Wael B. Hallaq and the late Charles J. Adams, who encouraged and supported me through the challenging and at times painful process of enlarging the scope of my research, namely putting my primarily literary focus into an interreligious, cross-cultural and interdisciplinary perspective. I am also grateful to the staff of the Islamic Studies Library and in particular Ms. Salwa Ferahian, the head of the public service, and Adam Gacek, the former Director, for counsel and help in collecting the research materials. Furthermore, I owe a considerable debt of friendship and gratitude to Yvonna Sarkees, a Senior Advisor from the Privy Council Office at the Treasury Board of Canada Secretariat, for her professional counsel on the issues of multiculturalism and leadership.

I must gratefully acknowledge the helpful and critical interest of Polish scholars, namely the late Professor Andrzej Kapiszewski, the founder of the Institute of the Middle and Far East at the Jagiellonian University in Krakow, where I presently work, Professor Bogdan Szlachta from the Jagiellonian University, Professor Jerzy Zdanowski from the Polish Academy of Sciences in Warsaw, and Professor Krzysztof Kościelniak from the Jagiellonian University. I owe a very special debt of gratitude to Professor Eugeniusz Sakowicz from the University of Cardinal Stefan Wyszyński in Warsaw, whose reading and critique of the manuscript was extremely helpful. I also thank my student Katarzyna Gorgoń, a Ph.D. candidate at the Pontifical University of John Paul II in Krakow, for her assistance in collecting Polish sources for my project. In addition, I extend words of gratitude to the staff of John Paul II's Institute of Intercultural Dialogue in Krakow for their helpful response to all my questions and requests.

Editing this book was not an easy task. Therefore, I would like to thank Emma Greeson, a Ph.D. student from the University of California, San Diego, for her creative assistance in preparing the final draft of my book in the most careful and accurate way.

My special thanks go to my friends: Elżbieta Górska, Laura Mitchell, Anna Sobczyk, Tadeusz Gałuszka, Paweł Siwiec, Anna and Tomasz Lasoń and Regina and Andrzej Szypuła. Their friendship and support has helped me through difficult times. I should also mention with gratitude the encouragement and advice of my teacher and friend, Professor Anna Marzec.

My profound thanks go to my sister Zofia for her love and support during this project. My special thanks to my daughter Judi and her father Abdulilah, who partly inspired me to write the book and helped me a great deal with gathering the research material. "Music begins where words end." The beauty of Judi's music was of considerable assistance in surpassing all the difficulties related to the project and at many times has made my constant work not only enjoyable but also possible.

Introduction

Hence, not the record of past events but only the story makes sense, and what is so striking in Kant's remarks at the end of his life is that he immediately understood that the subject of History's action would have to be Mankind, rather than man or any verifiable human community.[1]

General remarks

For over thirteen centuries, the relationship between Christianity and Islam has been one of military conflicts, bitter polemics, aversion, prejudice and reciprocal hostility. Despite the predominant negative Christian attitude toward Islam and Muslims that has marked this history, from time to time voices appeared in the Church advocating initiatives aimed at reciprocal understanding and feasible reconciliation. Finally, in the second half of the twentieth century, the efforts of the forerunners of Christian-Muslim dialogue, among them St. Francis of Assisi, Ramon Lull, St. Thomas Aquinas, Nicolas de Cusa, Louis Massignon and Victor Courtois, brought about a breakthrough that represented a real positive change in the Church's attitude towards Islam. The *aggiornamento*, the spirit of renewal and reform that characterized the pontificates of John XXIII and Paul VI, had opened the Church to the challenges of the modern world and dialogue with modernity. The "revolutionary" message of the Second Vatican Council, calling Christians to respect the spiritual, moral and cultural values of other religions, and in particular those of Islam, had found its

---

[1]   H. Arendt, *The Life of the Mind*, vol. 1, New York: Harcourt Brace Jovanovich, 1978, p. 117.

official recognition in crucial documents, such as the Dogmatic Constitution *Lumen Gentium* no.16 and the Declaration *Nostra Aetate* no. 3. Pope Paul VI left for his descendant a Church that had been "renewed" and opened for dialogue with non-Christians in the spirit of respect, tolerance and acceptance.

John Paul II[2] undertook this challenging task and from the beginning of his pontificate assured the world of his commitment to continue with the initiatives of his predecessor concerning interreligious dialogue, and in particular that between Christianity and Islam. On November 29, 1979, one year after his election, while addressing the Catholic community in Ankara, the Holy Father referred to the principles of *Nostra Aetate*, saying:

> Faith in God, professed by spiritual descendants of Abraham – Christians, Muslims and Jews – when it is lived sincerely, when it penetrates life, is a certain foundation of dignity, brotherhood and freedom of men and a principle of uprightness for moral conduct and life in society.[3]

John Paul II's message to the followers of the three great monotheistic religions was always simple and did not change after his address in Ankara: respect, love and help for each and every person. Interreligious dialogue, and particularly that with Islam, became for the Holy Father a vehicle facilitating his active engagement in the complex problems of the Middle East, an area where resolving political, religious and social tensions seemed impossible.

The Pope was always against any violence and military interventions. While engaging in the issue of the Palestinian-Israeli conflict, he condemned both the Israeli attacks on Palestinian cities and the Palestinian terrorist actions, emphasizing that such measures would certainly not contribute to the resolving of the conflict but rather to its escalation. The Gulf War in 1991, as well as the military intervention in Iraq in 2003, were strongly opposed by the Pontiff. As he had pointed out on numerous occasions, war with its tragic consequences could never be "just another means that one can choose to employ for settling differences between nations."[4]

The ultimate aim of John Paul II's engagement in resolving the socio-political and religious predicament of the Middle East was peace and security in this area. The most important path leading to the fulfillment of that goal was, according to the Holy Father, a dialogue of the Catholic Church with Islam and Judaism. Therefore,

---

[2]   The Blessed John Paul II (1920-2005); the Pope was beatified on May 1, 2012. The process of his canonization is ongoing.

[3]   John Paul II, "To the Catholic Community of Ankara" (Ankara, November 29, 1979), in: F. Gioia (ed.), *Interreligious Dialogue: The Official Teaching of the Catholic Church (1963-1995)*, Boston: Pauline Books & Media, 1997, p. 220, paragraph 339.

[4]   "Address of His Holiness John Paul II to the Diplomatic Corps" (January 13, 2003), no. 4, online: http://www.vatican.va/holy_father/john_paul_ii/speeches/2003/january/documents/hf_jp-ii_spe_20030113_diplomatic-corps_en.html, access: March 20, 2011. All papal documents are available online in the Holy See's archive (http://www.vatican.va/).

the Pope met on numerous occasions with Muslim and Jewish political and spiritual leaders and addressed his dialogical messages to common people during his pilgrimages to Middle Eastern countries. He also urged the participants of various conferences and gatherings not to spare their efforts to promote interreligious dialogue and cooperation and encouraged the followers of different religions to share their commitment in prayers for peace in the region. As the first Pope in history, John Paul II visited the Jewish synagogue in Rome (April 12, 1986) and the Muslim mosque in Damascus (May 6, 2001).

There is no doubt that the sincere interreligious dialogue conducted by John Paul II from the beginning of his pontificate resulted in many positive changes in the Middle East, including the establishment of diplomatic relations between the Vatican and Israel (1993) and between the Vatican and the Palestinian Autonomy (1996). Moreover, the systematic, persistent and tireless engagement of the Pontiff in resolving Middle Eastern conflicts contributed significantly to appeasing the socio-political and religious tensions in the area, so that despite the wars causing destruction in all spheres of life of the people living there, the international community undertook and still undertakes many consecutive efforts and initiatives that could stabilize the situation and keep the road to peace open. The Pope's vision of a Middle Eastern political order based on moral principles and his tremendous effort to implement it proved to be the protector of "a light" that saved both the region and the entire world from the eruption of a large scale, complex local conflict with unpredictable global consequences.

The purpose of my study is to present the history of John Paul II's dialogue with Islam and the Muslims, focusing on its role in resolving the socio-political and religious predicament in the Middle East region. The analysis of the uniqueness of John Paul II's dialogical path with the followers of Islam is placed in the context of the historical continuum of Christian-Muslim relations.

Chapter I contains a brief overview of the history of Christian-Muslim relations, focusing on the evolution of the Christian view and/or "image" regarding Islam in the light of not only a religious but also a broader socio-political context; that is, within the circumstances under which such a view and/or "image" of the Muslim religion was shaped. Within the few distinguished periods of that history, one may notice a gradual evolution of the Christian perception of Islam: from refusal and condemnation through various attempts to study the religion, up to a more objective search for commonalities that could possibly enable reciprocal understanding. Furthermore, the related discussion exposes a number of Christian voices advocating a more positive attitude towards Muslims and the need for dialogue and cooperation. A gradual, but eventually significant change in the Christian perception of Islam, as presented in this brief historical overview of Christian-Muslim relations, led to the construction of bridges for better reciprocal understanding. Finally, the twentieth century witnessed long-awaited and promising developments.

Chapter II of the study deals with the changes concerning the Catholic Church's approach to the modern world as had been indicated in *De Motione Oecumenica*

(1949), advocated by Louis Massignon (1883-1962) and Victor Courtois (1907-1960) and finally as introduced by the Second Vatican Council (October 11, 1962 – November 21, 1965). The discussion here addresses some important points, including (1) the significance of the *aggiornamento*, the spirit of changes as introduced by John XXIII, who with his encyclical *Pacem in Terris* opened the Catholic Church to the "outside world" and dialogue with modernity, (2) the decisive change in the attitude of the Church towards non-Christians, and in particular Muslims, as officially acknowledged in eleven documents of the Council (among them two with an explicit reference to Islam and Muslims) and (3) the role of Paul VI's initiatives in establishing the basic path for Christian-Muslim dialogue and cooperation. Moreover, this chapter contains references concerning the future pope Karol Wojtyła's engagement in the proceedings of the Second Vatican Council, which are crucial in understanding his vision of man in modern, rapidly-changing, diverse society and his relation to "the other" in the light of the pastoral mission of the Catholic Church.

The exposition of the issues included in the first two chapters constitutes a base, or a starting point, from which to present the historical path of John Paul II's dialogue with non-Christians, and in particular with Muslims. Drawing extensively from past Christian experiences, outlooks and approaches, such as those of St. Francis of Assisi and St. Thomas Aquinas, or more recent ones such as the decisions of the Second Vatican Council and related dialogical initiatives of Paul VI, John Paul II embarked on the task of elaborating his own unique path of dialogue with the followers of Islam.

The subsequent chapters are entirely devoted to the Pontiff's dialogue with Muslims and a presentation of how this sincere interreligious vehicle of communication and interaction served John Paul II as a powerful means and tool in his engagement with resolving Middle Eastern problems.

A presentation of the characteristic features of John Paul II's dialogue with the followers of Islam begins in Chapter III. The Holy Father undertook the task of building his dialogue with Muslims shortly after his election in 1978. Within the time span of his pontificate, three different phases of that dialogue are distinguished: the first (until 1980), the period of learning, which was the task of grasping the essence of the history of Christian-Muslim relations and, in particular, the conclusions of the Second Vatican Council and the dialogical teaching and initiatives of Paul VI; the second (the 1980s), the period of teaching the whole world about the meaning of and the need to conduct interreligious dialogue; and the third (from the 1990s until the end of the pontificate), the period of the Pope's active engagement in resolving political and religious tensions in the Middle East. An analysis of both important documents and related actions within the historical development of John Paul II's dialogue with Islam and the Muslims is followed by a conclusive discussion that (1) uncovers its meaning and its foundations, (2) outlines its aims and (3) practice and (4) presents the Holy Father's attitude towards difficulties and obstacles in the way of dialogical encounters.

The most important aim of John Paul II's dialogue with Muslims was the promotion of religious freedom, justice and peaceful coexistence between people of different religions and cultures. Therefore, the Pope believed that in the Middle East, an ethnic, religious and cultural mosaic, the need to strive for such a goal was the priority.

Chapter IV deals with the problem of religious freedom in the Middle East; the discussion here focuses on two main complex issues. The first relates to the Holy See's position on the issue of Jerusalem and the Holy Places and John Paul II's persistent appeal to the followers of Judaism, Christianity and Islam for peaceful coexistence in the Holy Land. The second complex issue concerns the Pontiff's visits to Muslim Middle Eastern countries with the aim of strengthening Christian minorities, in particular the Catholics, in their faith, and promoting the development of Christian-Muslim dialogue and cooperation in various spheres of life.

The last chapter is entirely devoted to a discussion of John Paul II's active engagement in resolving political problems in the region, and in particular his strong opposition to both terrorist attacks and military interventions. The issues addressed here are the Pope's quest to ease the Palestinian-Israeli conflict and settle the Palestinian question, his diplomatic struggle and his "No to war" mantra, i.e., his strong opposition to the Lebanese war, the Persian Gulf War of 1991 and the military intervention in Iraq in 2003.

Methodology and the state of research

The idea to engage in the research that resulted in publishing this book was rather spontaneous and came to me in 1994, after reading John Paul II's *Crossing the Threshold of Hope*, in which the Pope's words about Muslims and Islam sounded "very different" from those we usually heard from the media. These were words about dialogue, respect and tolerance in the spirit of *Nostra Aetate* and the Second Vatican Council. While collecting, reading and analyzing the related documents, articles and studies, I realized that although I was not fully aware of it, I had been "preparing" to write this book for many years. This "preparation" included my career-related experiences, such as a one-year stay in Egypt (1978-1979)[5] where

---

[5]   The historical news about Karol Wojtyła becoming the Pope reached me in Egypt. It happened in Luxor, at the train station, early morning, on October 17, 1978. I was there together with my friends Anna and Zbyszek Pomaz, a married couple of architects from Gdansk. While waiting for a train to Aswan, we learned from the owner of the hotel we stayed in that the Polish Cardinal had become the Pope. He even showed us the Arabic newspaper where I could clearly read: "The Polish Cardinal Karol Wojtyła was chosen the Pope and he took the name John Paul II." Certainly, on that day I could neither sense nor realize that an apparently accidental event, namely getting the historical news from a Christian (Copt) on the Egyptian,

I learned first-hand that Christians and Muslims are more similar than they are different, and my Ph.D. studies and work at the Institute of Islamic Studies at McGill University, a place known for its unique multicultural approach, where students and scholars from all over the world conduct an everyday dialogue of life and dialogue of experts. These experiences became my personal "lessons" on interreligious encounters, which enabled me to perceive John Paul II's dialogue with non-Christians with a more thorough understanding.

Many books and articles have been written about John Paul II and their authors have analyzed and discussed various aspects of his pontificate. However, in this enormous up-to-date scholarly output, there is not much about the Pope's persistent dialogue with Islam and the Muslims and his engagement in resolving the Middle Eastern predicament. This significant aspect of John Paul II's accomplishments still remains a rather unexplored area of studies and requires further academic discussion.

As already mentioned, the aim of this study is to analyze the development of John Paul II's dialogue with Islam and the Muslims, focusing on the uniqueness of his dialogical path and the Pope's way of applying dialogical means in resolving political and religious tensions in the Middle East, while placing this important aspect of John Paul II's pontificate in the historical continuum of Christian-Muslim relations.

Building dialogue has been one of the primary interests of historians for centuries. As already mentioned, in the history of Christian-Muslim relations, there were many initiatives to construct bridges of communication, and both Christians and Muslims had made various attempts to learn about each other's culture and faith. The next step was to build unity in diversity, which means establishing an interfaith dialogical path pioneered by the Second Vatican Council and the pontificate of Paul VI. Subsequently, this path was linked with the unprecedented leadership competency of John Paul II, which helped him build a collective consciousness that goes beyond religion. The Holy Father engaged himself in the task of focusing people's attention on spiritual activity directed to the self, to the other and to God, so they would be better prepared to face the challenges of today's global world.

In John Paul II's vision of Christian-Muslim relations, dialoguing with the aim of achieving spiritual union became the foundation for forming alliances based on faith and shared spiritual values. With time, he became a spiritual leader in conducting interreligious dialogue, which was perceived as a conflict-preventing and peace-building tool. The Pontiff was convinced that a sincere interreligious dialogue should become the primary means of resolving the complex of political, social and economic problems of today's Middle Eastern world, overcome by fearful conflicts and uncertainty. It seems historically significant that during the pontificate of John Paul II, the economic and political drivers of the conflicts in the Middle East were juxtaposed, for the first time, with the Pope's interventions based on morals and ethics and highlighted by his capacity-building of the intercultural competencies of

---

predominantly Muslim soil about Cardinal Wojtyła's becoming the spiritual leader of Christians would have symbolic implications for me some years later.

Christians and Muslims. The ultimate goal of John Paul II's interreligious dialogue, as exposed in this book, was to widen and enlarge people's horizons and perspectives, so that they would distance themselves from ethno-relativism and turn toward the path of pan-spiritualism. In other words, the dialogical strategy of John Paul II aimed at awakening the world's moral sensitivity and increasing people's awareness of the ethical dimension of their decisions and actions.

John Paul II left a large church-originated output as well as secular written works that either emphasized explicitly or alluded to the issue of building an interfaith dialogue. Therefore, one of the challenges that I endured during the process of my first methodological task in writing this dissertation was to put a significant effort into making an attentive selection of John Paul II's writings (in chronological order) while limiting the chosen elements to exclusively the necessary ones. Thus, the bulk of my initial analytical work was done by making textual choices, rather than interpreting the texts. The reasoning behind using this methodology reflects the clarity of John Paul II's written expression and the underlying assumption that John Paul II, as a charismatic spiritual leader, was following a spiritual strategy while using and developing his leadership competencies and adjusting to contemporary events.

The first methodological task (selection) described above was followed by the next one (analysis): an attempt to provide an analysis of the Pope's spiritual leadership in interfaith dialogue and present dialogical gains of interfaith relations of Christians and Muslims, seen through the prism of the Pope's tireless endeavors to implement interfaith dialogue in resolving the socio-political and economic Middle Eastern predicament. This task required a widening of the analytical perspective. This was achieved by adding a historical background and a brief political context of the presented elements in order to make it more instructive for readers who might have not witnessed the described events themselves. Therefore, original texts written by John Paul II were combined with a variety of descriptive sources from the specialists in related fields. The use of the chronological approach, simply following the steps of John Paul II as historically documented, was a continuation of the initial methodological approach (selection) that I applied in this dissertation.

With regard to primary sources, this book is based on a selection from John Paul II's magisterium and other writings referring to (1) interreligious dialogue, (2) dialogue with Islam and the Muslims, and (3) the Pope's involvement in resolving Middle Eastern socio-political and religious conflicts. In order to demonstrate the originality of John Paul II's mantra of "action and thought" in relation to his spiritual leadership in developing a dialogical path for the new history of Christian-Muslim relations, it was important to place it in the context of the changes in the attitude of the Catholic Church towards Christians, as introduced by the Second Vatican Council. Therefore, I had to work on additional primary material, namely on selections from the Council's documents and the magisterium of John XXIII and Paul VI.[6]

---

[6] Primary sources were taken from *Acta Apostolicae Sedis*, *Islamochristiana*, and a collection of documents prepared by the Pontifical Council for Interreligious Dialogue: F. Gioia (ed.),

The secondary sources, the up-to-date published works related to issues discussed in my book, could be divided into two groups. The first includes books and articles connected with the history of Christian-Muslim relations up until the late 1970s, namely: (1) historical overviews based on primary sources,[7] (2) books and collections of essays on various historical related topics grounded in adequate documents from the history of Christian-Muslim relations,[8] (3) complementary works,[9] (4) a substantial body of articles published in various academic journals,[10] and (5) collections of essays assessing the period of the Second Vatican Council and the pontificates of John XXIII and Paul VI.[11]

The second group of my secondary references is comprised of works and articles addressing the issue of John Paul II's dialogue with non-Christians, and in particular with the followers of Islam, represented by (1) a significant contribution of Professor Eugeniusz Sakowicz,[12] (2) more specific works,[13] (3) studies referring to the Pope's

---

Interreligious Dialogue... The English version of the documents quoted in the text is basically from the official Vatican Web Site (http://www.vatican.va/).

[7] Such as N. Daniel, *Islam and the West: The Making of an Image*, Oxford: Oneworld Publications, 1993; H. Goddard, *A History of Christian-Muslim Relations Relations*, Edinburgh: Edinburgh University Press, 2000 and B. Z. Kedar, *Crusade and Mission: European Approaches towards the Muslims*, Princeton, NJ: Princeton University Press, 1984.

[8] Such as D. J. Sahas, *John of Damascus on Islam: The "Heresy of Ishmaelites,"* Leiden: E. J. Brill, 1972; J. Kritzek, *Peter the Venerable and Islam*, Princeton, NJ: Princeton University Press, 1964; J. Hoeberichts, *Francis and Islam*, Quincy, IL: Franciscan Press, 1997; K. Kościelniak, *Grecy i Arabowie: Historia Kościoła melkickiego (katolickiego) na ziemiach zdobytych przez muzułmanów (634-1516)*, Kraków: Wydawnictwo UNUM, 2004; J. V. Tolan (ed.), *Medieval Christian Perceptions to Islam: A Book of Essays*, New York: Garland Pub., 1994; Y. Y. Haddad and W. Z. Haddad (eds.), *Christian-Muslim Encounters*, Gainesville: University Press of Florida, 1995.

[9] Such as R. W. Southern: *Western Views of Islam in the Middle Ages*, Cambridge: Harvard University Press, 1962; R. Armour: *Islam, Christianity and the West: A Troubled History*, Maryknoll, NY: Orbis Books, 2002 or W. M. Watt, *The Influence of Islam on Medieval Europe*, Edinburgh: Edinburgh University Press, 1972.

[10] Such as *Islamochristiana, Bulletin, Pro Dialogo, Islam and Christian-Muslim Relations, Encounter: Documents for Muslim-Christian Understanding, Muslim World*, etc.

[11] Namely J. J. Waardenburg (ed.), *Islam and Christianity: Mutual Perceptions since the Mid-20th Century*, Leuven: Peeters, 1998; M. L. Lamb and M. Levering (eds.), *Vatican II: Renewal within Tradition*, Oxford and New York: Oxford University Press, 2008 or W. Madges (ed.), *Vatican II: Forty Years Later*, Maryknoll, NY: Orbis Books, 2006.

[12] Namely related articles and books, such as E. Sakowicz, *Islam w dokumentach Kościoła i nauczaniu Jana Pawła II (1965-1996)*, Warszawa: Wydawnictwa Akademii Teologii Katolickiej, 1997 or idem, *Dialog Kościoła z islamem według dokumentów soborowych i posoborowych (1963-1999)*, Warszawa: Wydawnictwo Uniwersytetu Kardynała Stefana Wyszyńskiego, 2000.

[13] Such as M. Lelong, *L'Eglise catholique et l'islam*, Paris: Maisonneuve & Larose, 1993; B. L. Sherwin and H. Kasimow (eds.), *John Paul II and Interreligious Dialogue*, Maryknoll, NY: Orbis Books, 1999.

active engagement in the Middle Eastern affairs,[14] and (4) articles focusing on socio-political and religious problems of the Middle East, published in journals and (5) detailed biographies of John Paul II.[15]

This brief overview of my secondary sources, and in particular the second group of them, namely the up-to-date published books directly related to the topic of my study, represents the state of the present research on the issue. It clearly indicates that a complex analysis of John Paul II's spiritual leadership in developing a dialogical path for Christian-Muslim relations, an analysis discussing not only the features, the aims and the practice of such a path but also exposing the implementation of dialogical means in resolving the Middle Eastern predicament and placing the Pope's achievements in historical continuum of Christian-Muslim relations, has not yet been written. Therefore, I am convinced that my study will contribute to the currently increasing awareness on this important aspect of John Paul II's pontificate.

---

[14] Books, such as: G. E. Irani, *The Papacy and the Middle East: The Role of the Holy See in the Arab-Israeli Conflict, 1962-1984*, Notre Dame, IN: University of Notre Dame Press, 1986; A. Kreutz: *Vatican and the Palestinian-Israeli Conflict: The Struggle for the Holy Land*, New York: Greenwood Press, 1990; J. Moskwa: *Prorok i Polityk*, Warszawa: Świat Książki, 2003 and a collection of essays by K. C. Ellis (ed.), *The Vatican, Islam and the Middle East*, Syracuse, NY: Syracuse University Press, 1987.

[15] Such as T. Szulc, *Pope John Paul II: The Biography*, New York: Scribner, 1995; G. Weigel, *Witness to Hope: The Biography of John Paul II (1920-2005)*, New York: Harper Perennial, 2005; J. Kwinty, *Man of the Century: The Life and Times of Pope John Paul II*, New York: Henry Holt and Company Inc., 1997 or G. O'Connor, *Universal Father: A Life of Pope John Paul II*, London: Bloomsbury Publishing Plc., 2006.

I

Christianity and Islam

*From hostility and ignorance
to building bridges of reconciliation and understanding*

To a contemporary person, it seems that Christianity has always dominated Europe. Since the seventh century, Islam has been the religion of the Middle East. The common history of the two regions has manifested itself in continuous contact and various relations, such as religious confrontations, exchange of thought, trade, military encounters, colonialism, fights for independence, Islamization, Westernization, and after September 11th, in a Western war against Islamic fundamentalism and terrorism. Among all the religions that Christianity has had to confront, Islam was both misunderstood and attacked most intensely. For more than a millennium, this religion was considered a major threat to Europe and its followers were viewed as enemies of not only Christianity but also the entire Western civilization. With regard to its political aspect, this threat began with the Arab conquest of Spain at the beginning of the eighth century and ended with the siege of Vienna by the Ottoman Turks in 1683. However, "there were not only political reasons for Christian Europe's fear."[16] It should be noted that Islam is the only world religion that came into existence after Christianity. Therefore, it was unacceptable as a true religion and for centuries after the Byzantine apologetic writings, it was regarded as a mere heresy of Christianity. However, although the thirteen centuries of history between the two religions was dominated by wars of conquest and re-conquest, aversion, prejudice, hostility and bitter and often injurious polemics, there have always been voices on both sides advocating a more positive attitude and the need for dialogue and understanding.[17]

---

[16]   A. Schimmel, *Islam: An Introduction*, Albany: State University of New York Press, 1992, p. 1.

[17]   For an extensive discussion on Christian-Muslim relations, based on primary sources and references see the classic analysis, thoroughly revised and updated before the author's death

While discussing the issue of the relations between Christianity and Islam in history, one should bear in mind a number of considerations. First, it is important to realize that it was not the religious identity of the Arab conquerors that initially struck the European observers. What astonished them and prompted them to reflect were both the speed and the extent of the conquest itself, which in a few decades resulted in Arab domination of the eastern, southern and western shores of the Mediterranean Sea. Second, a presentation of Christian views regarding Islam should include their religious aspects as well as the political context, i.e., the circumstances under which such views of Islam as a religion actually appeared. Third, while discussing such views and outlooks, it is also important to realize the mental categories and capabilities that the authors had at their disposal which led to formulation of their ideas and statements.[18] Finally, one should also remember the fact that Islam features no separation between religious and non-religious matters.[19] In addition, for Muslims, their religion is not only a system of belief and worship; it embraces all aspects of the life of its followers: the rules of civil, constitutional and criminal law.

In the history of the relations between Christianity and Islam, a few different periods may be distinguished. For the purpose of our study, the historical overview of Christian-Muslim relations is focused on selected Christian views of Islam reflecting the evolution of reciprocal contact between the followers of the two religions from hostility and ignorance to attempts at building bridges of reconciliation and understanding.

---

in 1992, describing the formation of Western attitudes about Islam by tracing the development of Christian-Islamic interaction from medieval times to the present: N. Daniel, *Islam and the West*... Also refer to: R. Armour, *Islam, Christianity and the West*...; H. Goddard, *A History*...; Ch. J. Adams, "Islam and Christianity: The Opposition and Similarities," in: R. M. Savory and D. Agius (eds.), *Logos Islamicos: Studia Islamica in Honorem Georgii Michaelis Wickens*, Toronto: Pontifical Institute for Medieval Studies, 1984, p. 287-306.

[18] K. B. Wolf, "Christian Views of Islam in Early Medieval Spain," in: J. V. Tolan (ed.), *Medieval Christian Perceptions of Islam*..., p. 86.

[19] As stated by Lewis: "If the term "religion," in one sense, conveys much more to a Muslim than to a Christian, there is another sense in which it conveys much less. As a building, as a place of worship, the equivalent of the church among Muslims is the mosque. As an institution, as a power, the Church has no equivalent in Islam. Islam has no councils or synods, no prelates or hierarchies, no canon laws or canon courts. In classical Islamic history there could be no clash between pope and emperor, since the caliph, the titular head of the Islamic state and community, combined in himself both political and religious – though not spiritual – authority. There could be neither conflict nor cooperation, neither separation nor association between church and state, since the governing institution of Islam combined both functions" (*Islam and the West*, New York, Oxford University Press, 1993, p. 4).

The early history of Christian-Muslim relations

The first period is highlighted by the biography of the Prophet Muḥammad and the rise of Islam that lasted until the eleventh century. It is worth noting that Muḥammad met Christians on various occasions.[20] It was in the town of Bostra (Syria), an important junction on the caravan route and a great center of Christianity, where a significant incident is said to have taken place. Muḥammad accompanied his uncle Abū Ṭālib who led the caravan. In Bostra, they met a Christian monk named Baḥīrā.[21] He recognized that Muḥammad bore the signs of prophethood that the holy book had predicted, including "the seal of the prophethood between his shoulders."[22] Therefore, he believed that Muḥammad was the future "Envoy of Allah." Some years later, as Ibn Isḥāq reports, Waraqa Ibn Nawfal, the cousin of Muḥammad's first wife Khadīja Bint Khuwaylid, identified Muḥammad's experience in the cave of Hira as divine revelation.[23]

It appears as though Muḥammad was well aware of the already-existing idea of religious monotheism due to his numerous contacts with the followers of both Judaism and Christianity. As for the attitude of Muḥammad towards Christians, it may be considered ambivalent.[24] For example, as Ibn Isḥāq reported, when the Prophet received Christians from Najran, the delegation was invited to pray in the Prophet's mosque. However, when he negotiated a political treaty with them, his view concerning Christian beliefs had no room for compromise.[25]

---

[20] H. Goddard discusses five instances in which it is recorded that Muḥammad and the early Muslim community had some kind of direct encounter with Christians, as reported by Ibn Isḥāq (d. 767) in his *Sīrat Rasūl Allāh* (*The Life of Prophet of God*); see: H. Goddard, *A History...*, p. 19-28.

[21] In the Christian polemics against Islam, Baḥīrā became a heretical monk whose religious affiliations vary in different Christian sources. For a detailed discussion on related issues see: B. Roggema, *The Legend of Sergius Baḥīrā: Eastern Christian Apologetics and Apocalyptic in Response to Islam*, Leiden and Boston: E. J. Brill, 2009.

[22] 'Abd al-Malik Ibn Hishām, *The Life of Muḥammad: A Translation of Ibn "Isḥāq's Sīrat Rasūl Allāh,"* trans. A. Guillaume, London: Oxford University Press, 1955, p. 78-81. Also refer to: M. Rodinson, *Muḥammad*, trans. Anne Carter, New York: Pantheon Books, 1980, p. 46-47; M. Penn, "Syriac Sources for the Study of Early Christian-Muslim Relations," *Islamochristiana*, vol. 29 (2003), p. 72-73.

[23] Waraqa Ibn Nawfal was a *ḥanīf*, i.e., an Arab monotheist. He was familiar with the scriptures of both Judaism and Christianity. Khadīja consulted him concerning Muḥammad's prophetic experience. Waraqa assured Muḥammad that he received a great revelation like the one sent to Mūsā (Moses) ages before ('Abd al-Malik Ibn Hishām, *The Life of Muḥammad...*, p. 83, 107.

[24] See: B. F. Breiner and C. W. Troll, "Christianity and Islam," in: J. Esposito (ed.), *The Oxford Encyclopedia of Modern Islamic World*, vol. 1, New York: Oxford University Press, 1995, p. 280.

[25] 'Abd al-Malik Ibn Hishām, *The Life of Muḥammad...*, p. 270-277.

With regard to the Qur'anic image of Christians, one may say that in the fundamental source of Islam there is also some ambivalence in the attitude towards them.
As the Qur'an says, Muslims will find, among the People of the Book, Christians as
"nearest to them in love":

Strongest among men in enmity
To the Believers wilt thou
Find the Jews and Pagans;
And nearest among them in love
To the Believers wilt thou
Find those who say,
"We are Christians":
Because amongst these are
Men devoted to learning
And men who have renounced
The world, and they
Are not arrogant. [26]

However, at the same time, the Holy Book warns Muslims not to take Christians
or Jews as close friends:

O you who believe!
Take not the Jews
And the Christians
For your friends and protectors;
They are but friends and protectors
To each other. And he
Amongst you that turns to them
[For friendship] is of them.
Verily Allah guideth not
A people unjust. [27]

It also accuses Christians and Jews of disbelief:

The Jews call 'Uzayr [Ezra] a son
Of God, and the Christians
Call Christ the Son of God.
That is a saying from their mouth;
[In this] they but imitate
What the Unbelievers of old
Used to say. Allah's curse
Be on them: how they are deluded
Away from the Truth! [28]

---

[26]   The Qur'an, S: 5, v: 82. All the quotations are from: *The Meaning of the Holy Qur'ān*, trans.
       and comment. 'Abdullah Yūsuf 'Alī, Beltsville, MD: Amana Publications, 1989.

[27]   The Qur'an, S: 5, v: 51.

[28]   The Qur'an, S: 9, v: 30.

On the other hand, in the Qur'an there are important references to the acceptance of religious pluralism. According to Issa J. Boullata, religious pluralism may be considered "one of the doctrinal principles enunciated in the Qur'an."[29] In the light of the Qur'an, humankind was once made up of members of a single community. Then, with God's will, various human views resulted in religious pluralism. Prophets sent by God with divine revelations guided these communities in their beliefs. As the Qur'an says: "Unto every one of you We appointed a [different] law and way of life" (S.5: 48); and similarly: "for, every community faces a direction of its own, of which He is the focal point" (S. 2:148). Both verses, says Boullata, are followed by the command "*fa-stabiqū l-khayrāt*," which may be translated as "Vie, then, with one another in doing good works" (S. 5:48) or "Vie, therefore, with one another in doing good works" (S. 2:148). It is possible to assert that the Qur'an does not favor one religious community over another. However, as Boullata points out, according to the Qur'an "God has willed the Muslims to be a community of the middle way so that they might bear witness before humankind" (S.2:143). Furthermore, while dealing with people of other faiths, the Qur'an demands from Muslims that they be kind and tactful. Moreover, one should remember that, according to the Qur'an, "*lā ikrāha fī d-dīn*" (S. 2:256) which means, "there is no coercion or compulsion concerning religion"(S. 2:256).[30] All in all, after analyzing the related views of the famous Qur'anic exegetes, among them Aṭ-Ṭabarī (d. A.D. 923), Az-Zamakhsharī (d. A.D.1144), Jalāl ad-Dīn al-Maḥallī (d.1459), Jalāl ad-Dīn as-Suyūṭī (d.1505), Muḥammad 'Abduh (d.1905), Muḥammad Rashīd Riḍā (d.1935) and Sayyid Quṭb (d.1966), Boullata concludes that in the above-mentioned passages, "*fa-stabiqū l-khayrāt*" and "*lā ikrāha fī d-dīn*":

> We have the basis for interfaith dialogue and cooperation, which has the potential for leading us to a better world, if only people would heed and have good will toward one another.[31]

In the earliest history of Christian-Muslim relations, it is sometimes the positive and sometimes the negative aspect that has received greater emphasis. In the case of Muslims, according to Norman Daniel, the Qur'an itself determines the polemic area and the disputed matters are as follows: God is not three, Jesus is not Son of God, He was not crucified and the Bible has been falsified and misinterpreted.[32] The Muslims, then, considered Christianity an abrogated religion, whose followers refused to

---

29   I. J. Boullata, "*Fa-stabiqū'l-khayrāt*: A Qur'anic Principle of Interfaith Relations," in: Y. Y. Haddad and W. Z. Haddad (eds.), *Christian-Muslim...*, p. 43-53.

30   All the quotations from the Qur'an in this paragraph as cited by I. J. Boullata in his article "*Fa-stabiqū'l-khayrāt....*"

31   Ibid., p. 52.

32   N. Daniel, "Christian-Muslim Polemics," in: M. Eliade [et al.] (ed.), *The Encyclopedia of Religion*, vol. 11, New York: Macmillan, 1987, p. 402-404.

accept God's final word.[33] Therefore, under the circumstances, Christians could be tolerated if willing to submit to the authority of Muslim state.

The first Christian reaction to Islam was quite negative and Muslims were considered barbarians with whom friendly relations were rather impossible. However, a few decades later, with the expansion of the rapidly growing Islamic empire, the situation began to change. For many non-Muslim populations in Byzantine and Persian territories, Islamic rule meant only an exchange of old rulers for new ones. The non-Muslim population under Muslim rule was given three choices:

> (1) conversion to Islam and full membership in the community; (2) retention of one's faith and payment of a poll tax; or (3), if they refused Islam or "protected" status, warfare until Islamic rule was accepted.[34]

The Christians in the conquered lands belonged to *Ahl al-Kitāb* (The People of the Book), namely to one of three major "scriptural" communities, which included Christians, Jews and Zoroastrians, and as monotheists, aside from retaining their lands and possessions, they were allowed substantial religious freedom.[35] As Krzysztof Kościelniak has pointed out, despite the fact that religion was the fundament of medieval society, both Christians and Muslims surely perceived each other not only through the prism of religious differences. Other differences, such as sociological and cultural ones, were also important in stimulating the reciprocal contacts of both groups. All this influenced the status of Christians in Muslim societies, which differed considerably depending on place and historical time.[36] Sometimes the new Muslim rulers provided more local autonomy and the local population enjoyed more religious freedom, paying lower taxes than before.[37] The development of the *Dhimmī* (the protected) status gave non-Muslims, including Christians, some legal rights as subjects of Islamic government.[38] In fact, relations between Christians and Muslims

---

[33] Regarding early Muslim-Christian polemics see, for example: Muḥammad Ibn Hārūn al-Warrāq, *Anti-Christian polemic in early Islam: Abū 'Īsā al-Warrāq's "Against the Trinity,"* ed. and trans. David Thomas, Cambridge and New York: Cambridge University Press, 1992. For a contemporary discussion on Muslim-Christian polemics refer to: G. C. Anawati, *Polémique, apologie et dialogue islamo-chrétiens: Positions classiques médiévales et positions contemporaines*, Roma: Pontificia Universita Urbaniana, 1969; K. Zebiri, *Muslims and Christians Face to Face*, Oxford and Rockport, MA: Oneworld Publications, 1997.

[34] J. L. Esposito, *The Islamic Threat: Myth or Reality?*, New York: Oxford University Press, 1995, p. 39.

[35] B. Lewis, *The Middle East: 2000 Years of History from the Rise of Christianity to the Present Day*, London: Weidenfeld & Nicolson, 1995, p. 56-57. Also see: M. Arkoun, "The Notion of Revelation: From *Ahl al-Kitāb* to the Societies of the Book," *Die Welt des Islams*, vol. 28, 1988, p. 62-89.

[36] K. Kościelniak, *Grecy i Arabowie...*, p. 74-75.

[37] B. Lewis, *The Middle East...*, p. 56-57.

[38] See: Y. Bat, *The Dhimmi: Jews and Christians under Islam*, preface Jacques Ellul, trans. David Maisel, Paul Fenton and David Littman, Rutherford, CA: Fairleigh Dickinson

(especially the Muslim authorities) were generally good during the early period. The Muslims empire originally utilized the existing bureaucracy that included Christians, especially in Egypt, Syria and Persia. In general, the Islamic pattern of tolerance definitely contributed to the relatively peaceful Muslim-Christian coexistence. During its early period, Islam inherited the learning of the Hellenistic tradition due to some important scientific projects, including translations of works of science, philosophy and medicine from Greek into Arabic. Islam became the heir to the learning of the past and reached creative heights in architecture, science, technology and philosophy. The concept of legal rights for non-Muslims became an integral principle of Islamic law. Islamic learning and Islamic legal tolerance survived the disintegration of political unity in the ninth century and became important elements of the medieval period. The Islamic ideal, according to John Esposito, "was to fashion a world in which, under Muslim rule, idolatry and paganism would be eliminated, and People of the Book could live in a society guided and protected by Muslim power."[39]

With regard to the Christian polemic and apologetic literature from the early period of Christian-Muslim relations, it is represented by a substantial literary output including works by Oriental Christians and Christian authors from Byzantium and Muslim Spain.[40]

Oriental Christians, who had lived under Muslim rule since the seventh century, addressed Islam and its followers in a large number of apologetic and polemical works in Arabic, Syriac or Greek, such as epistles, tractates and single-theme dialogues in which the parties were identified as "Christians" and "Saracens."[41] The authors supported their arguments with both Biblical and Qur'anic quotations. Their attitude towards Islam and Muslims was diverse and ranged from hostility to conciliation. The early Christian polemicists were lacking a deeper knowledge and understanding of Islam. The main target of their criticism was the Prophet Muḥammad. He was usually depicted as a heretic, an impostor and a person of low moral values. Moreover, while discrediting the Prophet's reputation, they argued that His revelation was a false doctrine, and, at best, a mere heresy. As an example, one should mention here the polemics, or rather an attack on Islam by John of Damascus (655-747).[42]

University Press, London: Associated University Presses, 1985. For a thorough discussion about the *dhimmī* status concerning Christians, and in particular Arabs, see: K. Kościelniak, *Grecy i Arabowie...*, p. 75-86; R. Hoyland (ed.), *Muslims and Others in Early Islamic Society*, Aldershot and Burlington, VT: Ashgate Variorum, 2004.

[39] J. L. Esposito, *The Islamic Threat...*, p. 39.

[40] For a thorough discussion, based on primary sources, see: B. Z. Kedar, *Crusade and Mission...*, p. 3-41.

[41] B. Lewis explains: "For many centuries, both Eastern and Western Christendom called the followers of the Prophet *Saracens*, a world of uncertain etymology but clearly of ethnic and not religious connotation, since the term is both pre-Islamic and pre-Christian" (*Islam...*, p. 133).

[42] N. Daniel, *Islam and the West...*, p. 13-15; R. Armour, *Islam, Christianity and the West...*, p. 41-45. K. Kościelniak, *Grecy i Arabowie...*, p. 116-122. For a thorough discussion refer to: D. J. Sahas, *John of Damascus...*

In the section devoted to heresies from his major work *The Fount of Wisdom*, the author attempted to warn Christians about the evil of Islam, so they could save themselves from it. He saw Islam as a religion swaying away from the truth and as a preparation for the final "holocaust" heralded by the arrival of the Antichrist. His severe attack was also directed at the Prophet Muḥammad, whom he accused of immoral conduct. The lack of objectivity and the quite hostile attitude of John of Damascus towards Islam and Muslims may be surprising. According to traditional sources, he could have had some knowledge of Islam because he was employed, for several years, in the Arab administration in Damascus.[43]

The Christian polemics that came out of Byzantium were less voluminous and different with regard to the attitude they presented towards Islam. This literary heritage contains unfavorable accounts of Muḥammad and the rise of Islam, as well as letters attacking the new religion and tractates on early Christian-Muslim disputes.[44] The earliest Christian reaction to Islam that came from the Byzantine Empire was primarily negative. Muslims were considered barbarians and their religion viewed as not a true one but as a kind of Aryanism, a Christian heresy. Sophronius (560-638), the patriarch of Jerusalem and an eyewitness to the Arab conquest, complained about the cruelty, hostility and strength of the Saracens. While lamenting over the destruction of churches, the Patriarch viewed the fate of Christians as a result of their own wickedness.[45]

According to Kedar, one of the most influential Byzantine anti-Islamic works was the *Nicetae Byzantini Philosophi confutatio falsi libri quem scripsit Mohamedes Arabs*, written in the middle of the ninth century by Nicetas of Byzantium.[46] In his discussion of the Qur'an, in particular a detailed account of suras 2 to 18, he accused Muslims of adhering to an idolatrous conception of God.[47] There were also Byzantine authors who displayed more conciliatory stances. In 913 or 914, Patriarch Nicolas I of Constantinople sent a letter to the Caliph al-Muqtadir in which he stated that both he and the caliph had "obtained the gift of [their] authorities from a common Head."[48]

During the early period of Christian-Muslim relations, an important polemical Christian piece of literature came from Spain, a place that experienced the direct impact of Muslim rule and where "the favorable capitulation's terms meant that most

---

[43] R. Armour, *Islam, Christianity and the West…*, p. 41.

[44] For Christian-Muslim polemics from Byzantium see: J. Meyendorf, "Byzantine Views of Islam," *Dumbarton Oak Papers*, vol. 18 (1964), p. 113-132. Also refer to two important works by A. T. Khoury: *Polémique byzantine et l'Islam (VIIIe-XIIIe s.)*, Leiden: E. J. Brill, 1972 and *Les théologiens byzantins et l'Islam: Textes et auteurs (VIIIe-XIIIe s.)*, Louvain and Paris: Éditions Nauwelaerts and Beatrice-Nauwelaerts, 1969.

[45] J. C. Lamoreaux, "Early Christian Responses to Islam," in: *Medieval Christian Perceptions of Islam…*, p. 15.

[46] B. Z. Kedar, *Crusade and Mission…*, p. 21.

[47] Ibid.

[48] Ibid.

Spanish Christians were largely unaffected by the change of regime in 711."[49] At the beginning, the contact between Christians and Muslims[50] was limited due to some legal restrictions and social customs. However, as it turned out, with each generation born into Andalusian society the barriers that early Muslims created between themselves and the Christians began to disappear and within a century of the conquest, the sources revealed a high degree of assimilation and acculturation in both directions, especially towards Islam.[51] Many Christians became fond of the new, more refined culture. The assimilation of Christians into Islamic society was quite advantageous for them since it enabled active participation in a culturally diversified and economically prosperous environment that linked Spain with Africa, the Near East and Central Asia. Many Spanish Christians became successful merchants on both the local and international scale. Others embarked on the task of studying the Arabic language, theology and philosophy, enjoyed Arabic poetry; with time, while acquiring mastery in the refined Arab culture, they began to forget their own language and roots.[52] This situation seriously threatened Christian religious identity. The common practice among the Christians was to retain their religious identity. However, as Kenneth Baxter Wolf says:

> More typically Christians retained their religious identity, but did all they could to melt in the dominant society by avoiding anything that might, on the one hand, draw undue attention to their inferior status, and on the other, offend the religious sensibilities of their hosts. In short, they dressed like Muslims, they spoke like Muslims and lived like Muslims. While this process of acculturation contributed to the well-being of many Christians, other looked on with suspicion.[53]

With regard to the earliest accounts on the Muslims in Spain, one should mention two anonymous Latin Chronicles dating from 741 and 754. Apart from information about the Muslim conquest, there are some references to the Prophet Muḥammad, his followers and the distinct Muslim religious tradition.[54]

As for the Christian polemical literature, the earliest Latin works lack information about either their authors or their content. Among them are *Disputation Felicis cum Saraceno*, which survived only as a title mentioned in one letter of Alcuin to Charlemagne, and *Istoria de Mahomet*, written by an unknown author sometime before

---

[49]   K. B. Wolf, "Christian Views...," p. 92.
[50]   During the first few decades of the rise of Islam, the terms "Muslim" and "Arab" were practically synonymous. With the territorial spread of the new religion, the term "Muslim" was also applied to people of other ethnic origin.
[51]   K. B. Wolf, "Christian Views...," p. 92-93.
[52]   See: B. Lewis, *The Arabs in History*, Oxford and New York: Oxford University Press, 1993, p. 134.
[53]   K. B. Wolf, "Christian Views...," p. 93.
[54]   Ibid., p. 87-90.

850 and survived in its entirety.[55] The latter work presents the Prophet Muḥammad as a heretic who summoned his followers to abandon idolatry and adored a "corporeal God" in heaven. However, according to Wolf, *Istoria* also reveals the author's familiarity with Muslim tradition, presents Islam as a monotheistic religion, and acknowledges its missionary success among the Arabs.[56]

The "enforced success" of the Muslim religion and culture in Spain resulted in protests and even martyrdom of some Christians. In the late spring of the year 851, a monk named Isaac publicly denounced Muḥammad in front of a Muslim *qāḍī* (judge) and proclaimed the divinity of Christ, for which he was decapitated. Soon, a few monks and priests shared his fate, thus inaugurating the so-called "Cordovan martyr movement," which generated a number of victims.[57] The monastic communities supported the movement. However, given the advanced level of Christian assimilation and acculturation, which had been going on for one hundred and forty years in forced coexistence, it was expected that the martyr movement would be rather unpopular among the Christians in Córdoba and, following pressure from Muslim authorities, some Christians repudiated Isaac and others.

Among the men who led the reaction, one should mention the priest Eulogius (who died as a martyr in 859) and Paul Alvarus, a layman.[58] Their apocalyptic writings were inspired by the idea that the hegemony of Islam was a preparation for the appearance of the Antichrist. They believed that the Christians in Spain were fighting for survival under Muslim rule. *Liber apologeticus martyrum*, written by Eulogius sometime between 857 and his death, is a severe attack on Muḥammad, portraying him as heresiarch, the Antichrist and a false prophet and presenting Islam as a misguided derivative of Christianity rather than an entirely separate and rival system.[59] There is no doubt that approaching the matter from that standpoint enabled the author to picture Isaac and other martyrs as truly virtuous defenders of the faith who deserved to be honored by their community. Paul Alvarus similarly defended the martyrs and their actions in his *Indiculus luminosus*, written in 854.[60]

It is important to emphasize that the early Christian polemics that came out of Muslim Spain, in particular from Córdoba, shed some light on the nature of Chris-

---

[55] Ibid., p. 93.

[56] Ibid., p. 94.

[57] Ibid., p. 95-96; N. Daniel, *Islam and the West...*, p. 16-17. Also refer to: E. P. Colbert, *The Martyrs of Córdoba (850-859): A Study of the Sources*, Washington, DC: Catholic University of America Press, 1962; A. Cutler, "The Ninth-Century Spanish Martyrs' Movement and the Origins of Western Christian Missions to Muslims," *Muslim World*, vol. 55 (1965), p. 321-339; J. Waltz, "The Significance of the Voluntary Martyrs of Ninth-Century Cordoba," *Muslim World*, vol. 60 (1970), p. 143-59.

[58] See: C. M. Sage, *Paul Albar of Cordoba: Studies on His Life and Writings*, Washington, DC: Catholic University of America Press, 1943. This work includes a translation of Alvar's *Life of Eulogius*, p. 190-214.

[59] K. B. Wolf, "Christian Views...," p. 100.

[60] Ibid., p. 98.

tian-Muslim relations during that time and presented two opposing views on Islam: "one as a dangerous false prophecy and the other as a monotheistic religion based on a distinct revelation" that "may have been replicated in other Spanish communities under Muslim rule in that period."[61]

It is also worth noting that the authors who could observe and experience firsthand the outcome of Islamic rule and were influential in shaping views, according to Southern, demonstrated "ignorance of [a] peculiarly complex kind":

> They were ignorant of Islam, not because they were far from it like the Carolingian scholars, but for the contrary reason that they were in the middle of it. If they saw and understood little of what went on round them, and if they knew nothing of Islam as a religion, it was because they wished to know nothing.... Significantly they preferred to know about Mahomet from the meager Latin source which Eulogius found in Christian Navarre, rather then [*sic*] from the fountainhead of the Koran or the great biographical compilations of their Moslem contemporaries. [62]

This simplistic approach to Islam became a standard pattern for a few centuries to come.

It is rather hard to find anti-Islamic literature from before the twelfth century in early medieval Catholic Europe, with the exception of Spain and the effort of Charlemagne, who asked Alcuin in 799 for "the disputation of Felix with a Saracen."[63] The absence of Christian-Muslim polemics in Catholic Europe is usually wrongly explained by the fact that apart from in Spain, there was no direct contact with Muslims. In addition, it is mistakenly believed that in the early medieval times, practically no information about Muslim conquests or the beliefs or habits of Muslim people infiltrated Europe. Kedar argues with these incorrect assumptions by presenting examples of various reciprocal contacts in Italy and France and referring to works from a substantial body of Latin literature containing information about the Muslim conquests, beliefs and habits.[64]

---

[61] Ibid., p. 102.

[62] R. W. S o u t h e r n, *Western Views of Islam...*, p. 25-26.

[63] B. Z. K e d a r, *Crusade and Mission...*, p. 25.

[64] See: Ibid., p. 25-29.

Medieval polemics with Islam: from a fight to a sophisticated argument

By the middle of the eleventh century, Christian-Muslim history was approaching a new phase of its development, namely the period of the Crusades.[65] Although in the Middle East the strength of Islam was still unquestionable, the balance of power there shifted from the Arabs to the Turks. The Eastern Christian Empire, by then much reduced in size, was facing a new challenge, namely the expansion of the Seljuk Turks. Under the circumstances, the Byzantine Emperor Alexius I Comnenos realized that a stronger Europe that had been freed from barbarian invasions and that had already begun the successful military campaign against Muslim dominance in Spain, Portugal and Sicily, could offer help in recovering the Holy Land.

It all started on November 27, 1095, at the Council of Clermont in Le Puy (France), where in response to urgent appeals for help from the Byzantine emperor, Pope Urban II in his sermon called upon all Christians to march to the Holy Land and free Jerusalem. The Pontiff's plea launched a crusading effort that would endure for the next two centuries and had a tremendous impact on Western culture. For Urban II, the Crusades were an opportunity not only to strengthen his authority but also to enforce the papacy's role in legitimizing temporal rulers, and a chance to reunite the Eastern (Greek) and Western (Latin) Church. The Pope's plea mobilized Christian rulers and their subjects to unite and engage in a campaign that would present new political, military and economic advantages to stagnant Europe. Furthermore, especially for the nobles of France, it was also an opportunity to bring rowdy knights under control by directing their fighting potential to a good cause, namely the recovery of the Holy Land. The first Crusade was successful and resulted in the capture of Jerusalem (1099) and the establishment of four Latin Kingdoms. However, the success was short-lived and by the middle of the twelfth century, the Muslims mounted an effective military response. In 1187, the army led by Saladin (Ṣalāḥ ad-Dīn) recaptured Jerusalem.[66] The subsequent crusades did not bring significant changes since they "had degenerated into intra-Christian wars, wars against enemies who papacy denounced as heretics and schismatics.[67]

---

[65]   For a broad discussion of Christian-Muslim relations during the period of the Crusades, based on primary sources, see: Ibid., p. 57-203. Also refer to: J. Hoeberichts, *Francis*...; J. Riley-Smith, *The Oxford History of the Crusades,* New York: Oxford University Press, 2002; M. G. Bull and N. Housley (eds.), *The Experience of Crusading*, Cambridge and New-York: Cambridge University Press, 2003; K. Kościelniak, *Grecy i Arabowie*...; N. Housley, *Contesting the Crusade*, Malden, MA: Blackwell Publishing, 2006; J. Żebrowski, *Dzieje Syrii: Od czasów najdawniejszych do współczesności*, Warszawa: Dialog, 2006.

[66]   He was one of the most talented Muslim commanders. For a thorough study about Saladin and his achievements see: A. S. Ehrenkreutz, *Saladin*, Albany: State University of New York Press, 1972.

[67]   J. L. Esposito, *The Islamic Threat*..., p. 42.

There is no doubt that the period of the Crusades was a time of cruelty, hostility, vehemence and violence. Nevertheless, one may not underestimate the impact the Crusades had on the reciprocal contacts between Christians and Muslims. For the first time, Europe had the chance to get acquainted with the advancement and richness of Muslim civilisation. That experience gave the West an inspiration and motivation for change. Christian Europe came back to new life, entering a path of new developments. The Franks modernized their armies and arms, old cities were rebuilt and new ones established. Furthermore, the growth of new commercial enterprises and financial institutions stimulated economic prosperity. The Muslim East inspired a new, more sophisticated and refined lifestyle and supplied the West with "novelties," such as spices, perfume, satin, silk and various attributes of lavishness and luxury.[68]

Direct contact with Muslims, especially taking into account their spiritual life, let Christians get better acquainted with Islam and encouraged them to engage in systematic studies of that religion. The impulse to pursue such studies was stimulated by the writings of the noted abbot of Cluny monastery – Pierre Maurice de Montboissier, better known as Peter the Venerable (1092-1156),[69] who believed that in order to fight Muslims successfully, it was important for Christians to know the followers of Islam better.[70] During his stay in Spain, where he inspected Cluny's branch monasteries and conferred with the Spanish emperor Alfonso VII, he had the chance to observe Christians and Muslims living side by side and eventually engaging in a dialogue of life.[71] Moreover, while in Spain, he met Peter of Toledo and other skilled translators of Arabic.[72] Thus, Peter the Venerable was able to grasp and recognize the essence of the opportunities that his stay in Spain might bring about and had enough courage to initiate serious studies of Islam in Europe.

---

[68]   B. Lewis, *Arabs in History...*, p. 138.

[69]   See: J. Kritzek, *Peter the Venerable...*

[70]   A. Hourani, *Europe and the Middle East*, Berkeley: University of California Press, 1980, p. 9, 23.

[71]   See: M. R. Menocal, *The Ornament of the World: How Muslims, Jews, and Christians Created a Culture of Tolerance in Medieval Spain*, Boston: Little, Brown and Company (Inc.), 2002.

[72]   Under the Muslim government, Toledo, Córdoba and Seville became important scholarly centers where Muslims, Christians and Jews worked together on various translating projects. The school of Toledo specialized in translating Arabic, Syriac and Greek manuscripts, including scientific, philosophical and historical ones, into Latin. These writings from the ancient world had been lost to Western Europe during the barbarian invasions. Fortunately, they had survived in Greek in Byzantium and in Arabic and/or Syriac in Islamic centers in the Middle East, particularly in Baghdad [there worked Ḥunayn Ibn Isḥāq (809-873), known in Latin as Johannitus, a famous scholar and translator of Greek scientific treaties into Arabic and Syriac]. Finally, these important works became available to Western Europe through Spain. As J. Kritzek pointed out "there was no intellectual center in Europe that was not touched in some way by, that did not owe some debt to, the school of Toledo" (*Peter the Venerable...*, p. 54).

The abbot commissioned Peter of Toledo and some other scholars to embark on an important project, i.e., translating the *Apology* of al-Kindy,[73] the three other Arabic language tractates and the Qur'an itself into Latin.[74] The entire project formed the Toledan Collection.[75] At the head of it, Peter of Toledo placed *A Summary of the Entire Heresy of the Saracens*, his own apologetic work based on new, more reliable sources. Although the new sources helped Peter of Toledo to write with more accuracy and credibility, his final judgement of the Prophet Muḥammad and Islam was as negative as that of his predecessors. However, his idea to collect authentic Islamic sources and to make them available to Christians was an important step in Christian-Muslim relations.

In the meantime, Christian theologians engaged in sharp polemics with Muslims. The attitude of the Church toward Islam remained negative. Christians continued to reject Islam, considering it a heresy,[76] while the Qur'an and the Prophet Muḥammad remained the primary targets of their vicious attacks. With the Reconquest of Spain under way and the early successes of Crusaders, more and more Muslims came under Christian domination. Since the number of restrictions on reciprocal contacts implemented by Christian authorities was increasing, the dissonance between the two religions remained.

As mentioned earlier, in the middle of continuous Christian-Muslim confrontations, aside from reciprocal hostility and struggle, there were always some attempts to bridge the two separate worlds. This was the case of scholarly centers in Spain, such as Toledo and Córdoba, and in the Norman Kingdom in Sicily, where Muslims, Jews and Christians discussed, debated and studied together, relatively free of the religious coercion and bitterness that followed later.[77] Fortunately, the predominantly uncompromising Christian position concerning theological matters did not affect the sphere of other sciences. Christians embarked on the task of examining Muslim

---

[73]   The book is commonly called by its Arabic name *Risāla*. It consists of two parts: *The letter from a Saracen* (Al-Hāshimī) and *The Reply of a Christian* (Al-Kindy, also spelled Al-Kindī). Modern scholarship has not been able to reach a consensus on when the text was actually composed; estimates range from the ninth to the eleventh centuries. The translator of this famous text was Peter of Toledo, a Jew who converted to Christianity. Al-Kindy's *Apology* gained circulation and popularity among Christian scholars in the Middle Ages because it provided a model of argumentation against Islam. These attacks focused in particular on the Qur'an, the prophethood of Muḥammad and the spreading of the faith by conquest. These themes formed the main topics of Christian scholarship on Islam in the Middle Ages (N. D a n i e l, *Islam and the West...*, p. 29-30; R. A r m o u r, *Islam, Christianity and the West...*, p. 83).

[74]   The first Latin translation of the Qur'an by Robert Ketton appeared in 1143. For a thorough discussion refer to: T. E. B u r m a n, *Reading the Qur'ān in Latin Christendom, 1140-1560*, Philadelphia: University of Pennsylvania Press, 2007, p. 60-122.

[75]   See: R. A r m o u r, *Islam, Christianity and the West...*, p. 81-85.

[76]   Christians totally rejected Islam because the new religion did not accept the divinity of Jesus Christ and the doctrine of Trinity, namely the fundaments of Christian theology.

[77]   R. A r m o u r, *Islam, Christianity and the West...*, p. 96, 99-100.

scholars' achievements in astronomy, mathematics, medicine and philosophy.[78] As a result of these studies, Medieval Europe rediscovered ancient achievements which gave creative nourishment to its new quest for knowledge, learning and development.

One may say that the translation of Islamic sources, a project realized by Peter the Venerable, was an important step toward acquiring a more objective Christian view of Islam. However, the polemical activity of Christians known as Mozarabs, among them converted Jews, who lived in Spain and over the centuries of Muslim rule there became Arabicized in language and culture though maintaining their Christian belief and practice, was of much greater significance. As Thomas E. Burman points out:

> All these Spanish Christians "nurtured among Muslims," whether converted Andalusian Jews or Mozarabs had an intimacy with Islam that no other European Christian could match in the twelfth century. Known best collectively as Andalusian Christians... these Arabic-speaking Catholics had immediate and centuries' long experience of Islam, and as such they provided historians interested in Medieval-European perceptions of Islam with the opportunity to examine how Christians who knew Islam in the flesh attempted to understand and confront it intellectually.[79]

The apologetic and anti-Islamic writings of the eleventh- and twelfth-century Andalusian Christians reveal their authors' intellectual approach to Islam, namely how they studied Islam (sources and methods) while developing its image from their first-hand experience. In this regard, Burman says, practically all the Andalusian-Christian works share the tendency to draw on and interweave both material and methods from at least three crucial bodies of literature, namely "(1) the vast body of Islamic Traditional literature known usually as the *Ḥadīth*, (2) Middle-Eastern Christian theological and apologetic works written in Arabic; and (3) contemporary Latin theology."[80] All this enabled Andalusian-Christian scholars, among them Pedro de Alfonso (1062-1110), a Christian convert from Judaism, to apply both the methods and terms derived from Muslim sources in order to defend and explain Christian doctrines more convincingly. At the same time, the sources provided Christians with more thorough explanations of Muslim beliefs and practices.[81] Although this new approach did not change the overall medieval Christian image of Islam, it was an attempt to exchange the fight for a sophisticated argument and a sound preparation for more positive developments to come.

---

[78] See: W. M. Watt, *The influence of Islam...*, p. 30-44, 58-71.

[79] T. E. Burman,"*Tathlîth al-waḥdanîyâh* and the Twelfth-Century Andalusian-Christian Approach to Islam," in: J. V. Tolan (ed.), *Medieval Christian Perceptions to Islam...*, p. 110. For a further discussion on related issues see: idem, *Religious Polemic and the Intellectual History of the Mozarabs, 1050-1200*, Leiden and New York: E. J. Brill, 1994.

[80] T. E. Burman, "*Tathlîth al-waḥdanîyâh...*," p. 111.

[81] The works presenting such a tendency, and in particular an anonymous twelfth-century treatise known as *Thathlîth al-waḥdanîyâh* (Trinitizing the Unity of God or Confessing the Threefold Nature of the Oneness) are discussed at length by T. E. Burman: "*Tathlîth al-waḥdanîyâh...*," p. 109-128.

It should be pointed out that despite the predominantly reluctant and intolerant attitude of the Catholic Church towards Islam in medieval times, there were also some appeals for reconciliation and understanding. In 1076, Gregory VII (1015-1085),[82] a famous medieval Pope and a great reformer, in his letter to Emir An-Nāṣir referred to common roots in the "patriarch Abraham."[83] Furthermore, the Pope urged Christians and Muslim to enter the path of love and understanding based on the common belief in One God. In his monograph *L'Eglise catholique et Islam*, Michel Lelong points out that even the gloomy history of the Crusades is marked by some conciliatory initiatives, namely religious meetings and disputes.[84]

The results of such measures were diverse. The majority of Christians remained rather faithful to their inherited hostile attitude toward Muslims and still considered Islam to be a religion of faults and a threat. They criticized the lack of sincerity of Muslim practices and made little effort to understand Muslims' intentions. As Daniel points out, the term *heresy*, "treated as a common noun in referring to Islam, was used carelessly and casually in this connection."[85] All in all, Christians could view Islam only as "a corruption of Christian truth." Still, differences were counted and emphasized but similarities ignored. However, there was also a flicker of hope. For a number of Christians, a direct encounter with the followers of Islam and the observance of their deep religious belief was a breakthrough and an enriching experience. Opinions even appeared that the religious attitudes and practices of Muslims could become an inspiration for Christians.[86]

Medieval missionary activity: a hope for building bridges of understanding and reconciliation

The medieval time was marked by the development of the Christian missionary activity of the mendicant orders, such as Dominicans and Franciscans. They both worked for the conversion of Jews and Muslims in Spain, North Africa and the Holy Land. The Franciscans focused on mission work and direct preaching. The Dominicans' efforts were primarily directed towards training missionary monks. In order

---

[82] About the attitude of Pope Gregory VII to Muslims, see: A. Hourani, *Islam in European Thought*, Cambridge: Cambridge University Press, 1995, p. 9-10.

[83] See: *The Register o Pope Gregory VII 1073-1085: An English Translation*, trans. H. E. J. Cowdrey, Oxford and New York: Oxford University Press, 2002, p. 204-205.

[84] M. Lelong, *L'Eglise catholique...*, p. 44. For a polemic during the time of the Crusades see: R. Y. Ebied and D. Thomas (eds.), *Muslim-Christian Polemics during the Crusades: The Letter from the People of Cyprus and Ibn Abī Ṭālib al-Dimashqī's Response*, Leiden and Boston: E. J. Brill, 2005.

[85] N. Daniel, *Islam and the West...*, p. 213.

[86] M. Lelong, *L'Eglise catholique...*, p. 13.

to pursue their task effectively, they established several schools for learning Arabic. Dominicans also advocated continuing the Crusades alongside preaching activities.

Among the known Dominicans one should mention William of Tripoli (1220-1273), who was "relatively well informed about the beliefs and history of the Muslims."[87] His work *De Statu Saracenorum* reveals that William's good command of Arabic enabled him to not only get acquainted with the Qur'an and appreciate its unique style and language, but also to study the commentaries well. Therefore, in his discussions on related issues he was able to quote from different Islamic sources, well aware of their value. According to Daniel, "this careful distinction between the text, commentators and the Qur'an provides evidence showing respect and appreciation of the text."[88] His attitude towards the Prophet Muḥammad and Muslims rather parallels the previous negative images. However, the accounts are more substantial since the author quotes from Muslim sources. Furthermore, as Rollin Armour says, Tripoli "noted instances where Christianity and Islam agreed, citing passages on Jesus and Mary from the Qur'an and the *ḥadīth*, quoting from the Qur'an at length and quite accurately."[89]

Another famous Dominican missionary, Ricaldo da Monte di Croce (1243-1320), known as Ricoldo of Monte Croce, is credited with important works on Islam, among them *Contra Legem Sarracenorum* and *Itinerarium*. He joined the Dominican order in 1267 and in 1280 began a long journey of about twenty years to the Middle East with two aims: to learn about Islam and to work on converting Muslims. Ricoldo of Monte Croce succeeded in the first goal but not in the second.[90] His *Itinerarium* is an account of his travels that gave him the tremendous opportunity to explore the Muslim environment. The author began by visiting the Holy Land, travelled across Syria, through Mesopotamia and into Persia and stayed for some time in Baghdad, the city that witnessed the Muslim golden age, decline under Mongols rule, and still remained an important center for Islamic learning. His direct experience with the Muslims, their religion and their culture did not have much impact on his image of Islam, and his arguments resembled earlier ones, namely those from the medieval canon attacks against Islam, such as that the doctrines of the Qur'an were heresies and could not be God's law, that Muḥammad was an impostor and a forerunner of the Antichrist, etc.[91] However, it should be noted that Ricoldo of Monte Croce was among the few Christian polemicists who gained direct experience with the Muslims by living side by side with them and therefore his criticism acquired some moderation. He even praised Muslims for their "piety and morals."[92]

---

[87] B. Z. Kedar, *Crusade and Mission...*, p. 180.
[88] N. Daniel, *Islam and the West...*, p. 194.
[89] R. Armour, *Islam, Christianity and the West...*, p. 89-90.
[90] Ibid., p. 90.
[91] N. Daniel, *Islam and the West...*, p. 87-88.
[92] R. Armour, *Islam, Christianity and the West...*, p. 91.

As for the Franciscans, the missionary activity of Francis of Assisi (1181-1226) and Ramon Lull (1232-1315) deserves our special consideration.

St. Francis of Assisi's short trip to Egypt and his meeting with the Ayyubid sultan Malik al-Kāmil in 1219 in Damietta, the Egyptian village in the Nile Delta, is considered not only one of the best-known of the Franciscan's missionary efforts but is also one of the most significant examples of the medieval encounters between the followers of Christianity and Islam.[93] As mentioned, the initial purpose of that meeting was an attempt to convert the Sultan to Christianity.[94] However, the matter went in a different direction. It happened that on his way to Damietta, St. Francis visited the camps of the Crusaders. He was astonished to find his brothers in faith overcome by vehement hostility towards Muslims. Therefore, St. Francis realized that the words of the Gospel should be addressed first to his fellow believers. Another learning moment, this time a positive astonishment, was awaiting St. Francis in Damietta. The meeting with the Sultan proved to be different than expected. St. Francis of Assisi found out, to his surprise, that Malik al-Kāmil was not a barbarian, but a simple, pious man and a sensitive intellectual whose heart was full of love to One God – Allāh – and who spoke openly about the futility and harm of religious wars.[95]

As Christian Troll pointed out, the meeting in Damietta had a great impact on St. Francis of Assisi and significantly changed his view on Islam.[96] From that time, he was convinced that true faith and love for One God may be also found in the hearts of Muslims.[97] In Chapter 16 of his book *Regula non-boullata of 1221*, St. Francis advised the Christians of two ways of going "among" the Muslims.[98] The first way was to avoid quarrels and disputes and to be a subject to every human creature for God's sake (1 Peter 2:13), and in so doing bearing witness to the fact that they were Christians. The second was to proclaim the word of God openly, when they were able to see that it was God's will. According to Lelong,[99] the encounter in Damietta could have become a starting point for a dialogue with the followers of Islam. However, the vast majority of Christians were not ready yet for such a change.

---

[93] B. Z. Kedar, *Crusade and Mission...*, p. 119-126.

[94] The issue of St. Francis's journey to Damietta and his meeting with Malik al-Kāmil is presented by St. Bonaventure in his *Biography of St. Francis*. See: R. Prejs, Z. Kijas (eds.), *Źródła Franciszkańskie: Pisma św. Franciszka, źródła biograficzne św. Franciszka, pisma świętej Klary i źródła biograficzne, teksty ustalające normy dla braci i sióstr od pokuty*, trans. K. Ambrożbkiewicz, B. A. Gancarz [et al.], Kraków: Wydawnictwo OO. Franciszkanów "Bratni Zew," 2005, p. 914-916.

[95] *Dzieje Błogosławionego Franciszka i jego towarzyszy*, in: R. Prejs, Z. Kijas (eds.), *Źródła franciszkańskie...*, p. 1197-1198

[96] C. W. Troll, "Mission and Dialogue: The Example of Islam," *Encounter: Documents for Muslim-Christian Understanding*, no. 189-190 (November-December 1992), p. 12.

[97] For a detailed study on St. Francis's teachings concerning the relations with Muslims, see: J. Hoeberichts, *Francis...*

[98] For an analysis of Chapter 16, both its literary context and conceptual exegesis, see: Ibid., p. 43-138.

[99] M. Lelong, *L'Eglise catholique...*, p. 17.

The other famous Franciscan missionary was Ramon Lull (1233-1315), a poet, philosopher, theologian and mystic from Majorca.[100] Lull grew up during the times of the Reconquista, when Christianity was gaining back its influences on the island. His worldview was shaped by exposure to Catalonian culture, characterized by pluralism and even syncretism, and influences of Christian, Jewish and Muslim philosophical and mystical traditions. During the years 1262-1265, as a result of a Christ revelation, Lull decided to reform himself.[101] From that point, his entire life was devoted to the mission of spreading the Gospel to non-Christians, and in particular, Muslims.[102] He described himself as *Christianus arabicus*, which in modern language would mean a Specialist on Islam. Lull was a precursor to a modern missionary, a man of charisma and a scholar who was familiar with not only Islamic doctrine but also with Muslim tradition, philosophy, theology and mysticism.[103] Furthermore, he believed that in order to conduct his mission correctly and effectively, he should know the Arabic language. Only by knowing people's language could he initiate and conduct with them an honest, rational and sincere dialogue. It should be mentioned that Lull was neither afraid of Islam nor of entering into any kind of discussion with Muslim theologians. In his numerous works, among them the famous *Llibre del gentil e dels tres savis*,[104] he referred to Muslim doctrines and attempted to share his thorough knowledge with future generations of missionaries.[105] During the times of the Crusades, he proved that fighting Muslims by sword would not bring results and the only possible way to gain their hearts and even souls was to approach them with respect, tolerance and love. His unusual, in comparison with that of his contemporaries, attitude towards Muslims, and the originality of his mission among them, which focused not on negation of everything that was Islamic but on a sincere attempt to get to know and understand Islam and its followers, could enable us to consider him the first missionary-publicist.[106]

---

[100] See: S. M. Zwemer, *Raymund Lull: First Missionary to the Moslems*, Three Rivers: Diggory Press, 2006. This work was originally published by Funk and Wagnalls, New York, 1902.

[101] A. Sawicka, *Drogi i bezdroża kultury katalońskiej*, Kraków: Księgarnia Akademicka, 2007, p. 78-79.

[102] See: D. Urvoy, "Ramon Lull et l'Islam," *Islamochristiana*, vol. 7 (1981), p. 127-146.

[103] According to D. Urvoy, with regard to the opportunities of Christian-Muslim encounters and dialogues during the thirteenth and fourteenth centuries, sufism appeared as a possible common "field for exchanges in philosophy and theology." The author mentions Ramon Lull's spiritual dispute with Muslims ("Soufisme et dialogue islamo-chrétien, *Islamochristiana*, vol. 30 (2004), p. 55-64).

[104] See: R. Llull, *Llibre del gentil e dels tres savis*, Catala: Publicacions de l'Abadia de Montserrat, 2001. For recent edition R. Lull's works, containing all the previous critical editions, refer to: *Nova edicio de les obres de Ramon Llull*, Palma: Nabu Press, 1990.

[105] For a thorough discussion on Lull's writing related to Islamic philosophy, theology and mysticism refer to: J. Judycka, *Wiara i rozum w filozofii Rajmunda Lulla*, Lublin: Wydawnictwo Katolickiego Uniwersytetu Lubelskiego, 2005.

[106] T. Mastnak, *Crusading Peace: Christendom, the Muslim World, and Western Political Order*, Berkeley, CA and London: University of California Press, 2002, p. 104.

Another important voice that could change the history of Christian-Muslim relations, if taken into consideration in the right time, came from St. Thomas Aquinas. He was one of the greatest scholars who benefited from philosophical texts translated by Muslim, Jewish and Christian famous scholarly centers, such as Toledo, Cordoba and Sicily.

As pointed out by James Waltz, the literature devoted to St. Thomas Aquinas (1225-1274) and Islam had as its primary concern the impact of Islamic philosophy on his thought and hardly explored the issue of his attitude towards Muslims.[107] Furthermore, the scholar brings clear evidence of both the possibilities that St. Thomas had to acquire quite extensive knowledge about Islam and the results of such advantages as presented in his writings. He grew up in a family engaged in the service of the Emperor Frederic II, whose army boasted Muslim soldiers and whose court supported Muslim scholars.[108] Later, at the University of Naples, St.Thomas had the opportunity to study the works of Ibn Rushd, known in Europe as Averroes (1126-1198), the greatest Muslim Aristotelian, whose thought inspired a new and refreshing insight into major philosophical and religious themes. Finally, in Paris, he encountered and closely followed the theological formulations of Al-Farābī (870-950), and explored the scholarship of other Muslim thinkers.[109] It is worth noting that St. Thomas was also well aware of the main issues concerning Christian-Muslim polemics and disagreements. However, as pointed out by Waltz, "it appears rather unlikely that St. Thomas knew the disputation literature directly, although John of Damascus, whom he often cites, gave guidelines for disputations and composed a tract, *On Heresy of the Ismaelites*, which Thomas may have read and used."[110] However, Waltz argues that St. Thomas's knowledge of Islam "was yet severely limited," since:

> He could not consult the *sharī'a* or *hadīth* which embody Islamic law, he certainly manifests no knowledge of Islamic history, and, despite the claim that Muḥammad's perversions and fabrications "can be seen by anyone who examines his law," there is no evidence that he ever read the Qur'an, although Latin translations were available.[111]

---

[107] J. Waltz, "Muḥammad and the Muslims in St. Thomas Aquinas," *The Muslim World*, vol. 66/2 (April 1976), p. 81-95. The author mentions here an interesting study by M.-D. Chenu who proposed research on "Islam and Christendom" based on the *Summa contra Gentiles*. See: M.-D. Chenu, *Introduction à l'étude de Saint Thomas d'Aquin*, Montréal: Institut d'études médiévales de l'université de Montréal, 1950; eadem, *Toward Understanding St. Thomas*, trans. Albert M. Landry and Dominic Hughes, Chicago: H. Regnery Publishing, 1964, p. 295.

[108] See: Ph. Lomax, "Frederic II, His Saracens and the Papacy," in: J. V. Tolan (ed.), *Medieval Christian Perceptions to Islam...*, p. 175-197.

[109] J. Waltz, "Muḥammad and the Muslims...," p. 87. For a thorough discussion on the influence of Muslim thinkers on Western Medieval thought, see: R. Hammond, *The Philosophy of Alfarabi and its Influence on Medieval Thought*, New York: Hobson Book Press, 1947; E. A. Myers, *Arabic Thought and the Western World in the Golden Age of Islam*, New York: Ungar, 1964.

[110] J. Waltz, "Muḥammad and the Muslims...," p. 86.

[111] Ibid., p. 86-87.

St. Thomas Aquinas wrote about Islam in his *Summa contra Gentiles* and *De rationibus fidei contra Saracenos, Graecos et Armenos*. His attitude towards Islam, as revealed in these works, according to Waltz, seems to be far from objective or sympathetic and the arguments used against the Muslim religion are traditional Christian ones alleging violence or Muḥammad's lack of miracles. While St. Thomas acknowledged that Muḥammad taught some truth accessible to human reason, such as monotheism, he attempted to discredit his teaching by focusing on the Prophet's audience. He was convinced that Muḥammad's false doctrines could attract only brutes and nomads.[112] The major problem with Islam, as seen by Aquinas, "was its lack of authority, an authority that miracles could provide."[113] It should be pointed out that in St. Thomas's view of Islam, a new, important feature appeared which could explain the lack of positive outcomes from Christian-Muslim encounters.

In his book *Islam and the West: The Making of an Image*, Norman Daniel attempts to find the reasons for the persistent, intolerant and reluctant Christian attitude towards Islam. The author quotes St. Thomas Aquinas, who in the thirteenth century had pointed out the need to search for new moral and philosophical arguments that could be acceptable for Muslims. He emphasized that in the case of the polemics with Muslims, the use of both biblical authorities and rational methods of argument had proven futile. Aquinas suggested that theological discussions with the followers of Islam should instead focus on the defense of faith rather than on its proof. Most important was establishing a common ground for a possible way of communication and eventual understanding. Aquinas was convinced that the use of force was definitely inappropriate for converting Muslims "because to believe is a matter of will."[114] It was quite possible that the history of the relations between Christianity and Islam would have taken a different path and the bridges could have been built much earlier if the words of St. Thomas Aquinas had been taken into consideration.

It is worth noting that in the thirteenth century, the universities in Paris and Salamanca introduced studies of the Arabic language. It was a clear sign that the West had embarked on the serious task of examining the achievements of Muslim civilization using primary sources.

In the course of the thirteenth century, the West systematically grew stronger and was preparing for its next military campaigns. The subsequent Crusades, however, did not bring the awaited results. With the Mongol invasion and the fall of the Abbasid caliphate in 1258, Christian hopes for victory were once again raised. However, they quickly vanished, because in Egypt power was taken by an effective and strong dynasty, namely the Mamluks.[115] The Crusaders, then, were losing pre-

---

[112] Ibid., p. 83-84.

[113] R. Armour, *Islam, Christianity and the West...*, p. 98.

[114] J. Waltz, "Muḥammad and the Muslims...," p. 92.

[115] The Mamluks (1250-1517) were a local Muslim dynasty of slave origin that ruled in Egypt and Syria. They successfully challenged the Mongol threat. As defenders of Islamic orthodoxy, the Mamluks sponsored numerous religious buildings, including mosques, madrasas

viously-conquered cities one after the other. In 1291, ʿAkkā, the last fortress of the Crusaders, fell. In addition, a new force appeared in the Muslim West. A well-armed, well-trained and strong wave of Turkish tribes from Central Asia approached the Middle East. The Turks embraced Islam, established a dynasty[116] and with determination began to build their empire. In a relatively short period of time, the Ottomans became the champions and the defenders of their new faith.

During medieval times, the efforts of the Christian polemicists with Islam and missionaries engaged in contact with Muslims had two major aims: to discourage Christians from becoming Muslims and to encourage Muslims to become Christians. However, both proved to be rather idle goals, and, as Bernard Lewis concluded, "it took some centuries before they decided that the first was no longer necessary and the second was impossible."[117]

The renaissance's quest for knowledge, pragmatism and tolerance

The conquest of Constantinople in 1453 by the Ottoman Turks opened a new phase in the history of Christian-Muslim relations. With the final loss of hopes for military victory, some Christians gradually acquired a more balanced, pragmatic and tolerant attitude toward the Muslim East. However, the Church's position on the religion of Islam was very negative. Christians persistently continued to reject the possibility of a new revelation and proclamation of the rules of God by a new prophet. Furthermore, the polemics with the Muslims remained within the framework of formerly-established canons and limitations despite the fact that new Christian studies on Islam had been established.

From the time of the Renaissance in Europe, interest in the Muslim West began to increase. Many expeditions were organized. These included commercial, exploration and scientific expeditions. Furthermore, Islamic political, social and cultural issues quickly broadened the scope of religious themes. Increasing contact with the Muslim East and the possibility of watching "the living Islam" closely resulted in

---

and khanqahs. See: D. P. Little, *History and Historiography of the Mamlūks*, London: Variorum Reprints, 1986.

[116] The Ottomans (1281-1922) were a dynasty of Turkish sultans established by Osman (1258-1324) in Anatolia shortly after the Mongol's invasion. Following the conquest of Constantinople in 1453 and a successful military campaign in Asia and North Africa, they came to rule Islamic lands also threatening Europe; in the eighteenth century a gradual downfall of the Empire began. See: C. Imber, *The Ottoman Empire, 1300-1650: The Structure of Power*, New York: Palgrave, 2002; B. Tezcan, *The Second Ottoman Empire: Political and Social Transformation in the Early Modern World*, Cambridge and New York: Cambridge University Press, 2010.

[117] B. Lewis, *Islam...*, p. 13.

a gradual, although still slow and reluctant, change of the Western attitude towards Muslim civilization. With time a number of false images, wrong assumptions and stereotypes acquired some moderation.

It should be noted that with regard to religious dogmas, the medieval canons were still valid and obviously the Christian views of Islam remained negative. However, one may say that the Renaissance witnessed an important shift in attitude towards Muslim faith.[118] This change was associated with three fifteenth-century scholars, namely John of Segovia, Pope Pius II and Nicolas de Cusa, as well as one sixteenth-century Protestant theologian, Theodore Bibliander. It was their call to recognize legitimate religious values in Islam and to strengthen efforts to reach reciprocal understanding. A Spanish Franciscan, John of Segovia (1400-1458) proposed a new approach to Islam.[119] He was a professor at Salamanca and an advocate of Church reforms at the time of the Council of Basel (1431-1439). John of Segovia was dissatisfied with the lack of knowledge about Islam among Christians. He also argued that the problems that Christendom encountered with the Muslims and their religion could not be resolved by force. Therefore, he was convinced that the only solution to Christian-Muslim conflict was entering a path of peaceful negotiations while pursuing the task of increasing the knowledge of Islam. The last five years before his death in 1458 were spent in retirement at small monastery in Savoy, where he devoted himself to studies on Islam:

> And he did two things: made a new translation of the Koran, and he tried to interest his distinguished friends in his plans for solving the whole problem. Both these projects required a brief consideration and first of all the translation of the Koran, which was the foundation of his larger plans.[120]

Among the scholars addressed by John Segovia was Cardinal Nicolas of Cusa (1400-1464), a scholar and a churchman committed to reforms.[121] In his letter to Nicolas of Cusa, John of Segovia advocated a new approach to Islam, namely organisation of debates between Christian and Muslim leaders.[122] Nicolas of Cusa undertook the proposed new approach in his works *De pace fidei* and *Cribratio Alkorani*.[123]

---

[118] See: R. Armour, *Islam, Christianity and the West...*, p. 103-107.
[119] R.W. Southern, *Western Views of Islam...*, p. 89-92.
[120] Ibid., p. 87.
[121] Ibid., p. 92-94.
[122] Ibid., p. 93.
[123] See: J. E. Biechler, H. L. Bond (eds.), *Nicholas of Cusa on Interreligious Harmony: Text, Concordance, and Translation of De Pace Fidei*, Lewiston: Edwin Mellen Press, 1990; J. Hopkins (trans., analysis), *Nicholas of Cusa's "De pace fidei" and "Cribratio Alcorani,"* Minneapolis: Arthur J. Banning Press, 1994. For a discussion of Nicolas of Cusa's philosophy refer to: idem, *A Concise Introduction to the Philosophy of Nicholas of Cusa*, Minneapolis: University of Minnesota Press, 1978.

In *De pace fidei* he presented his vision of a conference with the participation of the leaders of major religious and ethnic groups. The aim of their discussion was to find out what they had in common. In that treatise, the author referred to Abraham as the father of the faith of all believers, namely Christians, Arabs and Jews.[124] Nicolas of Cusa emphasized Islam's strict monotheism. Moreover, while searching for similarities between Islam and Christianity, he focused on the Qur'anic passages that paralleled references in the Bible and common elements of the religious practices.

The other work, i.e., *Cribratio Alkorani*, represents a completely different approach to Islam.[125] While one may find here traces of the previously presented peaceful attitude to the Muslim religion, there is no doubt that in *Cribratio Alkorani*, Nicolas of Cusa returns to the earlier medieval views of discrediting the Qur'an, the Prophet Muḥammad and Islam. As Armour pointed out, the unexpected swaying away from a quite tolerant attitude towards Islam, as presented earlier in *De pace fidei*, was rather "disappointing" because "the *peace* proposed in the former is lacking in the latter."[126] Despite the unexpected shift in attitude toward Islam, it is important to credit Nicolas of Cusa for his innovative idea in *De pace fidei*. While stating that the common elements found in different religions could provide a basis for conversation, he definitely moved beyond polemical arguments in order to reach a mutual understanding. This, according to Armour, marked Nicolas of Cusa as "a notable innovator."[127]

Moreover, in the last month of his life John of Segovia sent a letter to Cardinal Aeneas Silvius Piccolomini (1405-1464), a respected Italian humanist who in 1458 was elected the Pope and took the name Pius II.[128] He criticized the Cardinal for calls to organize the new Crusades and advocated undertaking rather peaceful measures to reach the hearts of Muslims.[129] The Pope's reaction came two years later, when he wrote a letter to Mahomet II, the Turkish sultan and the commander of the army that captured Constantinople in 1453. In that letter, Pius II invited the Sultan to embrace Christianity. He pointed out the common features of the two religions and focused on the advantages of such a conversion, which would make Mehmet II the most powerful man of his day.[130]

There is no doubt that the Renaissance brought a noteworthy change in Christian thinking about Islam. One may share Southern's opinion that there was a "moment

---

[124] N. Daniel, *Islam and the West...*, p. 307.

[125] See: R. Armour, *Islam, Christianity and the West...*, p. 108-109.

[126] Ibid., p. 109.

[127] Ibid.

[128] As Pope, he was confronted with the pressing crisis of the advance of the Ottoman Turks, who in 1453 had captured Constantinople. He worked, albeit with little success, to organize a Christian crusade against Turks. His other chief concern was the decline of papal authority (M. Bunson, *The Pope Encyclopedia: An A to Z of the Holy See*, New York: Crown Trade Paperback, 1995, p. 276).

[129] R.W. Southern, *Western Views of Islam...*, p. 99.

[130] R. Armour, *Islam, Christianity and the West...*, p. 111.

of vision."[131] This "moment" had resulted from a gradual and shaky but meaningful evolution of the Christian approach to Islam. The previously discussed Renaissance scholars were not only able to learn a great deal about Islam while grasping its essence. In addition, they found common elements in both religions and acknowledged that the truth may be found in the other religion and, significantly, they proposed conversation. However, since the expected outcome of the conversation that they had in mind was Muslim conversion, they had little or no success in bringing their counterparts into discussions. Nevertheless, they had laid out the path of possible reciprocal understanding. This was the evident success of the Christian Renaissance scholars such as John of Segovia, Nicolas of Cusa and Pius II.

With the fall of the Byzantine and the rise of the Turkish power, the military threat of Islam to Europe constituted a great danger. The Ottoman armies had already moved into the lower Balkans and after the conquest of Constantinople pushed farther north into Hungary. Their presence in Europe was reversing the long Western offensive march against Islamic lands. By 1529, the army under Suleiman II (the Magnificent), the grandson of the conqueror of Constantinople, was at gates of Vienna. As it turned out, both in 1529 and later in 1532 the Turks had to retreat without taking the city.[132] However, for the next century and a half, the outcome of the possible Ottoman invasion was uncertain. It seems natural that under such circumstances the irenic approach to Islam was about to vanish. During the times of the Reformation there was not much interest in Islam and negative views were again surfacing. One may point out here the important contribution of the Swiss theologian and Renaissance scholar Theodore Bibliander (1504-1564),[133] and of Martin Luther (1483-1546).[134] In the face of constant severe military threat to Christendom from the Turks, culminating in the siege of Vienna in 1529, and the appearance in the same year of the Lutheran Augsburg Confession, Pope Clement VII (1478-1534) ordered the burning of the Arabic text of the Qur'an immediately after its publication in Venice.[135]

The sixteenth century witnessed considerable changes in the Muslim world, namely the expansion of the three Islamic Empires.[136] The Ottoman Turks moved into Southwest Asia and Southeast Europe, all the way to Vienna and across North Africa. The Safavids (1502-1736) established and developed a powerful empire in

---

[131] R.W. Southern, *Western Views of Islam...*, p. 103.

[132] The Turkish armies were at the gates of Vienna again in 1532. However, that time they also retreated without taking the city. The Turkish threat ended in 1683.

[133] See: K. Vehlow, "The Swiss Reformers Zwingli, Bullinger and Bibliander and their Attitude to Islam (1520-1560)," *Islam and Christian-Muslim Relations*, vol. 6 (1995), p. 229-254.

[134] See: A. S. Francisco, *Martin Luter and Islam: A Study in Sixteen-Century Polemics and Apologetics*, Leiden and Boston, E. J. Brill, 2007.

[135] H. Küng (et al.), *Christianity and the World Religions: Paths of Dialogue with Islam, Hinduism, and Buddhism*; trans. P. Heinegg, Garden City, NY: Doubleday, 1986, p. 20.

[136] See: M. G. C. Hodgson, *The Venture of Islam: Conscience and History in a World Civilization*, vol. 3: *The Gunpowder Empires and Modern Times*, Chicago and London: University of Chicago Press, 1974.

Persia.[137] Finally, the Great Mughals (1526-1858) flourished in India.[138] These empires represented the splendid achievements in all aspects of Muslim civilization. However, this last success did not last long, since the inevitable process of decline in the Muslim world had already begun.

While the Ottoman Empire posed a severe military threat to Europe during the days of Suleiman the Magnificent, his successor's armies and navies were unable to reach a comparable level of success. Therefore, the balance of power began to shift towards the Christian West. The Indian Ocean had been controlled for centuries by Arabs and subsequently by the Turks. With the success of the Portuguese navigators who rounded the Cape of Good Hope, the sea route to Asia was opened. Subsequently, the Western offensive continued: in 1509, the Arab-Egyptian fleet was destroyed and the Arabian Sea went under European control. Moreover, in 1510 and 1511, the Portuguese seized Goa and Malacca. Finally, with the capturing of Ormuz on the Persian Gulf, the Western military presence in South and Southeast Asia had begun.

The Turkish navy that had dominated the Mediterranean had been destroyed earlier at the Battle of Lepanto in 1571.[139] In 1683, Turkish troops withdrew from Vienna for the last time. The treaty of Carlovitz in 1699 was a clear sign that power had begun to shift to the Latin West.[140] The Islamic threat was limited to one area only, namely the Mediterranean coast of North Africa. In the seventeenth and into the eighteenth centuries, Algerian corsairs or pirates ventured into Mediterranean Sea lanes, attacking British, French and even American ships reaching as far as Iceland.

---

[137]   The Safavids (1502-1736) were one of the most significant ruling dynasties of Iran who established the *Ithnā 'asharī* (Twelve) school of Shi'a Islam as the official religion of their empire. They established control over all of Persia and reasserted the Iranian identity of the region, marking one of the most important turning points in the history of Islam. See: A. J. Newman, *Safavid Iran: Rebirth of a Persian Empire*, London: I.B. Tauris, 2006; Ch. P. Melville (ed.), *Safavid Persia: The History and Politics of an Islamic Society*, London: I. B. Tauris, 1996.

[138]   The Great Mughals (1526-1858) were descendants of the Timurids, who around 1700 controlled most of the Indian Subcontinent – from Bengal in the east to Balochistan in the west, Kashmir in the north to the Kaveri basin in the south. See: D. E. Streusand, *The Formation of the Mughal Empire*, Delhi and New York: Oxford University Press, 1989; J. F. Richards, *The Mughal Empire*, Cambridge and New York: Cambridge University Press, 1992.

[139]   On October 7, 1571, on the Gulf between mainland Greece and the Peloponnese, the fleets of the Ottoman Empire and the Holy League fought in a battle. The Ottoman fleet was destroyed. Victory gave the Holy League temporary control over the Mediterranean, protected Rome from invasion, and prevented the Ottomans from advancing further into Europe. For a thorough account of the battle and its historical and symbolic significance see: N. Capponi, *Victory of the West: The Story of the Battle of Lepanto*, London: Macmillan, 2006.

[140]   The Peace Treaty, concluding the Austro-Ottoman War of 1683-1697, in which the Ottoman side had finally been defeated at the Battle of Zenta and expelled from the Hungarian Kingdom after almost one and a half centuries of occupation, was signed on January 26, 1699, in Sremski Karlovci. Austria received all of Hungary and Transylvania except the Banat. Venice obtained most of Dalmatia along with the Morea. Poland recovered Podolia. The Ottomans retained Belgrade. The Treaty marked the beginning of the Ottoman decline, and made the Habsburg Monarchy the dominant power in Southeastern Europe.

The Latin West, long overshadowed by the Islamic world, became a challenging competitor. The sea power of the Portuguese and Spanish, joined by the Dutch and British, took Europeans directly to Asia. The West and its new flourishing science, movable technology, developing culture and literature was marching ahead, while the Islamic world moved into the defensive. Furthermore, the nineteenth century industrialization process enabled the West to gain a quite advantageous position. Subsequently, European rulers, emboldened by their underlying conviction of the religious and moral privileges of Christendom, started to look for new lands to conquer.

Acquiring knowledge from direct sources and approaching a new enlightened perspective

New and original studies on the Prophet Muḥammad and the Muslim religion were to be developed in Europe in the late sixteenth and seventeenth centuries. Among the reasons that had helped raise Western consciousness about Islam, one may point out the expansion of markets and military interests beyond the Mediterranean Sea. This expansion was a prelude to the development of colonial ventures, treaties and alliances with Muslims and Protestant-Catholic separation. Under the circumstances, anti-Muslim polemics gradually waned. Moreover, since the European interest in Islamic land stretched far beyond the scope of religious aspects, such interest could not be longer limited to theological disputes about the Qur'an, the Prophet and early Muslim history.

With the increase of Western power, starting from the seventeenth century and continuing on as the Islamic threat was significantly diminishing, Western scholars "found it easier to think of Islam as a religious movement rather than a direct enemy."[141] Therefore, they embarked on more organized and systematic studies. They began with the Arabic language[142] and on publication of Arab and Islamic sources. Finally, this developed into work by scholars who not only studied related literature but also acquired knowledge of the Muslim world from direct encounters with various manifestations of so-called "living Islam."

From the important works of that time, one should mention *Pansebeia* by Alexander Ross (1591-1654), published in 1649 (or 1650),[143] and *An Account of the*

---

[141] R. Armour, *Islam, Christianity and the West…*, p. 133.

[142] The Chair of Arabic was established at the College de France in 1539, at the University of Leiden in 1613 and at Oxford in 1636. The earlier charge of the fourteenth century Council of Vienna to establish schools for the study of Arabic, implemented briefly during the Renaissance, was coming to life once again.

[143] There are few editions of the work. See, for example: A. Ross, *Pansebeia: or, a View of All Religions in the World with the Several Church-Governments from the Creation, till these Times: also, a Discovery of All Known Heresies, in all Ages and Places, and Choice Observa-*

Rise and Progress of Mahometanism: With the Life of Mahomet and a Vindication of Him and His Religion from the Calumnies of the Christians by Henry Stubbe (1632-1676), which, according to Daniel, in many ways anticipated the Enlightenment.[144]

In 1705, the Dutch scholar Adrian Reland (1676-1718) published *De religione mohammedica*, considered by Hans Küng "the first reasonably objective work on Islam after Ross's *Pansebeia*."[145] It consisted of a translation of a compendium of Islamic theology and a systematic attempt by Reland to dispel popular misconceptions about the religion. As Daniel pointed out: "It is certainly the most important of several books that helped to clear away legend and substitute fact, and only fact; it can be studied with profit today."[146]

However, animosity against Islamic civilization still prevailed and so did the spirit of severe criticism and an anti-Islamic attitude. Clear evidence of such reluctance was the writing of Ludovico Maracci (1612-1700), one of the best Christian experts on the Arabic language and the Qur'an.[147] His polemical writing reveals a great deal of authentic knowledge derived from various Arabic sources. This good acquaintance with the sources enabled Maracci to master a new technique which he explained as follows: "When we act against the enemies of religion, we attack them more happily with their arms than with ours, and (thus) more happily overcome them."[148]

The Enlightenment thinkers brought an entirely new perspective to religion in general, namely seeing the "religion without mystery" (as stated by John Locke in the seventeenth century). They appealed to reason and to axioms of thought that were held to be self-evident and universal. Obviously this new approach concerned both Christianity and Islam. It is worth noting that this new approach to Islam was also linked with the new theory of religions of humankind, which called for both the recognition that other people had religions that were neither simply and necessarily heresies nor aberrations of Christianity, and for new methods for studying other religions, including Islam.[149] The biography of the Prophet Muḥammad written by Count Henri Boulainvilliers (1658-1722) is a clear example of such an approach.[150] Boulainvilliers presented the Prophet as a free thinker, the founder of a religion of reason which required no severe discipline and was stripped of miracles and mysteries. A similar interpretation can be found in the work of Claude Savary

---

tions and Reflections throughout the Whole, London: Printed for M. Gillyflower and W. Freeman, 1696.

[144] N. Daniel, *Islam and the West...*, p. 309.

[145] H. Küng (et al.), *Christianity and the World Religions...*, p. 20.

[146] N. Daniel, *Islam and the West...*, p. 318.

[147] M. Borrmans, "Ludovico Marracci et sa traduction latine du Coran," *Islamochristiana*, vol. 28 (2002), p. 73-86.

[148] L. Maracci, "Prefatory note" to his translation of the Qur'an, cited by N. Daniel in his book *Islam and the West...*, p. 322.

[149] Ibid., p. 315.

[150] R. Armour, *Islam, Christianity and the West...*, p. 135.

(1758-1788).[151] There is no doubt that this kind of image of Muḥammad certainly could not be acceptable and understandable for Muslims since they understand it through perceptions linked with the powerful Medinean and Meccan revelations.

During the Enlightenment, there was a revived interest in studying the Arabic language and translating the Qur'an. In 1734, George Sale (1697-1736) published a highly valued and appreciated translation of the Qur'an.[152] In his "Preliminary Treatise," Sale presents a relatively objective picture of Muḥammad. Unlike his predecessors, the scholar focuses on facts. His information is derived from a wide range of Muslim sources, among them works of Qur'anic commentators, such as Al-Bayḍāwī, Az-Zamakhsharī and Al-Jalālī. Therefore, as Daniel points out, with Sale's work "we meet the first considerable attempt at an entirely academic judgement."[153] However, his rather friendly attitude towards Islam could not "convince" his Muslim contemporaries and they considered him to be anti-Islamic.

Edward Gibbon's (1737-1794) *History of the Decline and Fall of the Roman Empire* (published in six volumes between 1776 and 1788) presented a comprehensive, balanced picture of the Prophet and Islam, created from a variety of sources displaying both positive and negative views. Although in his final judgement of Muḥammad and Islam the author was undecided, balancing between approval and disapproval:

> Gibbon's influence on the western perception of the Prophet, Islam, and their place in history was enormous. From recondite and learned books, most of them in Latin and little known outside the narrow world of clerics and scholars, he was able to present a picture of the Prophet and the rise of Islam that was clear, elegant, and above all convincing. Most important of all was that unlike previous writers, including the Arabists, he saw the rise of Islam not as something separate and isolated, nor as regrettable aberration from the onward march of the Church, but as a part of human history, to be understood against the background of Rome and Persia, in the light of Judaism and Christianity, and in complex interplay with Byzantium, Asia, and Europe.[154]

With time, the Enlightenment had won a place of honor and tolerance, which was presented in Germany by Gotthold Ephraim Lessing's (1729-1781) play *Nathan the Wise* (1783).[155] The author believed that the strength of a religion should be measured primarily by the credibility of its followers living in the spirit of peace, solidarity and tolerance with others.

---

[151] See: C. S a v a r y (ed.), *Le Koran: Traduit de l'arabe, accompagné de notes: Précédé d'un Abrégé de la vie de Mahomet tiré des écrivains orientaux les plus estimés par M. Savary*, Paris: Garnier, 1951.

[152] N. Daniel used Sale's version as "best expressing in English the meaning traditionally understood in Islam" in his book *Islam and the West...*, p. 32.

[153] Ibid., p. 322.

[154] B. L e w i s, *Islam...*, p. 98.

[155] G. E. L e a s i n g, *Nathan the Wise*, trans. and introduction W. F. Ch. A d e, Woodbury, NY: Barron's Educational Series, Inc., 1972. Also see: J.-J. E c k a r d t, *Lessing's Nathan the Wise and the Critics, 1779-1991*, Columbia, SC: Camden House, 1993.

Nineteenth and twentieth century progress in systematic studies of Islam

By the end of the eighteenth century, Europeans were ready to embark on more thorough studies on Islam than they had done before. With Napoleon Bonaparte's invasion of Egypt in 1798, the era of Western control over the Islamic world began. The French occupation was a brief episode in Egypt's long history, but it had a lasting significance. It not only aroused in the West a wave of interest in the Arab/ Islamic lands but also marked the opening of a prolonged struggle between the Western powers for influence and control over these territories. Moreover, it was also an advantageous opportunity for the West to learn a great deal about both Pharaonic Egypt and the contemporary world of Islam.[156] This, in turn, resulted in growing fascination with the Orient and the new impulse to develop related studies.

As the "remoteness" of the Middle East and other parts of the Islamic world began to disappear, Christian missionaries, scholars and theologians had more opportunities to encounter contemporary Muslim societies and engage in religious disputes. With the new ideas about religion and the evolution of the scholarly approach to human sciences, the terms of those disputes had changed. At the beginning of the nineteenth century, missionaries, scholars and theologians were divided concerning their attitude towards Islam. Some could see Islam only as the enemy and rival of Christianity, while others saw it as one of the many forms of human expression. Common to both approaches was the acceptance of the fact that Muḥammad and his followers had played an important part in the history of the world.[157] With the progression of the missionary movement in the nineteenth century, one could observe a stronger polarization concerning the Christian perception of Islam. Some missionaries and scholars still insisted on repeating the traditional unfavourable statements, while others were inclined to a more positive view.

Among those who continued the spread of former traditional negative views of Islam, one should mention Thomas Valpy (1825-1891) and William Muir (1819-1905). Valpy was the Principal of St. John's College at Aghra and later the Bishop of Lahore, and in his early work as a missionary believed that "Christianity and Muḥammadanism are distinct as earth as heaven, and could not possibly be true together."[158] Muir was a British official in India and a scholar who specialized in the history of Muḥammad and the early caliphate. In the 1850s, he wrote "The

---

[156] Napoleon Bonaparte brought with him to Egypt a group of 165 scientists, artists and men of letters. This mission set up Arabic and French printing-press in Cairo and founded Institut d'Egypte. The results of the research and studies conducted there were published in the twenty-volume work *Description de l'Egypte*. For a thorough account of Bonaparte's military campaign in Egypt and its long-lasting results see: P. Strathern, *Napoleon in Egypt: "The Greatest Glory,"* London: Jonathan Cape, 2007.

[157] A. Hourani, *Europe...*, p. 16.

[158] Ibid., p. 17.

Muḥammadan controversy," an article which demonstrated his complete opposition to the Muslim religion.[159] Similar views, as repeated later in his famous work *Life of Muḥammad*, were, according to Daniel, "no more sympathetic to Islam than the work of his medieval predecessors."[160]

However, as mentioned previously, the negative image of Islam was not the only one that had shaped the nineteenth century Christian attitude towards Islam. There was also a "positive" image related to the idea that religion is endemic to human nature. Common to both images was the acceptance of the fact that Muḥammad and his followers had played an important part in the history of the world.

Arguments about the character and work of the Prophet Muḥammad, viewed in secular and humanistic terms, continued to be rocked backwards and forwards throughout the nineteenth century. Thomas Carlyle's (1795-1881) lecture "The Hero as Prophet" caused a sensation by treating Muḥammad as a sincere and honest prophet.[161] Although in his image of the Prophet, Carlyle repeated some medieval accusations and was rather cautious about the final approval of Him and His mission, he was nevertheless keen to express a number of positive remarks while defending Muḥammad's sincerity.[162]

For Frederic Denison Maurice (1805-1872), a historian and theologian, who praised the charity of Carlyle's view of Muḥammad, the essence of religion was "the faith in men's hearts."[163] In his book *The Religions of the World and their Relations with Christianity*, he explained that Christians should accept "goodness" even in religions traditionally thought to be unworthy. Therefore, while rejecting the view that Islam was the enemy of Christianity, Maurice maintained that because of a number of reasons, such as its monotheism, high sense of morality and religious practices, Christians should accept this religion.[164]

Reginald Bosworth Smith (1819-1905) followed Maurice's argument, elaborating on the matter further.[165] He believed that in Islam there is a strong sense of ethical principle. According to Smith, Islam was an ally to Christianity since both religions aimed at the elevation of humanity. Therefore, he believed that the British should encourage Islam and get to know it better because peaceful Muslim-Christian relations could benefit from the overall situation in the British colonies.

---

[159]   Ibid., p. 19.

[160]   N. Daniel, *Islam and the West...*, p. 327.

[161]   A. Hourani, *Europe...*, p. 19. Also refer to: T. Carlyle, *The Best Known Works of Thomas Carlyle: Including Sartor Resartus, Heroes and Hero Worship and Characteristics*, New York: Book League of America, 1942.

[162]   See: N. Daniel, *Islam and the West...*, p. 313-314.

[163]   A. Hourani, *Islam...*, 1991, p. 20-21.

[164]   See: F. D. Maurice, *The Religions of the World and their Relations to Christianity Considered in Eight Lectures Founded by Robert Boyle*, London: J. W. Parker, 1848.

[165]   See: R. B. Smith, *Mohammed and Mohammedanism: Lectures Delivered at the Royal Institution in Great Britain in February and March, 1874 by Reginald Bosworth Smith with an Appendix Containing Emanuel Deutsch's Article on "Islam,"* appendix Emanuel Deutsch, New York: Harper & Bross, 1875.

Nineteenth century Romanticism brought some changes in the scope of scientific research pertaining to the perception of Islam. One effect of the Romantic period was taking Islam out of the area of religious disputation.[166] Instead, one could observe the growth of discussions on social, moral and political matters. The topics which attracted the greatest attention were those related to the problem of gender, such as the role of man, the situation of women and the issue of domestic violence. The Muslim East, with its fascinating exoticism, gave an impulse for further related studies. Moreover, artists' fascination with the oriental climate found its reflection in Romantic literature, especially poetry, and became a vital source of inspiration for Romantic fine arts.

Since the eighteenth century and in the nineteenth century in particular, a new science of Oriental studies had been developing. For the scholars in that new area of studies, the starting point was the religion of Islam. Subsequently, they embarked on the task of exploring the languages, the history and the culture of the nations that had formed Islamic civilization.[167] Throughout the nineteenth century and into the twentieth, the Orientalists undertook numerous projects in preparing scholarly editions of valuable Arabic texts surviving in manuscript form. These academic ventures resulted in a number of new translations of the Qur'an and new treaties shedding more light not only on the life and activities of the Prophet Muḥammad, but on various aspect of Islam. Since the Western scholars had become better acquainted with the achievements of Muslim civilization, their approach to it gradually changed, acquiring more objectivity. However, that objectivity did not embrace the attitude toward religion itself. The Catholic Church still condemned Islam, considering it a heresy, and refused to acknowledge Muḥammad as a prophet.

As underlined by Hans Küng, the nineteenth and twentieth centuries "have witnessed a tremendous upsurge in Orientalism and hence in scientific studies of Islam, which set the scene for a less polemical view of Islam on the part of Christian theologians and the Church."[168] Decisive progress was made on four fronts, namely (1) a historical assessment of Muḥammad, (2) a history of the Qur'an, (3) comprehensive research on Islamic culture from liturgy and mysticism through law and customs to literature and art, and (4) a historical evaluation of the image of Jesus in the Qur'an.

The visible signs of the inevitable dissolution of the Ottoman Empire, until then a strong defender of Islamic religious values, the increasing unresolved political and

---

[166]   N. Daniel, *Islam and the West...*, p. 314.

[167]   It is worth noting that among major world civilizations, medieval Islam left one of the richest legacies in the form of handwritten manuscripts. For Arabic manuscripts, see: A. Gacek, *Arabic Manuscripts: A Vademecum for Readers*, Leiden and Boston, E. J. Brill, 2009; idem, *The Arabic Manuscript Tradition: A Glossary of Technical Terms and Bibliography*. Leiden and Boston, E. J. Brill, 2001; idem, *The Arabic Manuscript Tradition: A Glossary of Technical Terms and Bibliography – Supplement*, Leiden and Boston, E. J. Brill, 2008.

[168]   See: H. Küng (et al.), *Christianity and the World Religion...*, p. 21. Also refer to: Ch. Adams, "Islam and Christianity...," p. 287-306.

social problems facing the Muslim East, together with the first signs of cultural decline, fortified the Western conviction of its unquestionable superiority in all spheres
of life. Obviously, that conviction in turn strengthened even more the persistent negative attitude towards Islam and the reciprocal relations between Christianity and
Islam. On the other hand, the development of *Religionswissenschaft*, i.e., a science
of the study of religion[169] and Friedrich Max Müller's idea that religion could only be
understood through comparison,[170] together with the above-mentioned evolution in
research and studies on Islam by both Western and Muslim scholars, brought about
positive changes in the overall Christian image of the Muslim world. Finally, the
twentieth century witnessed long-awaited positive developments.

Summary

For over thirteen centuries, the relationship between Christianity and Islam was
predominantly one of reciprocal hostility, wars and bitter polemics. The early Christian image of Islam was negative and, in fact, through the next centuries it retained its
basic features. However, in the course of history, due to a number of initiatives, this
negative Christian approach to Muslims and their religion acquired positive tones.

A letter, written in 1076, an important reference point in the Second Vatican
Council's Declaration *Nostra Aetate* no. 3 (1965), in which Pope Gregory VII had
called the Moroccan Emir Al-Nāṣir *his brother in Abraham* and urged Christians
and Muslims to enter the path of love and understanding based on the common
belief in One God, became a significant step on the path toward building bridges

---

[169] "A German technical term for the academic study of religions, apart from theology. Originally introduced by Friedrich Max Müller (1823-1900), it established itself as an academic
discipline in German universities by the end of the 19th century and at the beginning of
the 20th. The English translation of the word was always under debate because the term
Wissenschaft refers to both sciences and humanities. Max Müller himself used the English
form 'science of religion' but was not followed in this; later, translations such as 'comparative religion' or history of religion(s) had more success." Quoted from Blackwell Reference
Online, "Religionswissenschaft," available (http://www.blackwellreference.com/public/
tocnode?id=g9780631181392_chunk_g978063118139219_ss1-24 [access March 20, 2011]).

[170] As he famously put it, "He who knows one, knows one." One does not really understand
religion if he knows and acknowledges only his own. See: Encyclopaedia Britannica online,
"Max Müller," available (http://www.britannica.com/EBchecked/topic/396833/Max-Muller
[access March 20, 2011]). Refer to: F. Max Müller, *Introduction to the Science of Religion: Four Lectures Delivered at the Royal Institution in February and May 1870*, Varanasi: Bharata Manisha, 1972; idem, *The Essential Max Müller: on Language, Mythology, and
Religion*, J. R. Stone (ed.), New York: Palgrave MacMillan, 2002. Also see: H. Kasimow
and B. L. Sherwin (eds.), *No Religion is an Island: Abraham Joshua Heschel and Interreligious Dialogue*, Maryknoll, NY: Orbis Books, 1991.

of understanding and reconciliation. During the medieval period, Christian scholars and missionaries strengthened their efforts towards better perception of Muslims. First, by engaging in translating projects, they increased their knowledge of Islam by studying it from direct sources. Second, learning from direct experience, i.e., missionary activity, they became convinced that the true faith and love for One God may be also found in the hearts of Muslims (St. Francis of Assisi's assertion), that fighting them by sword would bring no results, and that the only appropriate way was to approach them with tolerance, respect and Christian love. Third, realizing that the most important issue was to establish common ground for a possible path towards communication and eventual understanding, they pursued their search for new moral and philosophical arguments that could be acceptable for Muslims.

During the Renaissance, the increased Christian quest for knowledge, recognition of the legitimacy of diverse religious values in Islam and the search for similarities between Islam and Christianity had made a substantial contribution towards reaching reciprocal understanding. Subsequently, the Enlightenment, with its new perspective of religion in general, called for both the recognition that other people had legitimate rights to other religions, which were neither simply and necessarily heresies or aberrations of Christianity, and for new methods for the study of other religions, including Islam. Finally, the nineteenth and the early twentieth centuries have witnessed amazing progress in scientific studies of Islam, leading to the development of Oriental studies, which resulted in a less polemical view of the Muslim religion on the part of Christian theologians and the Church.

There is no doubt that during the thirteen centuries of Christian-Muslim relations, the negative attitude of Christians towards the followers of Islam underwent a gradual positive evolution. One may say that by the first decade of the twentieth century, the Church was "prepared" to introduce in its teaching profound changes concerning relations with non-Christian religions, including Islam.

II

A dialogical approach to Islam

*The Catholic Church and its mission in the light
of the Second Vatican Council and the pontificate of Paul VI*

The dawn of the twentieth century witnessed a substantial improvement in the relations between Christianity and Islam. This more optimistic and promising approach was the result of well-organized Christian missionary work and the activity of Muslim reformers.[171] In their numerous writings, Sayyid Aḥmad Khan,[172] Jamāl ad-Dīn al-Afghānī,[173] Muḥammad ʿAbduh,[174] Rashīd Riḍā[175] and Muḥammad

---

[171] C. W. Troll, "Mission and Dialogue…," p. 3-14.

[172] Sayyid Aḥmad Khan (1817-1892) was a great Muslim thinker and reformer from the Indian Subcontinent. He was among the first who strongly advocated the need of making Islam compatible with modernity. For a recent study refer to: B. Belmekki, *Sir Sayyid Ahmad Khan and the Muslim Cause in British India*, Berlin: Klaus Schwarz, 2010.

[173] Jamāl ad-Dīn al-Afghānī (1838-1897) was a well-known Islamic activist and reformer. Originally from Afghanistan; traveled extensively to spread his teaching, especially the idea of pan-Islamism, in India and Arab lands; also active in the intellectual circles of Muslims living in Paris. See: N. R. Keddie and H. Algar, *An Islamic Response to Imperialism: Political and Religious Writings of Sayyid Jamāl ad-Dīn "al-Afghānī,"* Berkeley: University of California Press, 1983.

[174] Muḥammad ʿAbduh (1849-1905) was one of the most famous reformers of Islam from Egypt. He undertook the task of reforming the teaching at Al-Azhar, the most famous Islamic university. For a recent study refer to: S. Haj, *Reconfiguring Islamic Tradition: Reform, Rationality, and Modernity*, Stanford, CA: Stanford University Press, 2009.

[175] Rashīd Riḍā (1865-1935) was a Muslim revivalist who contributed greatly to the preservation and dissemination of the ideology of Islamic reform. For an interesting analysis of his three *fatwas* on missionary activities among Arab Muslims in Egypt delivered in *Al-Manār*, refer to: U. Riyad, "Rashīd Riḍā and a Danish Missionary: Alfred Nielsen and Three Fatwâs from *Al-Manâr*," *Islamochristiana*, vol. 28 (2002), p. 87-107. See also: E. E. Shahin,

Iqbāl[176] called upon the Muslims to reconcile Western modernity with the tradition of Islam in the spirit of mutual understanding, respect and tolerance.

The dissolution of the Ottoman Empire after the First World War, together with the growth of nationalistic aspirations, resulted in the formation of nation-states. Increasing migration and contact between people of different religions and cultures required that Christians and Muslims gain more knowledge of each other much more quickly than before. Furthermore, neighborly necessities required communication that would promote tolerance and reciprocal understanding.

The initiatives prior to the Second Vatican Council

The interwar era was the time of the pontificate of Pius XI (1857-1939), who had indeed responded to the needs of the new realities and contributed to the gradual positive modification of the Christian attitude towards Islam. Since the pontificate of Pius XI, the official texts of the Catholic Church began making a clear distinction between paganism and Islam.[177]

The outcome of the Second World War brought a further increase of nationalistic aspirations as well as interreligious encounters. Christian missionaries and scholars continued their reflection on related issues. They could look back into a long history of reciprocal contact, during which the attitude of the Catholic Church had undergone an evolution from a complete rejection, through attempts to learn about Islam from sources and direct encounters, to coping with it while aiming to understand it. Now, with the new world order and ethnic, cultural and religious diversity everywhere, there was a pressing need for a subsequent step in that evolution, namely to establish a way towards reciprocal relations between Christians and Muslims on the basis of full recognition and mutual respect.

On December 20, 1949, the Catholic Church published *De Motione Oecumenica*, a document about the ecumenical movement outlining the rules of contact between Catholics and non-Catholics.[178] In this document, the word *dialogue* is not mentioned and it does not deal with the relations of the Catholic Church with people other than Christians. However, one could agree with Eugeniusz Sakowicz that the

---

"Muḥammad Rashīd Riḍā's Perspectives on the West as Reflected in Al-Manār," *Muslim World*, vol. 79 (April 1989), p. 113-132.

[176] Muḥammad Iqbāl (1876-1938) was a famous poet and thinker from the Indian Subcontinent. He is known as the spiritual father of Pakistan. See: Sh. McDonough, *The Flame of Sinai: Hope and Vision in Iqbal*, Lahore: Iqbal Academy Pakistan, 2002.

[177] J. Urban, *Dialog międzyreligijny w posoborowych dokumentach Kościoła*, Opole: WT UO, 1999, p. 135.

[178] "*De Motione Oecumenica*," *Acta Apostolicae Sedis*, annus 42 (1950), series 2, vol. 17, p. 142-157.

instruction contains a meaningful description of the word *dialogue* as well as that there are statements of a general nature clearly indicating that the outlined methods of contact could be applied in relations with the outside world, including with the followers of non-Christian religions.[179]

The rarely-mentioned by scholars *De Motione Oecumenica* should, however, be considered an important document, indicating the forthcoming change in the Catholic Church's attitude not only towards ecumenism but, in consequence, also towards non-Christian religions. The significance of the document lies in the following points. First, the Catholic Church, fully aware of its perceived superiority as the depository of the truth, agreed on meetings with non-Catholics in which both parties would discuss the problem of faith and customs. Second, it was recommended that during such meetings, the questions should be discussed openly and without omitting difficult topics. Third, contact with others was, according to the Church, essential for increasing its awareness of the values present in the life of the others. Finally, as a result of such encounters, it appears as though both parties would not lose from whatever God had given them, but would instead attain a real fulfilment in Him. Moreover, these instructions also recommended that the ecumenical contact should include common prayers. Therefore, in a way, it became an inspiring signal for the future Catholic Church dialogue of religious experience, not only with non-Catholics, but with non-Christians as well. All in all, one may conclude that in the light of *De Motione Oecumenica*, the way for establishing a dialogical path in Christian-Muslim relations was laid.

Meanwhile, Christian reflection on the two religions as well as the reciprocal contacts between their followers continued and stimulated further changes.[180] Here one should mention the activity of Louis Massignon (1883-1962),[181] one of the greatest modern scholars in Islam, who significantly influenced the changes in Christian attitude towards the Muslims. Professor Massignon devoted his long and hardworking life to one goal: to increasing the Western awareness of the need, or rather, the imperative of discovering and appreciating the richness of Islamic civilisation. He was convinced that scholars should develop curious, inquisitive and objective research on various aspects of Muslim culture.[182] With regard to the characteristics of the three great monotheistic religions, Massignon wrote that Judaism was the

---

[179]   E. Sakowicz, *Dialog Kościoła z islamem...*, p. 41.

[180]   A. Siddiqui, "Fifty Years of Christian-Muslim Relations: Exploring and Engaging in a New Relationship," *Islamochristiana*, vol. 26 (2000), p. 51-77.

[181]   Ibid., p. 43-48. Also see: C. W. Troll, "Islam and Christianity Interacting in the Life of an Outstanding Christian Scholar of Islam: The Case of Louis Massignon (1883-1962)," *Islam and the Modern Age*, vol. 15 (August 1984), p. 157-166; G. Basetti-Sani, "A Catholic Islamist Louis Massignon (1883-1983)," *Bulletin*, vol. 18 (1983), no. 3, 258-265.

[182]   The study of Al-Hallāj (858-922), a famous Muslim mystic, was L. Massignon's doctoral dissertation, completed in 1914 and published in 1922. He continued to work on the subject for the rest of his life and a revised edition was published after his death. See: A. Hourani, *Islam...*, 1991, p. 46-48.

religion of hope, Christianity – the religion of love, and Islam – the religion of faith.[183] While sharing the conviction included in the Qur'an statement that all three religions had traced their origin from one source, Massignon did not hesitate to accept the affinity of Muslims with Abraham through Ismāʿīl. Moreover, the scholar maintained that Muslims were the people chosen and blessed by Abraham and that the Qur'anic assertion of the superiority of God's laws over human laws was bringing them closer to Christianity.[184]

Christian Troll wrote in one of his articles about the work of father Victor Courtois (1907-1960).[185] Despite the fact that he remains rather unknown, his contribution as an early proponent of Christian–Muslim dialogue seems to be of great importance. During the years 1946-1960 in Calcutta, Courtois was the editor of the magazine *The Notes of Islam: A Bulletin of Information about Islam with Special Reference to India.* The purpose of that periodical was to help to establish a better understanding of Islam. Courtois undertook the task of making the reader aware of Islam's mission, vision and path.[186] He attempted to present the religion of Islam in the most objective way, focusing on its beliefs, institutions and modern developments. While avoiding unnecessary comments and polemics, Courtois referred to the words of Ramon Lull (1232-1315), who in his studies of Islam always attempted to find common elements of both Islam and Christianity and maintained that eventually the two religions could be brought closer. Commenting on his own curriculum of Islamic studies courses designed for Christian seminars, Courtois remarked:

> Insistence should always be made not on what separates Christians from Muslims but on what may...bring them closer to each other and to the heart of Christ. We should study them not as enemies but as Brothers. To study we shall add much prayer.[187]

Courtois's articles reveal his insightful knowledge and thorough understanding of Islam, and in particular, an awareness of its dynamic character, the nature of its ever-present spirit of renewal and reform, as well as its great impact on all spheres of human life. He repeatedly stated the objective of the *Notes*: to contribute to a better appraisal of Islamic culture. Simultaneously he worked, reflected and wrote, although outside of the sphere of the *Notes*, to promote a better knowledge of Christ and his teachings among Muslims. Courtois called for a wider "ecumenism" between religions, especially Christianity and Islam. The main spring for Courtois's call laid in a clear perception of what unites all men most deeply: the common Fatherhood

---

[183] G. C. Anawati, "An Assessment of the Christian-Islamic Dialogue," in: K. C. Ellis (ed.), *The Vatican, Islam...*, p. 54.

[184] L. Massignon, "Les trois prières d'Abraham," Y. Moubarac (ed.), *Opera Minora*, vol. 3: *Arts et archéologie, la science de la compassion*, Beyrut: Dār al-Maʿārif, 1963, p. 804-816.

[185] C. W. Troll, "Christian-Muslim Relations in India: A Critical Survey," *Islamochristiana*, vol. 5 (1979), p. 119-149.

[186] Ibid., p. 126.

[187] Ibid., p. 127.

of God, which in turn he saw as the basis for the brotherhood of all humankind. Courtois focused on the Heart of Christ as the center of the hearts of men and the fulfilment of their deepest and best aspirations. Calling for reciprocal understanding between Christians and Muslims, he expressed his conviction that:

> Were they better known, they would surely be better loved, and where there is love there is God. *Ubi Caritas et Amor ibi Deus est.*[188]

The *Notes on Islam* succeeded, gained international recognition, and were increasingly read by Muslims. The periodical reported about the beginnings of Christian-Muslim "conversations" that were gradually developing into a world-wide dialogue. Courtois strongly advocated Christian-Muslim co-operation, and his contribution to fostering all the initiatives that could bring the two religions closer together is of great importance.

The efforts of all the early advocates of Christian-Muslim dialogue finally brought positive and promising results in the second half of the twentieth century.[189] *Aggiornamento*, the spirit of changes and reforms as introduced by the Pope John XXIII (1881-1963), opened the Catholic Church to the "outside world" and dialogue with modernity.[190] The new spirit introduced in the Church a process of active revitalisation, in which the faith was to undergo a broad and positive process of modernisation. Instantly, upon his advent to the Holy See, John XXIII saw that an ecumenical council was not only urgent but also essential in order to bring the Church up to date in the radically changed modern world. Therefore, on January 25, 1959, he decided to announce his intention to call forth such a council.[191] As George Weigel pointed out, the Pope wanted his council to be different from the previous one, i.e., less preoccupied with juridical and dogmatic matters and primarily focused on the pastoral and evangelical mission of the Church.[192] The Second Vatican Council

---

[188] Ibid., p. 128.

[189] See: H. Tessier, "Chretiens et Musulmans: Cinquante années pour approfondir leur relations," *Islamochristiana*, vol. 26 (2000), p. 33-50; A. Siddiqui, "Fifty years of Christian-Muslim Relations...," *Islamochristiana*, vol. 26 (2000), p. 50-77.

[190] For further details on the pontificate of John XXIII, see: P. Dreyfus, *Jean XXIII*, Paris: Artheme Fayard, 1979; P. Hebblethwaite, *John XXIII: Pope of the Council*, London: Geoffrey Chapman, 1984.

[191] In June 1959, the Ante-Preparatory Commission, established by John XXIII, wrote to Catholic bishops all over the world, requesting their suggestions for the Council's agenda. Karol Wojtyła sent the commissioners an essay proposing the Council's reflection on the human condition in the modern world. According to him, the crucial issue of the times was the human person, who while living in a material world, had intense spiritual longings. Therefore, it was important to address the issue of Christian humanism in relation to other humanisms and to see how the Church could pursue its evangelization mission in relation to the "others." For a further discussion see: G. Weigel, *Witness to Hope: The Biography of John Paul II (1920-2005)*, New York: Harper Perennial, 2005, p. 158-160.

[192] Ibid., p. 154.

opened on October 11, 1962.[193] The debates included four sessions.[194] Although the Holy Father would not live to see the completion of his work, he is credited for one of the most pivotal events in the history of the Church.

The Blessed John XXIII's *Pacem in Terris* as a tool for modern understanding of human rights and religious freedom

On April 11, 1963, John XXIII issued his most important encyclical: *Pacem in Terris*.[195] This document became both the inspiration and the basis for the new Church's approach to the modern world. The main issue discussed by the Pope was "peace among the nations," and as indicated in the opening lines, the encyclical was addressed not only

> To Our Venerable Brethren the Patriarchs Primates, Archbishops, Bishops and all other Local Ordinaries who are at Peace and in Communion with the Apostolic See, and to the Clergy and faithful of the entire Catholic World,

but, very significantly, also to

> all Men of Good Will.[196]

The encyclical *Pacem in Terris* focuses on the condition of modern man in society. Within the complex of problems facing man, John XXIII devoted his particular

---

[193] For a thorough discussion on a number of issues related to the "revolutionary transformation" and the new approach of the Catholic Church to the modern world as introduced by the Second Vatican Council, see: M. L. Lamb and M. Levering (eds.), *Vatican II: Renewal...*; W. Madges (ed.), *Vatican II...*; M. J. Wilde, *Vatican II: A Sociological Analysis of Religious Change*, Princeton, NJ: Princeton University Press, 2007.

[194] Karol Wojtyła was an active participant in all four sessions of the Council: he submitted both written and oral interventions and participated in working groups that refined draft documents between the Council's formal meetings in Rome. Furthermore, he knew a lot about the backstage informal discussions, that is, the backstage politics of the Council. During the post-councilor years both as the Cardinal and the Pope, he spoke frequently about the great debt he owed to Vatican II. As Weigel pointed out: "Anyone interested in understanding Wojtyła as bishop and as Pope must make the effort to "get inside" Vatican II, as he experienced it." G. Weigel, *Witness to Hope...*, p. 155.

[195] For John Paul II, this encyclical became one of the most important documents he referred to.

[196] John XXIII, "*Pacem in Terris*: Encyclical of Pope John XXIII on Establishing Universal Peace in Truth, Justice, Charity, and Liberty" (April 11, 1963), online: http://www.vatican.va/holy_father/john_xxiii/encyclicals/documents/hf_j-xxiii_enc_11041963_pacem_en.html, access: March 10, 2011.

attention to the issue of human rights. Referring to the question of religious belief, he said:

> Also among man's rights is that of being able to worship God in accordance with the right dictates of his own conscience, and to profess his religion both in private and public.[197]

According to the Pope, human rights can be observed only when all people are assured that they "are equal in natural dignity." This is the prerequisite for both "man's awareness of his rights" and, resulting from it, "the recognition of his duties."[198] Moreover, as John XXIII stated, "the possession of rights"[199] would encourage and convince man that it was essential to recognize and respect other people and would guide him in his search for real values in life:

> When society is formed on a basis of rights and duties, men have an immediate grasp of spiritual and intellectual values, and have no difficulty in understanding what is meant by truth, justice, charity and freedom. They become, moreover, conscious of being members of such a society. And that is not all. Inspired by such principles, they attain to a better knowledge of the true God – a personal God transcending human nature. They recognise that their relationship with God forms the very foundation of their life, which they live in the society of their fellows.[200]

While discussing the condition of modern man in a modern society, John XXIII pointed out that each person was unique and therefore "among the essential elements of the common good one must certainly include the various characteristics distinctive of each individual people." The common good, concluded the Holy Father, "can never exist fully and completely unless the human person is taken into account at all times."[201] According to him, the realities of the modern world required that the issue of common good be approached through a universal perspective and in a global context. John XXIII addressed the matter as follows:

> the universal common good requires the encouragement in all nations of every kind of reciprocation between citizens and their intermediate societies. There are many parts of the world where we find groupings of people of more or less different ethnic origin. Nothing must be allowed to prevent reciprocal relations between them. Indeed such a prohibition would flout the very spirit of an age which has done so much to nullify the distances separating peoples.
> Nor must one overlook the fact whatever their ethnic background, men possess, besides the special characteristics which distinguish them from other men, other very important elements in common with the rest of mankind. And these can form the basis of their

---

[197]   Ibid., no. 14.
[198]   Ibid., no. 44.
[199]   Ibid.
[200]   Ibid., no. 45.
[201]   Ibid., no. 55.

progressive development and self-realisation especially in regard to spiritual values. They have, therefore, the right and duty to carry on their lives with others in society.[202]

It seems obvious that in the modern world, where the domination of the stronger and richer over the weaker and poorer results in misunderstandings and conflicts, the use of force in resolving such problems never brings feasible solutions. Therefore, according to John XXIII:

> Men nowadays are becoming more and more convinced that any disputes which may arise between nations must be resolved by negotiation and agreement, and not by recourse to arms. … it no longer makes sense to maintain that war is a fit instrument with which to repair the violation of justice.[203]

Only by establishing contact with one another, the Pope believed, the nations around the world would come to "a better recognition of the natural ties that bind them together as men" and "a fairer realisation…that love, not fear, must dominate the relationships between individuals and between nations."[204]

Being aware of the fact that contact involving relations between people of different religious beliefs would pose a tremendous challenge for the Catholic Church, John XXIII did not hesitate to address the issue. With the conviction (1) that the realities of the twentieth century world required such a challenge, (2) that the principles set out in *Pacem in Terris* had arisen "from the very nature of things,"[205] and (3) that Catholics, firm in their belief, should be ready to listen and understand the others, the Pontiff explained:

> the putting of these principles into effect frequently involves extensive co-operation between Catholics and those Christians who are separated from this Apostolic See. It even involves the cooperation of Catholics with men who may not be Christians but who nevertheless are reasonable men, and men of natural moral integrity. "In such circumstances they must, of course, bear themselves as Catholics, and do nothing to compromise religion and morality. Yet at the same time they should show themselves animated by a spirit of understanding and unselfishness, ready to co-operate loyally in achieving objects which are good in themselves, or conducive to good."[206]

While analyzing *Pacem in Terris*, we may notice that despite the fact that John XXIII never mentioned the word *dialogue*, the whole text is about a dialogue of the Catholic Church with modernity. In addition, the encyclical stated the principles of conscious preparation for conducting such a dialogue; for establishing a new means

---

[202] Ibid., no. 100.
[203] Ibid., no. 126-127.
[204] Ibid., no. 129.
[205] Ibid., no. 157.
[206] Ibid., no. 157.

of communication and a new relation between people of different races, cultures and religious beliefs. The Pope believed that this was a new challenge for the twentieth century world. Therefore, he was convinced that Catholics should undertake "an immense task"[207] to meet that challenge with conscious reflection and responsible action, while being fully aware that a new understanding of global reality could only be built "little by little,"[208] and definitely within the framework of the Catholic Church's long historical tradition. "Establishing new relationships in human society, under the mastery and guidance of truth, justice, charity and freedom," the Holy Father stated, could bring about "true peace in accordance with divinely established order."[209] "Peace among the nations" was, according to John XXIII, not only the most important task but also the imperative and the ultimate aim of the modern world. All the nations, then, should strive for mutual understanding because:

> The world will never be the dwelling place of peace, till peace has found a home in the heart of each and every man, till every man preserves in himself the order ordained by God to be preserved.[210]

The dialogical message, as contained in *Pacem in Terris*, was a clear sign that the Catholic Church was finally entering a new era of its relations with non-Catholics and non-Christians. The aim of such relations, namely "peace among the nations," was clearly articulated, and so was the method to achieve it – "little by little." The encyclical outlined the prerequisites for the foreseen dialogical encounter, such as the focus on the situation of a human being in society, the need to preserve natural dignity and respect for the right to religious freedom. The message was there. Thus, it was up to the successor of John XXIII to grasp the message and carry on with "the immense task."

---

[207] Ibid., no. 163.
[208] Ibid., no. 161.
[209] Ibid., no. 163.
[210] Ibid., no. 165.

Documents of the Second Vatican Council referring to interreligious dialogue

The spirit of renewal and reform was continued by Paul VI (1897-1978). His new, related initiatives brought decisive changes in the attitude of the Church towards Islam and its followers.[211] The Second Vatican Council called upon Christians to respect the spiritual, moral and cultural values in other religions, including Islam.[212] On September 29, 1963, while opening the Second Session of the Second Vatican Council, Pope Paul VI addressed the issue of other monotheistic religions. The Holy Father said that the Catholic Church "looks beyond the horizon of Christianity," i.e., to the followers of other religions believing in one transcendent God.[213] It should be pointed out that, in his allocution, Paul VI spoke indirectly about dialogue as he neither mentioned any particular religion nor used the word dialogue. However, one may say that his speech clearly indicated and signalled an upcoming new approach, and in consequence, a new attitude of the Catholic Church towards non-Christians, and among them the followers of Islam. Furthermore, the discussed address became an inspiration for further argumentation of the need to conduct an interreligious dialogue as presented by Paul VI in his encyclical *Ecclesiam Suam* (October 6, 1964), as well as in the final documents of the Second Vatican Council, and in particular, in the Declaration on the Relationship of the Church to Non-Christian Religions, *Nostra Aetate* (October 28, 1965).

When discussing the Second Vatican Council's documents reflecting the Catholic Church's attitude towards non-Christians, including Muslims, one should remember that it is essential to view them within the living tradition of the Church. Moreover, it is also important to consider them in the context of the already-discussed long historical evolution of the Christian views related to Islam.[214]

Among the sixteen documents containing all the decisions of the Second Vatican Council, there are eleven that address the issue of interreligious dialogue. In five of them, one can find indirect references to the issue; the other four touch upon the matter directly. There are also two documents in which one finds statements focusing, in particular, on Islam and the Muslims.

Documents with indirect references to the issue of interreligious dialogue include following: Constitution on the Sacred Liturgy *Sacrosanctum Concilium* (December 4, 1963), Decree on Ecumenism *Unitatis Redintegratio* (November 21, 1964), Decree on Priestly Training *Optatam Totius* (October 28, 1965) and Declaration on

---

[211] See: M. Borrmans, "Le Pape Paul VI et les Musulmans," *Islamochristiana*, vol. 4 (1978), p. 1-10.

[212] For a broad discussion on related issues see: J. Waardenburg (ed.), *Islam and Christianity*...

[213] M. Borrmans, "Le Pape Paul VI...," p. 5.

[214] See: M. L. Lamb, "The Challenges of Reform and Renewal within Catholic Tradition," in: M. L. Lamb and M. Levering (eds.), *Vatican II: Renewal*..., 2008, p. 439-442.

Christian Education *Gravissimum Educationis* (October 28, 1965), as well as Decree on the Apostolate of the Laity *Apostolicam Actuositatem* (November 18, 1965).

Sacrosanctum Concilium indicates the Catholic Church's acceptance of the spiritual diversity of various ethnic groups and nations and expresses its willingness to incorporate some of these traditions into the liturgy.[215]

Unitatis Redintegratio outlines the rules of ecumenical encounter between Christians. The principles stated here are: (1) elimination of hostility and wrong doings, (2) the need to know each other better in order to conduct a theological dialogue, (3) undertaking common efforts to improve economic and social conditions and (4) a dialogue of action to eliminate injustice, promote culture and strive for peace. These are the same principles as those needed for dialogue and cooperation with all, that is, with non-Christians as well.[216]

Optatam Totius emphasizes the need to increase knowledge of other world religions, because according to the Catholic Church's view, "the seeds of the word," namely the elements of the truth and goodness, may also be found in other religions. Therefore, the document advocates that the seminarians should acquire a substantial knowledge of other religions and cultures.[217]

Gravissimum Educationis elaborates further on the necessity of Christian education, outlining the new goals and responsibilities of theological faculties at institutions of higher learning. The Declaration points out the need to develop theological research, in order for Christians to be able to reach a thorough understanding of the Revelation in the context of Christian wisdom as inherited from predecessors. Such research would help to deal with the problems of modernity, i.e., to accommodate the results of rapid development of science and technology and prepare specialists capable of conducting a dialogue of experts concerning crucial theological, philosophical and religious issues. Placing in *Gravissimum Educationis* a short reference to the encounter with non-Christians clearly signalled the Catholic Church's will and determination to undertake the immense task of education and preparation for a sincere dialogue with the followers of non-Christian religions.[218]

---

[215] "The Constitution on the Sacred Liturgy *Sacrosanctum Concilium* Solemnly Promulgated by His Holiness Pope Paul VI" (December 4, 1963), online: http://www.vatican.va/archive/hist_councils/ii_vatican_council/documents/vat-ii_const_19631204_sacrosanctum-concilium_en.html, access: March 10, 2011.

[216] "Decree on Ecumenism *Unitatis Redintegratio*" (November 21, 1964), no. 2, 3, 7, 12, online: http://www.vatican.va/archive/hist_councils/ii_vatican_council/documents/vat-ii_decree_19641121_unitatis-redintegratio_en.html, access: March 10, 2011.

[217] "Decree on Priestly Training *Optatam Totius* Proclaimed by His Holiness Pope Paul VI" (October 28, 1965), no. 16, online: http://www.vatican.va/archive/hist_councils/ii_vatican_council/documents/vat-ii_decree_19651028_optatam-totius_en.html, access: March 10, 2011.

[218] "Declaration on Christian Eduaction *Gravissimum Educationis* Proclaimed by His Holiness Pope Paul VI" (October 28, 1965), no.11, online: http://www.vatican.va/archive/hist_councils/ii_vatican_council/documents/vat-ii_decl_19651028_gravissimum-educationis_en.html, access: March 10, 2011.

With regard to the *Apostolicam Actuositatem*, one may find here a reference to the issue of cooperation with other people. According to the document, "the quasi-common heritage of the Gospel and the common duty of Christian witness resulting from it recommend and frequently require" to establish a closer cooperation between Catholics and other Christians. These common efforts should be realized by "individuals and communities within the Church, either in activities or in associations, in the national or international field." Furthermore, the realities of the modern world and "human values common to all mankind" make it essential that this cooperation also include those who "do not profess Christ's name but acknowledge these values." This dynamic and prudent cooperation, as stated in the Declaration, "which is of special importance in temporal activities," is a prerequisite to attaining "the unity of the human family."[219]

From an analysis of the documents of the Second Vatican Council with direct references to the issue of interreligious dialogue, a change in the Catholic Church's attitude towards others, namely other Christians and non-Christians, is revealed. The Dogmatic Constitution on Divine Revelation *Dei Verbum* (November 18, 1965) points out the need for Christians to embark on further studies of the Revelation in order to engage in a theological dialogue with "others." With respect to that task, reading and analyzing would be of great assistance. Therefore, the document states that:

> all the Christian faithful, especially Religious, … should gladly put themselves in touch with the sacred text itself, whether it be through the liturgy, rich in the divine word, or through devotional reading, or through instructions suitable for the purpose and other aids which, in our time, with approval and active support of the shepherds of the Church, are commendably spread everywhere. And let them remember that prayer should accompany the reading of Sacred Scripture, so that God and man may talk together; for "we speak to Him when we pray; we hear Him when we read the divine saying."[220]

According to the document, it is also important for Christians to engage themselves in translations of sacred texts, provided with the essential and adequate explanations, so "that the children of the Church may safely and profitably become conversant with the Sacred Scriptures and be penetrated with their spirit." Furthermore, Christians should also bear in mind the need of sharing their knowledge of the Bible with non-Christians as well, and for that reason:

---

[219] "Decree on the Apostolate of the Laity *Apostolicam Actuocitatem* Solemnly Promulgated by His Holiness, Pope Paul VI" (November 18, 1965), no. 27 online: http://www.vatican.va/archive/hist_councils/ii_vatican_council/documents/vat-ii_decree_19651118_apostolicam-actuositatem_en.html, access: March 10, 2011.

[220] "Dogmatic Constitution on Divine Revelation *Dei Verbum* Solemnly Promulgated by His Holiness Pope Paul VI" (November 18, 1965), no. 25, online: http://www.vatican.va/archive/hist_councils/ii_vatican_council/documents/vat-ii_const_19651118_dei-verbum_en.html, access: March 10, 2011.

editions of the Sacred Scriptures, provided with suitable footnotes, should be prepared also for the use of non-Christians and adapted to their situation. Both pastors of souls and Christians generally should see to the wise distribution of these in one way or another.[221]

As for the Decree *Ad Gentes Divinitus* on the Mission Activity of the Church (December 7, 1965), here the references to the issue of non-Christian religions reveal a few important points. First, in the light of *Ad Gentes Divinitus*, the Catholic Church views non-Christian religions as "diverse ways" of seeking God, to prepare for the encounter with God.[222] Second, the Decree points out that the "seeds of the word" are present in other religions and other contemplative cultural traditions.[223] Third, it encourages Christians to engage in an open, sincere and patient dialogue, i.e., "to carry out an apostolate by way of example," because Christians "are organized for this purpose; they are present for this, to announce Christ to their non-Christian fellow-citizens by word and example, and to aid them toward the full reception of Christ."[224] Finally, *Ad Gentes Divinitus* also affirms the role of lay people and their engagement in preparatory education for conducting dialogue with non-Christians. It is stated as follows:

Worthy of special praise are those laymen who, in universities or in scientific institutes, promote by their historical and scientific religious research the knowledge of peoples and of religions; thus helping the heralds of the Gospel, and preparing for the dialogue with non-Christians.[225]

Furthermore, the document emphasizes that such cooperation should be done "in a brotherly spirit with other Christians, and with non-Christians," and that the lives of laymen "may be a witness for Christ among non-Christians."[226]

With regard to the Declaration on Religious Freedom *Dignitatis Humanae* (December 7, 1965), one may notice that it not only confirms the statements concerning religious freedom from *Pacem in Terris* but also elaborates further on the issue.[227]

---

[221] Ibid.

[222] "Decree *Ad Gentes* on the Mission Activity of the Church" (December 7, 1965), no. 3, on line: http://www.vatican.va/archive/hist_councils/ii_vatican_council/documents/vat-ii_decree_19651207_ad-gentes_en.html, access: March 10, 2011.

[223] Ibid., no. 6.

[224] Ibid., no. 15.

[225] Ibid., no. 41.

[226] Ibid., no. 41.

[227] Karol Wojtyła participated actively in the third session of Vatican II's most controversial debate (on religious freedom) in one spoken and two written interventions. He was one of the proponents of a new *Declaration on Religious Freedom* who argued that the document should emphasize the fact that religious freedom was a matter of God's revealed will for the world and for human beings. Therefore, he was convinced that the *Declaration* should present religious freedom "substantially as revealed doctrine, which is entirely consonant with human

The document acknowledges that "the human person has a right to religious freedom," and that "the right to religious freedom has its foundation in the very dignity
of the human person as this dignity is known through the revealed word of God and
by reason itself." Furthermore, this right has its foundation in the very nature of
the human being and "not in the subjective disposition of the person." Therefore,
"the right to this immunity continues to exist even in those who do not live up to
their obligation of seeking the truth and adhering to it and the exercise of this right
is not to be impeded, provided that just public order be observed."[228] However, the
modern world is characterized by two important facts: (1) that "religious freedom
has already been declared to be a civil right in most constitutions, and it is solemnly
recognized in international documents," and (2) that "forms of government still exist
under which, even though freedom of religious worship receives constitutional recognition, the powers of government are engaged in the effort to deter citizens from
the profession of religion and to make life very difficult and dangerous for religious
communities."[229] Therefore, the document directs an urgent plea of the Council not
only to Catholics but to all men to reflect on the issue of religious freedom attentively, because:

> All nations are coming into even closer unity. Men of different cultures and religions
> are being brought together in closer relationships. There is a growing consciousness
> of the personal responsibility that every man has. All this is evident. Consequently, in
> order that relationships of peace and harmony be established and maintained within the
> whole of mankind, it is necessary that religious freedom be everywhere provided with
> an effective constitutional guarantee and that respect be shown for the high duty and
> right of man freely to lead his religious life in society.[230]

---

reason." According to Wojtyła, the modern world was in need of new teaching compatible
with the needs of modern societies that required a stronger protection of religious freedom.
The suggestions were taken into consideration and in the final text of *Dignitatis Humanae*
(no. 2), the passage related to the issue of religious freedom reads as follows: "This Vatican
Council declares that the human person has a right to religious freedom. This freedom means
that all men are to be immune from coercion on the part of individuals or of social groups and
of any human power, in such wise that no one is to be forced to act in a manner contrary to his
own beliefs, whether privately or publicly, whether alone or in association with others, within
due limits. The Council further declares that the right to religious freedom has its foundation
in the very dignity of the human person as known through the revealed word of God and by
reason itself. This right of the human person to religious freedom is to be recognized in the
constitutional law whereby society is governed and thus it is to become a civil right." See:
G. Weigel, *Witness to Hope...*, p. 163-166.

[228] "Declaration on Religious Freedom *Dignitatis Humanae* on the Right of the Person and of
Communities to Social and Civil Freedom in Matters Religious Promulgated by His Holiness
Pope Paul VI" (December 7, 1965), no. 2, online: http://www.vatican.va/archive/hist_coun-
cils/ii_vatican_council/documents/vat-ii_decl_19651207_dignitatis-humanae_en.html, access: March 10, 2011.

[229] Ibid., no. 15.

[230] Ibid.

Only when people are free in their religious belief does a dialogue become possible. In the realities of the modern world, people of various ethnic origins and different religious beliefs come closer together. They need to communicate. Therefore, in the light of *Dignitatis Humanae*, the Catholic Church's dialogue with non-Christian religions was and still is an imperative of our days.

The last document, i.e., the Pastoral Constitution on the Church in the Modern World *Gaudium et Spes* (December 7, 1965), addresses the issue of a dialogue between people. It reveals the Catholic Church's conviction that:

> By virtue of her mission to shed on the whole world the radiance of the Gospel message, and to unify under one Spirit all men of whatever nation, race or culture, the Church stands forth as a sign of that brotherhood which allows honest dialogue and gives it vigor.[231]

In order to carry on its dialogical mission effectively, the Church has to be united. Therefore, it is essential to "foster within the Church herself mutual esteem, reverence and harmony, through the full recognition of lawful diversity." Moreover, as stated in the document, it is of the utmost importance that:

> We do not forget that the unity of Christians is today awaited and desired by many, too, who do not believe in Christ; for the farther it advances toward truth and love under the powerful impulse of the Holy Spirit, the more this unity will be a harbinger of unity and peace for the world at large. Therefore, by common effort and in ways which are today increasingly appropriate for seeking this splendid goal effectively, let us take pains to pattern ourselves after the Gospel more exactly every day, and thus work as brothers in rendering service to the human family. For, in Christ Jesus this family is called to the family of the sons of God.[232]

In the light of *Gaudium et Spes*, the realities of the modern world require that the Church approaches the followers of non-Christian religions with esteem and respect:

> We think cordially too of all who acknowledge God, and who preserve in their traditions precious elements of religion and humanity. We want frank conversation to compel us all to receive the impulses of the Spirit faithfully and to act on them energetically.[233]

They should also engage with them in a dialogue:

> For our part, the desire for such dialogue, which can lead to truth through love alone, excludes no one, though an appropriate measure of prudence must undoubtedly be ex-

---

[231] "Pastoral Constitution on the Church in the Modern World *Gaudium et Spes* Promulgated by His Holiness, Pope Paul VI" (December 7, 1965), no. 92, online: (http://www.vatican.va/archive/hist_councils/ii_vatican_council/documents/vat-ii_cons_19651207_gaudium-et-spes_en.html, access: March 10, 2011.

[232] Ibid.

[233] Ibid.

ercised. We include those who cultivate outstanding qualities of the human spirit, but do not yet acknowledge the Source of these qualities. We include those who oppress the Church and harass her in manifold ways. Since God the Father is the origin and purpose of all men, we are all called to be brothers. Therefore, if we have been summoned to the same destiny, human and divine, we can and we should work together without violence and deceit in order to build up the world in genuine peace.[234]

With regard to the Pastoral Constitution on the Church in the Modern World *Gaudium et Spes*, it is important to note Karol Wojtyla's significant contribution to the essence of the text. As Weigel pointed out, this document "would retain a privileged place in the thinking and affections of Karol Wojtyła for the rest of his life" and two of its sections, namely 22 and 24, became the most-quoted citations from the Second Vatican Council in his papal teaching.[235]

There are two documents of the Second Vatican Council referring directly to Islam: the Dogmatic Constitution of the Church, *Lumen Gentium* (no. 16) and the Declaration on the Relationship of the Church to Non-Christian Religions, *Nostra Aetate* (no. 3).

Lumen Gentium is a document that is considered to be fundamental for the doctrinal teaching of the Second Vatican Council. The Constitution reveals the self-awareness of the Catholic Church of its nature, its doctrine and its mission. According to Sakowicz, this particular self-awareness enabled the Church to enter a new path of relations with non-Christians and, in a way, "to feel responsible" for their destiny.[236] Furthermore, both the Council and the entire Catholic Church were becoming increasingly aware of the fact that an interreligious dialogue in its universal dimension carries enormous potential. Since only individuals or communities who have become conscious of their identity can initiate and successfully conduct a sincere dialogue with others, in the light of *Lumen Gentium* the Catholic Church's prospects for such "an encounter" with non-Christians were quite promising.[237]

In *Lumen Gentium*, the Fathers of the Council presented their position concerning the relation of non-Catholics and non-Christians to the people of God. The Dogmatic Constitution of the Church states that:

All men are called to be part of this catholic [*sic*] unity of the people of God which in promoting universal peace presages it. And there belong to or are related to it in various

---

[234] Ibid.

[235] For an extensive account of Karol Wojtyła's involvement in the matter of wording the Pastoral Constitution on the Church in the Modern World *Gaudium et Spes*, see: G. Weigel, *Witness to Hope...*, p. 166-169.

[236] E. Sakowicz, *Dialog Kościoła z islamem...*, p. 49.

[237] See: F. Zapłata, "Misyjny charakter Kościoła w świetle konstytucji dogmatycznej *Lumen Gentium*," *Ateneum Kapłańskie*, vol. 58 (1966), no. 347, p. 326-336; M. Balwierz, "Katolickie podstawy dialogu z religiami niechrześcijańskimi," in: W. Hryniewicz, J. S. Gajek, S. J. Koza (eds.), *Ku chrześcijaństwu jutra: Wprowadzenie do ekumenizmu*, Lublin: Towarzystwo Naukowe Katolickiego Uniwersytetu Lubelskiego 1996, p. 676-701.

ways, the Catholic faithful, all who believe in Christ, and indeed the whole of mankind, for all men are called by the grace of God to salvation.[238]

Moreover, the Catholic Church recognizes that there are different links by which it is related to various religious and non-religious individuals or communities. The closest ties are with other Christian churches. As for the others, i.e., "those who have not yet received the Gospel," they are related to the people of God in various ways. In the first place are the Jews. Moreover, according to the Constitution, "the plan of salvation also includes" Muslims. One should point out here that in *Lumen Gentium* we encounter the Catholic Church's first official statement concerning Islam.

The text, adopted by the Council on November 21, 1964, is very brief and deals with Islam in the following words:

> But the plan of salvation also includes those who acknowledge the Creator. In the first place among these are Muslims, who professing to hold the faith of Abraham, along with us adore the same one and merciful God, who on the last day will judge the mankind.[239]

This text replaced the first draft:

> The sons of Ismael, who recognize Abraham as their father and believe in God of Abraham, are not unconnected with the Revelation made to the patriarchs.[240]

The Declaration on the Relationship of the Church to Non–Christian Religions *Nostra Aetate* is a crucial document of the Second Vatican Council entirely devoted to the issue of dialogue with non-Christians. Despite the fact that the Declaration is the shortest of all the Council's documents, it is unique because it reflects a real breakthrough in relations between the Church and the followers of non-Christian religions.

In *Nostra Aetate*, we find both statements of general nature (no. 1 and 5) and in relation to particular religions, namely Buddhism (no. 2), Judaism (no. 4) and Islam (no. 3).

The Declaration begins with a statement expressing the Church's intention to develop relations with non-Christians, focusing on the need to search for common features and values:

> In our time, when day by day mankind is being drawn closer together, and the ties be-tween different peoples are becoming stronger, the Church examines more closely her

---

[238] "Dogmatic Constitution on the Church *Lumen Gentium* Solemnly Promulgated by His Holiness Pope Paul VI" (November 21, 1964), no. 13, online: http://www.vatican.va/archive/hist_councils/ii_vatican_council/documents/vat-ii_const_19641121_lumen-gentium_en.html, access: March 10, 2011.

[239] Ibid., no. 16.

[240] R. Caspar, "Islam According to Vatican II: On the Tenth Anniversary of *Nostra Aetate*," *Encounter: Documents for Muslim-Christian Understanding*, no. 21 (January 1976), p. 2.

relationship to non-Christian religions. In her task of promoting unity and love among men, indeed among nations, she considers above all in this declaration what men have in common and what draws them to fellowship.[241]

The introductory remarks of general nature contain a few important points, namely (1) that God created all people and accepts each and every one:

One is the community of all peoples, one their origin, for God made the whole human race to live over the face of the earth. One also is their final goal, God. His providence, His manifestations of goodness, His saving design extend to all men, until that time when the elect will be united in the Holy City, the city ablaze with the glory of God, where the nations will walk in His light.[242]

(2) that people may differ in their ways of seeking the truth, although their vital questions remain practically the same:

Men expect from the various religions answers to the unsolved riddles of the human condition, which today, even as in former times, deeply stir the hearts of men: What is man? What is the meaning, the aim of our life? What is moral good, what sin? Whence suffering and what purpose does it serve? Which is the road to true happiness? What are death, judgment and retribution after death? What, finally, is that ultimate inexpressible mystery which encompasses our existence: whence do we come, and where are we going?[243]

(3) that there are "seeds of the truth" in other religions:

From ancient times down to the present, there is found among various peoples a certain perception of that hidden power which hovers over the course of things and over the events of human history; at times some indeed have come to the recognition of a Supreme Being, or even of a Father. This perception and recognition penetrates their lives with a profound religious sense.[244]

---

[241] "Declaration on the Relation of the Church to Non-Christian Religions *Nostra Aetate* Proclaimed by His Holiness Pope Paul VI" (October 28, 1965), no. 1, online: http://www.vatican.va/archive/hist_councils/ii_vatican_council/documents/vat-ii_decl_19651028_nostra-aetate_en.html, access: March 10, 2011. See: A. Kennedy, "The Declaration on the Relationship of the Church to Non-Christian Religions, *Nostra* Aetate," in: M. L. Lamb and M. Levering (eds.), *Vatican II: Renewal...*, p. 396-409; E. I. Cassidy, *Ecumenism and Interreligious Dialogue: Unitatis Redintegratio, Nostra Aetate,* New York: Paulist Press, 2005, p. 125-265; S. Nagy, "Wprowadzenie do Deklaracji o stosunku Kościoła do religii niechrześcijańskich," in: J. Groblicki and E. Florkowski (eds.), *Sobór Watykański II: Konstytucje, dekrety, deklaracje: Tekst polski*, Poznań: Wydawnictwo Pallottinum, 1968.

[242] "Declaration on the Relation of the Church to Non-Christian Religions *Nostra Aetate...*," no. 1.

[243] Ibid.

[244] Ibid., no. 2.

(4) that all people are brothers and, therefore, non-Christians should become partners in a dialogue with the Catholic Church:

> We cannot truly call on God, the Father of all, if we refuse to treat in a brotherly way any man, created as he is in the image of God. Man's relation to God the Father and his relation to men his brothers are so linked together that Scripture says: "He who does not love does not know God" (1 John 4:8).[245]

(5) that there should be no reason for discrimination of any kind:

> No foundation therefore remains for any theory or practice that leads to discrimination between man and man or people and people, so far as their human dignity and the rights flowing from it are concerned.[246]

because (6) the Church stands firmly against the mistreatment of people with regard to their ethnic, cultural and religious differences and encourages its followers to live in peace with non-Christians:

> The Church reproves, as foreign to the mind of Christ, any discrimination against men or harassment of them because of their race, color, condition of life, or religion. On the contrary, following in the footsteps of the holy Apostles Peter and Paul, this sacred synod ardently implores the Christian faithful to "maintain good fellowship among the nations" (1 Peter 2:12), and, if possible, to live for their part in peace with all men, so that they may truly be sons of the Father who is in heaven.[247]

In comparison with the first text on Islam in *Lumen Gentium*, the second one in *Nostra Aetate* (October 28, 1965) is much more developed.[248] It consists of two parts. The first, the doctrinal one, describes the values of the Muslim faith and worship and points out the values common to Islam and Christianity:

> The Church regards with esteem also the Moslems. They adore the one God, living and subsisting in Himself; merciful and all-powerful, the Creator of heaven and earth, who has spoken to men; they take pains to submit wholeheartedly to even His inscrutable decrees, just as Abraham, with whom the faith of Islam takes pleasure in linking itself,

---

[245] Ibid., no. 5.

[246] Ibid.

[247] Ibid.

[248] It should be noted that the task of compiling the Declaration *Nostra Aetate* from start to finish was within the responsibility of the Secretariat for Christian Unity. The experts on Islam were asked to work on the text in 1963. The Council finely adopted the Declaration on October 28, 1965. The Secretariat for Non-Christians, established to put this Declaration into practice, came into being only on Pentecost of 1964, and it did not really become valid before March of 1965. See: R. Caspar, "Islam According to Vatican II…," p. 2. Karol Wojtyła, attending the Council as a bishop, was one of the drafters of this document. See: T. Szulc, *Pope John Paul II…*, p. 107, 233.

submitted to God. Though they do not acknowledge Jesus as God, they revere Him as a prophet. They also honor Mary, His virgin Mother; at times they even call on her with devotion. In addition, they await the day of judgment when God will render their deserts to all those who have been raised up from the dead. Finally, they value the moral life and worship God especially through prayer, almsgiving and fasting.[249]

The second part of the text deals with practice and collaboration, calling upon the followers of both religions to work together:

> Since in the course of centuries not a few quarrels and hostilities have arisen between Christians and Moslems, this sacred synod urges all to forget the past and to work sincerely for mutual understanding and to preserve as well as to promote together for the benefit of all mankind social justice and moral welfare, as well as peace and freedom.[250]

While analyzing *Nostra Aetate* no. 3, it is important to look at footnote no. 5, namely "Cf St. Gregory VII, *letter XXI to Anzir (Nacir), King of Mauritania* (Pl. 148, col. 450f.)."[251] As already mentioned in the first chapter, in 1076 Gregory VII (1015-1085),[252] a famous medieval Pope and a great reformer, wrote a letter to "Al-Nāṣir, king of the province of Mauretania Sitifensis in Africa" to thank him "for his good will towards his Christian subjects and comments to him the messengers of Alberic and Cencius, associates of the papal household."[253]

This letter provides us with evidence about good, respectful relations between the Christian Pope Gregory VII and the Muslim Emir Al-Nāṣir, namely the exchange of cordial gestures, such as the Pope's fulfilment of the Emir's request to ordain "the priest Servanus as bishop according to the Christian dispensation," the Emir's already-implemented decision to free "Christians who were being held captives" and his promise to "free other captives."[254] In this letter, while expressing his gratitude for the exchange of such gestures, the Pope referred to common belief in "God the creator of all," explaining that:

> In truth, such charity both we and you owe more particularly to our own than the remaining peoples, for we believe and confess, albeit in a different way, the one God, and each day we praise and honour him as the creator of all ages and the ruler of this world. For as the Apostle says, 'He is our peace, who made both one.'(Eph. 2:14)[255]

---

[249] "Declaration on the Relation of the Church to Non-Christian Religions *Nostra Aetate…*," no. 3.

[250] Ibid.

[251] Ibid., footnote no. 5.

[252] About the attitude of Pope Gregory VII towards Muslims, see: A. Hourani, *Islam…*, p. 9-10.

[253] See: *The Register o Pope Gregory VII…*, p. 204-205.

[254] Ibid., p. 204.

[255] Ibid., p. 205.

All in all, it is important to point out that in referring to this letter (dated 1076), the Fathers of the Councils clearly indicated the fact that the essence of the Declaration *Nostra Aetate*, the basis and the will to conduct a sincere dialogue with Muslims was not new, and that the roots that let the dialogical spirit grow over the centuries can be traced to medieval times.

Paul VI and his dialogical initiatives concerning Islam and the Muslims

The question of Islam appeared during the second session in 1963 in relation to the issue of the Jews, namely the annex to the *Schema of Ecumenism* that had been prepared on the personal request of John XXIII. When the text was presented at the Council's session, it was met with strong opposition on the part of the bishops from the Middle Eastern region. It was obvious that in that area, the problem of Israel evoked strong emotions and the religious aspect was closely related to the growth of political tensions. Therefore, the bishops from the Middle East argued that if the Council called upon Christians for a more balanced, just and amiable attitude towards the Jews, it should then at the same time promote a similar approach toward Muslims.[256] The issue of Islam was brought to the attention of the Council at a very special moment. It was the beginning of the pontificate of Paul VI.[257] The new Pope was a person of great sensibility and openness and was particularly curious about the richness of other cultures and diverse ways of thinking and religious sentiments. It was due to his long-lasting friendship with the great scholar Louis Massignon and other specialists on Muslim civilisation that Paul VI had a very positive attitude towards Islam and its followers. Therefore, he had no hesitation in supporting the request of the Middle Eastern bishops.[258]

During the initial months of his pontificate, Paul VI undertook a number of initiatives to develop and promote a dialogue with other religions and particularly with Islam. It should be pointed out that his pontificate resulted in a number of documents dealing with the matter of interreligious dialogue, among them apostolic letters: *Spiritus Paracliti* (April 30, 1964) and *Progrediente Concilio* (May 18, 1964); apostolic exhortations: *Postrema Sessio* (November 4, 1965) and *Evangelii*

---

[256] R. Caspar, "Islam According to Vatican II…," p. 1.

[257] For a comprehensive discussion about the pontificate of Paul VI, see: P. Hebblethwaite, *Paul VI: The First Modern Pope*, New York: Paulist Press, 1993. Also refer to: F. X. Murphy, *The Papacy Today*, New York: MacMillan Publishing Co., Inc., 1981, p. 91-140.

[258] R. Caspar, "Islam According to Vatican II…," p. 2. Also refer to: N. Robinson, "Massignon, Vatican II and Islam as an Abrahamic Religion," *Islam and Christian-Muslim Relations*, vol. 2 (2) (December 1991), p. 182-205; M. Serafian, *The Pilgrim: Pope Paul VI, The Council and The Church in a Time of Decision*, New York: Farrar and Straus, 1964.

Nuntiandi (December 8, 1975); an apostolic constitution *Regimini Ecclesiae Universae* (August 15, 1967); and encyclicals, such as *Ecclesiam Suam* (August 6, 1964) and *Populorum Progressio* (March 26, 1967).[259]

As an institutional sign of the desire to meet and relate to followers of other faiths of the world, the Holy Father established the Secretariat for Non-Christians, in 1964, including the section for Muslims.[260] On that occasion, on May 18, 1964, Paul VI published his apostolic letter *Progrediente Concilio.* Referring to the words of Gospel, he mentioned: "I also have other sheep but they are not from the very same sheepfold. I have to lead them through" (J 10, 16). The Pontiff emphasized the need to strengthen the efforts on the path of dialogue and cooperation of the Catholic Church with non-Christian religions. The Secretariat began its activity on May 19, 1964. However, the mandate of that new institution was defined later by the Constitution *Regimini Ecclesiae* (August 15, 1967). The Secretariat was established with the following purpose:

> To search for methods and ways of opening a suitable dialogue with non-Christians. It should strive, therefore, in order that non-Christians come to be known honestly and esteemed justly by Christians and that in turn non-Christians can adequately know and esteem Christian doctrine and life.[261]

The new attitude towards non-Christian religions, including Islam, embraced the term *dialogue.* This term, which is both the norm and the ideal, was introduced to the Church in Paul VI's encyclical *Ecclesiam Suam*, on August 6, 1964.[262] Since that time, the word *dialogue*, which means not only a discussion but also includes all positive and constructive interreligious relations with individuals and communities of other faiths, has been frequently used by the Council as well as in Church-related teaching. The encyclical *Ecclesiam Suam* has been called "the great charter of dialogue."[263] In this document, Paul VI outlined for the Church the approaches to dialogue, especially emphasizing the need for missionary activity in the modern

---

[259] These documents are discussed by E. Sakowicz in *Dialog Kościoła z islamem…*, p. 82-98.

[260] For an overview concerning the activities of the Secretariat see: M. L. Fitzgerald, "The Secretariat for Non-Christians is Ten Years Old," *Islamochristiana*, vol. 1 (1975), p. 87-96; P. Rossano, "The Secretariat for Non-Christian Religions from the Beginnings to the Present Day: History, Ideas, Problems," *Bulletin*, vol. 14 (1979), no. 2-3, p. 88-109.

[261] "Address of the Pope at the Conclusion of the Plenary Assembly of the Secretariat," in: *The Attitude of the Church towards the Followers of Other Religions*, Vatican: Polyglot Press (English Edition), 1984, p. 8.

[262] *"Ecclesiam Suam*, Encyclical of Pope Paul VI on the Church" (August 6, 1964), online: http://www.vatican.va/holy_father/paul_vi/encyclicals/documents/hf_p-vi_enc_06081964_ ecclesiam_en.html, access: March 10, 2011.

[263] E. Sakowicz, "Dialog międzyreligijny," in: *Jan Paweł II: Encyklopedia dialogu i ekumenizmu*, E. Sakowicz (ed.), Radom: Polwen Polskie Wydawnictwo Encyklopedyczne, 2006, p. 136.

world. Furthermore, the encyclical had a great impact on the development of the term *dialogue* and its implementation in the teaching of the Church.

Ecclesiam Suam revealed the Church's deep self-awareness of its identity and its mission. The starting point was the Church's positive attitude towards the outside world and the spirit behind the *aggiornamento* as advocated by John XXIII. While marching on its way to Salvation through the history of cultures and societies, it was established that the Church needs constant renewal and reform. Although the Church identifies itself neither with a particular culture nor society, it is a part of them and a part of the entire world. Moreover, the Church is nourished by the richness of these cultures and these societies need to be supported by it, since it instils in them the word of God. The Church lives in the world and it is connected with all of humanity by unbreakable ties. Therefore, the Church, according to Paul VI, wants both to be understood by others and to understand the problems of others. Moreover, it desires to serve the needs of each and every human being. This conviction becomes the basis for a dialogue:

> This relationship, this dialogue, which God the Father initiated and established with us through Christ in the Holy Spirit, is a very real one, even though it is difficult to express in words. We must examine it closely if we want to understand the relationship which we, the Church, should establish and foster with the human race.[264]

As stated in *Ecclesiam Suam* "God Himself took the initiative in the dialogue of salvation. "He hath first loved us." (1 JN 4:10)," and it is upon us to be "the first to ask for a dialogue with men, without waiting to be summoned to it by others."[265]

The characteristic features of such a dialogue as described in *Ecclesiam Suam* are: (1) clearness:

> Clarity before all else… In order to satisfy this first requirement, all of us who feel the spur of the apostolate should examine closely the kind of speech we use. Is it easy to understand? Can it be grasped by ordinary people? Is it current idiom?[266]

(2) meekness:

> Christ bade us learn from Himself: "Learn of me, for I am meek and humble of heart." (Mt 11:29) It would indeed be a disgrace if our dialogue were [sic] marked by arrogance, the use of bared words or offensive bitterness. What gives it its authority is the fact that it affirms the truth, shares with others the gifts of charity, is itself an example of virtue, avoids peremptory language, makes no demands. It is peaceful, has no use for extreme methods, is patient under contradiction and inclines towards generosity.[267]

---

[264] "*Ecclesiam Suam*, Encyclical of Pope Paul VI on the Church" (August 6, 1964), no. 71, online: http://www.vatican.va/holy_father/paul_vi/encyclicals/documents/hf_p-vi_enc_06081964_ ecclesiam_en.html, access: March 10, 2011.

[265] Ibid., no. 72.

[266] Ibid., no. 81.

[267] Ibid.

(3) trust:

> Confidence is also necessary; confidence not only in the power of one's own words, but also in the good will of both parties to the dialogue. Hence dialogue promotes intimacy and friendship on both sides. It unites them in a mutual adherence to the Good, and thus excludes all self-seeking.[268]

and (4) prudence:

> The prudence of a teacher who is most careful to make allowances for the psychological and moral circumstances of his hearer, (Mt 7:6) particularly if he is a child, unprepared, suspicious or hostile. The person who speaks is always at pains to learn the sensitivities of his audience, and if reason demands it, he adapts himself and the manner of his presentation to the susceptibilities and the degree of intelligence of his hearers.[269]

The dialogue, as discussed by Paul VI in his encyclical, embraces four circles. The first "comprises the entire human race, the world";[270] the second is made up of "all those men who worship the one supreme God, whom we also worship";[271] the third "is nearest to us" and "comprises all those who take their name from Christ";[272] and the fourth "is the one, holy, Catholic, and apostolic Church of which the Roman Church is *mother and head.*"[273]

As revealed in *Ecclesiam Suam* as well as in other documents and a number of related initiatives, opening a dialogue with the people of the world, among them the followers of non-Christian religions, was the Pontiff's priority. According to Paul VI, such a dialogue was a tremendous challenge for both Christians and non-Christians and engaging in it was not only a need, but also an imperative of those days and the days to come. In *Ecclesiam Suam*, the Holy Father said:

> Then we see another circle around us. This too is vast in extent, yet not so far away from us. It comprises first of all those men who worship the one supreme God, whom we also worship. We would mention first the Jewish people, who still retain the religion of the Old Testament, and who are indeed worthy of our respect and love.
> Then we have those worshipers who adhere to other monotheistic systems of religion, especially the Moslem religion. We do well to admire these people for all that is good and true in their worship of God. And finally we have the followers of the great Afro-Asiatic religions.[274]

---

[268]   Ibid.
[269]   Ibid.
[270]   Ibid., no. 97.
[271]   Ibid., no. 107.
[272]   Ibid., no. 109.
[273]   Ibid., no. 113.
[274]   Ibid., no. 107.

While aware of both the considerable differences between Christianity and non-Christian religions and the Catholic Church's conviction that "there is but one religion, the religion of Christianity," Paul VI acknowledged that:

> We do, nevertheless, recognize and respect the moral and spiritual values of the various non-Christian religions, and we desire to join with them in promoting common ideals of religious liberty, human brotherhood, good culture, social welfare and civil order. For our part, we are ready to enter into discussion on these common ideals, and will not fail to take initiative where our offer of discussion in genuine, mutual respect would be well received.[275]

The positive attitude of Paul VI towards Islam and his will and determination to develop a dialogue with its followers met with a quite sympathetic reception and amiable gestures from the Muslims. During his visit to Egypt in March 1965, the Cardinal Francis Koenig, archbishop of Vienna, was invited by Sheikh Aḥmad Ḥasan al-Bāqūrī, the principal of Al-Azhar (the most famous Muslim university), to give a lecture in reference to the issue of interreligious dialogue. On May 31, 1965, in the amphitheatre of Al-Azhar in Cairo, and in the presence of nearly two thousand Muslims, the Christian Cardinal addressed the audience, reading a paper entitled "Monotheism in the Contemporary World." The paper was received very well and later a large number of copies in Arabic were distributed all over the Muslim world.[276]

All the initiatives and efforts of Paul VI related to the development of a dialogue of the Catholic Church with non-Christians, and particularly with the followers of Islam, were finally officially acknowledged in two significant documents, namely the Dogmatic Constitution of the Church, *Lumen Gentium* (no. 16), and the Declaration on the Relationship of the Church to Non-Christian Religions, *Nostra Aetate* (no. 3).[277]

As mentioned previously, from the beginning of his pontificate Pope Paul VI was convinced of the need and importance of developing the dialogue with the Muslims. Furthermore, he found the basis of undertaking such an initiative quite clear and convincing. At this point, it is important to remember what he said about the matter during his *Angelus* prayer on October 17, 1965. While informing the people about the decision of the Second Vatican Council to announce the Declaration *Nostra Aetate*, the Pope called upon all Catholics to pray for non-Christians, and particularly for those who trace the roots of their faith to Abraham, that is, for Jews and Muslims, because, as he concluded: "The Heavenly Mother surely loves them (Jews and Muslims) and we should pray for them to her."[278]

---

[275] Ibid., no. 108.

[276] F. Koenig, "Le monothéisme dans le monde contemporain," *MIDEO*, vol. 8 (1964-1966), p. 407-422.

[277] For an analysis of both documents, see p. 68-73 of this work. Also refer to: R. Caspar, "Islam According to Vatican II...," p. 1-7.

[278] Paul VI, "To the Faithful at the *Angelus Domini*, Rome" (October 17, 1965), in: F. Gioia (ed.), *Interreligious Dialogue...*," p. 140.

As pointed out previously, the Secretariat for non-Christians was founded in 1964. It is symbolic and worth noting that the name was changed later (1988) to the Pontifical Council for Interreligious Dialogue. However, its special Section for Islam has been quite active only since 1965. The Section has hosted many delegations from all parts of the Muslim world. For example, in December 1970, representatives of the highest Islamic Council from Cairo came to the Vatican, and in October 1974, a delegation of experts in Islamic law was received. Those visits were accompanied by re-visits: representatives of the Vatican met with the Egyptian President Anwar Sādāt and the Saudi King Fayṣal.[279] In attempts to promote the idea of interreligious dialogue and, in particular, that of a dialogue with Islam, the Secretariat began to issue a special bulletin and other publications.[280]

Every year, the Section for Islam addresses Muslims all over the world with special wishes and words of friendship on the occasion of ʿĪd al-Fiṭr, a holiday at the end of Ramadan, the month of fasting. The wishes are broadcasted by the Vatican Radio in Arabic, translated into other languages and officially published. This gesture of friendship and respect coming from the Vatican has definitely contributed to the substantial improvement of Christian-Muslim relations in recent decades, promoting friendly and fruitful contacts between them. In 1967, the end of Ramadan almost coincided with the Christian New Year of 1968. While addressing pilgrims gathered in Mecca, the late King Fayṣal referred to that fact in the following words:

> I do not wish to miss this opportunity of pointing out that Islam is the religion of truth, the religion of freedom, the religion of co-operation and the religion of tolerance. So, when a message was sent out from the Vatican on the occasion of the Christian New Year, through a spokesman for his holiness Pope Paul, greeting Muslims and saluting the religion of Islam, this was given a very warm welcome by Muslims and received by them gratefully.[281]

During his pontificate, Paul VI made pilgrimages to several countries. He went on pastoral visits to the Holy Land (1964), India (1964), Portugal (1967), Turkey (1967), Columbia (1968), Switzerland (1969), Uganda (1969), the Philippines, Austria, Indonesia, Hong Kong and Ceylon (1970).[282] The program of those visits included meetings with local Muslim populations and their leaders. Paul VI welcomed the establishment of diplomatic relations with countries with a majority or a significant number of Muslims, and Muslim leaders were cordially received at the Vatican.

---

[279] See: G. C. Anawati, "An Assessment of the Christian-Islamic Dialogue," in: *The Vatican, Islam...*, p. 55-56.

[280] M. L. Fitzgerald, "The Secretariat for Non-Christians...," p. 92-93.

[281] Ibid., p. 94.

[282] For the important addresses related to Christian-Muslim dialogue during these visits see: F. Gioia (ed.), *Interreligious Dialogue...*, p. 117-119 (Bethlehem, January 6, 1964), p. 149--150 (Istanbul, July 25, 1967), p. 168 (Kampala, August 1, 1969), p. 173-175 (Manila, November 29, 1970), p. 176-177 (Djakarta, December 3, 1970).

Furthermore, thanks to an initiative of the Pontiff, various meetings and conferences were organized to promote the development of Christian-Muslim relations.

A closer look at the texts of the speeches given by Paul VI proves his commitment to developing and promoting interreligious dialogue. The Holy Father was convinced that only sincere reciprocal contact between the various religious and ethnic groups in the Middle East could possibly ease the existing tensions and ultimately lead to peaceful solutions.

On January 4, 1964, while addressing the King of Jordan, during his pilgrimage to the Holy Land, Paul VI made a reference to the issue of dialogue in universal terms. He said:

> We, Peter's Successor, remember his reference to the Psalms in his first Epistle: "He who would love life and see good days…let him turn away from evil and do good, let him seek after peace and pursue it" (Ps. 23, 13-15). Saint Peter also wrote: "Honour all men; love the brother-hood; fear God; honour the King" (1 Peter, 11, 17)
>
> May God grant Our prayer, and that of all men of good will, that living together in harmony and accord, they may help one another in love and justice, and attain to universal peace in true brotherhood.[283]

A few years later, the Pope discussed the matter of dialogue and reciprocal relations in more precise terms. On September 18, 1969, in his welcome address to the new Ambassador of Pakistan, the Holy Father remarked:

> The Catholic Church, in fact, teaches that "Faith needs to prove its fruitfulness by penetrating the believer's entire life, including its worldly dimensions, and by activating him towards justice and love, especially regarding the needy" (*Gaudium et Spes*, N. 21). She also recognizes that "in the first place among" those who acknowledge the Creator "there are the Moslems, who, professing to hold the faith of Abraham, along with us adore the one and merciful God, Who on the last day will judge mankind" (*Lumen Gentium*, N.16). Hence the Church strives, through this common belief, to foster concord and peace among individuals, families, nations, and races, by the observance of social and international justice for the fruit of justice is peace.[284]

On December 8, 1975, Paul VI announced his apostolic exhortation *Evangelii Nuntiandi*. While explaining the evangelical mission of the Catholic Church, as seen through the light of the decisions and documents acknowledged by the Second Vatican Council, the Holy Father addressed the issue of interreligious dialogue. It should

---

[283] "Pilgrimage to the Holy Land Address of Paul VI to the King of Jordan" (January 4, 1964), online: http://www.vatican.va/holy_father/paul_vi/speeches/1964/documents/hf_p-vi_spe_19640104_jordania_en.html, access: March 10, 2011.

[284] "Address of Paul VI to the Ambassador of the Republic of Pakistan to the Holy See" (September 18, 1969), online: http://www.vatican.va/holy_father/paul_vi/speeches/1969/september/documents/hf_p-vi_spe_19690918_ambasciatore-pakistan_en.html, access: March 10, 2011.

be noted that the new attitude of the Church, adopted by the Council, had great impact on the theological justification of the Church's dialogical mission, as discussed by Paul VI in *Evangelii Nuntiandi*. In his apostolic exhortation addressed to "The Episcopate, the Clergy and to all the Faithful of the Entire World," the Pontiff pointed out the unique character and the role of Christianity among other world religions. However, at the same time, he acknowledged that "good" and "truth" might also be found in other religions. For Paul VI, an interreligious dialogue did not necessarily mean a dialogue of religions, but rather a dialogue of religious people. The Pope's aim was to inspire religious people to participate in dialogical encounter and cooperation, so they could overcome existing barriers and prejudices, and eventually reach mutual understanding. As the Holy Father explained:

> This first proclamation is also addressed to the immense sections of mankind who practice non-Christian religions. The Church respects and esteems these non-Christian religions because they are the living expressions of the soul of vast groups of people. They carry with them the echo of thousands of years of searching for God...They possess an impressive patrimony of deeply religious texts. They have taught generations of people how to pray. They are all impregnated with the "seeds of the Word."[285]

There is no doubt that for Paul VI the question of interreligious dialogue, and, in particular, a dialogue with the followers of Islam, was an important task, and an imperative of the twentieth century and the century to come, and he considered it essential for peace and security in modern world. Therefore, until the end of his pontificate, the Holy Father addressed this issue on many occasions. On April 8, 1976, while receiving the Egyptian President at the Vatican, the Pope said:

> We also express at this time our great desire that the Muslim-Christian dialogue should continue and make progress among you people, in that fraternal spirit which ought to characterize all those who adore one God – just and merciful.[286]

The task of developing interreligious dialogue, and in particular one with Islam, was undertaken and pursued in an unprecedented way by John Paul II.

---

[285] *"Evangelii Nuntiandi*: Apostolic Exhortation of His Holiness Pope Paul VI to the Episcopate, to the Clergy and to All the Faithful of the Entire World" (December 8, 1975), no. 53, online: http://www.vatican.va/holy_father/paul_vi/apost_exhortations/documents/hf_p-vi_exh_19751208_evangelii-nuntiandi_en.html, access: March 10, 2011.

[286] "Address of the Holy Father Paul VI to the Egyptian President Visiting for the First Time the Apostolic See" (April 8, 1976), online: http://www.vatican.va/holy_father/paul_vi/speeches/1976/documents/hf_p-vi_spe_19760408_presidente-egitto_en.html, access: March 10, 2011.

Summary

The twentieth century, and in particular the post-World War II era, brought new positive changes in the Christian attitude towards non-Christian religions, as indicated by *De Motione Oecumenica* (1949), a significant document, in the light of which the approach to establishing a dialogical path for interreligious dialogue, including that with Islam, had begun. Furthermore, those changes were also stimulated by continued scholarly Christian reflection on the two religions and the reciprocal contact of their followers. Finally, the efforts of all the early proponents of Christian-Muslim dialogue provided an impulse to this pivotal event in the Church's history.

Aggiornamento, the spirit of changes and reforms as introduced by John XXIII, had opened the Catholic Church to the "outside world," and his encyclical *Pacem in Terris* became both the inspiration and the basis for the Church's new approach to dialogue with modernity. The heart of *aggiornamento* was the Second Vatican Council (1962-1965), which called upon Christians to respect the spiritual, moral and cultural values in other religions, including Islam.

The specific question of Islam appeared during the second session in 1963. It was the beginning of the pontificate of Paul VI. The new Pope was a person of a great sensitivity and openness. Furthermore, he was particularly curious about the richness of other cultures and diverse ways of thinking and religious sentiments. He introduced to the Church's teaching the term *dialogue* and undertook many initiatives, among them establishing the Secretariat for Non-Christians, as well as published a number of documents, including the encyclical *Ecclesiam Suam*, designed to develop and promote a dialogue with other religions and particularly with Islam. Finally, during the Second Vatican Council, Paul VI announced two Church documents referring directly to Islam, namely the Dogmatic Constitution of the Church, *Lumen Gentium* (no. 16) and the Declaration on the Relationship of the Church to Non-Christian Religions, *Nostra Aetate* (no. 3).

Pope Paul VI left for his successor a Church opened to and prepared for dialogue with the followers of Islam in the spirit of respect, tolerance and understanding. It was upon John Paul II to undertake the important task of continuing this work by preparing an actual action plan and following through with it.

III

Opening a new chapter in the history of Christian-Muslim relations

The meaning, the foundations, the aims and the practice of John Paul II's dialogue with the followers of Islam

In human relations all over the world, a dialogue, which commonly means a meeting and/or a conversation between two persons, plays a fundamental role as a means of communication. The term *dialogue* has entered widespread circulation from the language of literature and philosophy. Dialogue forms the basic language structure in drama. There are also literary and philosophical works written in a form of conversation that has been known since Plato. Despite the fact that in the course of history dialogue has entered different spheres of life, its basic structure practically has not changed. One may say that a dialogue meant and still means an exchange of thoughts that would not necessarily mean confrontation. Instead, such an exchange of outlooks should rather serve a clarification of the interlocutor's views and, in consequence, lead to an easier grasping and better understanding of what one side wanted to communicate to the other. Nowadays, the meaning of the term *dialogue* has been enriched by a pragmatic aspect. In such an understanding, a *dialogue* means a meeting of various groups of people who intend to engage in a constructive and respectful discussion that could lead to an acceptance and a better understanding of each other and initiate their common work for a common goal, i.e., for a better and safer world.

In the past few decades, and especially since the changes concerning the Catholic Church's approach to the modern world, as introduced by the Second Vatican

Council and the pontificate of Paul VI, the concept of such a dialogue has become very important in the Church's relations with non-Christians. As discussed in the previous chapter, Paul VI not only introduced to the Church's teaching the term *dialogue* but also undertook a number of measures to initiate and promote a dialogical encounter with the followers of non-Christian religions, including Muslims.

All the important initiatives of Paul VI concerning interreligious dialogue were continued and developed in an unprecedented way by his great successor John Paul II, who since the beginning of his pontificate had held out an open hand to all world religions.[287] Making it a point to travel widely and to address diverse groups, including Muslims, Jews, Buddhists, Shintoists and Hindus in sites all over the world, he had enthusiastically embraced religious diversity and called for a sincere interreligious dialogue and an end of religious prejudice, racial antagonism and xenophobia. For John Paul II, the continuous and persistent development of interreligious dialogue, and, in particular the one with the followers of Islam, always remained one of the focal points of his mission.[288]

As for the Pontiff's encounter with Muslims prior to his election, we may refer to his book *Crossing the Threshold of Hope*. John Paul II recalled there an episode from the period of his studies in Rome:

> I remember an event from my youth. In the convent of the Church of Saint Mark in Florence, we were looking at the frescoes by Fra Angelico. At a certain point a man joined us who, after sharing his admiration for the work of this great religious artist, immediately added: "But nothing can compare to our magnificent Muslim monotheism." His statement did not prevent us from continuing the visit and the conversation in a friendly tone. It was on that occasion that I got a kind of first taste of the dialogue between Christianity and Islam, which we have tried to develop systematically in the post-conciliar period.[289]

Although prior to his election John Paul II did not have much contact with Muslims, one may say that he came to the Vatican relatively "well-prepared" for a dia-

---

[287] For a further discussion including a brief overview of John Paul II's contribution to the development of interreligious dialogue illustrated by the edited excerpts from his writings and speeches on dialogue with Buddhism, Judaism and Islam see: B. L. Sherwin and H. Kasimow (eds.), *John Paul II...* Also refer to: E. Sakowicz, *Pryncypia dialogu Kościoła katolickiego z religiami Dalekiego Wschodu i Indii w w świetle nauczania Soboru Watykańskiego II oraz dokumentów posoborowych*, Warszawa: Wydawnictwo Uniwersytetu Kardynała Wyszyńskiego, 2006.

[288] In his book *Jean-Paul II et l'Islam* (Paris: François-Xavier de Guilbert, 2003) Michel Lelong presents a brief overview of selected issues, such as history of Christian-Muslim relations, common values of both religions and discusses the role of John Paul II in developing a sincere dialogue between the Catholic Church and the followers of Islam. The book also contains some reflections about the future of Christian-Muslim dialogue of life.

[289] John Paul II, *Crossing the Threshold of Hope*, Toronto: Alfred A. Knopf Canada, 1994, p. 92.

logical encounter with the followers of Islam. First, Karol Wojtyła, the future Pope, was well acquainted with the thought and works of St. Francis of Assisi, St. Thomas Aquinas and Ramon Lull and their role in the history of Christian-Muslim relations.[290] Moreover, he was fascinated by the philosophy of dialogue and the works of Martin Buber, Emamuel Levinas and Franz Rosenzweig, which definitely influenced his dialogical approach. Second, as a bishop Karol Wojtyła actively participated in the sessions of the Second Vatican Council.[291] Therefore, he was well aware of all the efforts of John XXIII and Paul VI related to the matter of decisive changes concerning the attitude of the Church towards non-Christians.[292] Furthermore, as it has been already mentioned, the future Pope was a member the Council's Committee that prepared the Constitution *Gaudium et Spes*, the document dealing extensively with the issue of the Church's dialogical mission in the context of the modern changing world.[293] Following the Council, Wojtyła actively implemented its decisions, in Poland and in Rome, attending four out of five general synods it set up.[294] It is also worth mentioning that, as Weigel suggests, the experience of the Council, namely working with Popes John XXIII and Paul VI and spending hours everyday in St. Peter's Basilica, not far from the apostle's tomb, had itself deepened Karol Wojtyła's understanding the office of Peter and had enabled him to grasp well "what that office exacted from the man who held it."[295] Third, the future Pope had a special, so to say, a unique way of dealing with people. No matter how "difficult" was the partner of his conversation, Wojtyła was ready to listen and willing to search for compromising solutions despite obstacles. So, sometimes even "impossible" conclusions were reached. Fourth, while living in Poland he could observe the tradition of religious tolerance with regard to Polish Muslims, namely the Tartars.[296] Moreover, the direct

---

[290] Their approach to Muslims and Christian-Muslim contacts, as discussed in Chapter I of this work, found its reflection in Pope John Paul II's related thought and actions.

[291] As G. Weigel underlined, K. Wojtyła's scholarly and unusual pastoral background along with his interest in everything from history, culture and politics to social ethics and family matters placed him in an advantageous position for participation in the Second Vatican Council. About K. Wojtyła's active participation in the debates of the Council, and in particular concerning the issue of religious freedom see: G. W e i g e l, *Witness to Hope...*, p. 159-166. K. W o j t y ł a, *The Acting Person*, trans. A. P o t o c k i, Dordrecht and London: D. Reidel Publishing Company, 1979.

[292] For Karol Wojtyła's assessment of the realization of the Council's teaching, including a discussion on the relation between dialogue and faith see: *U podstaw odnowy: Studium o realizacji Vaticanum II*, Kraków: Polskie Towarzystwo Teologiczne, 1972; English edition: *Sources of Renewal: The Implementation of the Second Vatican Council*, trans. P. S. F a l l a, San Francisco: Harper and Row, 1980.

[293] About the references of *Gaudium et Spes* to the issue of the Catholic Church's dialogue with non-Christian religions see: Chapter II of this work, p. 67-68.

[294] See: G. O ' C o n n o r, *Universal Father...*, p. 159-160.

[295] G. W e i g e l, *Witness to Hope...*, p. 155.

[296] The Polish Tartars are the descendants of the Tartar tribes who in the 13th century reached the territory of Poland and Lithuania with the aim to conquer some lands. From the 14th century they began to settle on the territory of Poland and over the centuries they

observance of Muslims living side by side with Christians during his pilgrimage to the Holy Land in 1963[297] and his trip to the Philippines (1973), a country with a substantial Muslim minority, increased his awareness of Islam and the Muslim world. Fifth, when he became Pope, John Paul II had at his disposal all the official documents of the Second Vatican Council, including the most important one, namely *Nostra Aetate* and the example of Paul VI's initiatives towards conducting a sincere dialogue with Muslims, such as the encyclical *Ecclesiam Suam* and the establishment of the Secretariat for Non-Christians.[298] All in all, one may say that prior to John Paul II's election, the basic guidelines for the Catholic Church's dialogical encounter with Islam were already drawn. It was up to the new Pope to elaborate further the already initiated, post-Vatican II path of Christian-Muslim relations.

When we reflect on John Paul II's life and work during the pre-election period and take into consideration his love for poetry, drama and mysticism, we may notice that those experiences were also important for his "preparation" to meet the dialogical challenges of his pontificate.[299] The Holy Father's devotion to prayer and his mystical way of losing himself in God had strengthened his inner spirit. Moreover, his subtle nature as a poet and a man of theatre made him capable of listening at-

---

assimilated well with the Polish society, retaining their religion (they are Sunni Muslims of ḥanafī rite). See: K. Warmińska, *Tatarzy polscy: Tożsamość religijna i etniczna*, Kraków: Towarzystwo Autorów i Wydawców Prac Naukowych "Universitas", 1999. Also refer to: E. Sakowicz, "Islam and Christian-Muslim Relations in Poland," *Islamochristiana*, vol. 23 (1997), p. 139-146.

[297] During the Second Vatican Council, Karol Wojtyła followed Pope Paul VI's suggestion that bishops should visit the Holy Land prior to the Pope's own pilgrimage there in 1964. See: G. Weigel, *Witness to Hope...*, p. 156-157.

[298] Karol Wojtyła had his first audience with Pope Paul VI on November 30, 1963. After that Wojtyła's meetings with Paul VI became increasingly frequent. See: G. O'Connor, *Universal Father...*, p. 158-159.

[299] See: K. Wojtyła, *The Collected Plays and Writings on Theater*, trans. and introduction B. Taborski, Berkeley: University of California Press, 1987; John Paul II, *The Place Within: The Poetry of John Paul II*, trans. J. Peterkiewicz, London: Hutchinson, 1994; John Paul II, *Poezje – Poems*, trans. J. Peterkiewicz, afterward K. Dybciak, Krakow: Wydawnictwo Literackie, 1998; John Paul II, *Tryptyk rzymski: Medytacje – Roman Triptych: Meditations*, trans. J. Peterkiewicz, Kraków: Wydawnictwo Literackie, 2003; Karol Wojtyła, John Paul II, *Poezje, dramaty, szkice, tryptyk rzymski*, foreword M. Skwarnicki, Kraków: Wydawnictwo Znak, 2003; W. P. Szymański, *Z mroku korzeni: O poezji Karola Wojtyły*, Kraków: Księgarnia Akademicka, 2005; J. Machniak, *Bóg i człowiek w poezjach i dramatach Karola Wojtyły – Jana Pawła II*, Kraków: Wydawnictwo Św. Stanisława BM Archidiecezji krakowskiej, 2007. For a thorough discussion on literary work of Karol Wojtyła – John Paul II see a recent publication: Z. Zarębianka and J. Machniak (eds.), *The Space of the Word: The Literary Activity of Karol Wojtyła – John Paul II*, Cracow: John Paul II Institute of Intercultural Dialogue, 2011 (English version of iidem (eds.), *Przestrzeń słowa: Twórczość literacka Karola Wojtyły – Jana Pawła II*, Kraków: Wydawnictwo św. Stanisława BM Archidiecezji Krakowskiej, 2006).

tentively to people, sensing their feelings, "feeling" their problems, so he could truly share their happiness, sorrows and pains. As Williams remarked, while performing his duties as the Supreme Pastor, John Paul II had persistently "resisted the usual institutionalization of his person as Pope."[300] He used to take time to perform duties as a parish priest in solemnizing a marriage, console the sick in a hospital, share a humble meal with the homeless, pick up and hug a child, laugh with the young and sing with them. His "uniqueness" as Pope, according to Williams, was based on the fact that he had never been "depersonalized":

> His charm for the whole world, in fact lies in the fact that John Paul II Wojtyła is a whole person with a personal history like everyone else, and thus a model person in any age when in all Three Worlds the sense of personhood has been imperiled.[301]

The history of the life and work of Karol Wojtyła and then John Paul II clearly reveals that, regardless of place, time and circumstances, the value of being with people was the most important for him. John Paul II was well aware of the "uniqueness" of each and every person. His "intercultural sensitivity" together with his deep concern for human beings, who nowadays often face different cultures, ethnic origins and religions, convinced him that each and every person needs to be approached with love, respect and tolerance and be accorded a sense of self-esteem and responsibility for things. As Williams pointed out, John Paul II's unusual ability of remaining "so much a vibrant human being, himself palpably savoring life as well as serving others," meant that every man and woman had "in some way been encouraged to feel less helpless before the seemingly vast and irrational forces within and around societies, and more helpful."[302] In the modern, politically, socially and culturally "complicated world," according to the Pope, a dialogue of a human being with "the other," a conversation based on mutual respect and tolerance and enriching the awareness of each other was the only beneficial and constructive means of contact between both individuals and diverse groups of people. All in all, during his entire life John Paul II sought to "build the bridges" to "bring together his intellectual and intuitive sides, his respect for religions, and his love for others, to promote understanding of the nobility and dignity of each human being."[303]

---

[300] G. H. Williams, *The Mind of John Paul II: Origins of His Thought and Action*, New York: The Seabury Press, 1981 p. 262. George Hunston Williams (1914-2000), a Church historian and professor of Harvard Divinity School, who attended the Second Vatican Council as an invited Protestant "observer," met with K. Wojtyła and was impressed with the personality of the bishop from Krakow. In 1978, he predicted (writing for Harvard University's newspaper *Crimson*) that Wojtyła would be the next Pope (T. Szulc, *Pope John Paul II...*, p. 218).

[301] Ibid.

[302] Ibid.

[303] L. Allen-Shore, *Building the Bridges: Pope John Paul II and the Horizon of Life*, foreword S. Dziwisz, Ottawa: Novalis Press and Saint Paul University, 2004, p. 69.

Three distinctive phases of dialogue

Analyzing of the history of John Paul II's dialogue with Islam and the Muslims is not an easy task because since the beginning he was engaged in practically simultaneous, numerous endeavors and actions promoting such a dialogue. The Pope was spreading his dialogical message through a number of means and ways, such as publication of related documents, speeches given on various occasions, meetings with Muslim leaders and addressing people during his pilgrimages around the world. However, when getting into the core of the matter, one may notice in this history three distinguished phases.

First phase: grasping the essence of the Church's dialogical history

The first phase began with Karol Wojtyla's election on October 16, 1978 and lasted until the end of the 1970s. This was a period of "intensive learning," that is, grasping the essence of the Second Vatican Council's conclusions related to the issue of interreligious dialogue and of the dialogical teaching and initiatives of Paul VI. Moreover, during that time the Pope expressed, on several occasions, his commitment to continue a sincere interreligious dialogue, and in particular, that with the followers of Islam.

As indicated by the choice of his name, right from the beginning of his pontificate John Paul II embarked on the task of following the path of changes in the spirit of modernity as it had been introduced by the Second Vatican Council led by John XXIII and Paul VI, and desired by John Paul I, who on August 27, 1978 in the radio message *Urbi et Orbi*, announced that the dialogue with the world would be the priority of his pastoral mission.[304] With regard to the issue of interreligious dialogue, and particularly the development of a dialogue with the followers of Islam, John Paul II indeed continued the policy of his predecessor Paul VI. Undertaking such a challenging task was clear proof of John Paul II's evangelical bravery. On December 10, 1978, only a few weeks after his election, during the Sunday prayer, while appealing for peace in Lebanon, the Pope did not hesitate to call Muslims, "who refer their roots to Abraham," his "brothers and sisters" in faith.[305] A few months later,

---

[304]   John Paul I said: "We wish to pursue with patience but firmness that serene and constructive dialogue that Paul VI had at the base of his plan and program for pastoral action. The principal theme for this was set forth in his great encyclical *Ecclesiam Suam;* namely that men, as men should know one another, even those who do not share our faith." "Radio Message *Urbi et Orbi*" in: F. Gioia (ed.), *Interreligious Dialogue...*, p. 211, paragraph 329.

[305]   John Paul II, *"Angelus"* (December 10, 1978), online: http://www.vatican.va/holy_father/ john_paul_ii/angelus/1978/documents/hf_jp-ii_ang_19781210_en.html, access: March 15, 2011.

on March 4, 1979, John Paul II published his first encyclical *Redemptor Hominis.*[306] While referring directly to Paul VI's "great charter of dialogue", i.e., the encyclical *Ecclesiam Suam*, the Holy Father reminded the people of the achievements of the Second Vatican Council in opening the Church to the modern world and introducing it to the sphere of universal awareness. The Pope remarked:

> This awareness – or rather self-awareness – by the Church is formed in "a dialogue"; and before this dialogue becomes a conversation, attention must be directed to "the other", that is to say: the person with whom we wish to speak. The Ecumenical Council gave a fundamental impulse to forming the Church's self-awareness by so adequately and competently presenting to us a view of the terrestrial globe as a map of various religions.[307]

Well aware of the fact that the modern world had become the sphere of cultural and religious pluralism, John Paul II addressed the issue of interreligious dialogue, pointing out that attention should be paid to the "seeds of the Word," which could be found in different religions.[308] As the Holy Father explained:

> The Fathers of the Church rightly saw in the various religions as they were so many reflections of the one truth, "seeds of the Word", attesting that, though the routes taken may be different, but there is a single goal to which is directed the deepest aspiration of the human spirit as expressed in its quest for God and also in its quest, through its tending towards God, for the full dimension of its humanity, or in other words the full meaning of human life.[309]

Furthermore, while referring to the Declaration on the Relationship of the Church to Non-Christian Religions *Nostra Aetate*, the Pontiff stated that:

> The Council gave particular attention to the Jewish religion, recalling the great spiritual heritage common to Christians and Jews. It also expressed its esteem for the believers of Islam, whose faith also looks to Abraham.[310]

---

[306] In his book *Crossing the Threshold...* (p. 48) John Paul II said: "You will remember that my first encyclical on the Redeemer of man (*Redemptor Hominis*) appeared a few months after my election on October 16, 1978. This means that I was actually carrying the contents *within me*. I had only to copy from memory and experience what I had already been living on the threshold of the papacy."

[307] John Paul II, "*Redemptor Hominis* to his Venerable Brothers in the Episcopate the Priests the Religious Families, the Sons and Daughters of the Church and to All Men and Women of Good Will at the Beginning of his Papal Ministry" (March 4, 1979), no. 11, online: http://www.vatican.va/holy_father/john_paul_ii/encyclicals/documents/hf_jp-ii_enc_04031979_redemptor-hominis_en.html, access: March 15, 2011.

[308] See: E. Sakowicz, *Dialog Kościoła z islamem...*, p. 71.

[309] John Paul II, "*Redemptor Hominis...*," no. 11.

[310] Ibid.

The publication of *Redemptor Hominis* was a clear confirmation of John Paul II's will and determination to carry on with the task of promoting and developing a sincere dialogue with non-Christians, including Muslims, in the spirit of *Nostra Aetate*. The following months of his pontificate brought about new significant developments.

While looking at the history of John Paul II's dialogue with the followers of Islam we should keep in mind that, as Williams pointed out, the Pope's theoretical investigations embodied in a number of documents, books and other writings should be viewed parallel to his actions and all his experiences prior to his election, such as being a seminarian, priest, professor or prelate, and should be considered a compelling part of a man who had spoken with the authority of the Successor of St. Peter.[311] As observed throughout his entire pontificate, the Holy Father persistently followed and demonstrated his conviction that the appearing of important ideas and problems should be signaled right away, the most appropriate solutions applied and related tasks undertaken as soon as possible.

On April 27, 1979, John Paul II addressed the members of the Secretariat for Non-Christians who gathered in Rome for their first Plenary Assembly. While referring to the work of Paul VI, the Pontiff mentioned his predecessor's love, interest, care and attention devoted to the world of non-Christian religions. John Paul II expressed his gratitude for the efforts of the Secretariat to seek out the forms and the methods that were suitable for conducting what Paul VI called "the dialogue of salvation" with non-Christians. He said:

> Nearly fifteen years of experience has taught many things, and with clear vision your Plenary Assembly is able to describe the present state of dialogue with non-Christians in the various cultural areas, identifying the difficulties, problems and results attained in each area, and deciding short-term and long-term programs for the coming years.[312]

A few months later, John Paul II went to Turkey. Obviously, the Catholic community living there was the Pope's primary concern. However, the pastoral visit to a country inhabited by a Muslim majority gave the Holy Father an opportunity to speak publicly, for the first time, about the matter of the Christian attitude toward Islam. On November 29, 1979, while addressing the Catholic Community in Ankara, John Paul II pointed out the significance of the Second Vatican Council. Referring to its documents, namely the Constitution of the Church *Lumen Gentium* no. 16 and the Declaration of the Church to Non-Christian Religions *Nostra Aetate* no. 3, as well as to his own encyclical *Redemptor Hominis*, the Holy Father spoke about the patrimony of Islam and its great spiritual values. He also expressed his esteem and respect for the Muslims and spoke special words of friendship to his Islamic brothers and sisters.

---

[311]   G. H. Williams, *The Mind of John Paul II...*, p. 261.
[312]   John Paul II, "To the Secretariat for Non-Christians" (Rome, April 27, 1979), in: F. Gioia (ed.), *Interreligious Dialogue...*, p. 217, paragraph 333.

While discussing the spiritual heritage of Christianity and Islam and its impact on both human life and society as a whole, the Pontiff remarked that:

It would be rather essential for the Christians and the Muslims to enter a new history, i.e., to acknowledge and develop spiritual ties that unite them, so that they could guard together social justice, moral values, peace and freedom.[313]

John Paul II was convinced that in the modern pluralistic world of ethnic, cultural and religious diversity, the only way to build a safer future was to choose dialogue as a means of communication. For the Pope an interreligious dialogue, and in particular a dialogue between Christians and Muslims, could also become a powerful vehicle of cooperation. Resulting from the inner impulse of love, it could help in establishing and safeguarding the proper order in society and increase respect for true spiritual values. Therefore, in his address in Ankara he appealed to each and every member of the Catholic community there to give some thought to the issue of Christian-Muslim dialogue and cooperation. He said:

I would like to encourage you to an every day reflection on the very roots of the faith in God, in whom also believe your fellow citizens Muslims. From that you would be able to draw the rules of reciprocal cooperation for the progress and the betterment of the society as well as for peace and brotherhood in free manifestation of each other own religious beliefs.[314]

Second phase: establishing the Pope's own dialogical path

During the second phase, namely the period of the 1980s, John Paul II was focused on establishing his own dialogical path with Muslims and while consequently confirming his commitment to dialogue, the Holy Father embarked on the task of teaching the whole world, in simple words, about the philosophy of a dialogue, its meaning and its aims, and making people of different cultures and religions aware of the necessity to engage in such a dialogue.

According to the Pope, only while engaged in a sincere dialogue could people develop their intercultural sensitivity and thus contribute to a better world through better perception of self and more skillful understanding of others.

In the early 1980s, during his pilgrimages to several countries while addressing different groups of people, including Muslims, the Pope focused on confirming his commitment to continue, promote and develop his dialogue with the Muslims in the spirit of *Nostra Aetate*. On May 7, 1980, in his speech to Muslims in Nairobi (Kenya) he said:

---

[313] John Paul II, "To the Catholic Community of Ankara...," p. 219-222, paragraph 337-341.
[314] Ibid., p. 222, paragraph 341.

The Catholic Church realizes that the element of worship given to the one living subsistent merciful and almighty creator of heaven and earth is common to Islam and herself and that is a great link uniting all Christians and Muslims…From my part I wish, therefore, to do everything possible to help develop the spiritual bonds between Christians and Muslims…Our relationship of reciprocal esteem and the mutual desire for authentic service to humanity urge us on to joint commitment in promoting peace, social justice, moral values and all the freedom of man.[315]

The following day, during a meeting with Muslims in Accra (Ghana) John Paul II clearly expressed his wish:

Where Muslims and Christians live as neighbors, mutual respect will be constantly present in social life also, and common action to promote the acceptance and the defense of man's fundamental rights.[316]

On the 31st of May (1980) in Paris, during a meeting with the representatives of the Muslim community in France, while referring to the principles of *Nostra Aetate*, the Pope once again reaffirmed to the world his commitment to develop and promote a sincere dialogue between the Catholic Church and the followers of Islam.[317] The Holy Father also directed similar words to both Christians and Muslims during his subsequent pilgrimages to Pakistan,[318] the Philippines (1981), Portugal (1982), Belgium (1985) and Morocco (1985).

It should be emphasized that while addressing both Christians and Muslims, he often referred to their everyday problems and on many occasions expressed his concerns about the social, cultural and religious problems that immigrant workers, either Muslim or Christian, may encounter in their host country. While addressing Muslims in Paris, on May 31, 1980, he said:

I know that not all of your problems have been solved, no more than those of other workers around the world, no more than those of many Christians living and working in a number of Islamic countries. Yet, we are convinced that goodwill, sincere efforts toward understanding and the common quest for solutions with a real desire for conciliation can, with the assistance of the one God in whom we all believe, help to find satisfactory solutions.
Our common ideal is a society in which men can recognize each other as brothers walking in God's light and striving for what is good.[319]

---

[315] "John Paul II's Address during the Meeting with Muslims in Nairobi (Kenya)" (May 7, 1980), *Islamochristiana*, vol. 6 (1980), p. 211.

[316] "John Paul II's Address during the Meeting with Muslims in Accra (Ghana)" (May 8, 1980), *Islamochristiana*, vol. 6 (1980), p. 212.

[317] See: John Paul II, "To the Representatives of the Muslim Community in France" (Paris, May 31, 1980), in: F. Gioia (ed.), *Interreligious Dialogue…*, p. 233-234, paragraph 360.

[318] About the visit see: Chapter IV of this work, p. 141.

[319] John Paul II, "To the Representatives of the Muslim Community in France…," p. 233-234, paragraph 360.

As mentioned previously, during the 1980s the main task of John Paul II concerning the issue of Christian-Muslim relations was widespread teaching about the need, the basis and the significance of interreligious dialogue. The best example of the Pope's lessons on such a dialogue seems to be his address to young Muslims in Casablanca.

John Paul II's visit to Casablanca was an unprecedented event. It was the first time that a Pope had ever formally addressed a Muslim audience at the invitation of a Muslim leader. The visit came on August 19, 1985, the last day of John Paul II's third African pilgrimage, which had taken him to Togo, Ivory Coast, Cameroon and the Central African Republic, where he participated in the 43rd International Eucharistic Congress in Nairobi. The few hours' stop in Casablanca was arranged at the personal request of Morocco's ruler, King Ḥasan II, who had invited John Paul II to his country during his royal visit to the Vatican.[320] At the stadium in Casablanca the Pope met with approximately 80,000 young Muslims.

While presenting himself as both the Bishop of Rome and the head of the Catholic Church, John Paul II indicated that he had come to Casablanca to speak as a believer in God to other believers in God:

> It is as a believer that I come to you… simply… to give here today the witness to what I believe, what I wish for well-being of my brothers, mankind, and what, through experience, I consider to be useful for all.[321]

Then, he approached the audience with words that focused on the common Christian and Muslim belief in one God, common roots traced to Abraham and "many things in common" that Christians and Muslims had "as believers and as human beings." He said:

> We live in the same world, marked by many signs of hope, but also by multiple signs of anguish. For us, Abraham is a very model of faith in God, of submission to his will and of confidence in his goodness. We believe in the same God, the one God, the living God, the God who created the world and brings his creatures to their perfection.[322]

Referring to the spirit of the Second Vatican Council and its *Nostra Aetate* Declaration, the Pope called for a common belief in God, appealed for common witness to man's dignity, for a pluralistic and jointly-responsible world and stressed an urgent need for growth in the spiritual life. While addressing one of the most difficult issues in Christian-Muslim relations, that is, religious freedom, the Holy Father explained

---

[320] About John Paul II's visit to Morocco see: G. Weigel, *Witness to Hope…*, p. 498-500.
[321] "The Speech of the Holy Father John Paul II to Young Muslims during his Meeting with them in Casablanca (Morocco, August 19, 1985)," *Encounter: Documents for Muslim-Christian Understanding*, no. 128 (August 1986), p. 2.
[322] Ibid.

that religious faith, not a secular indifference or neutrality toward religion, was the most secure ground for religious liberty:

> Obedience to God and this love for man ought to lead us to respect human rights, these rights which are the expression of God's will and demands of human nature such as it was created by God. Therefore, respect and dialogue require reciprocity in all spheres... more particularly religious freedom. They favour peace and agreement between the peoples. They help to resolve together the problems of today's men and women, especially those of the young.[323]

The reception of John Paul II's speech, as Cardinal Dziwisz recalled, was astonishing; the young people listened to the Pope attentively and reacted to his words spontaneously:

> It was extraordinary how the young people applauded at all the right moments. It's clear that they couldn't have known where he was going or have been coached in any way. So, we finally reached the amazing conclusion that they were simply listening with attentive interest to what the Holy Father was telling them.[324]

On many occasions, while addressing various personalities and groups of people, John Paul II explained that interreligious dialogue did not grow out of opportunism of the tactics of the moment, but from reasons which experience and reflection, and even difficulties themselves, had only deepened. He emphasized that in interpersonal dialogue one experiences one's own limitations as well as the possibility of overcoming them. Therefore, the best way to resolve the greatest concerns of our century was to work together with the other person toward that goal. Religious experiences and outlooks, explained the Pope, could themselves be purified and enriched in this process of encounter. John Paul II was convinced that socio-cultural changes in the world together with their inherent tensions and difficulties render a dialogical style of human relationship. Furthermore, growing interdependence, in all sectors of society, necessary for living together, for human promotion and, above all, for pursuing the demands of peace had made, according to the Pope, the need for dialogue even more urgent.

John Paul II strongly believed that an interreligious dialogue, and in particular a sincere dialogue with Muslims, was essential for the Church, which had been called to collaborate in God's plan with its methods of presence, respect and love toward all persons. Therefore, since his first encyclical *Redemptor Hominis*, and during his numerous meetings with various personalities and above all on the occasion of his journeys, the Pope often emphasized the need to conduct such a dialogue.

---

[323] "The Speech of the Holy Father John Paul II to Young Muslims...," p. 5.
[324] S. Dziwisz, *A Life with Karol: My Forty-Year Friendship with the Man Who Became Pope: Cardinal Stanislaw Dziwisz in Conversation with Gian Franco Svidercoschi*, New York: Doubleday, 2008, p. 239-240.

In 1984, while addressing the Plenary Assembly of the Secretariat, twenty years after both the publication of *Ecclesiam Suam* and the foundation of the Secretariat for Non-Christians, the Pope once again pointed out the importance of an interreligious dialogue in the view of increasing social and cultural changes in all parts of the modern world:

> In fact, no one can fail to see the importance of and the need which interreligious dialogue assumes for all religions and all believers, called today more than ever to collaborate so that every person can reach his transcendent goal and realize his authentic growth and to help cultures to preserve their own religious and spiritual values in the presence of rapid social changes.[325]

During the 1980s, John Paul II published several documents where we may find multiple references to the issue of Christian-Muslim dialogue. Among them are the following: apostolic exhortations *Familiaris Consortio*, November 22, 1981, *Christifideles Laici*, December 30, 1988; encyclicals: *Dominum et Vivificantem*, May 18, 1986, *Sollicitudo Rei Socialis*, December 30, 1987; apostolic letter *Redemptionis Anno*, April 20, 1984; and Apostolic Constitution *Pastor Bonus*, June 28, 1988.

In *Familiaris Consortio*, while referring to the spirit of the Second Vatican Council the Pope emphasized:

> Love, too, goes beyond our brothers and sisters of the same faith since "everybody is my brother or sister." In each individual, especially in the poor, the weak, and those who suffer or are unjustly treated, love knows how to discover the face of Christ, and discover a fellow human being to be loved and served.[326]

In this exhortation John Paul II also addressed important issues concerning Christian-Muslim relations, and in particular the question of mixed marriages. While pointing out the role of the family and family values in the modern world and expressing his observations about the increasing number of mixed marriages between Catholics and non-baptized persons, he explained the need for respect for each other's religious beliefs:

> In many such marriages the non-baptized partner professes another religion, and his beliefs are to be treated with respect, in accordance with the principles set out in the

---

[325] John Paul II, "Address of the Pope at the Conclusion of the Plenary Assembly of the Secretariat" (March 3, 1984), in: *The Attitude of the Church towards the Followers of Other Religions: Reflections and Orientations on Dialogue and Mission*, Vatican: Polyglot Press, 1984, p. 3.

[326] John Paul II, "Apostolic Exhortation *Familiaris Consortio* of Pope John Paul II to the Episcopate to the Clergy and to the Faithful of the Whole Catholic Church on the Role of the Christian Family in the Modern World" (November 22, 1981), no. 64, online: http://www.vatican.va/holy_father/john_paul_ii/apost_exhortations/documents/hf_jp-ii_exh_19811122_familiaris-consortio_en.html, access March 15, 2011.

Second Vatican Council's Declaration "Nostra Aetate" on relations with non-Christian religions.[327]

In *Christifideles Laici*, the Pontiff appealed to the lay people to engage themselves in various social, political and cultural activities and initiatives leading to the rapprochement and cooperation between people of different cultures, traditions and religious beliefs. John Paul II addressed the matter in the following words:

> The Synod Fathers have mentioned that the lay faithful can favour the relations which ought to be established with followers of *various religions* through their example in the situations in which they live and in their activities: "Throughout the world today the Church lives among people of various religions... All the Faithful, especially the lay faithful who live among the people of other religions, whether living in their native region or in lands as migrants, ought to be for all a sign of the Lord and his Church, in a way adapted to the actual living situation of each place. Dialogue among religions has a preeminent part, for it leads to love and mutual respect, and takes away, or at least diminishes, prejudices among the followers of various religions and promotes unity and friendship among peoples"(129).[328]

As for John Paul II's encyclical *Dominum et Vivificantem*, while referring to the Holy Spirit, he explained that "within the perspective of the great Jubilee," the Catholic Church needed to "look further and go further a field, knowing that *the wind blows where it wills*, according to the image used by Jesus in his conversation with Nicodemus," and following the example of Jesus, it should strengthen its efforts to reach out to all the people of "good will." He said:

> The Second Vatican Council, centered primarily on the theme of the Church, reminds us of the Holy Spirit's activity also "outside the visible body of the Church." The Council speaks precisely of "all people of good will in whose hearts grace works in an unseen way. For, since Christ died for all, and since the ultimate vocation of man is in fact one, and divine, we ought to believe that the Holy Spirit in a manner known only to God offers to every man the possibility of being associated with this Paschal Mystery."[329]

In his encyclical *Sollicitudo Rei Socialis*, the Pope emphasized the need for trust among all people, so they could share their commitment in the defense of the poor

---

[327]   Ibid., no. 78.

[328]   John Paul II, "Post-Synodal Apostolic Exhortation *Christifideles Laici* of His Holiness John Paul II on the Vocation and the Mission of the Lay Faithful in the Church and in the World" (December 30, 1988), no. 35, online: http://www.vatican.va/holy_father/john_paul_ii/apost_exhortations/documents/hf_jp-ii_exh_30121988_christifideles-laici_en.html, access: March 15, 2011.

[329]   John Paul II, "*Dominum et Vivificantem:* On the Holy Spirit in the Life of the Church and the World" (May 18, 1986), no. 53, online: http://www.vatican.va/holy_father/john_paul_ii/encyclicals/documents/hf_jp-ii_enc_18051986_dominum-et-vivificantem_en.html, access: March 15, 2011.

while working in the various spheres of social economic and political engagement and thus contribute to the betterment of their families and the societies in which they live. The Holy Father stated:

> Consequently, following the example of Pope Paul VI with his Encyclical *Populorum Progressio*, I wish to appeal with simplicity and humility to everyone, to all men and women without exception. I wish to ask them to be convinced of the seriousness of the present moment and of each one's individual responsibility…I likewise address this appeal to the Jewish people, who share with us the inheritance of Abraham, "our father in faith"…as well as to the Muslims who, like us, believe in a just and merciful God. And I extend it to all the followers of the world's great religions.[330]

On June 28, 1988, John Paul II announced the Apostolic Constitution *Pastor Bonus*.[331] With regard to the issue of dialogue with non-Christians, the related articles of the Constitution confirmed the character of the Church's teaching[332] and concerning the matter of Christian-Muslim relations, it is important to note that in Art. 162 of *Pastor Bonus* it was stated: "This Council has a Commission, under the direction of the president of the Council, for fostering relations with Muslims from a religious perspective."

Furthermore, on the basis of this document, some important changes related to the facilitating of the functioning of Roman Curia offices were introduced. In particular, the name of the Secretariat for Non-Christians was changed into the Pontifical Council for Inter-Religious Dialogue.[333] One may certainly agree with Sakowicz that

---

[330] John Paul II, "*Sollicitudo Rei Socialis:* To the Bishops, Priests, Religious Families, Sons and Daughters of the Church and all People of Good Will for the Twentieth Anniversary of *Populorum Progressio*" (December 30, 1987), no. 47, online: http://www.vatican.va/holy_father/john_paul_ii/encyclicals/documents/hf_jp-ii_enc_30121987_sollicitudo-rei-socialis_en.html, access : March 15, 2011.

[331] John Paul II, "Apostolic Constitution *Pastor Bonus*" (June 28, 1988), online: http://www.vatican.va/holy_father/john_paul_ii/apost_constitutions/documents/hf_jp-ii_apc_19880628_pastor-bonus-index_en.html, access: March 15, 2011.

[332] Art. 159 – The Pontifical Council for Inter-Religious Dialogue fosters and supervises relations with members and groups of non-Christian religions as well as with those who are in any way endowed with religious feeling. Art. 160 – The Council fosters suitable dialogue with the followers of other religions and encourages various kinds of relations with them. It promotes appropriate studies and conferences to develop mutual information and esteem, so that human dignity and the spiritual and moral riches of people may ever grow. The Council sees to the formation of those who engage in this kind of dialogue. Art. 161 – When the matter under consideration so requires, the Council must proceed in the exercise of its own function in consultation with the Congregation for the Doctrine of the Faith, and, if need be, with the Congregations for the Oriental Churches and for the Evangelization of Peoples.

[333] The Council conducts important publishing activity. Besides books and various documents from dialogue meetings it organizes, it also publishes regularly three times a year a bulletin called *Pro Dialogo* (up until 1988 known as *Bulletin*) containing significant Church texts on dialogue, articles, and news of dialogue activities throughout the world. For the profile of the

change of the name was not only a formal matter, but the elimination of word *non* in the new name also reflects a radical change in the attitude of the Church to other faiths, including Islam.[334]

From the beginning of his pontificate, John Paul II supported the activity and initiatives of the Secretariat for Non-Christians.[335] In the 1980, the Secretariat published important documents dealing in detail with both the theoretical and practical aspects of Christian-Muslim dialogue, namely *Guidelines for Dialogue between Christians and Muslims* (1981)[336] and *The Attitude of the Church towards the Followers of Other Religions* (1984).[337]

It is important to emphasize that during the 1980s, John Paul II began his active involvement in easing the political and religious tensions the Middle East. For the Pope, the crucial issue was to assure a peaceful coexistence between Christians, Muslims and Jews, i.e., to resolve in a mutually acceptable way the question of Jerusalem and the status of the Holy Places which the Holy Father addressed in his apostolic letter *Redemptionis Anno,* published on April 20, 1984.[338]

Third phase: employing dialogical means in resolving modern world problems

The third phase of the history of John Paul II's dialogue with Islam and the Muslims began in the early 1990s and lasted until the end of his pontificate. The main tasks of the Pope during this period, as revealed in published documents and demonstrated by related actions were: (1) to continue his mission around the world while convincing people that dialogue of life is not a possibility but the only alternative and a must, (2) to increase awareness of the multicultural world and the challenges of the era of globalization, (3) to introduce new means of developing interreligious dialogue and (4) to strengthen his active engagement in resolving religious and political conflicts in the Middle East with particular focus on the Palestinian-Israeli conflict

---

Pontifical Council for Interreligious Dialogue see the Holy See's archive: http://www.vatican.va/roman_curia/pontifical_councils/interelg/documents/rc_pc_interelg_pro_20051996_en.html, access March 15, 2011.

[334] See: E. Sakowicz, *Dialog Kościoła z islamem...*, p. 167.

[335] See: "Address of John Paul II to the Members of the Secretariat for Non-Christians" (April 27, 1979), online: http://www.vatican.va/holy_father/john_paul_ii/speeches/1979/april/documents/hf_jp-ii_spe_19790427_segret-non-cristiani_en.html, access: March 15, 2011.

[336] M. Borrmans, *Guidelines for Dialogue between Christians and Muslims*, trans. R. Marston Speight, New York: Paulist Press, 1990.

[337] *The Attitude of the Church towards the Followers of Other Religions: Reflections and Orientations on Dialogue and Mission*, Vatican: Polyglot Press, 1984.

[338] For a thorough discussion on this issue, including the significance of *Redemptionis Anno*, see: Chapter IV of the work, p. 131-137.

the war in Lebanon and Iraq,[339] the question of Jerusalem and the status of the Holy Places and the protection of Christian minorities living in Middle East.[340]

On December 7, 1990, twenty-five years after the Second Vatican Council's Decree on Missionary Activity *Ad Gentes* and fifteen years after the Apostolic Exhortation *Evangelii Nuntiandi* issued by Pope Paul VI, John Paul II published his encyclical *Redemptoris Missio*, entirely devoted to the mission of the Church on the threshold of the third millennium. As stated in the document, both experiences and conclusions from traveling around the world to meet people of different religions, cultures and ethnic origins convinced the Pope of the urgency and the need of renewing the missionary commitment of the Church in the spirit of dialogue that "revitalizes faith and Christian identity, and offers fresh enthusiasm and new incentive."[341]

In *Redemptoris Missio*, there are specific references to the dialogue of the Catholic Church with non-Christians, including Muslims. As it had been already stressed in previously discussed papal documents, and as it was consequently repeated in *Redemptoris Missio*, for John Paul II, such a dialogue was an important part of the evangelization mission of the Church because it would enable Christians to get acquainted with and to respect the spiritual richness of others. According to the Pope, an interreligious dialogue "understood as a method and means of mutual knowledge and enrichment... is not in opposition to the mission *ad gentes*; indeed, it has special links with that mission and is one of its expressions."[342] Moreover, the Church's mission should be addressed to people of other religions, including Muslims because God "wishes to share with them (all the people) the fullness of His revelation and love," and makes Himself present "in many ways, not only to individuals but also to entire peoples through their spiritual riches, of which their religions are the main and essential expression, even when they contain 'gaps, insufficiencies and errors' (Paul VI, *Evangelii Nuntiandi*, 53)."[343]

According to the Pope, there was neither conflict nor contradiction between the evangelization and engaging in interreligious dialogue. In the context of the Church's mission *ad gentes*, they are both linked and because "the Church... by her nature is missionary (*Ad Gentes*, 2)."[344] However, as pointed out by the Holy Father:

> These two elements must maintain both their intimate connection and their distinctiveness; therefore they should not be confused, manipulated or regarded as identical, as though they were interchangeable.[345]

---

[339] See: Chapter V of this work, p. 155-193.

[340] See: Chapter IV, p. 119-154.

[341] John Paul II, "*Redemptoris Missio:* On the Permanent Validity of the Church's Missionary Mandate" (December 7, 1990), no. 1, 2, online: http://www.vatican.va/holy_father/john_paul_ii/encyclicals/documents/hf_jp-ii_enc_07121990_redemptoris-missio_en.html, access: March 15, 2011.

[342] Ibid., no. 55.

[343] Ibid.

[344] John Paul II, *Crossing*..., p. 115.

[345] Ibid., no. 55.

Although dialogue and proclamation, the Holy Father believed, should serve one mission, it was also important to remember that they could not be considered equal.[346] As stated in *Redemptoris Missio*, and emphasized by John Paul II on many other occasions, a sincere dialogue, based on hope and love, was "an activity with its own guiding principles, requirements and dignity."[347] The Pope was convinced that through such a dialogue that constituted a positive and creative challenge for the Church and commanded "respect for everything that has been brought about in human beings by the Spirit who blows where he wills (*Redemptor Hominis*, 12), the Church should seek to uncover the 'seeds of the Word' (*Ad Gentes*, 11, 15), a 'ray of that truth which enlightens all men' (*Nostra Aetate*, 2)."[348]

According to John Paul II, an interreligious dialogue as perceived in the context of the Church's mission should be consistent with Christian religious traditions and convictions, open to understanding the other party, characterized by truth, humility and frankness and by the sincere conviction that "dialogue can enrich each side."[349] Furthermore, while conducting such a dialogue both parties should demonstrate patience, persistence and consequence in the search for common values and religious experiences, so they could eliminate irenicism, prejudice, lack of tolerance and misunderstandings. Only an open and sincere dialogue, the Holy Father believed, would lead to inner purification of each party's own faith and become a way to "turn" to each other and to "recognize" in the partner of dialogue his or her brothers and sisters. As John Paul II explained in *Redemptoris Missio*, all Christians, including the laity, should be involved in interreligious dialogue, "even in places where their efforts are not well received," so they could contribute in many different and complementary ways to the betterment of humanity. As the Pope explained:

A vast field lies open to dialogue, which can assume many forms and expressions: from exchanges between experts in religious traditions or official representatives of those traditions to cooperation for integral development and the safeguarding of religious values; and from a sharing of their respective spiritual experiences to the so-called "dialogue of life," through which believers of different religions bear witness before each

---

[346] The document *Dialogue and Proclamation*, published on May 19, 1991 by the Pontifical Council for Interreligious Dialogue, had been prepared since 1986 but published after the encyclical *Redemptoris Missio*. Therefore, as Sakowicz pointed out, the statement by John Paul II in the encyclical should be "read parallel with the content of *Dialogue and Proclamation*." (E. Sakowicz, *Dialog Kościoła z islamem...*, p. 163. For a further discussion see: F. Arinze, "The Place of Dialogue in the Church's Mission: Reflections on *Redemptoris Missio*," *Bulletin*, vol. 26 (1991), no. 1, p. 20-23; J. Dupuis, "Dialogue and Proclamation in Two Recent Documents," *Bulletin*, vol. 27 (1992), no. 2, p. 165-172; J. Tomko, "Dialogue and Proclamation: Its Relation to the Encyclical *Redemptoris Missio*," *Bulletin*, vol. 26 (1991) no. 2, p. 204-209.

[347] John Paul II, "*Redemptoris Missio...*," no. 56.

[348] Ibid.

[349] Ibid.

other in daily life to their own human and spiritual values, and help each other to live according to those values in order to build a more just and fraternal society.[350]

John Paul II's encyclical *Redemptoris Missio* is considered one of the crucial documents of the Catholic Church on interreligious dialogue, outlining its features, how it appears in practice and expected outcomes for the third millennium. It is also worth noticing that in the 1990s, the Pope published other documents in which he once again referred to and stressed the importance of interreligious dialogue, and in particular that with Islam and the Muslims. These documents were related to the preparation of the Church for the Jubilee of the Year 2000 and among them was the most important one, the apostolic letter *Tertio Millenio Adveniente*, announced on November 10, 1994.[351]

In this letter, John Paul II pointed out the need for a deeper reflection on the issue of interreligious dialogue including the examination of Christian conscience, the value of penance and forgiveness of sins with regard to non-Christians.[352] He also discussed the Church's progress in the process of opening up to a dialogue with the modern world, in the spirit of the profound changes as introduced by the Second Vatican Council, and the contribution of the Popes connected with the Council, starting with John XXIII, continuing with Paul VI and John Paul I, including his own related endeavors.[353] The Pope said:

> The Council's guidelines – set forth in *Gaudium et Spes* and other documents – of open, respectful and cordial dialogue, yet accompanied by careful discernment and courageous witness to the truth, remain valid and call us to a greater commitment.[354]

According to the Pontiff, in its preparation the Great Jubilee, the Church needed to continue its commitment to dialogue with great religions, already demonstrated in a number of ways, so the crisis of civilization "which is highly developed from the standpoint of technology but is interiorly impoverished by its tendency to forget God or to keep him at a distance,"[355] could be countered and eventually cured by the civilization of love based on the universal values of peace, solidarity, justice and liberty. According to John Paul II, the eve of the Year 2000 provided a great opportunity to renew the call of the Second Vatican Council pronounced in its famous Declaration *Nostra Aetate* and advance the development of dialogue with non-Christian religions,

---

[350] Ibid., no. 57.
[351] John Paul II, "Apostolic Letter *Tertio Millenio Adveniente* of His Holiness Pope John Paul II to the Bishops, Clergy and Lay Faithful on Preparation for the Jubilee of the Year 2000" (November 10, 1994), online: http://www.vatican.va/holy_father/john_paul_ii/apost_letters/documents/hf_jp-ii_apl_10111994_tertio-millennio-adveniente_en.html, access: March 15, 2011.
[352] Ibid., no. 32, 35.
[353] Ibid., no. 18, 19.
[354] Ibid., no. 36.
[355] Ibid., no. 52.

in which "the Jews and the Muslims ought to have a pre-eminent place."[356] In the light of the progress that had already been made in the Church's dialogue with the great monotheistic religions, it was anticipated by the Pope that the occasion of the Jubilee would make it possible "to hold *joint meetings* in places of significance for the great monotheistic religions."[357] As for the realization of related hopes and expectations, the Pope addressed the matter in the following words:

> In this regard, attention is being given to finding ways of arranging historic meetings in places of exceptional symbolic importance like Bethlehem, Jerusalem and Mount Sinai as a means of furthering dialogue with Jews and the followers of Islam, and to arranging similar meetings elsewhere with the leaders of the great world religions. However, care will always have be taken not to cause harmful misunderstandings, avoiding the risk of syncretism and of a facile and deceptive irenicism.[358]

During the 1990s and the first three years of the third millennium, John Paul II published subsequent important documents, namely the apostolic exhortations *Ecclesia in Africa*, *Ecclesia in Asia*, *Ecclesia in Oceania*, and *Ecclesia in Europe*, in which he continued his reflections on the issue of dialogue with non-Christians and in particular with Muslims in the context of the preparation for the Great Jubilee of the Year 2000.

In *Ecclesia in Africa*, announced on September 14, 1995,[359] the Pope focused on the need of respecting the values and religious traditions of each person and of sharing the commitment to work together for human progress and development at all levels. Furthermore, the Holy Father pointed out that Christians and Muslims should respect "on both sides the principle of religious freedom with all that this involves, also including external and public manifestations of faith," and commit themselves to promoting a dialogue "free from the risks of false irenicism or militant fundamentalism," and to protesting "against unfair policies and practices, as well as against the lack of reciprocity in matters of religious freedom."[360]

The apostolic exhortation *Ecclesia in Asia,* announced and signed by John Paul II on November 6, 1999 in Delhi, during the closing session of the Special Assembly for Asia of the Synod of Bishops,[361] emphasized the role of interreligious dialogue as an important aspect of the Church's evangelization mission.

---

[356] Ibid., no. 53.

[357] Ibid., no. 53.

[358] Ibid.

[359] John Paul II, "Post-Synodal Appostolic Exhortation *Ecclesia in Africa of the Holy Father John Paul II to the Bishops, Priests and Deacons, Men and Women Religious and All the Lay Faithful on the Church in Africa and its Evangelizing Mission towards the Year 2000*" (September 14, 1995), online: http://www.vatican.va/holy_father/john_paul_ii/apost_exhortations/documents/hf_jp-ii_exh_14091995_ecclesia-in-africa_en.html, access: March 15, 2011.

[360] Ibid., no. 66.

[361] John Paul II, "Post-Synodal Apostolic Exhortation *Ecclesia in Asia* of the Holy Father John Paul II to the Bishops, Priests and Deacons, Men and Women in the Consecrated Life

While assessing relevant experiences as well as progress in the development of dialogue with non-Christians, and in particular the one with Muslims, "which the Second Vatican Council bequeathed to the whole Church as a duty and a challenge," the Pope emphasized that "only those with a mature and convinced Christian faith are qualified to engage in genuine interreligious dialogue." Both maturity and sincere commitment, the Pope believed, would assure respect for principles, avoiding the risk of irenicism, promoting mutual advancement on the road of religious inquiry and experience, and the elimination of prejudice, intolerance and misunderstandings. In the light of the socio-political predicament of the modern world, according to the Pope, it was important for the Church of Asia "to provide suitable models of interreligious dialogue – evangelization in dialogue and dialogue for evangelization – and suitable training for those involved." This "new evangelization" needed "*a dialogue of life and heart*" which required openness to other believers, a willingness to listen, mutual respect and tolerance. Furthermore, the Holy Father pointed out the necessity to "continue to strive to preserve and foster at all levels this spirit of encounter and cooperation between religions." While recalling the meeting held in Assisi, the city of Saint Francis, on October 27, 1986, between the Catholic Church and representatives of the other world religions, the Pope put a special emphasis on the value of popular piety and the importance of revitalizing prayer and contemplation in the process of dialogue.[362]

As previously mentioned, during the 1990s one of the most important tasks of John Paul II's dialogue with non-Christians and in particular Muslims was to increase awareness of the multicultural world and the challenges of the era of globalization. He addressed these issues in his two apostolic exhortations, namely *Ecclesia in Oceania,* published on November 22, 2001, and *Ecclesia in Europe*, published on June 28, 2003.[363]

In *Ecclesia in Oceania*, while reflecting on the "unprecedented encounters among the cultures of the world" resulting from both easier migration and increasing opportunities to travel, the Pope pointed out the pressing need for the Catholic Church in Oceania to reach a better understanding of non-Christian religions, their teachings, ways of life and worship, so it could provide various educational, cultural and social services in multireligious and multicultural society more efficiently, thus pursuing a fruitful dialogue of life with these religions. Moreover, taking into

---

and All the Lay Faithful on Jesus Christ the Saviour and his Mission of Love and Service in Asia: '...That They May Have Life, and Have it Abundantly' (Jn 10:10)" (November 6, 1999), online: http://www.vatican.va/holy_father/john_paul_ii/apost_exhortations/documents/hf_jp-ii_exh_06111999_ecclesia-in-asia_en.html, access: March 15, 2011.

[362] Ibid., no. 31.

[363] John Paul II, "Post-Synodal Apostolic Exhortation *Ecclesia in Europa* of His Holiness Pope John Paul II to the Bishops Men and Women in the Consecrated Life and All the Lay Faithful on Jesus Christ Alive in His Church the Source of Hope for Europe" (June 28, 2003), online: http://www.vatican.va/holy_father/john_paul_ii/apost_exhortations/documents/hf_jp-ii_exh_20030628_ecclesia-in-europa_en.html, access: March 15, 2011.

account the growth of the non-Christian population in Oceania, including the Muslim one, John Paul II also explained that the Church there needed "experts in philosophy, anthropology, comparative religions, the social sciences and, above all, theology."[364]

The apostolic exhortation *Ecclesia in Europe* also contains references to the issue of profound and perceptive interreligious dialogue. While addressing the problem, the Pope explained that European Christians need to acquire a better knowledge of other religions "in order to establish a fraternal conversation with their members who live in today's Europe." Well aware of the fact that the number of Muslims living in Europe had significantly increased in recent years, John Paul II pointed out that "a *proper relationship with Islam* is particularly important."[365] The Holy Father explained:

> Christians living in daily contact with Muslims should be properly trained in an objective knowledge of Islam and enabled to draw comparisons with their own faith. Such training should be provided particularly to seminarians, priests and all pastoral workers.[366]

However, as John Paul II emphasized at the same time, it was also important for the Catholic Church to engage actively in ensuring, through both its own activity and appropriate measures undertaken by the European institutions, the promotion of "religious freedom in Europe," and to feel free "to insist that reciprocity in guaranteeing religious freedom also be observed in countries of different religious traditions, where Christians are a minority."[367]

In relation to the issue of John Paul II's interreligious dialogue, one should also mention his apostolic letter *The Rapid Development*, that was announced on January 24, 2005, the day of the Feast of Saint Francis de Sales, Patron Saint of Journalists.[368] In this letter the Pope addressed the issue of modern means of communication, pointing out that "the *world of communications*" has a tremendous potential because it is "capable of unifying humanity and transforming it into – as it is commonly referred to – *a global village*." In the context of rapid technological changes in the sphere of communication, the role of the mass media has "acquired such importance as to be

---

[364] John Paul II, "Post-Synodal Apostolic Exhortation *Ecclesia in Oceania* of His Holiness Pope John Paul II to the Bishops Priests And Deacons Men and Women in the Consecrated Life and All the Lay Faithful on Jesus Christ and the Peoples of Oceania: Walking His Way, Telling His Truth, Living His Life" (November 22, 2001), no. 25, online: http://www.vatican.va/holy_father/john_paul_ii/apost_exhortations/documents/hf_jp-ii_exh_20011122_ecclesia-in-oceania_en.html, access: March 15, 2011.

[365] John Paul II, "Post-Synodal Apostolic Exhortation *Ecclesia in Europa*," no. 57.

[366] Ibid.

[367] Ibid.

[368] John Paul II, "Apostolic Letter the Rapid Development of the Holy Father John Paul II to those Responsible for Communications" (January 24, 2005), online: http://www.vatican.va/holy_father/john_paul_ii/apost_letters/documents/hf_jp-ii_apl_20050124_il-rapido-sviluppo_en.html, access: March 15, 2011.

the principal means of guidance and inspiration for many people in their personal, familial, and social behavior."[369] Furthermore, in the age of global communication, the people are constantly exposed to and confronted by mass media which, without any doubt, influence "the formation of personality and conscience," but also stimulate "the interpretation and structuring of affective relationships, the coming together of the educative and formative phases, the elaboration and diffusion of cultural phenomena, and the development of social, political and economic life."[370] Therefore, according to the Pope, attention should be paid to the proper implementation of new means of communication:

> The mass media can and must promote justice and solidarity according to an organic and correct vision of human development, by reporting events accurately and truthfully, analyzing situations and problems completely, and providing a forum for different opinions. An authentically ethical approach to using the powerful communication media must be situated within the context of a mature exercise of freedom and responsibility, founded upon the supreme criteria of truth and justice.[371]

Among the documents containing references to Christian-Muslim dialogue that were published by the Holy See in the 1990s, it is also important to note two, namely *The Code of Canons of the Oriental Churches*, promulgated by John Paul II on October 18, 1990 and *The Catechism of the Catholic Church,* approved by the Pope on June 25, 1992 and published on October 11, 1992. Moreover, one should also mention in this context *Christianity and Other Religions*, a significant document, prepared and announced by the International Theological Committee on September 30, 1996.[372]

A closer look at John Paul II's dialogical initiatives concerning Christian-Muslims relations during the three-phase history of his dialogue with Islam and the Muslims as well as getting into the core of the Pope's related speeches and official documents from that period enable us to sketch the overall characteristics of his path of dialogue with Islam and the Muslims. The following discussion will address its most important points, i.e., the questions of (1) the meaning and the basis of this dialogue, (2) the major aims and (3) the framework in which it was conducted by John Paul II. Furthermore, it will also address the issue of (4) the Pontiff's risk management plan – his way of dealing with differences and obstacles that could jeopardize his efforts.

---

[369] Ibid., no. 3
[370] Ibid.
[371] Ibid.
[372] For an overview of the document see: E. Sakowicz, *Dialog Kościoła z islamem...*, p. 168-171.

The meaning and the foundations of dialogue

How did John Paul II understand and explain the meaning of the word *dialogue* and what were, according to him, the qualities of a true dialogue? The answer could be found in his official documents, speeches and writings. The matter was addressed clearly in his Message for the World Day of Peace (January 1, 1983). According to the Pope, dialogue was "a central and essential element of ethical thinking among people, whoever they may be" that presupposed "the *search for what is true, good and just* for every person, for every group and every society." As for dialogue's prerequisites, it demanded "*openness and welcome*: that each party should explain its thoughts, but should also *listen* to the explanation of the situation such as the other party describes it." A sincere engagement in dialogue, according to the Pope, presupposed "that each party should accept the *difference* and the *specific nature* of the other party." The power of that means of communication laid in the fact that through dialogue it was possible to search successfully for "what is and *which remains common to people*, even in the midst of tensions, opposition and conflicts." As the Pope explained:

> Finally, true dialogue is the search for what is good by peaceful means. It is the persistent determination to have recourse to all the possible formulas of negotiation, mediation and arbitration…It is recognition of the inalienable dignity of human beings. It rests upon respect for human life. It is a *wager upon the social nature of people*, upon their calling to go forward together, with continuity, by a converging meeting of minds, wills, hearts, towards the goal that the Creator has fixed for them. This goal is to make the world a place for everybody to live in and worthy of everybody.[373]

John Paul II's way of understanding the essence of a sincere dialogue with people of other religions was explained further on April 28, 1987 in his address to the members and staff of the Secretariat for Non-Christians. The Pope stated:

> [The dialogue with people of other religions] is a complex of human activities. All founded upon respect and esteem for people of different religions. It includes the daily living together in peace and mutual help, with each bearing witness to the values learned through the experience of faith. It means a readiness to cooperate with others for the betterment of humanity and a commitment to search together for peace. It means the encounter of theologians and other religious areas of convergence and divergence. Where circumstances permit, it means a sharing of spiritual experience and insight. This sharing can take the form of coming together as brothers and sisters to pray to God in ways which safeguard the uniqueness of each religious tradition.[374]

---

[373] John Paul II, "Message for the World Day of Peace" (Rome, December, 1982); F. Gioia (ed.), *Interreligious Dialogue…*, p. 263-264, paragraph 412.

[374] A fragment from John Paul II's address to the Members and Staff of the Secretariat for Non-Christians (April 28, 1987), quoted in: N. Bakalar and R. Balkin (eds.), *The Wisdom of*

For John Paul II, conducting a sincere interreligious dialogue, and in particular that between the Christians and the Muslims, was not an easy task because religion itself could be made an instrument and become an excuse for polarization and division. Therefore, he was convinced that nowadays, taking into account the present conditions of the existing world, engaging in such a dialogue should primarily mean learning to forgive, since both Christians and Muslims could point to possible wrongs suffered through the centuries. Then, it should mean trying to understand the hearts of others, which was particularly difficult when there was a lack of agreement and engaging themselves in mutual cooperation in various areas. During his pastoral visit to Nigeria, on February 14, 1982 in Kaduna, the Pope explained that as follows:

> We [Christians and Muslims] can engage in dialogue in order to understand each other better at both the level of the scholars and in person-to-person relationship, in the family and in places of work and play. We can promote honesty and discipline in private and public life, greater courage and wisdom in politics, the elimination of political antagonisms, and the removal of discrimination because of a person's race, colour, ethnic origin, religion or sex.[375]

But first of all, John Paul II emphasized, the dialogue between the Christians and the Muslims should mean putting oneself at the service of all humanity and the one God who according to Christian and Muslim belief is the source of all the rights and values of humankind.

"Dialogue is not so much an idea to be studied," the Pope often explained, "as it is a way of living in positive relationship with others."[376] He was convinced that only in that daily dialogue of life could people come to know and understand, through personal contact and experience, the religious convictions of others. Such a mutual encounter would indeed enrich all those who participate:

> The transmission of human and spiritual values to new generations, human rights and responsibilities, ways to support the struggle of the poor, the hungry, the sick and the homeless for a dignified life; preservation of God's creation, his original gift to humanity; the search for peace, the call for justice: those were some of the issues which would have to be solved, according to the Pope, through encounter and cooperation with others through a sincere dialogue of the two great religions Christianity and Islam.[377]

With regard to the basis of his dialogue with Muslims, John Paul II frequently referred to the principles of *Nostra Aetate,* pointing out that Islam "deserves

---

John Paul II: The Pope on Life's Most Vital Questions, introduction John W. White, San Francisco: HarperSanFrancisco, 1995, p. 124.

[375] "Pope John Paul II's Address to the Muslim Population of Kaduna" (February 14, 1982), *Islamochristiana*, vol. 8 (1982), p. 241.

[376] "The Address of the Holy See to the Members of the Plenaria of the Pontifical Council for Interreligious Dialogue" (April 26, 1990), *Islamochristiana*, vol. 16 (1990), p. 295.

[377] Ibid., p. 297.

special attention by reason of its *monotheistic* character and its link with the *faith of Abraham*."[378] On June 5, 1985, during the General Audience in Rome he explained:

> The Muslims "*adore one God*, living and enduring, merciful and all-powerful, *Maker* of heaven and earth and *speaker of men*. They strive to submit wholeheartedly, even to his inscrutable decrees, just as did *Abraham*, with whom the Islamic faith is pleased to associate itself (NA 3). But there is more: The followers of Muhamet even honour Jesus: "Though they do not acknowledge Jesus as God, they revere Him as a prophet. They honour *Mary, His virgin mother*; at times they call on her too with devotion. In addition they wait the day of judgement when God will give each man his due *after raising him up*. Consequently they prize the *moral life* and give worship to God especially through prayer, almsgiving and fasting" (NA 3).[379]

In his book *Crossing the Threshold of Hope*, John Paul II stated: "As a result of their monotheism, believers in Allah are particularly close to us."[380] There were also other religious values that Christians and Muslims had in common and the Pope spoke about them frequently. On August 19, 1985, during his meeting with young Muslims at Casablanca, John Paul II explained the matter at length in the following words:

> Christians and Muslims, we have many things in common, as believers and as human beings. We live in the same world, marked by many signs of hope, but also by multiple signs of anguish. For us, Abraham is a very model of faith in God, of submission to his will and of confidence in his goodness. We believe in the same God, the one God, the living God, and the God who created the world and his creatures to their perfection... Both of us believe in the importance of prayer, of fasting and alms giving, of repentance and of pardon; we believe that God will be a merciful judge to us at the end of time, and we hope that after resurrection he will be satisfied with us and we know that we will be satisfied with him.[381]

John Paul II's teaching on the fundaments of the Catholic Church's dialogue with Islam and Muslims was rooted in all the positive moments from the thirteen centuries of Christian-Muslim relations that contributed to building the bridges of reciprocal acceptance, tolerance and understanding as already exposed in the first chapter, and was primarily based on the official conclusions of the Second Vatican Council and the example of the work of Paul VI as discussed at length in the second chapter. However, one may find in the Pope's teaching its own distinguishing ele-

---

[378] John Paul II, "To the Faithful in General Audience" (Rome, June 5, 1985), in: F. Gioia (ed.), *Interreligious Dialogue...*, p. 287, paragraph 448.

[379] Ibid., p.287-288. For a discussion on Muslim links with Abrahamic traditions see: B. E. Hinze and I. A. Omar, *Heirs of Abraham: The Future of Muslim, Jewish and Christian Relations*, Maryknoll, NY: Orbis Books, 2005. About Jesus in Muslim tradition, see: See: T. Khalidi, *The Muslim Jesus: Sayings and Stories in Islamic Literature*, Cambridge, MA: Harvard University Press, 2001.

[380] John Paul II, *Crossing...*," p. 91.

[381] "The Speech of the Holy Father John Paul II to Young Muslims...," p. 2, 9.

ments, namely the emphasis on the notion of humanism and the idea of brotherhood as unifying factors for Christians and Muslims. As the Holy Father stated in his encyclical *Redemptor Hominis*, the Church should pay attention to every single person because "by his Incarnation, he, the son of God, *in a certain way united himself with each man.* He worked with human hands, he thought with a human mind. He acted with a human will, and with a human heart he loved."[382] Moreover, through interreligious dialogue, both Christians and Muslims could assure "the dignity of each and every human being, whatever his or her ethnic origin, religious affiliation, or political commitment."[383] On many occasions, while emphasizing the close bonds linking Christianity and Islam, John Paul II wanted to encourage the followers of both religions to "become *fraternal allies in service* to human family."[384] In his speeches directed to Muslims, the Pope presented himself as a brother. This could be seen as an evident sign of Pope's sincerity in his dialogue with the followers of Islam. On February 20, 1981, while addressing the Muslim representatives at Davao Airport in the Philippines, the Pope explained this characteristic feature of his dialogical teaching as follows:

> I deliberately *address you as brothers*; that is certainly what we are, because we are members of the same human family, whose efforts, whether people realize it or not, tend toward God, who created us and whom we are trying to reach, in our own ways, through faith, prayer and worship, through the keeping of his laws and through the keeping of his law and through submission to his designs.[385]

The aims of dialogue

As reflected in John Paul II's teaching and the initiatives he undertook, his dialogue with Muslims had a number of aims that could be summarized as follows. First, for John Paul II the prerequisite of dialogue as well as its fundamental aim was religious freedom leading to the elimination of hostility, preservation of human spirituality and fostering harmony and peaceful coexistence. The Pope believed that when the right to religious freedom was complemented by the right to religious education, the prospect for the well-being of society was even greater.[386]

---

[382] John Paul II, "*Redemptor Hominis...*," no. 8.

[383] John Paul II, "To the Participants in the Sixth Assembly of the World Conference on Religion and Peace (WCRP) at the Synod Hall" (Rome, November 3, 1994), in: F. Gioia (ed.), *Interreligious Dialogue...*, p. 529, paragraph 814.

[384] John Paul II, "To Muslim and Hindu Representatives of Kenya" (Nairobi, August 18, 1985), in: Ibid., p. 296, paragraph 463.

[385] John Paul II, "To the Representatives od Muslims of the Philippines" (Davao, February 20, 1981), in: Ibid., p. 235, paragraph 363.

[386] On February 14, 1982, in his address to the communities of the State of Kaduna (Nigeria) and in particular to the Muslim population, the Pope said: "Both of us can spearhead the principle

Second, dialogue was essential to understand each other better. Only thorough knowledge and understanding could help to fight hostility and abandon wrong assumptions and stereotypes. Moreover, the increased awareness of each others' spiritual heritage and finding common values could establish the links and ties of trust and thus contribute to the well-being of whole societies.[387] According to the Pope, dialogue would help Christians and Muslims in their search for truth. Christians should accept the elements of truth in the faith of their partners in dialogue; the spiritual tradition of the others should be affirmed and acknowledged because it contains "the seeds of the truth."

Third, for the Pope, dialogue should aim to create of "a climate" for cooperation and harmony. Most important was the attitude of friendship and tolerance. Such "a climate" could be created on the basis of Christian-Muslim dialogue, namely love for the one and only God. Engaging in a conversation with Muslims, John Paul II believed, would help Christians understand their religiosity, observe their fidelity to prayer and eventually to get closer to their "feeling or sensing God."[388] Moreover, all that would definitely contribute to the establishment of new or "renewed" reciprocal relations. For the Pope the "renewal" meant both (1) significant changes in perception of each other, modification of views and outlooks and (2) a decisive change in the way of approaching each other, namely the abandoning the attitude of rejection and indifference and opening to each other in the spirit of tolerance. This would help to accept differences.[389]

Fourth, John Paul II was convinced that Christians and Muslims should join their efforts to meet the challenges of the modern world, in particular growing atheism and the disrupted balance between technological development and ethics that results not only in poverty but is also the main cause of man's alienation, isolation and loneliness. In the light of John Paul II's teaching, dialogue should aim at the defense of family as the fundamental institution (defense of life, family's dignity, against abortion, pornography). Christians and Muslims should work together for the cause of bettering human beings and for establishing strong ties within humankind. Their sincere dialogue and cooperation should prove that "the children of the same God"

---

and practice of religious freedom, ensuring its application especially in the religious education of children. When the right of each child to worship God is complemented by his or her right to religious education, then all society is enriched and its members are well equipped for life. Religious education takes on increased importance today, since certain elements in society seek to forget and even to destroy the spiritual aspect of man." "Pope John Paul II's Address to the Muslim Population of Kaduna," p. 241.

[387] See: John Paul II, "To the People of Pakistan" (Karachi, February 16, 1981), in: F. Gioia (ed.), *Interreligious Dialogue...*, p. 235, paragraph 361.

[388] See: Idem, "To the Bishops of Mali on Their *ad limina* Visit" (Rome, November 26, 1981), in: F. Gioia (ed.), *Interreligious Dialogue...*, p. 248, paragraph 386.

[389] See: Idem, "To Representatives of the Muslims of Cameroon" (Yaoundé, August 12, 1985), in: F. Gioia (ed.), *Interreligious Dialogue...*, p. 290, paragraph 451. "In his address the Pope said: "For us the true path remains that of *dialogue*, which has many aspects. First of all it means to learn to know one another's faith, overcome prejudices and misunderstandings. It means being tolerant with regard to differences."

are bound together by unbreakable ties of friendship and respect for each other that could protect them against anti-religious and anti-human tendencies and the increasing secularization of the modern world.[390]

Fifth, while referring to the Middle East, the crucial aim of John Paul II's dialogue with Muslims (and Jews) living there was to resolve the major political, social and religious problems, such as the Palestinian-Israeli conflict, the status of Jerusalem and the Holy Places, protection of Christian minorities and spreading the message of peace. This included convincing the people that nowadays the predicament of the area could not be resolved by military conflicts and wars.

All in all, according to John Paul II's teaching, a sincere interreligious dialogue in all its forms, i.e., dialogue of specialists, dialogue of religious experience, dialogue of deeds and dialogue of life, has only one aim. It should be conducted with the purpose that all people, among them Christians and non-Christians, become aware that God has created them and God is the One who embraces them all in love and that they should join their efforts in building a better and a safer world.

The practice of dialogue

John Paul II conducted his dialogue of life in a very simple way. From the beginning of his pontificate, the Holy Father engaged himself in a mission that had as its aim both dialogue and proclamation addressed to the people of the whole world. With the humanity and generosity of spirit for which he had been known, the Pope spoke directly and forthrightly to all people, regardless of their religion, color or race. No matter how difficult the circumstances were, he always tried to find a simple way to present his message. He always sought to console, to understand and to give. He suggested reflection, he provided an inspiration and motivational support and helped find a feasible solution.

There is no doubt that a sincere dialogue with Islam and the Muslims was a part of John Paul II's mission. This task the Holy Father pursued in a number of ways. He received the Muslim leaders at the Vatican and met them during his pilgrimages to Muslim and non-Muslim countries. When the circumstances did not favor official contacts he was always ready for unofficial meetings.

---

[390] See: Idem, "To Bishops from Indonesia on Their *ad limina* Visit" (Rome, May 20, 1989), in: F. Gioia (ed.), *Interreligious Dialogue…*, p. 406, paragraph 638. The Pope said: "Dear brothers Bishops, it is your particular pastoral responsibility to adopt the means most appropriate for proclaiming the message of salvation. The Church does not hesitate to show a deep respect for other religions which are the living expression of the soul of peoples. When Christians and the followers of other religious traditions are united in their belief in the Creator, there exists a profound basis for mutual understanding and peaceful exchange. I encourage you to continue and intensify your collaboration with your Moslem brethren in meeting the challenges of increasing secularization."

As a religious leader and a scholar, John Paul II met influential Muslim theologians, such as Ḥasan at-Turābī from Sudan and Fataḥ ash-Shaykh from Egypt.[391] Moreover, the Pope encouraged and supported the organization of various interreligious conferences, colloquia and gatherings. John Paul II actively participated in such meetings organized in Rome and used to send his addresses and greetings to the ones taking place elsewhere.[392]

For John Paul II it was important to meet with the Muslim leaders. However, it was the common people that were the Holy Father's greatest concern. It was with them, the Muslims all over the world, that the Pope used to share his reflections about the urgent issues of the contemporary world. His message was simple, and since his first address in Ankara in 1979 and up until his death had remained the same: respect, love and help for every human being. Wherever the Pope travelled and whomever he addressed, he always repeated his call for a dialogue of life between Christians, Muslims and other believers to promote moral values, justice, liberty and peace.

During his numerous travels to countries all over the world, the Pope always emphasized the eminently religious and pastoral character of his trips.[393] The well-being of Christians, whether they were the majority or minority in a visited country, and their harmonious coexistence with Muslims and believers of other faiths was always the primary focus of John Paul II. However, the pastoral journeys also gave John Paul II occasion to address universal issues such as social justice, cultural progress and international cooperation. For John Paul II, the dialogue with Muslims meant sharing their concerns and defending their rights. He was also aware that in the current world situation it was not possible to isolate the Christian-Muslim dialogue from the political context. Therefore, his voice in defense of weak and poor sounded firmly and strongly. The Pope never hesitated to appeal to the various governments for changes in their policy and for the respect of human dignity. It is obvious that the political authority of the Pope was limited only to the Vatican. However, as a religious leader, John Paul II did take a firm stand concerning political events. He discussed urgent issues with the heads of states on the occasions of his pastoral visits and when he received politicians at the Vatican.

The Pope frequently visited Africa, a continent troubled for centuries by conflict, famine and mass displacement, not only to promote Christian-Muslim dialogue there but also to keep the public informed about the world's responsibilities toward the people living there.[394] He was also particularly concerned with the Middle East and

---

[391]   T. Szulc, *John Paul II…*, p. 463.

[392]   See the list of the meetings and conferences (1970-1988) in: M. Borrmans, *Guidelines for Dialogue…*, p. 115-121.

[393]   John Paul II made 104 pilgrimages to the countries all over the world.

[394]   For example, in 1993 during his visit to Uganda, he said: "I return to Africa at a decisive moment. A world divided into opposing economic and military blocs is being replaced by a world increasingly affected by a distressing imbalance between a developed North and a struggling South. … As a new structure of international relationships emerges … Africa should be given its proper place. … Neglect must not follow the former exploration … Surely

devoted much of his effort to resolving political problems in the area by his tireless striving to promote religious freedom, justice and peace in this region.

It should be noted that in his commitment to developing interreligious dialogue, the Pope was open to quite unusual initiatives.

The World Day of Prayer for Peace, involving non-Catholic and non-Christian religious leaders, was one of the most innovative initiatives of John Paul II's pontificate. The Pope announced it on January 25, 1986 and the negative reactions were almost instantaneous. However, despite some setbacks and controversy, the preparations and arrangements continued and finally the prayer was successfully held in Assisi, on October 27, 1986.[395]

In January 1993, moved by his concern for the continuing tragedy of war in Bosnia-Herzegovina and other parts of Europe, the Pope and the Presidents of the Episcopal Conferences of Europe gathered anew in the city of St. Francis to pray for peace. They were joined by a total of forty-seven delegations, including Christians of other confessions, Muslims[396] and Jews, to fast and pray for the gift of peace. "There can be no genuine peace unless believers stand together in rejecting the politics of hate and discrimination and in affirming the right to religious and cultural freedom in all human societies."[397] This was the conviction John Paul II wanted to share with the Muslims who gathered in Assisi to join the Day of Prayer for Peace in the Balkans and Europe. In his address to the Muslim delegation, the Pope said:

> We stand in solidarity with these victims of oppression, hatred and atrocities, with all those whose villages have been burned and bombed, with those who flee their homes and take refuge elsewhere...
> The call of the Second Vatican Council for Christians and Muslims to work together remains valid today...
> Your presence in Assisi on this occasion is of great significance: it proclaims the genuine religious belief is a source of mutual understanding and harmony, and the only perversion of religious sentiment leads to discrimination and conflict.[398]

---

the nations of Africa have a right to expect disinterested help in securing genuine independence, so that at last they will be able to build their own future in their own way." "John Paul II's speech during the welcome ceremony at Uganda's Entebbe Airport" (February 5, 1993), *Islamochristiana*, vol. 19 (1993), p. 301.

[395] The Community of Sant'Egidio has continued living the spirit of the Assisi World Day of Prayer, proposed by John Paul II in 1986, by accepting the Pope's final invitation of that historical meeting: "Let's keep spreading the message of Peace and living the spirit of Assisi." The two first meetings were in Rome in 1987 and 1988 and those subsequent were organized in other European, Mediterranean and American cities year after year. The 1995 meeting was a special one: it took place in Jerusalem, in the heart of the Holy City. The title was "Together in Jerusalem: Jews, Christians and Muslims." In 2009 the meeting was held in Krakow, Poland at the special invitation of Cardinal Stanisław Dziwisz.

[396] There were 31 Muslim delegations from all over the world.

[397] "The Holy Father's Homily during the Ecumenical Prayer Vigil," *Islamochristiana*, vol. 19 (1993), p. 251.

[398] Ibid., p. 251-252.

In his attempts to reach a better understanding between Christians, Muslims and Jews, John Paul II decided to entrust the power of art, namely of music.[399] On January 17, 2004, John Paul II attended the special *Concert of Reconciliation*, organized by the Vatican. The concert took place in the Paul VI Audience Hall and the performers came from Ankara, Krakow, London and Pittsburgh. The program included John Harbison's sacral motet *Abraham*[400] and Gustav Mahler's 2nd Symphony *Resurrection*, directed by Gilbert Levine. In the audience next to the Pope were sitting Elio Toaff,[401] the Chief Rabbi of Rome and ʿAbd al-Wahhāb Ḥusayn Jumʿa, the Imam of the mosque in Rome.[402] At the end of the concert while addressing the audience, John Paul II said:

> The history of relations between Jews, Christians and Muslims is marked by patches of light and shadow and has unfortunately known some painful moments. Today we are aware of the pressing need for sincere reconciliation among believers in the one God. This evening we are gathered here to give concrete expression to this commitment to reconciliation, entrusting ourselves to the universal message of music…Yes! We must find within us the courage for peace. We must implore from on High the gift of peace. And this peace will spread like a soothing balm if we travel non-stop on the road to reconciliation. Then the wilderness will become a garden in which justice will flourish, and the effect of justice will be peace (cf. Is 32: 15-16).[403]

One may say that in his tireless efforts to develop and promote the Catholic Church's dialogue with Islam and the Muslims, John Paul II was always ready to use any suitable occasion to explain over and over that only in dialogue could people of different religions get to know each other and reach reciprocal understanding.

---

[399] On April 4, 1999, John Paul II published his *Letter to Artists* where he spoke about their responsibility as "gifted" to convey to the people, through their creativity, the message of goodness and beauty. See: "Letter of His Holiness Pope John Paul II to Artists" (April 23, 1999), online: http://www.vatican.va/holy_father/john_paul_ii/letters/documents/hf_jp-ii_let_23041999_artists_en.html, access: March 15, 2011.

[400] The motet "Abraham," for double choir and 13 brass instruments, was especially composed for the *Concert of Reconciliation*. In its official invitation, the Vatican noted, "This initiative has assumed a special significance in view of the current world context, the event entrusts to the powerful efficacy of music the commitment to reconciliation that all the children of Abraham – Jews, Christians and Muslims – must embrace with conviction." G. Schirmer, "John Harbison: Abraham," online: http://www.schirmer.com/default.aspx?TabId=2420&State_2874=2&workId_2874=24143, access: March 17, 2011.

[401] John Paul II was the first pope in history to visit the Jewish synagogue. On April 12, 1986, Chief Rabbi Elio Toaff received him in the Synagogue in Rome.

[402] The Mosque and Islamic Cultural Centre in Rome was officially inaugurated on June 21, 1995 (the foundation stone had been laid in December 1984).

[403] "Address of John Paul II at the Conclusion of the Concert Dedicated to the Theme of Reconciliation among Jews, Christians and Muslims" (January 17, 2004), no. 2, 3: online: http://www.vatican.va/holy_father/john_paul_ii/speeches/2004/january/documents/hf_jp-ii_spe_20040117_concerto-riconciliazione_en.html, access: March 15, 2011.

Differences and obstacles

How did the Pope deal with doctrinal differences between Christianity and Islam? He was well aware that the doctrinal differences between Christianity and Islam could break the dialogue. Therefore, while talking about the common religious values, he also spoke openly about religious differences: "Not only is the theology but also the anthropology of Islam very distinct from Christianity."[404] His attitude toward doctrinal differences between Christianity and Islam and his way of dealing with this issue reflects his strong faith in the good will of human beings. The Holy Father addressed the matter in simple and clear words:

> Loyalty demands also that we should recognize and respect out differences. Obviously the most fundamental is the view that we hold on the person and work of Jesus of Nazareth. You know that, for the Christians, this Jesus causes them to enter into an intimate knowledge of the mystery of God and into a filial communion of his gifts, so that they recognize him and proclaim him Lord and Savior.[405]

Those were, the Pope stated, important differences. However, he believed that they were not an obstacle on the path of a sincere dialogue, and that both the Christians and the Muslims could accept them with humility, respect, and in the spirit of mutual tolerance.

John Paul II was convinced that Christians, while engaged in dialogue with Muslims, should pay attention to one-sided views and eliminate opinions that could lead to domination of one of the partners or cause "dangerous misunderstandings." In his message for the celebration of the 1983 World Day of Peace, while discussing the obstacles of dialogue, he said:

> I am thinking of what *damages or prevents the normal process of dialogue*. I have already let it be understood that dialogue is blocked by an a priori decision to concede nothing, by a *refusal to listen*, by a claim to be – oneself and only oneself – the measure of justice.[406]

John Paul II was also convinced that both Christians and Muslims should become alert to the dangers of irenic views and relativism that could lead to syncretism. As Sakowicz pointed out, the Holy Father saw in the care for preservation of

---

[404] John Paul II, *Crossing the Threshold...*, p. 93.
[405] "The Speech of the Holy Father John Paul II to Young Muslims...," p. 9.
[406] "Message of His Holiness Pope John Paul II for the Celebration of the Day of Peace" (January 1, 1983), no. 7, online: http://www.vatican.va/holy_father/john_paul_ii/messages/peace/documents/hf_jp-ii_mes_19821208_xvi-world-day-for-peace_en.html, access: March 15, 2011.

Christian identity the best way of protecting Christianity against the danger of syncretism.[407] The Pontiff also warned against the dangers of postmodernism that promote the type of liberty featuring disrespect (for liberty). So, eventually liberty becomes anti-liberty. Both Christians and Muslims are facing the danger of the spread of postmodern ideas, so they should be alert to it and capable of detecting their destructive influence and protecting themselves against it. On many occasions, John Paul II reminded Christians that they should not be discouraged by difficulties that might arise in their dialogue with Muslims. Instead, they should actively engage in interreligious dialogue with the conviction that Jesus Christ, who himself had fought all the obstacles, would be the example to follow.

Although John Paul II was welcomed with great hospitality and was listened to with graciousness in numerous countries all over the world, there were also people, both Muslims and Christians, who opposed his mission and proposed dialogue and rejected his solutions as well. As for the Muslim scholars, some of them questioned the fundaments and the ways of John Paul II's engagement in a dialogue with the followers of Islam.[408]

How did the Pope deal with these setbacks and occasional controversies? He never engaged in any polemics with his opponents. Instead, with patience, and strong belief in the good will of the people, he constantly renewed his appeal for mutual understanding, pointing out that the Church remains always open to dialogue and cooperation. "Everything is possible," the Pope used to say, "if only people want it."[409] Everything needed patience, understanding and time, he emphasized. Some years ago we could not have even imagined that the leaders of diverse religions would pray together.

There is no doubt that today both Christianity and Islam play the most important roles in the spiritual life of the people of the world. Therefore, the Pope constantly urged his audience not to forget that a sincere dialogue between the Christians and the Muslims was not only a possibility but rather an imperative of our days. In 1995 in his address in Rome, the Pope said:

> Both Christians and Muslims are called to defend the inviolable right of each individual freedom of religious belief and practice...We should work together, bearing witness before modern civilization to the divine Presence and loving Providence, which guide our

---

[407] See: E. Sakowicz, *Dialog Kościoła z islamem...*, p. 251-252.

[408] For example: In 1984, Aḥmad Dīdāt (1918-2005), a Muslim scholar, writer, charismatic public speaker and Islamic missionary, challenged John Paul II to a public debate. John Paul II only agreed to a closed conference. Dīdāt wrote back insisting that such a debate should take place in public. When the Pope stopped answering, Dīdāt distributed a pamphlet in January 1985 headlined *His Holiness Plays Hide and Seek with Muslims*. For a variety of Muslim scholars' views on related issues refer to a collection of articles published in: "Le dialogue vu par les musulmans," *Etudes Arabes*, (1995), no. 88-89.

[409] A fragment from John Paul II's Homily at Otranto, Italy (October 5, 1980), quoted in: N. Bakalar and R. Balkin (eds.), *The Wisdom of John Paul II...*, p. 122.

steps. Together we can proclaim that He who has made us and called us to live in harmony and justice.[410]

No one can deny the impact that the pontificate of John Paul II had on many spheres of life of the people all over the world and, in particular, his great contribution to the development of interreligious dialogue. Why, despite many setbacks and controversies, was John Paul II eventually successful in conducting his dialogue with Islam and the Muslims?

The Pope's success came from his sincere approach to the partners of his dialogue, his deep spirituality, his unquestionable moral authority as defender of family values admired by Muslims, his simplicity, his openness and, above all, from the strong desire to put all his efforts in the service of God and humanity. In 1987, in his speech to religious leaders in Los Angeles, he quoted St. Francis of Assisi:

> O Divine Master, grant that I may not so much seek to be consoled as to console, to be understood as to understand, to be loved as to love, for it is in giving that we receive, it is in pardoning that we are pardoned, and it is in dying that we are born to eternal life.[411]

"What unites us Christians is much greater than what separates us," was a conviction often repeated by John XXIII. John Paul II gave these words a new, more universal meaning: What unites us Christians and Muslims, believers in one God, is much greater than what separates us.

John Paul II's persistent search for new means for a sincere dialogue between Christians and Muslims continued until the end of his pontificate. Consistency, objectivity and pragmatism, but most of all, a clear view of long-standing goals shaped all the papal endeavors related to the development of Christian-Muslim dialogue. The most important aims of his dialogical efforts were freedom, justice and peace in the Middle East.

The following two chapters will shed some light on related matters.

---

[410] "John Paul II's Address at the Audience with the Officials of the Pontifical Council for Interreligious Dialogue and the Representatives of the World Islamic Call Society" (February 15, 1990), *Islamochristiana*, vol. 16 (1990), p. 295.

[411] A fragment from John Paul II's speech to Interreligious Leaders at Los Angeles (September 16, 1987), quoted in: N. Bakalar and R. Balkin (eds.), *The Wisdom of John Paul II...*, p. iix.

Summary

All the significant initiatives of Paul VI concerning interreligious dialogue were continued and developed in an unprecedented way by his great successor John Paul II. The history of his dialogue with Muslims, as revealed through both the Pontiff's multiple documents and actions, includes three distinguished phases. The First Period (1978-1980) was a preparatory time devoted to learning. This represented grasping the essence of the Second Vatican Council's conclusions related to the issue of building interreligious dialogue and reflecting on Paul VI's dialogical teaching and initiatives, as well as confirming the commitment to continue with these tasks. The Second Period (the 1980s) was devoted to teaching the whole world, using simple words, about the philosophy of dialogue of life, its meaning and its aims and making people of different cultures and religions aware of the necessity to engage in such a dialogue. Last and not least, it was followed by the Final Period (from the 1990s until the end of the pontificate), that was focused on increasing people's awareness of the multicultural world, preparing to face the challenge of the era of globalization and strengthening his active engagement in resolving religious and political conflicts in the Middle East.

For the Pope, a sincere dialogue with Muslims was "not so much an idea to be studied" but rather "a way of living in positive relationship" with them. Therefore, he was convinced that in the contemporary world, engaging in such a dialogue meant learning to forgive, trying to understand the hearts of Muslims through better perception of oneself and more skillful understanding of them, engaging in mutual cooperation in various areas. First and foremost, it meant putting oneself at the service of humanity and while helping others to develop intercultural sensitivity, to ultimately contribute to a better and safer world.

John Paul II pursued these tasks in a number of ways. He received Muslim leaders at the Vatican and met them during his pilgrimages to Muslim and non-Muslim countries. When the circumstances did not favor official contacts, he was always ready for unofficial meetings. While visiting Muslim countries, he met and addressed the common people. Moreover, the Pope encouraged and supported the organization of various interreligious conferences, colloquia and gatherings. John Paul II actively participated in such meetings and educational activities organized in Rome and often sent his addresses and greetings to the ones that were taking place elsewhere. His message to Muslims all over the world was simple and since his first address is Ankara in 1979 and up until his death had remained the same: respect, love and help for every human being. Wherever the Pope traveled and whomever he addressed, he always repeated his call for a dialogue of life between the Christians, the Muslims and other believers to promote moral values, justice, liberty and peace.

IV

John Paul II and the issue
of religious freedom
in the Middle East

The question of Jerusalem and the protection
of Christian minorities in Muslim countries

As mentioned in Chapter III, for John Paul II the period of 1980s was dedicated to teaching the whole world about the meaning of, the aim of and the need for inter-religious dialogue. This dialogue was for the Pope essential "to serve peace, respect freedom," to promote "religious freedom: [a] condition for peace" and "to build peace, [and] respect minorities." In other words, his constant objective to refuse any falsehood preventing the spread of "truth, the power of peace," was the core of his "dialogue of peace, a challenge for our time."[412]

Peaceful coexistence in the Middle East, where people of different cultures and religious beliefs live side by side, was always on John Paul II's agenda. Since his first address on Middle Eastern soil, in Ankara, the Holy Father repeated his message frequently. On the occasion of the Fourteenth World Day of Peace (January 1, 1981), the Pontiff invited "men and women of good will" to think about the state of the world and about the great cause of peace, saying:

---

[412] These five quotations are the respective titles of Messages of His Holiness John Paul II for the Celebration of the World Day of Peace: "Serve Peace, Respect Freedom," 1981; "Religious Freedom: Condition for Peace," 1988; "To Build Peace, Respect Minorities," 1989; "Truth, the Power of Peace,"1980; "Dialogue of Peace, A Challenge for Our Time," 1983.

I do this from a powerful conviction: that peace is possible, but that it is also something that has to be continually won, a good thing that has to be attained through ever renewed efforts. Each generation feels in a new way the permanent need for peace in the face of the daily problems of life. Yes, it is every day that the ideal of peace has to be made into a concrete reality by each one of us.[413]

Following the line of Pope John XXIII's encyclical *Pacem in Terris*, where he put forward freedom as one of the "four pillars that support [the] house of peace," John Paul II considered freedom, and in particular, religious freedom "a cornerstone of the structure of human rights, and for this reason, an irreplaceable factor in the good of individuals and of the whole of society, as well as of the personal fulfillment of each individual."[414]

In the Middle East, an area inhabited by numerous ethnic, national, linguistic and religious groups, the question of assuring religious freedom to each and every individual living there was of primary importance in John Paul II's opinion. Moreover, it also became a prerequisite for establishing the "proper" status of Jerusalem and the Holy Places and respecting religious minorities. Therefore, the Holy Father devoted much of his attention to both issues. He participated actively in all diplomatic efforts to resolve the issue of Jerusalem and the Holy Places and while visiting Muslim countries continued to both strengthen Christian minorities in their faith and encourage them to engage in a fruitful dialogue of life with Muslims.

The Holy See's position on the issue of Jerusalem and the Holy Places prior to the Second Vatican Council

In the course of history and for different reasons, Jerusalem has become central to the sacred geography of adherents of the three religions of Abraham.[415] However,

---

[413] "Message of His Holiness John Paul II For the Celebration of the Day of Peace: *To Serve Peace, Respect Freedom*" (January 1, 1981), online: http://www.vatican.va/holy_father/john_paul_ii/messages/peace/documents/hf_jp-ii_mes_19801208_xiv-world-day-for-peace_en.html, access: March 25, 2001.

[414] "Message of His Holiness John Paul II for the Celebration of the World Day of Peace: *Religious Freedom: Condition for Peace*" (January 1, 1988), online: http://www.vatican.va/holy_father/john_paul_ii/messages/peace/documents/hf_jp-ii_mes_19871208_xxi-world-day-for-peace_en.html, access: March 25, 2001.

[415] For a balanced account of Jerusalem as a Holy City for Jews, Christians and Muslims see: K. Armstrong, *Jerusalem: One City, Three Faiths*, New York: Alfred A. Knopf, 1996; S. Goldhill, *The Temple of Jerusalem*, Cambridge, MA: Harvard University Press, 2005. Also refer to E. F. Peters's broad collection of sources on the city, its visitors, and their impressions from the earliest days to the 1830s, i.e., *Jerusalem: The Holy City in the Eyes of chroniclers, Visitors, Pilgrims, and Prophets from the Days of Abraham to the Beginning of Modern Times*, Princeton, NJ: Princeton University Press, 1985. Also refer to: S. D. Goitein,

the city has been not only a symbol of God but also a deeply-rooted part of Jewish, Christian and Muslim identities. The religious importance of Jerusalem for Jews, Christians and Muslims is rooted in the holy shrines revered by the followers of all three monotheistic religious.

For Jews, Jerusalem represents redemption from centuries of persecution.[416] In Christianity, the city of Jerusalem is a symbol, both historical and geographical, of Christ's life on Earth.[417] This is the place of Jesus' suffering, death and resurrection. As for the Muslims, Jerusalem is sacred for them because of its association first with Abraham and his descendants, and then with the Prophet Muḥammad, who is believed to have made his miraculous night journey on a winged steed (Burāq) from Mecca to the Al-Aqṣā Mosque in Jerusalem. From there he ascended into heaven until he reached the seventh Heaven.[418]

In the course of history, the competition to gain influence over Jerusalem, a holy city for the three religions, led to many clashes, conflicts, invasions and occupations resulting from rivalries between powers aspiring for control in the Middle East.[419] At the end of World War I, Jerusalem was captured by British troops representing

---

"al-Ḵuds: Part A. History," in: *Encyclopaedia of Islam*, vol. 5, Leiden: E. J. Brill, 1960, p. 322-339; O. Grabar, "al-Ḵuds: Part B. The Monuments," in: *Encyclopaedia of Islam*, vol. 5, p. 339-344.

[416] The Jewish holy places include the Tomb of Absalom, the Cemetery on the Mount of Olives, the Tomb of David, the Wailing Wall, Rachel's Tomb and a number of ancient and modern synagogues. (K. Armstrong, *Jerusalem…*, p. 21-102).

[417] The Christian holy places include the Holy Sepulchre, the Cenacle, the Church of Saint Anne, the Tomb of Virgin, the Garden of Gethsemani, the Sanctuary of the Ascension and the Mount of Olives. (Ibid., p. 194-216).

[418] The night journey is described in the Qur'an (S: 17, v: 1):
> Glory to [Allah]
> Who did take His Servant
> For a Journey by night
> From the Sacred Mosque
> To the Farthest Mosque,
> Who precincts We did
> Bless – in order that We
> Might show him some
> Of Our Signs: for He
> Is the One heareth
> And seeth [all things]. (*The Meaning of…*).

From then on the Al-Aqṣā Mosque has been the sacred place of worship (after Mecca and Medina) for Muslims all over the World. For a related discussion refer to: M. Borrmans, "Jérusalem dans la tradition religieuse musulmane," *Islamochristiana*, vol. 7 (1981), p. 1-18.

[419] The longest occupation was that of the Ottoman Turks. They controlled Jerusalem and the Holy Places from 1517 to 1917. During the Turkish times, Jerusalem enjoyed a special administrative status. According to the *Administrative Regulations of 1877-1888*, the city had an autonomous or independent status. However, as Cattam pointed out, this was not autonomy in a real sense, but "meant only that it was linked directly to Constantinople, the capital of the Ottoman Empire, instead of being under the jurisdiction of the governor of the province."

Allied forces. Subsequently, following the peace treaty that ended the war, Palestine was detached from the Ottoman Empire and designated to be administrated by the British mandate, granted by the League of Nations, on terms stipulated in the Balfour Declaration (November 2, 1917).[420] This Declaration provided for the facilitation of Jewish immigration, land purchase and the implementation of public works and services, and allowed the major religious communities to be involved in the administration of the Holy Places. However, since the Balfour Declaration promised the Jews a national home in Palestine, the Vatican opposed it, fearing that the establishment of a Jewish state would threaten the rights of Christians and endanger peace and stability in the Holy Land.

It should be noted here that following the defeat of the Ottoman Empire and the considerable resulting changes in the spheres of influence in the area of Jerusalem and the Holy Places, the Vatican began to get involved in related religious and political problems. Since the end of World War I, the Holy See's policy towards Jerusalem has evolved from one of supremacy to one fostering ecumenism and interreligious dialogue.

Benedict XV (1854-1922) and Pius XI (1857-1939) encouraged and promoted the preeminence of Catholic rights and privileges. When in 1937 the Palestine Royal Commission recommended the partition of Palestine into Jewish and Arab states and a British mandate area that would include Jerusalem, Bethlehem and Jaffa, the Holy See did not support the proposal, maintaining that both its interests and the cause of peace in the area would be best served if Britain continued to run the Mandate or if the Mandate were given to some other Christian nation. During and after World War II, the Vatican expressed its concerns that either an Arab or a Jewish domination in Palestine would prejudice Catholic interests in the Holy Land and provoke an Arab-Jewish conflict and thus threaten the peace of the Holy Places.

The important evolution of the Holy See's position on Jerusalem and the status of the Holy Places was related to years of the pontificate of Pius XII (1939-1958) who, as seen through his encyclicals, introduced a new, both pastoral and political, element into the Middle East issue, assuring the world about the impartiality of the Holy See regarding the problem of the Holy Land and condemning violence.

In the summer of 1947, the United Nations Special Committee for Palestine, established by the United Nations General Assembly, recommended that Palestine be partitioned into Arab and Jewish states and Jerusalem, with its environs, be made into a *corpus separatum* under United Nations control, to guarantee the preservation of the rights of all religious groups related to the Holy Places.[421] The Vatican gave its

---

(H. Cattan, "The Status of Jerusalem under International Law and United Nations Resolutions, *Journal of Palestine Studies*, vol. 10/3 (1981), p. 3-4.)

[420] For a discussion on related issues, see: L. Stein, *The Balfour Declaration*, Jerusalem and London: Magnes Press, Hebrew University and Jewish Chronicle Publications, 1983 and I. Friedman, *The Question of Palestine, 1914-1918: British-Jewish-Arab Relations*, London: Routledge & K. Paul, 1973.

[421] F. J. Khouri, "The Jerusalem Question and the Vatican," in: K. C. Ellis (ed.), *The Vatican, Islam...*, p. 144.

support to the above-mentioned plan. Since the included recommendations provided for a full internationalization of Jerusalem and its environs, the partition plan was, according to the Vatican, the best way to resolve its basic concerns because it would (1) protect both the Holy Places and the Catholic community in Palestine, (2) ensure the universal character of the city and (3) prevent Jerusalem from being included into an Arab or a Jewish state. The Holy See also hoped that the internalization of Jerusalem would stop the exodus of Christians and therefore strengthen their community.[422]

The Arab community reacted strongly to the partition plan and in the fall of 1947, fighting broke out between the Arab and the Jewish communities in Palestine.

In February and March 1948, the United Nations Trusteeship Council met to draw up a statute establishing a *corpus separatum* for the Jerusalem area. The document provided for a governor with broad executive authority, a legislative council, and various safeguards for human rights in the Holy Places. However, the final vote on the statute was postponed because a special session of the General Assembly had been called to review the entire Palestine question.[423]

The issue of Palestine was addressed on May 1, 1948 by Pius XII in his encyclical *Auspicia Quaedam*. While expressing his concerns about the situation in the area, he emphasized the religious significance of the Holy Land and urged the international community to establish justice and peace there.[424]

On May 15, 1948, following Britain's military evacuation of Palestine, Israel proclaimed itself an independent state. War broke out between Israel and the Arab states. Following the Israeli-Transjordan Armistice Agreement, Jerusalem was divided between Jordanians and Israelis.[425] The Old City, with the Holy Places, came under control of Transjordan (later to be known as Jordan), and the Western (or New) City fell under Israeli dominance. Although the Agreement did not include any reference to the internationalization of Jerusalem, the international community, including the Holy See, still fully supported that solution.[426]

---

[422] S. Ferrari, "The Vatican, Israel and the Jerusalem Question (1943-1984)," *The Middle East Journal*, vol. 39 (1985), no. 2, p. 318-319.

[423] F. J. Khouri, "The Jerusalem Question...," p. 145.

[424] The Pope said: "Indeed, if there exist any place that ought to be most dear to every cultured person, surely it is Palestine, where, from dawn to antiquity, such great light of truth shone for all men, where the Word of God made flesh, announced, through the angels' choir, peace to all men; where finally, Christ hanging on the Cross acquired salvation for all mankind … We desire, therefore … that the situation in Palestine may at long be settled justly and thereby concord and peace be also established." "*Auspicia Quaedam* Encyclical of Pope Pius XII on Public Prayers for World Peace and Solution of the Problem of Palestine to Patriarchs, Primates, Archbishops, Bishops, and Other Ordinaries *In Peace and Communion with the Holy See*" (May 1, 1948), no. 13-14, online: http://www.vatican.va/holy_father/pius_xii/encyclicals/documents/hf_p-xii_enc_01051948_auspicia-quaedam_en.html, access: March 25, 2011.

[425] F. J. Khouri, *The Arab-Israeli Dilemma*, Syracuse: Syracuse University Press, 1985, p. 103.

[426] Ibid., p. 104.

On October 24, 1948, Pope Pius XII issued a new encyclical, *In Multiplicibus Curis.* Well aware of the fact that continued fighting would result in tremendous personal sufferings and bring damage to religious sanctuaries and institutions, the Pontiff condemned "any recourse to violence" and manifested his "lifelong solicitude for peace in Palestine."[427] Furthermore, Pius XII appealed to leaders of the international community "to assure, with international guarantees, both free access to the Holy Places scattered throughout Palestine, and the freedom of worship and respect of customs and religious traditions."[428]

Meanwhile, the international community continued its support for the implementation of the partition resolution's provisions concerning Jerusalem, confirmed on December 11, 1948, by the United Nations General Assembly in Resolution no 194 (III).[429] In late 1948 and early 1949, Israeli and the Vatican emissaries met to work out their differences. However, those attempts did not result in a feasible solution.

On April 15, 1949, in his subsequent encyclical, i.e., *Redemptoris Nostri Cruciatus,* Pius XII once again referred to the issue of Palestine and the Holy Places. The Pope revealed his concerns about "the difficulty and uncertainty of the situation" in the Holy Land.[430] While referring to his previous encyclical, *Multiplicibus Curis,* Pius XII renewed his support for the internationalization of Jerusalem to protect the Holy Places and ensure peace and stability there. Furthermore, the Pope expressed his conviction that the Catholic institutions which had been founded in Palestine to help the poor educate youth and give hospitality to visitors should continue their work as "they did so laudably in the past."[431] Pius XII insisted that "all the rights

---

[427] The Pope declared that "peace could only be realized in truth and justice; that is by respecting the rights of acquired traditions, especially in the religious field, as well as by the strict fulfillment of the duties and obligations of each group of inhabitants." "*In Multiplicibus Curis:* Encyclical of Pope Pius XII on Prayers for Peace in Palestine to the Venerable Brethren, the Patriarchs, Primates, Archbishops, Bishops, and Other Ordinaries in Peace and Communion with the Apostolic See" (October 24, 1948), no. 3, online: http://www.vatican.va/holy_father/pius_xii/encyclicals/documents/hf_p-xii_enc_24101948_in-multiplicibus-curis_en.html, access: March 25, 2011.

[428] Ibid., no. 8.

[429] H. Cattam, "The Status of Jerusalem...," p. 9-10.

[430] He said: "Although the actual fighting is over, tranquility in Palestine is still very far from having been restored. We are still receiving complaints from those who have every right to deplore the profanation of sacred buildings, images, and charitable institutions, as the destruction of peaceful homes of religious communities. Piteous appeals still reach us from numerous refugees, who have been forced by disastrous war to emigrate and even live in exile in concentration camps, the prey to destitution, contagious disease and perils of every sort." "*Redemptoris Nostri Cruciatus:* Encyclical of Pope Pius XII on the Holy Places in Palestine to the Venerable Brethren the Patriarchs, Primates, Archbishops, Bishops, and Other Ordinaries in Peace and Communion with the Apostolic See" (April 15, 1949), no. 5, online: http://www.vatican.va/holy_father/pius_xii/encyclicals/documents/hf_p-xii_enc_15041949_redemptoris-nostri-cruciatus_en.html, access: March 25, 2011.

[431] Ibid., no. 15.

to the Holy Places, which Catholics during the centuries have acquired...should be preserved inviolate."[432]

In the summer and fall of 1949, there were further talks between the Vatican and Israeli officials. However, the two parties were unable to reach any agreement.

Until the early 1949, the Arab states continued to oppose both the partition plan and the establishment of a *corpus separatum* for Jerusalem. However, with the changing situation, after Israel won the Palestine war, they began to realize that they would have more to gain than to lose from the United States' enforcement of the partition resolution, since it would compel Israel to give up a large part of its occupied areas, including West Jerusalem, and allow many Palestinian refugees to return to their homes. Therefore, under the circumstances, the Arab states, except for Jordan, began to support the United Nations resolutions recommending the full internationalization of the Holy City.[433]

In the fall of 1949, the United Nations embarked on the consequential task of examining the matter. There were various proposals to resolve the issue. However, the majority of the United Nations members, among them Arab States excluding Jordan, the Soviet block and Catholic countries encouraged by the Vatican, continued their support or even insistence upon the full internationalization of Jerusalem.[434] On December 9, 1949, the United Nations General Assembly passed a resolution calling for the internationalization of Jerusalem and requesting the Trusteeship Council to prepare a statute establishing permanent international control, in accordance with the 1947 partition resolution, for the Jerusalem area.

Due to difficulties in implementing the Trusteeship Council's Statute, the issue of Jerusalem was back on the agenda of the United Nations General Assembly in the fall of 1950. In light of the continuous opposition of both Israel and Jordan to the internationalization of the Holy City, a number of the United Nations members began to withdraw their support from that plan and began searching for a solution that would be more acceptable to Israel and Jordan. As for the existing resolutions, they remained unimplemented and the issue of Jerusalem was not undertaken by the United Nations General Assembly until after the 1967 war.

The Holy See continued to support the full internationalization of Jerusalem, calling for justice and peace in Middle East. Moreover, with the threat of conflict over the Suez Canal, in his encyclical *Laetamur Admodum,* issued on November 1, 1956, Pius XII reminded the leaders of the international community that "differences among men are not resolved by arms, bloodshed, or destruction, but only by reason, law, prudence, and justice."[435]

---

[432] Ibid., no. 16.

[433] F. J. Khouri, *The Arab-Israeli...*, p. 106.

[434] S. Ferrari, "The Vatican, Israel and the Jerusalem...," p. 321-322.

[435] "*Laetamur Admodum:* Encyclical of Pope Pius XII Renewing Exhortation for Prayers for Peace for Poland, Hungary, and the Middle East to the Venerable Brethren, the Patriarchs, Primates, Archbishops, Bishops, and Other Local Ordinaries in Peace and Communion with

Paul VI's quest to establish a special status for Jerusalem and the Holy Places

In the years of the Second Vatican Council (1962-1965), the issue of Jerusalem and the status of the Holy Places once again became the focus of the Catholic Church's concerns. During the pontificate of Paul VI, the Vatican called for a just solution, pointing out the urgent need to establish a special status for Jerusalem and the Holy Places, guaranteed by an international authority that would assure the preservation of the civil and religious rights of all the communities in question. In addition, the Holy See began to emphasize the equality of all three monotheistic religions and encourage the followers of Judaism, Christianity and Islam to enter the path of dialogue and cooperation.

In 1964 (January 4-6), Pope Paul VI visited the Holy Land. Although his pilgrimage had a primarily spiritual character, it also had important implications, both religious and political. However, as for the issue of Jerusalem, the matter remained untouched.[436]

Israel's victory over the Arab States in June of 1967 brought under its control all of the Jordanian territory west of the Jordan River, including East Jerusalem. Many Israelis insisted that the Holy City should be permanently under their sovereignty. However, the Papacy did not approve the annexation of East Jerusalem and continued its support for the full internationalization of the Holy City.[437]

---

the Apostolic See" (November 1, 1956), no. 8, online: http://www.vatican.va/holy_father/pius_xii/encyclicals/documents/hf_p-xii_enc_01111956_laetamur-admodum_en.html, access: March 25, 2011.

[436] The Pope received an enthusiastic welcome from Christians and Muslims and met with Orthodox and Catholic patriarchs and Jordanian and Israeli heads of states. For a detailed description of the entire papal visit, see: *Jérusalem: Le Moniteur Diocésain du Patriarcat Latin de Jérusalem*, vol. 1-2 (January-February (1964); *Proche Orient Chrétien*, vol. 14 (1964), p. 1-71).

[437] On June 9, 1967, an official Vatican spokesman stated that the United Nation's partition resolution of 1947 had been and still was "in accordance with the wishes of the Holy See" (F. J. Khouri, "The Jerusalem Question...," p. 150). Subsequently, on June 23, the Vatican observer to the United Nations circulated an official document declaring that the Holy See was "convinced that the only solution which offers a sufficient guarantee for the protection of Jerusalem and its Holy Places is to place the city and its vicinity under an International regime." S. Ferrari, "The Vatican, Israel and the Jerusalem...," p. 323; Also see related articles in *L'Osservatore Romano* (June 6, 1967) and (June 11, 1967). In addition, the document explained that "the term of 'internationalization' in its proper sense should mean a separate territory, a *corpus separatum*, subject to International regime" (S. Ferrari, "The Vatican, Israel and the Jerusalem...," p. 324). On June 26, Paul VI himself expressed this view (M. Benvenisti, *Jerusalem: The Torn City*, Minneapolis: University of Minnesota Press, 1976, p. 264). A few days later, on June 30, a group of Latin American countries presented to the United Nations General Assembly a draft resolution supporting the Vatican's position concerning Jerusalem. However, the proposed document did not obtain a sufficient majority

On June 27, 1967, the Knesset passed a law enabling the Minister of Interior to proclaim Jerusalem a single city under the Israeli administration and approved a measure providing for the protection of the Holy Places and guaranteeing freedom of access to them by all the religious groups. The following day, Israel formally united the two sections of the city and extended its borders to include Kallandia Airport and Mount Scopus to the north and northwest and the Mount of Olives to the east, as well as several Arab villages to the south.[438]

The Vatican condemned the annexation and undertook diplomatic measures aimed at easing the political tension. As Ferrari reported, a number of meetings were held in Rome between the Israeli Ambassador and Vatican officials, including Paul VI. However, due to the fact that the two parties' positions still remained irreconcilable, the talks eventually failed.[439]

Israel's annexation of Jerusalem was condemned by many states, including the United States.[440] Therefore, on July 4, 1967, the United Nations General Assembly easily passed *Resolution 2253-ES-V*, dismissing the annexation as invalid and calling upon Israel to rescind all measures taken to alter the city's status.[441] It should be noted that Israel ignored the above resolution.[442]

The fact that neither the United Nations nor the major powers took any serious action to stop Israel from consolidating its claim to the entire city of Jerusalem, together with Israel's willingness to continue negotiations concerning the status of the Holy Places, led the Vatican to reconsider its position. From August 1967, the Holy See continued to call for an internationally guaranteed statute for Jerusalem without making references to the territorial internationalization of the city, the *corpus*

---

to be accepted by the General Assembly. It was evident that most of the nations represented at the United Nations no longer considered the *corpus separatum* a feasible solution.

[438] F. J. K h o u r i, *The Arab-Israeli…*, p. 113.

[439] S. F e r r a r i, „The Vatican, Israel and the Jerusalem…," p. 324.

[440] F. J. K h o u r i, „The Jerusalem Question…," p. 150.

[441] "2253 (ES-V): Measures Taken by Israel to Change the Status of the City of Jerusalem" (July 4, 1967), online: http://unispal.un.org/UNISPAL.NSF/0/A39A906C89D3E98 685256C29006D4014, access: March 27, 2011.

[442] However, the Israeli government, fully aware of the importance of the Jerusalem issue for the members of the international community, was willing to reach an agreement regarding the status of the Holy Places with the Pope and Christian leaders. Representatives of Israel met with officials from the Vatican, the World Council of Churches, and other Christian groups, as well as with delegations from a number of Christian countries. The majority of other religious leaders refrained from supporting Israel's position (F. J. K h o u r i, "The Jerusalem Question…," p. 151). Israel's position was that while retaining sovereignty over the entire city, it would give the Holy Places extraterritorial, "universal" status, under the supervision of the religious communities themselves. Furthermore, Israel was willing to grant quasi-diplomatic status to the Church's official delegations stationed in Jerusalem and to work out the final detailed arrangements with representatives of the various religious organizations. The Israeli government was convinced that peace in Jerusalem and the safety of the Holy Places could be better assured by a unified city administration than a divided one (Ibid., p.151). The Pope, as well as the majority of other religious leaders, refrained from supporting Israel's position.

separatum. On December 22, 1967, in his Christmas message, Paul VI clarified the newly-modified position more by indicating the two features that the Vatican considered "essential and impossible to evade" in any possible solution to the problem of Jerusalem and the Holy Places. The Pope explained:

> There are two essential aspects...The first concerns the Holy Places properly so called and considered as such by the three great monotheistic religions, Judaism, Christianity and Islam. It is a matter of guaranteeing freedom of worship, respect for preservation of and access to the Holy Places, protected by special immunities thanks to a special status, whose observation would be guaranteed by an institution, International in character, taking into particular account of the historic and religious personality of Jerusalem. The second aspect of the question refers to the free enjoyment of the legitimate civil and religious rights of persons, residences, and activities of all communities present on the territory of Palestine.[443]

It is important to notice that the above address contained a new element. Unlike Benedict XV, Pius XI and Pius XII, Pope Paul VI placed the three religious communities present in Jerusalem on equal footing in his speech. Furthermore, the Pope emphasized his concern for the people, as well as for the religious institutions in Palestine, referring to the need to guarantee their civil as well as religious rights. In his Christmas address of December 1967, Paul VI made it clear and definite that while the Vatican was prepared to abandon Jerusalem's territorial internationalization and consider alternative solutions, it was not prepared to compromise on the fundamental requirements that had urged the Holy See in the years 1948-50 to forward requests for a *corpus separatum*. The Pope insisted that the fulfillment of these requirements would have to be satisfied in any new formula put forward.[444]

As the Israeli position on Jerusalem remained rather non-negotiable and its proposal for extraterritoriality for the Holy Places was in no way considered acceptable for the Vatican, the talks between Israel and the Vatican continued to be without prospects for a feasible solution.[445]

The Vatican concerns with regard to the Jerusalem issue increased in the early 1970s, after the Israeli government announced its "master plan" for the future of the city: to double the Jewish population of the city by 1980. Despite protests from the international community, including the United States and other western countries, and the multiple United Nations General Assembly and Security Council resolutions

---

[443] Quoted by G. E. Irani (*The Papacy and the Middle East...*, p. 80) from B. Collin, *Recueil de documents concernant Jérusalem et les lieux saints*, Jérusalem: Franciscan Printing Press, 1982, p. 36.

[444] G. E. Irani, *The Papacy and the Middle East...*, p. 81-82.

[445] The definite breakdown came at the beginning of 1971, when Paul VI sent a letter informing the Israeli President that he could not agree to any agreement with a country that the Holy See did not officially recognize. Furthermore, the Holy Father refused the Israeli proposal to recognize "the Pope as the representative of all Christian groups" (M. Benvenisti, *Jerusalem...*, p. 268).

condemning Israeli policies and actions, the Israeli government continued to implement its plan.[446]

In an attempt to ease the rising tensions and find an accommodation with the Israeli government regarding the status of the Holy Places and the fate of the Catholics living in the Holy Land, on January 15, 1973, Paul VI met with Israeli Prime Minister Golda Meir.[447] However, despite attempts to narrow differences, the conducted talk did not bring results and the positions of the Vatican and Israel remained irreconcilable.[448]

In the 1970s, the situation in Middle East and in particular in the Holy Land remained one of the Papacy's main concerns. The preoccupation of the Holy See with the fate of Christians living there and the call to maintain and preserve the unique and universal character of the city was the focus of the apostolic exhortation *Nobis in Animo* (March 25, 1974), where Paul VI once again expressed his conviction that peace in the Holy Land could not be achieved without respecting equal rights of all the religious groups living there.[449]

The publication of *Nobis in Animo* and the Pope's evidently stated disapproval of the exclusive Israeli control over the Holy City resulted in a severe attack by the Israeli rabbi Shlomo Goren,[450] and led to further discontent between the Vatican and Israel. There was also an embarrassing incident during the Seminar on Islamic-Christian dialogue that was held in Tripoli, Libya, on February 1-6, 1976, with the participation of Arab religious and political leaders, under the joint sponsorship of the Libyan government and the Holy See.[451] The Seminar issued a twenty-four-paragraph statement on number of issues, such as religion and science, religious freedom and cooperation, as well as related matters. Among the twenty-four paragraphs

---

[446] The plan envisaged the expansion of the Jewish population in the surrounding area. In order to realize that task, vast housing projects were to be developed in and around the city. Many Arab properties were to be sequestered and in some sections of Jerusalem and its suburbs the Arab inhabitants were to be removed from their homes to make room for the coming immigrant Jews (F. J. Khouri, "The Jerusalem Question...," p. 152).

[447] G. E. Irani, *The Papacy and the Middle East...*, p. 37-38.

[448] After the audience, the Holy See issued a *communiqué* stating that "Pope Paul VI, after having recalled the history and the suffering of the Jewish people, explained the viewpoint of the Holy See on questions that touch most closely its humanitarian mission, such as the problem of the refugees and the situation of the various communities living in the Holy Land, as well as questions regarding Holy Places and the sacred and universal character of the city of Jerusalem." Quoted by G. E. Irani (*The Papacy and the Middle East...*, p. 38) from *L'Osservatore Romano* (January 15-16, 1973).

[449] See: "*Nobis in Animo*: Esortazione apostolica di sua santità Paolo pp. VI all'episcopato, al clero ed ai fedeli di tutto il mondo sulle accresciute necessità della Chiesa in terra santa" (March 25, 1974), online: http://www.va/holy_father/paul_vi/apost_exhortations/documents/hf_p-vi_exh_19740325_nobis-in-animo_it.html access: March 27, 2011.

[450] G. E. Irani, *The Papacy and the Middle East...*, p. 85.

[451] For a detailed account of the Tripoli Seminar refer to: M. Borrmans, "Le séminaire du dialogue Islamo-Chrétien de Tripoli (Libye, 1-6 février 1976)," *Islamochristiana*, vol. 2 (1976), p. 135-170.

there were two considered controversial, i.e., paragraphs 20 and 21. Paragraph 20 referred to the Israeli-Palestinian dispute and contained a statement saying that "the two parties...distinguish between Zionism and Judaism, considering Zionism an aggressive, racist movement, alien to Palestine and the whole Levant."[452] Paragraph 21 addressed the problem of Jerusalem, stating that the two parties "affirm the national rights of the Palestinian people and its right to return to its land, assert that 'Jerusalem is an Arab city,' and call for the setting up of a permanent commission to investigate attempts to change the character of Islamic and Christian places."[453]

As Irani pointed out, the Vatican delegation did not approve paragraphs 20 and 21, and in particular, "the assertion that 'Jerusalem is an Arab city,' without making a distinction between the Western Sector, which has been Israeli since 1948, and the old City, conquered in the aftermath of June 1967."[454] He said:

> In essence, what Rome wanted to demonstrate by its rejection of the two paragraphs in the Tripoli statement was that (1) the Papacy refused to be dragged into the Arab-Israeli quarrel in order to champion the cause of either party, and (2) the Holy See considers the Holy City as the common heritage to the three monotheistic religions on an equal basis without differentiation.[455]

In the late 1970s, the position of the Holy See concerning the issue of Jerusalem remained roughly the same. Vatican-Israeli relations were characterized by both increasing tensions and a number of attempts to improve them. In November 1977, President Sādāt went to Jerusalem and one year later the Camp David agreements were signed.[456]As Ferrari pointed out, those facts "at least partially unblocked the impasse in which all the previous initiatives designed to resolve the Middle East conflict had foundered,"[457] and despite the fact that the positions of Israel and Egypt concerning the issue of the Holy City were rather irreconcilable, "the Vatican could not overlook the possibility that during the course of the diplomatic negotiations between these two countries the question of Jerusalem might find a stable outcome."[458] While following the related political developments and negotiations closely, the Holy See remained firm in its already known position.

---

[452] Ibid.
[453] Ibid.
[454] G. E. Irani, *The Papacy and the Middle East...*, p. 86.
[455] Ibid., p. 86-87.
[456] For a broad discussion on related issues, see: C. E. Swisher, *The Truth about Camp David: The Untold Story about the Collapse of the Middle East Peace Process*, New York: Nation Books, 2004.
[457] S. Ferrari, "The Vatican, Israel and the Jerusalem...," p. 328.
[458] Ibid., p. 329.

John Paul II's call upon the followers of Judaism, Christianity and Islam for peaceful coexistence in the Holy Land

With regard to the issue of Jerusalem and the status of the Holy Places, Pope John Paul II steadily continued the policy of his predecessor. On October 2, 1979, he visited the United Nations, and in his speech to the General Assembly reaffirmed, following the line of Paul VI's statements, his "hope for a special statute that, under international guarantees…would respect the particular nature of Jerusalem, a heritage sacred to the veneration of millions of believers of the three great monotheistic religions, Judaism, Christianity and Islam."[459] The position presented by John Paul II was explained further by a detailed note prepared by the Vatican's Permanent Observer at the United Nations.

The document confirmed the Holy See's customary demand for "a special statute internationally guaranteed for Jerusalem."[460] However, as Ferrari mentioned, this demand was placed in the context of a more specifically religious context. The statement pointed out the need to preserve the unique identity of Jerusalem as a religious center and a place of fruitful encounter and cooperation of the three great monotheistic religions. Furthermore, it elaborated on the significance of historical and religious pluralism, calling for full respect of equal rights of all communities present in the Holy City, exclusion of both political and religious dominance, and encouraging all initiatives that could forward the development of a reasonable human and religious dialogue. In addition, the document also mentioned the need "to define the territory and list the Holy Places, as well as provide for the guarantees and for the supervision which the international community will have to give to the 'statute' and for a juridical form of this commitment and of the accord of the interested parties."[461]

Although the position of the Holy See on the issue of Jerusalem and the Holy Places, as revealed from the note drawn up by the Vatican's Permanent Observer to the United Nations, basically stayed in line with Paul VI's previous statements, one may easily notice a new element, namely the importance attributed to the need to guarantee equal rights for the Jewish, Christian and Muslim communities present in the Holy Land. In the view of the Papacy, the religious pluralism that makes Jerusalem so special and absolutely unique could become a source of the needed dialogue and cooperation.

---

[459] "Apostolic Journey to the United States of America: Address of His Holiness John Paul II to the 34th General Assembly of the United Nations" (New York, October 2, 1979), no. 10, online: http://www.vatican.va/holy_father/john_paul_ii/speeches/1979/october/documents/hf_jp-ii_spe_19791002_general-assembly-onu_en.html, access March 27, 2011.

[460] For a brief overview of UN Document S/13679 (December 1979), refer to: S. Ferrari, "The Vatican, Israel and the Jerusalem…," p. 329-330.

[461] Ibid.

Following the publication of the above-mentioned document, a number of proposals appeared, defining more precisely the content of the basic guidelines coming
from the Vatican. The proposals were particularly focused on the system of international guarantees for Jerusalem and the potential involvement of particular countries
that could gain political influence in the Middle East.[462]

A few months later, in an article published shortly before the Israeli government
enacted its *Basic Law* to formalize the annexation of Jerusalem,[463] *L'Osservatore Romano* warned against solutions based on either unilateral initiatives by one state or
bilateral agreements between one and more states, pointing out the risk of a solution
negotiated between Israel and Arab states that might leave the Christian communities without sufficient protection. The newspaper, once again, emphasized the need
for an adequate legal system guaranteed by a higher international authority: in that
case, most probably the United Nations. The basic requests of the Holy See were
outlined as follows:

1.   that the overall character of Jerusalem as sacred heritage shared by the three mono-
     theistic religions be guaranteed by appropriate measures;
2.   that religious freedom in all its aspects be safeguarded for them;
3.   that the complex of rights acquired by the various communities over the shrines
     and the centers for spirituality, study, welfare be protected;
4.   that the continuance and development of religious, educational, and social activity
     of each community be ensured;
5.   that this be actuated with equality of treatment for all three religions;
6.   that this be achieved through an "appropriate juridical safeguard" that does not de-
     rive from the will of only one of the parties interested.[464]

The article confirmed the Holy See's position, calling firmly for the implementation of a special statute for Jerusalem, defined here as an "appropriate juridical safeguard." It was also evident that, in the view of the Vatican, the significance and value
of Jerusalem are such as to surpass the interest of any single state or bilateral agreements between one state and others."[465] However, the article also presented a new
element by indicating the evolution in the Holy See's position on Jerusalem. The
Vatican requests, published by *L'Osservatore Romano*, clearly revealed an evidently
increasing awareness that under the "difficult circumstances," the Holy See would

---

[462] Ibid., p. 330.

[463] *The Basic Law: Jerusalem, Capital of Israel* declares that United Jerusalem is the capital of
       Israel. It was passed July 30, 1980. It began as a private initiative of Knesset Member Geula
       Cohen, who opposed the peace treaty with Egypt, and was adopted by the government of
       Menachem Begin. See: "Basic Law: Jerusalem" (July 30, 1980), online: http://zionism-israel.
       com/hdoc/Basic_Law_Jerusalem.html, access: March 27, 2011.

[464] Quoted by G. E. Irani (*The Papacy and the Middle East…*, p. 87) from *L'Osservatore Ro-
       mano*, English ed., (July 1, 1980).

[465] The article referred to the UN 1947, 1948 and 1949 Resolutions and the 1950 Special Statute
       approved by the Trusteeship Council.

have to consider a conditional acceptance of the sovereignty of some "power," in this case Israel, provided that an international body would guarantee the special status of the Holy City. The article stated that:

> The Holy See considers the safeguarding of the sacred and universal character of Jerusalem to be of such primary importance as to require any power that comes to exercise sovereignty over Holy City to assume the obligation, before the three religious confessions spread throughout the world, to protect not only the special character of the city but also the rights connected with the Holy Places and with the religious communities concerned, on the basis of an appropriate International body.[466]

The position adopted by the Holy See, as presented in the article discussed above, resulted in a strong reaction from the members of Jewish religious community, and in particular from two American rabbis, i.e., Rabbi Martin A. Cohen and Rabbi David H. Panitz, who sent a letter to the Vatican's Secretary of State, Cardinal Cassaroli.[467] The letter once again confirmed considerable differences with regard to the issue of Jerusalem. Furthermore, it pointed out the Holy See's questionable acknowledgement of Israel's efficient administration and its constant preoccupation with the preservation of Jerusalem's historical and spiritual heritage.

In Jerusalem, religious feelings are very strong and the emotional attachment of millions of Jews, Christians and Muslims to the city is unparalleled in today's world. The Pope believed that this historical phenomenon had made the Holy City unique and emphasized its universal symbolic character. Furthermore, John Paul II was convinced that the level of emotional attachment of Jews, Christians and Muslims to the Holy City could carry at the same time both a great danger for conflict and a tremendous potential for peace and reconciliation. On January 1, 1982, in his Message for the World Day of Peace, John Paul II referred, once again, to the symbolic meaning of the Holy City, pointing out that:

> In Jerusalem, on the day of Pentecost, the Holy Spirit caused the first disciples of the Lord to rediscover, beyond the diversity of languages, the royal road to peace in brotherhood. The Church remains the *witness of this great hope.*[468]

In the following years, his position on Jerusalem remained attuned with that of his predecessor, Paul VI. Its essence was fully elaborated by John Paul II in his apostolic letter *Redemptions Anno*, published on April 20, 1984.[469] In the introduction,

---

[466] Quoted by G. E. Irani (*The Papacy and the Middle East…*, p. 88) from *L'Osservatore Romano*, English ed., (July 1, 1980).

[467] G. E. Irani, *The Papacy and the Middle East…*, p. 89-90.

[468] "Message of His Holiness Pope John Paul II for the Celebration of the Day of Peace" (January 1, 1983).

[469] "From the Apostolic Letter of John Paul II *Redemptionis Anno*" (April 20, 1984), online: http://www.biblebelievers.org.au/redempti.htm, access: March 27, 2011. The text of the letter follows the English translation by *L'Osservatore Romano*.

while mentioning Paul VI's visit to Jerusalem and the Holy Places, the Pontiff expressed his personal hope for such a pilgrimage. John Paul II referred to both the historical and spiritual significance of the Holy Land, and of Jerusalem in particular, for the followers of the three great monotheistic religions. He said:

> Christians honor her [Jerusalem] with a religious and intent concern because there the words of Christ so often resounded, there the great events of the Redemption were accomplished...the first Christian community sprang up and remained throughout the centuries of continual ecclesial presence despite the difficulties. Jews ardently love her and every age venerate new memory, abundant as she is in many remains and monuments from the time of David who chose her as the capital, and of Salomon who built the Temple there. Therefore, they...point to her as the sign of their nation. Muslims also call Jerusalem "Holy," with a profound attachment that goes back to the origins of Islam and springs from the fact that they have there many special places of pilgrimage and for more than a thousand years have dwelt there, almost without interruption.[470]

The emotions binding each of the faiths to Jerusalem have grown in the course of its history. As a result, the Pope believed, Jerusalem had been such a deeply-embedded ideal that objectivity had become rather impossible. While referring to the recent history of the Holy Land, the Pope referred to "the violent events which have afflicted Jerusalem for many decades."[471] John Paul II expressed both his and his predecessors' concern with the situation in Jerusalem. Furthermore, he pointed out that the Pontiffs had always followed closely all the related initiatives and resolutions of the United Nations, and, on many occasions, have called "for reflection" and "urged that an adequate solution be found to this difficult and complex issue."[472]

A closer look at the content of *Redemptionis Anno* reveals that the Holy See's already known stand on Jerusalem sounds firmer and is more explicit in this document. One may also notice that, although the presented position seems to be rather flexible regarding the legal framework of the special statute for Jerusalem and even the geographical area in which it would be implemented, the expected tasks of the international community, as discussed by John Paul II, are precisely defined and stated. The first represents the protection with complete equality of the religious and civil rights of the communities present in Jerusalem. It should be emphasized that the Pope put this particular task in a crucial and sensible political context, as he acknowledged both the right of Israel to secure borders and the right of the Palestinians to a homeland. As the Holy Father explained:

> For the Jewish people who live in the State of Israel and who preserve in that land such precious testimonies to their history and their faith, we must ask for the desired security and the due tranquility...The Palestinian people, who find their historical roots in that land and who

---

470 Ibid.
471 Ibid.
472 Ibid.

for decades have been dispersed, have the natural right in justice to find once a homeland and to be able to live in peace and tranquility with the other people of the area.[473]

It was a deep conviction of John Paul II that Jerusalem stands as a sacred symbol of universal peace for the human family. Therefore, he believed the second task of the international community should be not only to safeguard this unique character of the city and the Holy Places, but at the same time to protect the equality of the followers of the three great monotheistic religions and encourage them to engage in dialogue and cooperation. The Pope explained:

> The entire human race and especially the peoples and nations who have in Jerusalem brothers in faith: Christians, Jews and Muslims have reason to feel themselves involve in this matter and to do everything possible to preserve the unique and sacred character of the Holy City. Not only the monuments or the sacred places, but the whole historical Jerusalem and the existence of religious communities.[474]

In the 1990s, his position concerning Jerusalem did not change. In his speeches delivered to various communities and authorities around the world, the Pope continued to emphasize the need to assure religious freedom for each and every person. On October 5, 1995, while addressing the 50th General Assembly of the United Nations in New York, the Pontiff reminded his audience "how important it is to safeguard *the fundamental right to freedom of religion and freedom of conscience*, as the cornerstones of the structure of human rights and the foundation of every truly free society."[475] In all his statements related to the Middle East, John Paul II continued to express his deep conviction that the hope for real peace in this area could prove ephemeral if a just and adequate solution were not found to the particular problem of Jerusalem. On January 13, 1996, while addressing the diplomats accredited to the Holy See, John Paul II once again pointed out that:

> The religious and universal dimension of the Holy City demands a commitment on the part of the whole International community, in order to ensure that the City preserves its uniqueness and retains its living character. The Holy Places, dear to the three monotheistic religions, would lose much of their significance if they were not permanently surrounded by active communities of Jews, Christians and Muslims, enjoying true freedom of conscience and religion, and developing their own religious, educational and social activities.[476]

---

[473]   Ibid.

[474]   Ibid.

[475]   "Apostolic Journey of His Holiness John Paul II to the United States of America: The Fiftieth General Assembly of the United Nations Organization: Address of His Holiness John Paul II" (New York, October 5, 1995), no. 10, online: http://www.vatican.va/holy_father/john_paul_ii/speeches/1995/october/documents/hf_jp-ii_spe_05101995_address-to-uno_en.html, access: March 27, 2011.

[476]   John Paul II, "Address of the Holy Father on the Occasion of the Exchange of Greetings with the Diplomatic Corps Accredited to the Holy See" (January 13, 1996), no. 2,

The Pope's long struggle for dialogue and peace in the Middle East resulted in some positive changes, including the establishment of diplomatic relations between the Holy See and Israel and then with the Palestinian Autonomy.[477] All that, together with increased diplomatic contacts between the Vatican and the Arab states, eventually led to an easing of the tensions between the Palestinians and the Israelis. Therefore, John Paul II decided to fulfill his dream and in the year 2000, the year of the 2000th anniversary of the birth of Jesus Christ, he went on a pilgrimage to the Holy Land.

On March 20, 2000, during the welcome ceremony at the airport in Amman, while referring to the long tradition of harmonious coexistence between Christians and Muslims in the Hashemid Kingdom, John Paul II explained that only the development of a sincere dialogue between the three monotheistic religions would lead to a long-lasting peace settlement in the area. Three days later, in Jerusalem, during the interreligious meeting at the Notre Dame Pontifical Institute, the Pope elaborated on the matter even further. He said:

> For all of us Jerusalem, as its name indicates, is the "City of Peace". Perhaps no other place in the world communicates the sense of transcendence as divine election that we perceive in her stones and monuments, and in the witness of the three religions living side by side within her walls. Not everything has been easy in this co-existence. But we must find in our respective religious traditions the wisdom and the superior motivation to ensure the triumph of mutual understanding and cordial respect…If the various religious communities in the Holy Land succeed in living and working together in friendship and harmony, this will be of enormous benefit not only to them but also to the whole cause of peace in this region.[478]

However, the first years of the twenty-first century saw that the political situation in the Middle East become more complicated again. With the events of September 11, 2001, and subsequently the American intervention in Afghanistan, tensions in this region have risen again. The Palestinian-Israeli dispute entered a very difficult stage. John Paul II, appalled by these dangerous developments, engaged himself again, urging the international community on many occasions to undertake initiatives aimed at easing the political and religious tensions in the Middle East, and in particular in the Holy Land. In January 2002, while addressing the Diplomatic Corps accredited to the Holy See, the Pope said:

> The Holy Land is still, through man's fault, a land of fire and blood…Weapons and bloody attacks will never be the right means for making a political statement to the

online: http://www.vatican.va/holy_father/john_paul_ii/speeches/1996/documents/hf_jp-ii_spe_13011996_diplomatic-corps_en.html, access: March 27, 2011.

[477] For a thorough discussion on related issues see Chapter V, p. 175-178.

[478] "Jubilee Pilgrimage of His Holiness John Paul II to the Holy Land (March 20-26, 2000: Address of John Paul II: Interreligious Meeting at the Notre Dame Pontifical Institute" (Jerusalem, March 23, 2000), no.1, online: http://www.vatican.va/holy_father/john_paul_ii/travels/documents/hf_jp-ii_spe_20000323_jerusalem-notre-dame_en.html, access: March 27, 2011.

other side…As I have already stated on many occasions, only respect for others and their legitimate aspirations, the application of international law, the evacuation of the occupied territories and an internationally guaranteed *special status for the most Holy Places* in Jerusalem can bring about a beginning of pacification in that part of the world and break the hellish cycle of hatred and vengeance.[479]

There is no doubt that the interest shown by John Paul II in the Holy Land reflected one of the primary concerns of his pontificate. The Pontiff's numerous interventions and statements related to the problems and situations associated with the Holy Land not only demonstrated the importance attributed to that area, but above all emphasized his conviction that all those sincere and tireless efforts to seek peace could also become an example and inspiration for so many other analogous situations throughout the world. All in all, one may say that John Paul II's concern for the adequate status of Jerusalem and the Holy Places revealed his deep conviction that religious freedom is a natural right of each and every human being and therefore should always remain above the interests of any given state.

"To build peace, respect minorities":[480] John Paul II's dialogical mission to protect Christian minorities in the Middle East

With Pope John Paul II, the activity of the Holy See, based essentially on law and justice, moved beyond the present circumstances and looked to the future, towards the interchange between nations, religions and the whole human race. In his efforts to teach the whole world about dialogue and peace, he continued with the task of Paul VI, who in 1967 launched the idea of a World Day of Peace[481] with the aim that "widely differing communities" would meet "to celebrate the inestimable benefit of

---

[479] "Address of His Holiness Pope John Paul II to the Diplomatic Corps" (January 10, 2002), no. 3, online: http://www.vatican.va/holy_father/john_paul_ii/speeches/2002/january/documents/hf_jp-ii_spe_20020110_diplomatic-corps_en.html, access: March 27, 2011.
[480] This is the title of John Paul II's Message for the 1989 World Day of Peace.
[481] The themes of Paul VI's Messages are as follows:
     1968: *1 January: World Day of Peace*
     1969: *The Promotion of Human Rights, the Road to Peace*
     1970: *Education for Peace Through Reconciliation*
     1971: *Every Man is My Brother*
     1972: *If You Want Peace, Work for Justice*
     1973: *Peace is Possible*
     1974: *Peace Depends on You Too*
     1975: *Reconciliation, The Way to Peace*
     1976: *The Real Weapons of Peace*
     1977: *If You Want Peace, Defend Life*
     1978: *No to Violence, Yes to Peace*

peace and to affirm their willingness to defend and serve it."[482] The first Message sent to the world by John Paul II on January 1, 1979, was entitled, as his predecessor had decided shortly before his death, "To Reach Peace, Teach Peace." Since then, each year the Pope continued his "lessons" by repeating essential points and placing them in the context of new themes.[483] While broadening the scope of discussed issues, he worked on increasing people's awareness of the fact that "peace is a dynamic process which must take account of the many conditions and factors that can either favor it or disturb it."[484]

Among the problems that needed special consideration was, according to the Pope, the question of minorities. John Paul II addressed this issue in his 1989 Message for the World Day of Peace. While referring to the words of John XXIII, who

---

[482] "Message of His Holiness Pope John Paul II for the Celebration of the Day of Peace: *To Reach Peace, Teach Peace*" (January 1, 1979), online: http://www.vatican.va/holy_father/john_paul_ii/messages/peace/documents/hf_jp-ii_mes_19781221_xii-world-day-for-peace_en.html, access: March 27, 2011.

[483] These are the themes of the successive twenty-seven World Days of Peace:
1979: *To Reach Peace, Teach Peace*
1980: *Truth, the Power of Peace*
1981: *To Serve Peace, Respect Freedom*
1982: *Peace: A Gift of God Entrusted to Us!*
1983: *Dialogue for Peace, A Challenge for Our Time*
1984: *From a New Heart, Peace is Born*
1985: *Peace and Youth Go Forward Together*
1986: *Peace is a Value with No Frontiers North-South, East-West: Only One Peace*
1987: *Development and Solidarity: Two Keys to Peace*
1988: *Religious Freedom, Condition for Peace*
1989: *To Build Peace, Respect Minorities*
1990: *Peace with God the Creator, Peace with All of Creation*
1991: *If You Want Peace, Respect the Conscience of Every Person*
1992: *Believers United in Building Peace*
1993: *If You Want Peace, Reach Out to the Poor*
1994: *The Family Creates the Peace of the Human Family*
1995: *Women: Teachers of Peace*
1996: *Let Us Give Children a Future of Peace*
1997: *Offer Forgiveness and Receive Peace*
1998: *From the Justice of Each Comes Peace for All*
1999: *Respect for Human Rights: The Secret of True Peace*
2000: *"Peace on Earth to Those Whom God Loves!"*
2001: *Dialogue Between Cultures for a Civilization of Love and Peace*
2002: *No Peace Without Justice, No Justice Without Peace*
2003: *"Pacem in Terris": A Permanent Commitment*
2004: *"An Ever Timely Commitment: Teaching Peace"*
2005: *"Do Not Be Overcome by Evil but Overcome Evil with God"*

[484] "Message of His Holiness Pope John Paul II for the Celebration of the World Day of Peace: *To Build Peace, Respect Minorities*" (January 1, 1989), no. 1, online: http://www.vatican.va/holy_father/john_paul_ii/messages/peace/documents/hf_jp-ii_mes_19881208_xxii-world-day-for-peace_en.html, access: March 15, 2011.

in *Pacem in Terris* pointed out that "ethnic minorities are often included within the national borders of a different ethnic group, and this leads to quite complex problems,"[485] and to the Second Vatican Council's statement affirming that "peace is not merely the absence of war, nor can it be reduced solely to the maintenance of a balance of power between enemies,"[486] the Holy Father remarked:

> It is clear that at this time of increased international *détente* resulting from agreements and mediations which allow us to look forward to solutions in favour of peoples who have been the victims of bloody conflicts, the question of minorities is assuming a notable importance. Consequently, it constitutes a matter for careful reflection on the part of political and religious leaders and all men and women of good will.[487]

Nowadays, minority groups exist in almost all societies and they differ in terms of cultural traditions, ethnic origins, historical experiences, race and religious beliefs. Their harmonious coexistence with majority groups contributes to the well-being of the human family. There are, according to the Pope, two fundamental principles that should constitute the basis of all social organization in a nation made up of diverse groups of people: (1) the assurance of "the inalienable dignity of every human person, irrespective of racial, ethnic, cultural or national origin, or religious belief" and (2) the requirement "that the whole of humanity, beyond its ethnic, national, cultural and religious differences, should form a community that is free of discrimination between peoples and that strives for reciprocal solidarity."[488] The implementation of these principles both by the state and the people – the acceptance and the respect of diversity – helps to eliminate attitudes of prejudice, thus contributing to healthy social relations.

There is no doubt that the protection of Christian minorities in the Middle East, and in particular of Catholics living side by side with Muslims, was one of the Pope's main objectives from the beginning of his pontificate.[489] The Holy See followed the situation in the area closely and the Pope often received at the Vatican delegations representing Christian minorities from the Middle East, including those of Bishops on their *ad limina* visits. However, most important were his pilgrimages to Muslim

---

[485]   "*Pacem in Terris*: Encyclical of Pope John XXIII…," no. 93.

[486]   "Pastoral Constitution on the Church in the Modern World *Gaudium et Spes*…," no.78.

[487]   "Message of His Holiness Pope John Paul II for the Celebration of the World Day of Peace: *To Build Peace, Respect Minorities*" (January 1, 1989), no. 3.

[488]   Ibid.

[489]   The number of Christians in the Middle East is shrinking each and every year. Therefore the problem has become one of the Papacy's main concerns. For discussions on related issues, see: *The Middle East Quarterly*, vol. 8 (2001), no. 1: *Disappearing Christians in the Middle East*. Also refer to: A. Sfeir, "Chrześcijanie na wschodzie," in: E. Guerriero and M. Impagliazzo (eds.), *Najnowsza historia Kościoła: katolicy i kościoły chrześcijańskie czasie pontyfikatu Jana Pawła II*, trans. J. Partyka, Kraków: Wydawnictwo M, 2006, p. 123-139. For an overview of the status of Christianity in the Middle Eastern countries that John Paul II visited, refer to: D. M. McCurry (ed.), *World Christianity, Middle East*, Monrovia, CA: MARC, 1979.

countries. These pilgrimages had a three-fold aim: (1) strengthening Catholics in their faith, (2) promoting unity among Christians and (3) encouraging Christian-Muslim dialogue and cooperation in the various spheres of life. One may notice that the focal points of his visits differed, depending on the overall socio-political situation, the condition of Christian community and possible prospects for successful development of Christian-Muslim dialogue.

John Paul II began his direct encounter with Christian minorities living in Middle Eastern Muslim majority countries in 1979. His first three pilgrimages included Turkey (1979), Pakistan (1981) and Morocco (1985).

John Paul II's encounter with Muslim majority countries began with Turkey.[490] During his visit there, the Pope was focused on two issues, namely the "rapprochement" between Catholics and Orthodox and the initiation of Christian-Muslim dialogue and cooperation.[491] The Holy Father met with political and religious authorities, including the President, the diplomatic corps and the patriarchs. The visit resulted in Pope John Paul II and the Ecumenical Patriarch Dimitrios I signing the official *Joint Declaration*, in which they expressed their gratitude to Pope Paul VI and Patriarch Athenagoras I "for everything they did to reconcile our Churches and cause them to progress in unity" and affirmed their "resolute determination to do everything possible to hasten the day when full communion will be reestablished between the Catholic Church and the Orthodox Church."[492] Furthermore, as stated in the document, the Holy Father and the Patriarch indicated their will to follow the path towards unity:

> We want the progress in unity to open up new possibilities of dialogue and collaboration with believers of other religions, and with all men of goodwill, in order that love and brotherhood may prevail over hatred and opposition among men. We hope to contribute in this way to the coming of true peace in the world. We implore his gift of him who was, who is, and who will be, Christ our one Saviour and our real peace.[493]

---

[490]   Turkey: population 78,785,548, Muslim 99.8% (mostly Sunni), other 0.2% (mostly Christians and Jews); "Turkey," online: https://www.cia.gov/library/publications/the-world-factbook/geos/tu.html, access: October 30, 2011.

[491]   See: G. O'Connor, *Universal Father...*, p. 230-231. Pope Paul VI visited Turkey on July 25, 1967. For his address to the religious leaders of the Muslim community see: "Voyage Apostolique à Istanbul, Ephèse et Izmir: Discours du Pape Paul VI au Chef des Musulmans" (Istanbul, Juillet 25, 1967), online: http://www.vatican.va/holy_father/paul_vi/speeches/1967/july/documents/hf_p-vi_spe_19670725_comunita-musulmana_fr.html, access: March 27, 2011.

[492]   The *Joint Declaration* was proclaimed and signed in Phanar, on the feast of St. Andrew, 1979. See: "Joint Declaration of Pope John Paul II and the Ecumenical Patriarch Dimitrios I" (November 30, 1979), online: http://www.vatican.va/roman_curia/pontifical_councils/chrstuni/ch_orthodox_docs/rc_pc_chrstuni_doc_19791130_jp-ii-dimitrios-i_en.html, access: March 27, 2011.

[493]   Ibid.

In 1981, the Holy Father used the occasion to benefit from a four-hour techni-cal stop on the way to the Philippines during his ninth foreign pastoral visit, and on February 16, the Pope met with the Pakistani people in Karachi.[494] The main goal of his visit was to strengthen the small Catholic community in their faith and pro-mote dialogue with Muslims.[495] In both his welcome and farewell addresses, as well as in the homily during the Holy Mass at Cricket Garden Stadium in Karachi, the Pope expressed his satisfaction about the fruitful cooperation between the Catholic Church and the Pakistani (Muslim) Government in the spheres of education, social and charity work. Moreover, in his farewell speech to the people of Pakistan, John Paul II expressed his appreciation for their rich cultural heritage. While addressing the issue of interreligious dialogue, the Holy Father emphasized the role of such a dialogue for the development and benefit of society and pointed out the need "to discover common concerns which are shared by all men and women of goodwill."[496] Furthermore, with regard to the issue of Christian-Muslim cooperation, the Pontiff expressed his gratitude for the strengthening of the bonds which unite the followers of both religions and urged them to continue on the path of dialogue. He said:

> I am thinking in a particular way of the bonds of dialogue and trust which have been forged between the Catholic Church and Islam. By means of dialogue we have come to see more clearly the many values, practices and teachings which both our religious tra-ditions embrace…I pray that the mutual understanding and respect between Christians and Muslims, and indeed between all religions, will continue and grow deeper, and that we will find still better ways of cooperation and collaboration for the good of all.[497]

John Paul II's visit to Morocco in 1985, a country with a very small Catholic minority (0.2% of the population), was primarily directed towards encouraging and promoting Christian-Muslim dialogue.[498] In his homily, during the Mass at the Insti-tute of Charles de Foucault,[499] attended by representatives of the Moroccan Catholic

---

[494] John Paul II's ninth pilgrimage included Pakistan, the Philippines, Guam (USA), Japan, and Anchorage (USA), (February 16-27, 1981). Paul VI visited Pakistan on November 27, 1970.

[495] Pakistan: population187,342,721, Muslim 95% (Sunni 75%, Shi'a 20%), other (includes Christian and Hindu) 5%; "Pakistan," online: https://www.cia.gov/library/publications/the-world-factbook/geos/pk.html, access: October 30, 2011.

[496] John Paul II, "To the People of Pakistan" (Karachi, February 16, 1981), in: F. Gioia (ed.), *Interreligious Dialogue…*, p. 235, paragraph 361.

[497] Ibid., p. 235, paragraph 362.

[498] Morocco: population 31,968,361, Muslim 99%, Christian 1%; "Morocco," online: https://www.cia.gov/library/publications/the-world-factbook/geos/mo.html, access: October 30, 2011.

[499] Charles de Foucault (1858-1916) was a priest and a missionary, who from 1901 lived among the Tuaregs of the Hoggar and had a great respect for their culture and faith. He wanted to be among those who were abandoned and needed help. De Foucault wanted all who drew close to him to find in him a brother, "a universal brother." See: A. Merad, *Christian Hermit in an Islamic World: A Muslim's View of Charles de Foucauld*; trans., foreword and afterword Z. Hersov, New York: Paulist Press, 1999.

community, the Holy Father spoke about the gift of love and respect towards Muslims. He also emphasized the need for further development of the Christian-Muslim dialogue and cooperation in the spirit of the Second Vatican Council and related efforts of Pope Paul VI.[500]

There is no doubt that the most important point from the program of John Paul II's visit to Morocco was his meeting with young Muslims in Casablanca. The reception of the Pope's words about the past and present state of Christian-Muslim dialogue and cooperation, together with his reflections on future perspectives in this domain as well as on general human concerns, was astonishing.[501] This meeting left a long-lasting impression on the Pope and he recalled it in his book *Crossing the Threshold of Hope*:

> The trip I made to Morocco at the invitation of King Hasan II can certainly be defined as a historic event. It was not simply a courtesy visit, but an event of a truly pastoral nature. The encounter with the young people at Casablanca Stadium (August 19, 1985) was unforgettable. The openness of the young people to the Pope's words was striking when he spoke of faith in one God. It was certainly an unprecedented event.[502]

In the 1990s, John Paul II went on pilgrimages to Sudan (1993), Tunisia (1996) and Lebanon (1997).

With John Paul II's growing involvement in resolving the Middle Eastern political problems, his voice in the defense of religious freedom for Christian minorities sounded stronger; the best example was his visit to Sudan, considered one of the most difficult pastoral missions undertaken during his pontificate. For ten years, the country had been overcome by civil war between the North (inhabited by Arab Muslims) and the South (inhabited by Christians), considered by many to be a religious war. Although Christians were suffering the tragic consequences of this war, the government repeatedly denied such facts. The official announcement of the Pope's visit to Khartoum for the first liturgical celebration of Blessed Bakhita was issued on December 22, 1992, by both the Holy See and the Sudanese Government. The reaction from mass media was rather positive and quite optimistic. Two Arabic newspapers, *Al-Inqādh Al-Waṭanī (The National Salvation)* and *As-Sūdān Al-Ḥadīth (The Modern Sudan)*, pointed out that, for the first time in history, a Pope was coming to Sudan, a country of dialogue, good relations and of well-known religious tolerance, and that this important event would take place at the same time as the scheduled Confer-

---

[500]   See: "Voyage Apostolique au Togo, en Côte D'Ivoire, au Cameroun, en République Centrafricaine, au Zaïre, au Kenya, au Maroc: Messe à L'Institut 'Charles de Foucauld': Homélie du Pape Jean-Paul II" (Casablanca, Août 19, 1985), online: http://www.vatican.va/holy_father/john_paul_ii/homilies/1985/documents/hf_jp-ii_hom_19850819_casablanca_fr.html, access: March 27, 2011.

[501]   The meeting with young Muslims in Casablanca, and in particular the address of John Paul II, was already discussed in Chapter III, p. 92-94.

[502]   John Paul II, *Crossing...*, p. 94.

ence on Religious Dialogue. Muslim preachers supported the Pope's visit from the pulpits, considering it a good occasion for the Pope to see for himself the peaceful co-existence, the religious tolerance and the rights enjoyed by the Ahl al-Kitāb (the People of the Book), among them Christians. The comments coming from Muslim fundamentalists were far from favorable ones. As for the reaction from the Catholics, the mass media rather refrained from commenting on this matter.[503]

Under the circumstances, during his Pastoral mission to Sudan (February 10-11, 1993), John Paul II's objective was to strengthen Christians in their faith, making them aware that, although a minority, they were a very active and very important minority whose existence should not be ignored. There is no doubt that the Pope's visit raised both hopes and fears in those who were well aware of the real situation in the country and not comfortable with the present attitude of the political authorities. However, it might have been expected that Pope John Paul II, who was already known for his courage and determination in the defense of human rights, would not refrain from addressing the issue of the civil war in Sudan and would stand in solidarity with Christians suffering from discrimination, being deprived of their basic rights, in particular that of religious freedom. On February 10, 1993, in his homily delivered during the Eucharistic Celebration in Khartoum at Green Square in honor of blessed Josephine Bakhita, while greeting the entire Muslim community, the Holy Father stated that he came to Sudan to appeal for "*a new relationship between Christians and Muslims in this land*," saying:

> I repeat now the conviction which I know was shared by the Muslims present at that meeting: "that genuine religious belief is a source of mutual understanding and harmony, and that only the perversion of religious sentiment leads to discrimination and conflict".[504]

Furthermore, John Paul II explained that under no circumstances was it permissible "to use religion as an excuse for injustice and violence" and that such an abuse deserved to "be condemned by all true believers in God."[505] Appalled by the continuous religious conflict in the South, he said:

> Religious freedom is a right which every individual has because it springs from the inalienable dignity of each human being. It exists independently of political and social structures and, as has been stated in a host of international Charters, the State has the obligation to defend this freedom from attack or interference...Today the Successor of

---

[503] See: "The Pope's Visit to the Sudan: A Survey through the Sudanese Press," *Encounter: Documents for Muslim-Christian Understanding*, no. 195-196 (1993), p. 3-27.

[504] "Apostolic Journey to Benin, Uganda and Khartoum (Sudan): Eucharistic Concelebration in Honor of Blessed Josephine Bakhita: Homily of His Holiness John Paul II" (Khartoum, February 10, 1993), no. 3, online: (http://www.vatican.va/holy_father/john_paul_ii/homilies/1993/documents/hf_jp-ii_hom_19930210_khartoum_en.html, access: March 27, 2011.

[505] Ibid., no. 3.

Peter and the whole Church reaffirm their support of your Bishops' insistent call for respect of your rights as citizens and as believers.[506]

A complete lesson on the rights of religious minorities, and in particular the right of religious freedom, was given in John Paul II's address during his meeting with General Al-Bashīr, the President of the Republic of Sudan. While expressing his hope, born of confidence that "peace is always possible," the Pope explained that man "is capable of finding just solutions to situations of conflict, no matter how long they have been going on and no matter how intricate the motives which caused them" and that the "efforts to restore harmony depend on the parties involved being willing and determined to implement the conditions required for peace."[507]

There is no doubt that in the course of the twentieth century, mistreatment of minorities prompted the international community to enshrine in international accords the rights of such groups. However, as John Paul II emphasized, in this case "the translation of intent into law and behavior in each nation is the measure of that country's maturity, and the guarantee of its capacity to foster peaceful coexistence within its own borders and to contribute to peace in the world."[508] The Church, the Pope continued, "approaches this question from an eminently moral and humanitarian point of view," calling for observation of "the universal obligation to understand and respect the variety and richness of other peoples, societies, cultures and religions," so that "minorities within a country have the right to exist, with their own language, culture and traditions, and the state is morally obliged to leave room for their identity and self-expression."[509] Moreover, it is upon the state "to respect and defend the differences existing among its citizens, and to permit their diversity to serve the common good." Also, the experience shows that "peace and internal security can only be guaranteed through respect for the rights of all those for whom the state has responsibility."[510] Therefore, as the Holy Father stated:

> In such a perspective, the freedom of individuals and communities *to profess and practice their religion* is an essential element for peaceful human coexistence. Freedom of conscience and freedom to seek the truth and to act according to one's personal religious beliefs are so fundamentally human that any effort to restrict them almost inevitably leads to bitter conflict.

All in all, with regard to the well-being of the society, the Pope concluded:

---

[506]   Ibid., no. 4.

[507]   "Pastoral Journey to Benin, Uganda and Khartoum (Sudan): Meeting with General Omar Hassan Ahmed Al-Bashir, President of the Republic of the Sudan: Address of His Holiness John Paul II" (Khartoum, February 10, 1993), no. 2, online: http://www.vatican.va/holy_father/john_paul_ii/speeches/1993/february/documents/hf_jp-ii_spe_19930210_presidente-sudan_en.html, access: March 27, 2011.

[508]   Ibid., no. 4.

[509]   Ibid., no. 5

[510]   Ibid.

Where relations between groups within a Nation have broken down, dialogue and negotiation are the obligatory paths to peace. Reconciliation in accordance with justice, and respect for the legitimate aspirations of all sectors of the national community must be the rule. To guarantee the participation of minorities in political life is a sign of a morally mature society, and brings honor upon those nations in which all citizens are free to share in national life in a climate of justice and peace.[511]

As mentioned previously, John Paul II's pastoral visit to Sudan was considered a real challenge for two reasons: his charisma and diplomacy. As recalled by Arturo Mari, because of the weight of the issues addressed, the Pope's meeting with the President required a second unofficial session.[512]

During the other two pastoral missions in the 1990s, namely to Tunisia (1996) and Lebanon (1997), John Paul II's attention was focused on the development of Christian-Muslim dialogue as a vehicle for both strengthening Christians in their faith and helping them to engage without fear in everyday mutual cooperation with Muslims in various spheres of life.

The visit to Tunisia was one of the shortest but the mission with which John Paul II went with there was of great importance.[513] The Holy Father met with 600 representatives of the world of culture, politics and religion at the Presidential Palace of Carthage (April 14, 1996). While referring to the glorious history of Christianity in Tunisia and the great contribution of Arab civilization to the development of the region, admiring the achievements of Ibn Khaldūn (1332-1406), the precursor of modern "historical and sociological thought," the Pope pointed out the importance of cultural exchange between people from Christian and Islamic worlds. Furthermore, he encouraged undertaking new initiatives and following successful already-realized ones, such as Islamic-Christian colloquia and a variety of common projects organized by the Centre d'Études et de Recherches Économiques et Sociales in Tunisia.[514]

The issue of the peaceful coexistence of various religious groups in Lebanon had been on John Paul II's agenda since the beginning of his pontificate.[515] Therefore,

---

[511]   Ibid.

[512]   As Arturo Mari recalled, the Pope's straightforward appeal to end the war and implement justice and respect for human rights in Sudan during the unofficial meeting with the President 'Umar Ḥasan Aḥmad al-Bashīr was deliberate and emotional. John Paul II did not spare his efforts to articulate his decisive stand on people's right to religious freedom. See: A. Mari, *Do zobaczenia w raju*, in conversation with J. Mikołajewski, foreword S. Dziwisz, Poznań: TVP Promotion Design, 2005, p. 99.

[513]   Tunisia: population 10,629,186, Muslim 98%, Christian 1%, Jewish and other 1%; "Tunisia," online: https://www.cia.gov/library/publications/the-world-factbook/geos/ts.html, access: October 30, 2011.

[514]   See: "Voyage Apostolique en Tunisie: Rencontre avec les représentants du monde politique, culturel et religieux: Discours du Saint-Père Jean-Paul II" (Avril 14, 1996): online: http://www.vatican.va/holy_father/john_paul_ii/speeches/1996/april/documents/hf_jp-ii_spe_19960414_world-culture_fr.html, access: March 27, 2011.

[515]   Lebanon: population 4,143,101 Muslim 59.7% (Shi'a, Sunni, Druze, Isma'ilite, Alawite or Nusayri), Christian 39% (Maronite Catholic, Greek Orthodox, Melkite Catholic, Armenian

the Pope's pilgrimage to this country was very much awaited.[516] In his speech during the welcome ceremony, John Paul II mentioned the heritage of his predecessor Paul VI, and in particular his concern for Lebanon, which he considered a living example of harmonious coexistence between Christians and Muslims. He also pointed out that this country, "while preserving her particular treasures and remaining faithful to herself, must be able to embrace new realities of the modern society and to take full place in the community of nations."[517] Therefore, the main aim of his pastoral visit to Lebanon on May 10-11, 1997 was to conclude the Special Assembly for Lebanon of the Synod of Bishops, i.e., the signing and proclamation of the apostolic exhortation *New Hope for Lebanon*.[518] In his homily during Mass at the Naval Base in Beirut, the Holy Father explained:

> Almost two years ago the Synodal Assembly conducted its work in Rome. But the solemn part of it, the publication of the Post-Synodal Document, is taking place now, here in Lebanon. These circumstances enable me to be in your land, for the first time, and to tell you of the love that the Church and the Apostolic See have for your nation, for all Lebanese people: for the Catholics of the different rites — Maronite, Melkite, Armenian, Chaldean, Syrian, Latin; for the faithful belonging to other Christian Churches; as well as for the Muslims and the Druze, who believe in the one God.[519]

This document, as the Pope emphasized, not only confirmed the importance of Lebanon, its historical mission of proving how different faiths can live together in peace, brotherhood and cooperation, but should also become "the contribution of the universal Church to the greater unity of the Catholic Church in Lebanon, to the overcoming of divisions between the different Churches and to the development of the country, in which all Lebanese are called to take part."[520] The Pope renewed, once again, his appeal to stop fighting and strive for peace and reconciliation.

Orthodox, Syrian Catholic, Armenian Catholic, Syrian Orthodox, Roman Catholic, Chaldean, Assyrian, Coptic, Protestant), other 1.3%; "Lebanon," online: https://www.cia.gov/library/publications/the-world-factbook/geos/le.html, access: October 30, 2011. About the situation of Christians in Lebanon, see: A. Sfeir, "Chrześcijanie...," p. 130-133.

[516] After three cancelled attempts John Paul II finally visited Lebanon in 1997 (G. O'Connor, *Universal Father...*, p. 339).

[517] "Apostolic Journey of His Holiness John Paul II to Lebanon (May 10-11, 1997): Arrival Ceremony at Beirut International Airport, Speech of Pope John Paul II" (May 10, 1997), no. 2, online: http://www.vatican.va/holy_father/john_paul_ii/travels/documents/hf_jp-ii_spe_10051997_lebanon-arrival_en.html, access: March 27, 2011.

[518] "Exhortation apostolique post-synodale: une espérance nouvelle pour le Liban de sa sainteté Jean-Paul II aux patriarches, aux évêques, au clergé, aux religieux, aux religieuses et à tous les fidèles du Liban," online: http://www.vatican.va/holy_father/john_paul_ii/apost_exhortations/documents/hf_jp-ii_exh_19970510_lebanon_fr.html, access: March 27, 2011 .

[519] "Apostolic Journey of His Holiness John Paul II to Lebanon (May 10-11, 1997): Homily during Mass at a Naval Base in Beirut" (May 11, 1997), no. 1, online: http://www.vatican.va/holy_father/john_paul_ii/travels/documents/hf_jp-ii_hom_11051997_en.html, access: March, 27, 2011.

[520] "Apostolic Journey of His Holiness John Paul II to Lebanon (May 10-11, 1997): Arrival Ceremony..."

The last three pilgrimages, namely to Egypt (2000), Jordan (2000) and Syria (2001), related to the "Jubilee Pilgrimage to the Holy Land" were ones of great significance and universal dimension.

In February 2000, the Holy Father went to Egypt with his Jubilee Pilgrimage to Mount Sinai ("in the footsteps of Moses"). On February 24, during his welcome address at the airport in Cairo, where he was greeted by the highest political and religious authorities, John Paul II expressed his gratitude for the possibility to "[visit] and [pray] at the places specially linked to God's interventions in history," and "to go to where God revealed his name to Moses and gave his Law as a sign of his great mercy and kindness towards his creatures."[521]

While referring to the historical significance of Egypt, the Pope stated that "[t]his is the land of a five thousand-year-old civilization…where different cultures met and mingled," which had made a significant contribution to "preserving the spiritual and cultural traditions of the church" and bringing Islamic "splendors of art and learning which have had a determining influence on the Arab world and on Africa."[522] Moreover, "Egypt has for centuries pursued the ideal of national unity," and, as he emphasized, "differences of religion were never barriers, but a form of mutual enrichment in the service of the one national community."[523] According to the Holy Father, the new millennium required that the Egyptian people not only continue along the lines of their glorious past but also that they meet the challenges of the modern world by strengthening religious bonds among Catholics, promoting Christian unity, and pursuing the task of developing Christian-Muslim dialogue and cooperation.[524]

Concerns for the Catholic minority were addressed by John Paul II in his homily during Mass in the Indoor Stadium in Cairo attended by representatives of all of Egypt's Catholic Churches, namely Coptic, Latin, Maronite, Greek (Melkite), Armenian, Syrian and Chaldean.[525] Having in mind the need of strengthening the Egyptian Catholics in their faith, John Paul II called upon the older generation to help young people to discover "the face of God, to show them the path to follow, the path of personal encounter with God and the human acts worthy of our divine filiation, a path which is certainly demanding, but a path of liberation which alone will fulfill their desire for happiness."[526]

---

[521] "Jubilee Pilgrimage of His Holiness John Paul II to Mount Sinai: Speech of the Holy Father John Paul II at the Arrival Ceremony" (Cairo, February 24, 2000), no. 1, online: http://www.vatican.va/holy_father/john_paul_ii/travels/documents/hf_jp-ii_spe_20000224_egypt-arrival_en.html, access: March 27, 2011.

[522] Ibid., no. 1, 2.

[523] Ibid., no. 2.

[524] About the situation of Christians in Egypt, see: A. Sfeir, "Chrześcijanie…," p. 128-130.

[525] Egypt: population 82,079,636, Muslim (mostly Sunni) 90%, Coptic 9%, other Christian 1%; "Egypt," online: https://www.cia.gov/library/publications/the-world-factbook/geos/eg.html, access: October 30, 2011.

[526] "Jubilee Pilgrimage of His Holiness John Paul II to Mount Sinai: Mass in the Indoor Stadium of Cairo, Homily of the Holy Father John Paul II" (February 25, 2000), no. 8, online: http://

The issue of Christian unity was elaborated by John Paul II at the Ecumenical Meeting at the New Cathedral of Our Lady, where he met with His Holiness Pope Shenouda, the head of the Orthodox Coptic Church, His Beatitude Patriarch Stephanos II Ghattas, the Patriarch of Catholic Copts, the Distinguished Representative of His Holiness Petros and Bishops and Dignitaries of the Churches and Ecclesial Communities of Egypt. In his speech, the Holy Father referenced the *Common Declaration* (1973) of Pope Paul VI and Pope Shenuda III. While referring to all Christians' "communion in the one Lord Jesus Christ, in the one Holy Spirit and in one baptism," he appealed for better understanding, reconciliation and unity among the Egyptian Christians. The Holy Father also pointed out that at the beginning of the new millennium, the matter of bearing common witness to Christian faith "in a whole range of ways" posed "enormous challenges to the human family."[527] He said:

> There is no time to lose!…We must avoid anything which might lead, once again, to distrust and discord…We do not know each other sufficiently: let us therefore find ways to meet! Let us seek viable forms of spiritual communion…Let us find forms of practical cooperation, especially in response to the spiritual thirst of so many people today, for the relief of their distress, in the education of the young, in securing humane conditions of life, in promoting mutual respect justice and peace, and in advancing religious freedom as a fundamental human right.[528]

In Egypt, the majority of the population is Muslim, and, therefore, it was very important for the Pope, during his visit there, to take the opportunity to speed up the process of developing interreligious dialogue and cooperation. John Paul II met and spoke with Muḥammad Sayyid Ṭanṭāwī, the Grand Sheikh of al-Azhar and religious leader of the Muslim community. It was the Pope's wish that during the Jubilee Pilgrimage to Mount Sinai, the representatives of non-Christian religions would pray together there. However, for various reasons, this was impossible, and the Holy Father had to pray "alone." His visit to Saint Catherine's Monastery at the foot of Mount Sinai was not only "a moment of intense prayer for peace and for interreligious harmony," but also a confirmation of the Pope's sincere "commitment to interreligious dialogue, a great sign of hope for the peoples of the world."[529] In his homily during the celebration of the Word at Mount Sinai, John Paul II expressed his great

---

www.vatican.va/holy_father/john_paul_ii/travels/documents/hf_jp-ii_hom_20000225_cairo_en.html, access: March 27, 2011.

[527] "Jubilee Pilgrimage of His Holiness John Paul II to Mount Sinai: Ecumenical Meeting at the New Cathedral of Our Lady of Egypt, Speech of the Holy Father John Paul II" (Cairo, February 25, 2000), no. 5, online: http://www.vatican.va/holy_father/john_paul_ii/travels/documents/hf_jp-ii_spe_20000225_egypt-ecumen_en.html, access: March 27, 2011.

[528] Ibid.

[529] "Jubilee Pilgrimage of His Holiness John Paul II to Mount Sinai: Celebration of the Word at the Mount Sinai, Homily of the Holy Father John Paul II" (February 26, 2000), no. 1, online: http://www.vatican.va/holy_father/john_paul_ii/travels/documents/hf_jp-ii_hom_20000226_sinai_en.html, access: March 27, 2011.

joy to be in the place where God revealed "the magnificent mystery of his faithful Love for all humankind," where "he revealed his name!" and "he gave his Law, the Ten Commandments of the Covenant!"[530] Using the occasion, the Pope addressed the issue of the universal meaning of this Law, saying:

> The Ten Commandments are not an arbitrary imposition of a tyrannical Lord. They were written in stone; but before that, they were written on the human heart as the universal moral law, valid in every time and place. Today as always, the Ten Words of the Law provide the only true basis for the lives of individuals, societies and nations. Today as always, they are the only future of the human family. They save man from the destructive force of egoism, hatred and falsehood.[531]

John Paul II continued his catechesis related to the issue of peace in the Middle Eastern region in March 2000, during his visit to Jordan. After his pastoral mission to Egypt, this was the subsequent stage of his Jubilee Pilgrimage to the places connected with the life and mission of Jesus.[532] In Jordan, the overwhelming majority of population, i.e., almost 99% is Muslim, and Catholics of different rites constitute about 1% of the population.[533] As for the Palestinians, among them are refugees from Israel, who constitute about 40% of the population. Under the circumstances, for John Paul II, it was not only important to strengthen the local Catholics in their faith, but also to encourage them to engage in a dialogue with Muslims, so that together they could reach a peaceful resolution of the conflicts in the Middle East. On March 20, 2000, during his speech at the welcome ceremony in Amman, the Holy Father addressed this issue as follows:

> In this area of the world there are grave and urgent issues of justice, of the rights of peoples and nations, which have to be resolved for the good of all concerned and as a condition for lasting peace. No matter how difficult, no matter how long, the process of seeking peace must continue. Without peace, there can be no authentic development for this region, no better life for its peoples, no brighter future for its children... Building a future of peace requires an ever more mature understanding and ever more practical cooperation among the peoples who acknowledge the one true, indivisible God, the Creator of all that exists. The three historical monotheistic religions count peace, goodness and respect for the human person among their highest values.[534]

---

[530] Ibid., no. 1.

[531] Ibid., no. 3.

[532] The Pope visited the Monastery of Moses on Mount Nebo, Madaba, the Jordanian Christian center with the sixth-century mosaic map of the Holy Land, and Wādī al-Kharrār, where he met with the Latin Patriarch of Jerusalem, Mīshīl Ṣabbāḥ.

[533] Jordan: population 6,508,271, Sunni Muslim 92% (official), Christian 6% (majority Greek Orthodox, but some Greek and Roman Catholics, Syrian Orthodox, Coptic Orthodox, Armenian Orthodox, and Protestant denominations), other 2% (several small Shi'a Muslim and Druze populations); "Jordan," online: https://www.cia.gov/library/publications/the-world-factbook/geos/jo.html, access: October 30, 2011.

[534] "Jubilee Pilgrimage of His Holiness John Paul II to the Holy Land (March 20-26, 2000): Speech of the Holy Father John Paul II at the Welcome ceremony in Jordan" (Amman, March

Referring to the role of the Catholic Church in Jordan, the Pope pointed out that it "is always eager to cooperate with individual nations and people of goodwill in promoting and advancing the dignity of the human person." Moreover, the Holy Father spoke about his appreciation for the Church's engagement in "its schools and education programs, and through its charitable and social institutions."[535]

As for the Papal concern for peace in the Middle East, this issue was addressed further during Mass at the Amman Stadium. John Paul II spoke there about the urgent need for greater Christian unity and interfaith cooperation, assessing the progress already made in those domains. He said:

> During the last five years, the Church in this region has been celebrating the Pastoral Synod of the Churches in the Holy Land. All the Catholic Churches together have walked with Jesus and heard his call anew, setting out the path ahead in a General Pastoral Plan...The Synod has made clear that your future lies in unity and solidarity. I pray today, and I invite the whole Church to pray with me, that the Synod's work will bring a strengthening of the bonds of fellowship and cooperation between the local Catholic communities in all their rich variety, between all the Christian Churches and Ecclesial Communities, and between Christians and the other great religions which flourish here.[536]

In May 2001, the Pope visited Syria. This was the Jubilee Pilgrimage "in the footsteps of Saint Paul the Apostle." The visit to Syria was a part of John Paul II's ninety-third apostolic journey, considered one of the most difficult pilgrimages of his pontificate. It was an occasion for the Holy Father to address once again the issue of Christian unity, interreligious dialogue and to repeat his tireless appeal for peace in the entire Middle Eastern area.

The Christian minority in Syria constitutes about 10% of the population.[537] There are six Catholic Churches, namely Latin, Maronite, Greek (Melkite), Armenian, Syrian and Chaldean and three Orthodox Churches, i.e., Greek, Syrian and Jacobite. It is worth mentioning that in modern Syria there are important places related to the history of Christianity, in particular Antioch.[538]

---

[535] 20, 2000), no. 2, online: http://www.vatican.va/holy_father/john_paul_ii/travels/documents/ hf_jp-ii_spe_20000320_jordan-arrival_en.html, access: March 27, 2011.

Ibid., no. 3.

[536] "Jubilee Pilgrimage of His Holiness John Paul II to the Holy Land (March 20-26, 2000): Homily of the Holy Father, Jordan – Amman Stadium" (Amman, March, 21, 2000), no. 5, online: http://www.vatican.va/holy_father/john_paul_ii/travels/documents/hf_jp-ii_hom_ 20000321_amman_en.html, access: March 27, 2011.

[537] Syria: population 22,517,750, Sunni Muslim 74%, other Muslim (includes Alawite, Druze) 16%, Christian (various denominations) 10%, Jewish (tiny communities in Damascus, Al Qamishli, and Aleppo); "Syria," online: https://www.cia.gov/library/publications/the-world-factbook/geos/sy.html, access: October 30, 2011. About the situation of Christians in Syria, see: A. Sfeir, "Chrześcijanie...," p. 133-136.

[538] This city was known as an important spiritual center during the first centuries of Christianity in the East. For a thorough account on the history of the Melkite Church in Syria, see:

On May 6, 2001, during the welcome ceremony in Damascus, the Pontiff recalled Syria's "magnificent" contribution to the history of Christianity, emphasized the significance of "the great cultural influence of Syrian Islam" and expressed his hopes that this country would "spare no effort to work for greater harmony and cooperation among the peoples of the region, in order to bring lasting benefits not only to [the Syrian] land, but also to other Arab countries and the whole international community."[539] The Holy Father addressed the complex problems of modern Syria later the same day, in his homily at the Abbassyin Stadium. He said:

> With all your compatriots, without distinction of community, continue tirelessly your efforts to build a society marked by fraternity, justice and solidarity, where everyone's human dignity and fundamental rights are recognized. In this Holy Land, Christians, Muslims and Jews are called to work together, with confidence and boldness, and to work to bring about without delay the day when the legitimate rights of all peoples are respected and they can live in peace and mutual understanding.[540]

Furthermore, the Pontiff appealed to Christian families to remain strong in their faith and "give significant time to prayer, to listening to God's word and to Christian education" in order to "find effective support to tackle the difficulties of daily life and the great challenges of today's world."[541] He also expressed his deep conviction that if they put themselves "enthusiastically at the service of others," they would "find meaning" in their lives, because "Christian identity is not defined by opposition to others but by the ability to go out of oneself towards one's brothers and sisters."[542]

In his efforts to strengthen Christians in their faith, the Pope met with Christian youth. In his address at the Greek-Catholic Cathedral in Damascus, the Holy Father emphasized the need for better relations and closer cooperation between the Churches and Ecclesial Communities, and expressed his gratitude for the initiatives and activities that they had already undertaken. Moreover, John Paul II also urged and encouraged young Christians to reflect together on their Christian identity and work together for their future as Christians in Syria. He said:

> Strengthen the things that unite you. Meditate together on the Gospel, call upon the Holy Spirit, listen to the testimony of the Apostles, and pray with joy and thanksgiving. Love your ecclesial communities. They have handed on to you the faith and the testi-

---

K. Kościelniak, *Grecy i Arabowie...*

[539] "Welcome Ceremony in Damascus: Address of John Paul II" (May 5, 2001), no. 3-4, online: http://www.vatican.va/holy_father/john_paul_ii/speeches/2001/documents/hf_jp-ii_spe_20010505_president-syria_en.html, access: March 27, 2011.

[540] "Holy Mass at the Abbassyin Stadium of Damascus: Homily of John Paul II" (May 6, 2001), no. 4, online: http://www.vatican.va/holy_father/john_paul_ii/homilies/2001/documents/hf_jp-ii_hom_20010506_damascus_en.html, access: March 27, 2011.

[541] Ibid., no. 5.

[542] Ibid.

mony for which your forefathers often played a high price. They are counting on your courage and your holiness, which are the foundation of all true reconciliation. May the prayer of Christ "that all may be one" always resound in your hearts as an invitation and a promise! Your country is marked by fellowship between all parts of society.[543]

Moreover, the Pontiff expressed his conviction that thanks to the spirit of fraternity, Christians with a firm identity would feel like a real part of Syrian society and would be able "to make their own contribution, in freedom, to the common good."[544]

It is worth mentioning that the Holy Father's visit to Syria was an occasion to repeat his persistent call for peace in the Middle East. On May 7, 2001, during a prayer for peace at the Greek Orthodox Church in Quneitra at the Golan Heights, he said:

> *"Blessed are the peacemakers, for they shall be called sons of God"* (Mt 5:9). From this place, so disfigured by war, I wish to raise my heart and voice in prayer for peace in the Holy Land and in the whole world. Genuine peace is a gift from God. Our openness to that gift requires a conversion of heart and a conscience obedient to his Law. Mindful of the sad news of the conflicts and deaths which even today arrive from Gaza, my prayer becomes more intense.[545]

While discussing the significance of John Paul II's pilgrimage to Syria, it is important to point out that during his visit there, the world witnessed one of the most important events in the history of Christian-Muslim relations. On May 6, 2001, John Paul II was the first Pope in history to enter the Muslim mosque, namely the Umayyad Grand Mosque in Damascus.[546] This fact not only demonstrated his respect for Islam and the achievements of Muslim civilization, but also signified the importance attributed to Christian-Muslim dialogue and cooperation. The address of John Paul II to Muslim leaders during his historic visit to the Umayyad Grand Mosque in Damascus marked the beginning of a new stage in the relations between Christianity and Islam. The Pope said:

> I truly hope that our meeting today in the Umayyad Mosque will signal our determination to advance interreligious dialogue between the Catholic Church and Islam. This dialogue has gained momentum in recent decades; and today we should be grateful for the road we have traveled so far...The positive experiences must strengthen our com-

---

[543] "Youth Meeting at the Greek-Catholic Cathedral – Damascus: Address of John Paul II" (May 7, 2001), no. 6, online: http://www.vatican.va/holy_father/john_paul_ii/speeches/2001/documents/hf_jp-ii_spe_20010507_youth_en.html, access March 27, 2011.

[544] Ibid.

[545] "Prayer for Peace at the Greek-Orthodox Church in Quneitra: Address of John Paul II" (Golan Heights, May 7, 2001), online: http://www.vatican.va/holy_father/john_paul_ii/speeches/2001/documents/hf_jp-ii_spe_20010507_prayer-peace_en.html, access: March 27, 2011.

[546] This place is connected in particular way with St. John the Baptist. The mosque holds a shrine which still today contains the head of St. John the Baptist (Yaḥyā), honored as a prophet by both Christians and Muslims alike.

munities in the hope of peace…It is important that Muslims and Christians continue to explore philosophical and theological questions together, in order to come to a more objective and comprehensive knowledge of each other's religious beliefs. Better mutual understanding will surely lead, at the practical level, to a new way of presenting our two religions not in opposition as has happened too often in the past, but in partnership for the good of the human family.[547]

Moreover, this historic visit could be also considered a symbol of the Pope's concerns and his active engagement and tireless efforts in promoting religious freedom, justice and peace in the Middle East, i.e., in resolving the social and political predicament of this area that is so important for the whole world.

Summary

Peaceful coexistence in the Middle East, an area inhabited by numerous ethnic, national, linguistic and religious groups, was always on John Paul II's agenda, and the question of assuring religious freedom to each and every person living there of primary importance. Moreover, for John Paul II, assuring this fundamental human right was also a prerequisite for establishing a special conciliatory status for Jerusalem and the Holy Places that would respect religious minorities. Therefore, the Holy Father devoted much of his attention to both issues. He participated actively in all diplomatic efforts to resolve the issue of Jerusalem, and while visiting Muslim countries continued to both strengthen Christian minorities in their faith and encourage them to engage in a fruitful dialogue of life with Muslims.

As for to the issue of Jerusalem and the status of the Holy Places, Pope John Paul II consistently continued the policy of his predecessor, opposing any projects that would make Jerusalem a city belonging to a specific nation or coming under control of a particular religious group, and requesting a special status that would be guaranteed internationally. However, his position, as explained in *Redemptionis Anno*, was precisely defined and put in a receptive political context. According to the Pope, the internationally guaranteed special status of Jerusalem and the Holy Places should ensure special protection with complete equality of the religious and civil rights of the communities present in the city and safeguard both the right of Israel to secure borders and the right of the Palestinians to a homeland.

---

[547] John Paul II, "Meeting with the Muslim Leaders, Omayyad Great Mosque, Damascus: Address of the Holy Father" (May 6, 2001), no. 4, online: http://www.vatican.va/holy_father/john_paul_ii/speeches/2001/documents/hf_jp-ii_spe_20010506_omayyadi_en.html, access: March 27, 2011.

IV

Among the Middle Eastern problems involving the issue of religious freedom that needed special consideration was, according to the Pope, the protection of Christian minorities in the Middle East, and, in particular, of Catholics living side by side with Muslims. John Paul II closely followed the situation in the area at question and he received delegations representing Christian minorities from the Middle East, including those of Bishops on *ad limina* visits, at the Vatican. However, it appears as though the most important were his pilgrimages to Muslim countries. These pilgrimages had a three-fold aim: (1) strengthening Catholics in their faith, (2) promoting unity among Christians and (3) encouraging Christian-Muslim dialogue and cooperation in the various spheres of life. One may notice that the focal points of his visits significantly differed, depending on the overall socio-political situation, the condition of the Christian community and possible prospects for the successful development of Christian-Muslim dialogue. However, all his speeches to various communities and authorities in the Middle East had one point in common: the Pope's persistent appeal for assuring religious freedom to each and every person.

V

Engaging in resolving political problems in the Middle East

*The Holy Father's quest for dialogue and peaceful settlement
in the areas the Palestinian-Israeli conflict
and the war in Lebanon and in Iraq*

Since the middle of the twentieth century, the political tensions in the Middle East have been either focused on or related to the issue of the unresolved Palestinian-Israeli conflict, which over the last few decades has caused the outbreak of violence in different parts of the region as well as clashes of conflicting religious and political interests. Therefore, all the Middle Eastern problems, among them the Lebanese war that erupted in 1975, appear to be somehow related to the Palestinian-Israeli conflict and it is rather unlikely that other long-lasting peaceful settlements will be possible unless a suitable agreement between the Palestinians and the Israelis is reached.

The Palestinian-Israeli dispute began early in the twentieth century and it culminated with a clash between the Palestinian and the Israeli claims over the land of Palestine. This dispute has evolved into an open conflict with complex dimensions and many layers – political, socio-economic and psychological. The essence of the problem lies in the disjunctive claims of the Israelis and the Palestinians concerning the territory of Palestine.

As for the political causes of the conflict, the local Palestinian population ascribed them to the Zionist struggle and the determination to establish a state for the Jews in Palestine and a total rejection of such of aspirations. The creation of Israel in 1948 was met with military opposition from the local Palestinian population, and subsequently led to open armed conflicts between Arabs and Israelis in 1948, 1956,

1967 and 1973.[548] Over the past four decades, the existing tensions have resulted in numerous tragic events in the disputed area. With regard to the socio-economic dimension of the Palestinian-Israeli conflict, it has been manifested by the clash of a rich, well-organized, well-developed and industrial establishment of Jewish settlers supported by the West, with the Palestinian and Arab population still struggling to overcome their unresolved socio-economic predicament inherited from the times of the Ottoman Turks' domination.[549] The conflict also has an important psychological aspect that lies in a constant feeling of insecurity experienced by the involved parties. There is no doubt that the Israelis and the Palestinians are both victims and victimizers aspiring to secure some kind of firm psychological identity for themselves. They are in constant fear of one another. Their sense of insecurity and instability is rooted in the attachment that both groups have to the land of Palestine. As Irani points out, the rights of Israelis and Palestinians are in radical and apparently irreconcilable opposition.[550] The Israelis strongly deny the existence of Palestinian rights, and the Palestinians assert that their national claims are of more importance, as they are justified by historical fact and societal realities.

There is no doubt that the Palestinian-Israeli conflict has placed the papacy and the Church in a difficult position. They have been forced to reassess their attitudes and revise long-held prejudices with respect to both Jews and Muslims. Also, the Holy See has held a firm position for centuries about maintaining an impartial stand and therefore was destined to occasionally face various related challenges from Eastern Christian, especially Catholic, communities. Furthermore, it should be noted that the predicament of the Holy See that has been outlined was further complicated by the fact that the three monotheistic religions, namely Judaism, Christianity and Islam, have been fighting for survival, struggling with ethno-nationalistic implications and the incongruent interests of the various groups.

The Holy See's engagement in Middle Eastern political problems prior to the pontificate of John Paul II: the Palestinian-Israeli conflict and the Lebanese war

The Papacy's involvement in the complex of interrelated political, religious and social problems in the Middle East prior to the election of John Paul II was focused on three major issues: (1) the Palestinian-Israeli conflict, (2) the Lebanese war, and (3) the question of Jerusalem with the status of the Holy Places.

---

[548] For a complex discussion on the issues related to the establishment of Israel and the subsequent Arab-Israeli wars, see for example: W. L. Cleveland, *A History of the Modern Middle East*, Boulder: Westview Press, 1994, p. 222-258.

[549] See: P. Mansfield, *A History of the Middle East*, Toronto: Penguin Books: 1992, p. 24-34.

[550] G. E. Irani, *The Papacy and the Middle East...*, p. 12.

The Holy See's involvement in the issue of the Palestinian-Israeli conflict has been manifested on two interrelated and complementary levels: humanitarian-religious and diplomatic. The first one reveals the Papacy's full commitment to defending the right of people to self-determination and to justice and peace. The second, diplomatic, has been focused on three outcomes. The Holy See was determined (1) to recognize the legitimate rights of both the Palestinians and the Israelis, (2) to facilitate contact between the two parties involved in the conflict while using its capacity as a religious institution and (3) to act as a mediator between the Arabs and the Israelis.

As already mentioned, the main interest of the Holy See in the Middle East is the welfare of the Catholic minorities living in the region, among them many Palestinians. Therefore, from the beginning of the Palestinian-Israeli dispute, the Papacy adopted a sympathetic and supportive attitude to the plight of the Palestinians. Humanitarian help for refugees following the wars between Arabs and Israelis has remained one of its primary concerns. In order to respond adequately to the various needs of the Palestinian refugees, the Holy See established two important institutions, namely the Pontifical Mission for Palestine[551] and Bethlehem University.[552]

Since the beginning of its involvement in the Palestinian-Israeli conflict, the Holy See has always advocated the consolidation of peace through justice. Moreover, following the policy outlined by Vatican II, and especially after Paul VI's encyclical *Populorum Progressio*,[553] that advocacy evolved into a rather decisive stand.

---

[551] The Pontifical Mission for Palestine was founded in 1949 by Pope Pius XII in the view of the Church mission to secure immediate help and relief. The mission has provided goods and services for educational, religious, cultural and humanitarian needs. The main offices of the Pontifical Mission are in New York, regional offices in Beirut, Jerusalem, and Amman, and a liaison biuro is located in Rome. The fact that the activity of the Mission has remained one of the main concerns of the Papacy's policy in the Middle East had been clearly pointed out in a letter sent by Paul VI on July 16, 1974, to Monsignor John G. Nolan. In the letter, the Pope spoke about his "heartfelt sharing" in the suffering of the Palestinian people, and gave his "support for their legitimate aspirations." However, while sharing the Palestinian sense of frustration, Holy Father firmly condemned the recourse to arms and the violence. See: G. E. Irani, "The Israeli-Palestinian Conflict," in: K. C. Ellis (ed.), *The Vatican, Islam...*, p. 131.

[552] The establishment of Bethlehem University (October 1, 1973) was a result of Paul VI's efforts to improve the situation of young Palestinians. In order to prevent their exodus, the Pope undertook the task of providing them with a good-quality education and possible prospects for the future. Together with other academic institutions on the West Bank, Bethlehem University has quickly become a center for training young people to prepare them for the leadership of a possible future Palestinian state. The establishment of the University, directly supervised by the Holy See, proved to be an effective response to the Palestinians' educational needs. Furthermore, taking into consideration the Papal authority, the Israeli government had to become more careful in possible restrictions concerning the activities of that important institution of learning. See: Ibid., p. 133-136.

[553] The encyclical was published on March 26, 1967. In this document, Paul VI addressed the issue of dialogue between civilizations, pointing out that such a dialogue, an imperative of the

Since the mid 1960s, the Popes have condemned acts of terrorism and the use of force from both sides and have called for a just and equitable solution in the framework of adequate resolutions adopted by the United Nations. After the defeat of Arab armies in 1967, the Palestinians resorted to guerrilla warfare. The leaders of the Palestine Liberation Organization (PLO)[554] supported the guerrilla actions and the plans for the acquiring all of Palestine. Obviously, under the circumstances, that kind of response was not acceptable for Israel and the international community, including the Holy See. However, the events of 1973 convinced the PLO, led by Yāsir 'Arafāt,[555] to reassess and revise their policy. So, eventually, PLO leaders realized that the elimination of Israel and establishment of a single Palestinian state was no longer an advantageous solution. Moreover, that kind of program could even stand in the way of the PLO becoming the representative of the Palestinian people that would be accepted by most nations of the world. Taking into consideration the given realities, the moderate leaders under Yāsir 'Arafāt definitively changed their attitude, indicating their willingness to accept a more reasonable solution, namely a smaller Palestinian state, to be established on the West Bank of the Jordan River and the Gaza Strip. In order to pursue their goal, they turned to diplomatic and political means. That change of attitude on the part of the Palestinian leaders was met with a supportive response from most of the international community. They were convinced that a long-lasting solution to the Arab-Israeli dispute could not be achieved without providing for the political rights of the Palestinians. Therefore, most nations began to acknowledge the PLO as the legitimate representative of the Palestinian people and support the establishment of a Palestinian state. These new and promising developments also made it easier for the Holy See to publicly acknowledge Palestinian rights and establish official contacts with PLO representatives.

All the above-mentioned facts had an impact on Paul VI's public statements related to the Palestinian-Israeli dispute, and, from the mid-1970s, the Pope demonstrated his profound solicitude for the problem of peace in the Middle East and

---

modern society, should be focused on man: "Sincere dialogue between cultures, as between individuals, paves the way for ties of brotherhood. Plans proposed for man's betterment will unite all nations in the joint effort to be undertaken, if every citizen – be he a government leader, a public official, or a simple workman – is motivated by brotherly love and is truly anxious to build one universal human civilization that spans the globe. Then we shall see the start of a dialogue on man rather than on the products of the soil or of technology." *"Populorum Progressio:* Encyclical of Pope Paul VI on the Development of Peoples" (March 26, 1967), no. 73, online: http://www.vatican.va/holy_father/paul_vi/encyclicals/documents/hf_p-vi_enc_26031967_populorum_en.html, access: March 10, 2011.

[554] Palestine Liberation Organization (PLO): a political and paramilitary organization founded in 1964 by the Arab League, regarded by the Arab states as "sole legitimate representative of the Palestinian people."

[555] Yāsir 'Arafāt (1929-2004): the leader of the Palestine liberation movement, one of the founders of al-Fataḥ and the chairman of the PLO since 1969; Nobel Peace Prize winner (1994) and the first President of the Palestinian National Authority (1996-2004). See: S. K. Aburish, *Arafat: From Defender to Dictator*, New York & London: Bloomsbury Press, 1998.

firmly recognized the right of both peoples, namely the Palestinians and the Israelis, to self-determination and nationhood. On April 8, 1976, in his address to the Egyptian President Anwar Sādāt, who was visiting the Holy See for the first time, Paul VI stated:

> With deep concern for this generation and the generations yet to come, we extend our sincere encouragement to continue to seek the peaceful and just solution to the Arab-Israeli crisis. This must include an equitable solution also to the problem of the Palestinian people, for whose dignity and rights we have repeatedly expressed humanitarian and friendly interest.[556]

On December 15, 1977, Paul VI received the new ambassador of the Syrian Republic to the Holy See. In his address, the Pope once again spoke about the lot of the Palestinian people and his words related to their tragic experiences sounded even stronger.[557] In the last year of Paul VI's pontificate, his position on the Palestinian-Israeli problem remained the same. On April 29, 1978, in his address to Ḥusayn Ibn Ṭalāl, the King of Jordan, the Holy Father assured the world about his constant preoccupation with the situation in the Middle East and his commitment to the search for peace based on recognition of the legitimate demands of the involved parties. Furthermore, the Pope spoke about his particular concern with the problem of the Arab-Israeli crisis, and once again expressed his hope that:

> A just end may be put to the sad situation of the Palestinians, and that Jerusalem, the Holy City for the three great monotheistic religions of Judaism, Christianity and Islam, may really become the "high place" of peace and encounter for peoples from every part of the world who, in spite of their diversity, are joined in brotherhood by the worship they offer to the one and only God.[558]

In 1949, the Holy See established diplomatic relations with Lebanon. Since that time Lebanon has been important for the Papacy, as it is considered a living example and model of multiethnic and multireligious groups, in particular those of Christians and Muslims living together. After the Second Vatican Council, which gave both in-

---

[556] "Address of the Holy Father Paul VI to the Egyptian President…"

[557] The Pope said: "The Palestinian people…are of particular concern to us, since among others they have suffered and are suffering the most. On various occasions we have declared our profound sympathy with them. We consider that, in spite of the deplorable acts of violence with which their cause is at times proposed to world attention, it ought to be given most serious and generous consideration." "Address of the Holy Father Paul VI to the New Ambassador of the Syrian Arab Republic to the Holy See" (December 15, 1977), online: http://www.vatican. va/holy_father/paul_vi/speeches/1977/december/documents/hf_p-vi_spe_19771215_ambasciatore-rep-araba_en.html, access: March 29, 2011.

[558] "Address of the Holy Father Paul VI to King Hussein Ibn Talal of Jordan" (April 29, 1978), online: http://www.vatican.va/holy_father/paul_vi/speeches/1978/april/documents/hf_p-vi_spe_19780429_re-hussein-giordania_en.html, access: March 29, 2011.

spiration and encouragement for the ecumenical and interfaith movement officially acknowledged in related documents, Lebanon has become an ideal place for the application of the principles advocated during the Council, i.e., pluralism and respect for human rights.

From the beginning of the Lebanese war in 1975, the fundamental objective of the Holy See was to protect the Christian presence in Lebanon; in other words, to save the territorial integrity of the country and preserve the Lebanese formula of co-existence. The war in Lebanon itself became a series of confrontations between the Arabs and the Israelis. The country had been already involved passively in the Arab-Israeli conflict by giving asylum to waves of refugees since 1948. In 1970, with the Jordanian subjugation of the PLO, its involvement became active. Furthermore, with the increased engagement of the regional powers, namely Syria and Israel, Lebanon became a center of confrontation between the East and the West.

Since the beginning of the Lebanese war in 1975, as Irani pointed out, the role of the Holy See was guided by three major principles:

(1) no party in Lebanon should jeopardize Christian-Muslim dialogue, (2) the behaviour of some elements in the Christian community should not compromise the formula of coexistence sanctioned in the 1943 National Covenant and (3) the Palestinians, who for years have suffered exile, should not fall victims to a "new injustice in Lebanon.[559]

Obviously, the Lebanese war posed a serious threat to these objectives. Therefore, and in order to prevent the disruption of the Lebanese formula, the Holy See dispatched mediation and fact finding-missions to Lebanon.

The first mission, headed by Cardinal Paolo Bertoli, was sent in 1975, seven months after the beginning of the war. Its aim was to gather firsthand information. Furthermore, the delegation focused on establishing a dialogue between the parties in conflict, so the Lebanese formula of Christian-Muslim coexistence could be saved and the territorial integrity of Lebanon maintained.[560] The second mission in 1976, led by Monsignor Mario Brini, was organized primarily for pastoral and humanitarian considerations. Moreover, for the Holy See, it was also important to express his solicitude toward the Christian community in Lebanon and help the victims of the war.[561] Those missions confirmed that ecumenism and peaceful coexistence had high priority in Papal diplomacy in relation to Lebanon.

There is no doubt that in conflicts having ethnic and nationalistic aspects, any significant divisions, namely ideological, political and religious ones within the various groups, would definitely limit the effectiveness of the Holy See's involvement. This situation occurred in Lebanon. One could notice that the longer the conflict between

---

[559] G. E. Irani, *The Papacy and the Middle East...*, p. 102.
[560] See: Ibid., p. 126-131.
[561] See: Ibid., p. 131-134.

the various parties lasted, the more difficult the Papacy's role was, i.e., the harder it was to advocate and implement a frank and peaceful dialogue among the Lebanese.

As pointed out previously, the main objective of the Holy See was to preserve both the territorial integrity of Lebanon and the Lebanese formula of coexistence. Therefore, Pope Paul VI in his addresses and written statements emphasized his total support for the legitimate authorities represented by the President of the Republic of Lebanon and the conviction that since the war in Lebanon was a civil war, the Lebanese were alone capable of solving their problems.[562] The Holy See opted to act as a mediator and conciliator among various groups, emphasizing the inherent limits in the spiritual nature of his mission. However, there were many tensions between various Christian groups in Lebanon. Moreover, with the Holy See's perception that there was a definite link between the war in Lebanon and the Palestinian-Israeli conflict, there were misunderstandings and tensions between the Papacy and the Maronite leaders who opted for detaching the Lebanese war from regional problems.[563]

It should be mentioned that since the outbreak of the war, the Holy See had been in continuous contact with France, the United States and Syria in order to participate actively in the task of finding a suitable resolution to the strife in Lebanon. Furthermore, the Holy See coordinated his efforts with the American Catholic hierarchy, and, as Irani pointed out, "the active involvement of the Catholic community in the United States may have had an impact on US policy toward Lebanon."[564]

John Paul II's commitment to the struggle for justice and peace in the Middle East

There is no doubt that John Paul II unified the religious and the socio-political dimensions of the Church in an unprecedented fashion.[565] From the beginning of his pontificate, John Paul II displayed intense interest and involvement in peacekeeping and social justice in the Third World, linked with religious freedom and the observance of human rights everywhere. He modernized the Vatican, making it into a modern nation-state, turned it into a full-fledged player in world affairs, and established it as a state with ever-expanding diplomatic ties around the globe.[566] Further-

---

[562] For further discussion, refer to: G. E. Irani, *The Papacy and the Middle East...*, p. 116-123.

[563] There were controversies and polemics between Pope Paul VI and some Maronite religious and political leaders. The decision by Christian militias to establish contact with Israel was viewed negatively in Rome in the light of the harm it could do to the other Christian communities living in Arab countries. See: G. E. Irani, *The Papacy and the Middle East...*, p. 157.

[564] Ibid., p. 124.

[565] For a broad discussion on the issue, refer to: F. X. Murphy, *The Papacy...*, p. 177-239.

[566] See: R. B. Shelledy, "The Vatican's Role in Global Politics," *SAIS Review*, vol. 24 (Summer-Fall 2004), no. 2, p. 149-162.

more, he also stressed his particular concern with the situation in the Middle East, an area where political, social and religious tensions come to the fore and where a sincere dialogue seemed to fail.[567]

The Pope's strong voice was ever present in Middle Eastern affairs. John Paul II expressed his deep concern about the situation in the region on a number of occasions, constantly renewing his appeal for peace. He condemned the brutality of force in the area, demanded rapid political decisions concerning the conflicts in the Holy Land and in Lebanon, strongly opposed military interventions in Iraq, defended the rights of Palestinians and appealed for undertaking political measures "aimed at ensuring both to the State of Israel the just conditions of its security and to the Palestinian people their own indisputable rights."[568]

In his numerous speeches, letters and messages referring to the Middle East, John Paul II always focused on the special importance of the area and his conviction that "these lands, filled with history, the cradle of three great monotheistic religions, ought to be places where respect for the dignity of man as a creature of God, and for reconciliation and peace are self-evident."[569]

The Pope's involvement in the Middle East was essentially motivated by his desire to protect the welfare of Catholic minorities. John Paul II was alarmed to discover that the prospects for the survival of the indigenous Christian communities in the Holy Land were extremely precarious.[570] Thousands of Palestinians had left Jerusalem after 1967, under the pressure of Israeli occupation.[571] Therefore, from the beginning of his pontificate, the main focus of John Paul II's diplomacy in the Middle East was on the Palestinian-Israeli dispute. However, the election of John Paul II and his preoccupation with the situation in Lebanon also raised hopes among Lebanese people that the new Pope, because of his Polish background, his own traumatic experience with the destructive consequences of war, together with his strong determination to work for the cause of peace, would be more receptive to the plight of their country. The first few months of his pontificate proved that these hopes were correct.

On October 2, 1979, in his address to the United Nations, while referring to the situation in the Middle East, the Holy Father reasserted his commitment to justice and peace in the area and expressed his conviction that the just settlement of the Palestinian-Israeli conflict was the priority. Following the policy of his predecessor Paul VI, John Paul II explained:

---

[567] A. Kreutz, "The Vatican and the Palestinians: A Historical Overview," *Islamochristiana*, vol. 18 (1992), p.121.

[568] "The Holy Father's Address to the Diplomatic Corps Accredited to the Holy See" (January 12, 1991), *Islamochristiana*, vol. 17 (1991), p. 278.

[569] Ibid., p. 277. John Paul II was well aware that with regard to the question of peace in the Middle East, the interreligious dialogue there had to include a third party, namely the followers of Judaism, and therefore, as it is discussed later in this chapter, since the beginning of his pontificate he undertook the task of developing his dialogue with the Jews.

[570] About the situation of Christians in the Holy Land, see: A. Sfeir, "Chrześcijanie...," p. 137.

[571] A. Kreutz, *Vatican and the Palestinian-Israeli Conflict...*, p. 153-154.

While being prepared to recognize the value of any concrete step or attempt made to settle the conflict, I want to recall that it would have no value if it did not truly represent the "first stone" of a general overall peace in the area, a peace that, being necessarily based on equitable recognition of the rights of all, cannot fail to include the consideration and just settlement of the Palestinian question.[572]

The Pope then raised the issue of Lebanon which, according to him, was very much connected with the Palestinian-Israeli conflict and pointed out that "the tranquility, independence and territorial integrity of Lebanon within the formula that has made it an example of peaceful and mutually fruitful coexistence between distinct communities,"[573] should be assured due to the common efforts of the international community. Finally, following the policy line of his predecessor, John Paul II emphasized the need for "a special statute that, under international guarantees… would respect the particular nature of Jerusalem, a heritage sacred to the veneration of millions of believers of the three great monotheistic religions, Judaism, Christianity and Islam."[574]

The Pope's speech at the United Nations revealed a good grasp of the Middle Eastern predicament and indicated his strong determination to work for the cause of justice and peace in that area. During the subsequent months, John Paul II followed the situation in the region with attentiveness. In December (6-19, 1978), the third pontifical mission headed by Cardinal Paolo Bertoli was sent to Lebanon. This was a conciliatory mission with three purposes: (1) to unite and reconcile the Maronites, (2) to revive the formula of coexistence between Christians and Muslims and (3) to work on formulating a unified Lebanese position with regard to the possibility of permanent settlement of Palestinians in Lebanon. It should be mentioned that the Holy See's decision to send the mission to Lebanon was made in coordination and agreement with the United States, France, Great Britain and West Germany.[575]

The subsequent pontifical mission to Lebanon headed by Cardinal Agostino Cassaroli, the Holy See's Secretary of State, was sent in March (29-April 2), 1980, and it was primarily of a pastoral nature. However, the visit included talks with the Maronite leaders aimed at narrowing differences within the community and convincing them that, according to the Holy See, there was a definite link between the war in Lebanon and the Palestinian-Israeli conflict and that an "adequate resolution to the Palestinian question was of fundamental importance in order to attain peace in Lebanon."[576]

---

[572] "Apostolic Journey to the United States of America: Address of His Holiness John Paul II to the 34th General Assembly…," no. 10.

[573] Ibid.

[574] Ibid.

[575] As Irani mentioned, two weeks before dispatching the mission the Holy See sent letters to President Carter, President Valery Giscard d'Estaing, Prime Minister James Calahan and Chancellor Helmut Schmidt, and all of them approved that initiative (G. E. Irani, *The Papacy and the Middle East*…, p. 135).

[576] G. E. Irani, *The Papacy and the Middle East*…, p. 140.

The course of political developments in the region, as followed closely by John Paul II during first three years of his pontificate, including the Geula Cohen *Basic Law* to annex Jerusalem, as well as the Pope's official and unofficial meetings with political leaders, such as President Carter, King Ḥasan of Morocco, King Ḥusayn of Jordan, Vice-President Mubārak of Egypt, Israeli officials and PLO envoys, contributed significantly to his increased understanding of Middle Eastern problems, especially the Palestinian-Israeli dispute. The Pope's growing awareness of that issue was emotionally expressed in his speech delivered in Otranto, on October 5, 1980:

> The terms of the Middle East drama are well-known: the Jewish people, after tragic experiences connected with the extermination of so many sons and daughters, driven by the desire for security, set up the state of Israel. At the same time, the painful condition of the Palestinian people was created, a large part of whom are excluded from their land. These are facts that are before everyone's eyes. And other countries, such as Lebanon, are suffering as a result of a crisis that threatens to be a chronic one.[577]

As Weigel pointed out, the homily in Otranto "set the strategic framework for the Holy See's Middle East policy in the 1980s and 1990s.[578] Since John Paul II had not been part of the Vatican diplomatic process in the Middle East prior to his election, he was in a good position to look at the related issues from a new perspective. Furthermore, the Pontiff was fully aware and convinced that in the Middle East the political problems were interwoven with religious issues. He had at his disposal both the Second Vatican Council's teaching (*Nostra Aetate* no. 3 [on Islam] and no. 4 [on Judaism]) and the dialogical path established by Paul VI and outlined above. Therefore, he was not only able, but as his actions demonstrated, determined to introduce into the Middle Eastern policy a new, interreligious context and pursue the path of religious reconciliation between the followers of Judaism, Christianity and Islam.

The Otranto speech was a clear affirmation of the Holy See's recognition of the political rights of both the Jews and the Palestinians. With regard to the Palestinian-Israeli conflict, John Paul II fully supported the policy of Paul VI[579] and he began to take a firmer stand in defense of the rights of the Palestinian people. The moral conviction of the Pope that the security of one nation, namely the Israelis, could not be established by the violation of the rights of another one, i.e., the Palestinians, became the fundament of the Holy See's official position on the Israeli-Palestinian conflict for the years to come.

---

[577] "Visita pastorale ad Otranto: Omelia di Giovanni Paolo II" (October 5, 1980), no. 6, online: http://www.vatican.va/holy_father/john_paul_ii/homilies/1980/documents/hf_jp-ii_hom_19801005_otranto_it.html, access March 29, 2011. (English translation: *The Washington Post*, (October 6, 1980) quoted by G. E. Irani, *The Papacy and the Middle East...*, p. 29.)

[578] G. Weigel, *Witness to Hope...*, p. 701.

[579] A. Kreutz, "The Vatican and the Palestinians...," p. 120.

Israeli invasion of Lebanon and the Palestinian problem

Since the outbreak of war in 1975, the issue of Lebanon, considered a living example of a formerly relatively harmonious Christian-Muslim coexistence, had been one of the Papacy's priorities. Therefore, as previously mentioned, from the beginning of his pontificate, John Paul II followed the matter closely.

When in June 1982, Israel invaded Lebanon, John Paul II became the most outspoken defender of the Palestinians.[580] The day after the invasion (June 7, 1982), the Pope told President Regan, on an official visit to the Vatican, that the crisis in Lebanon "merits the attention of the world because [of] the danger it contains of further provocation in the Middle East with immense consequences for world peace."[581] On June 8, he sent a telegram to the Lebanese President Ilyās Sarkīs to express his preoccupation with the situation. He also gave his blessing to Mother Teresa of Calcutta, who was going to West Beirut to demonstrate solidarity with the victims of Israeli bombardment.[582] On September 15, the Pope met with Yāsir 'Arafāt.[583] During the audience, the Pontiff spoke against "recourse to arms and violence in any form and above all, to terrorism and reprisals," and once again called for a Middle East peace settlement that recognized "the right of the Palestinians to a country of their own."[584] The meeting was concluded by a joint statement condemning terrorism. The audience was strongly criticized by the Israelis.[585]

John Paul II's meeting with 'Arafāt also caused a further deterioration in the Holy See's relations with several personalities in the Maronite community who believed that Christians in the Middle East had no other recourse than armed self-defense against Muslims.[586] One day after the meeting, Israeli-sponsored Christian militias perpetrated a massacre against Palestinian civilians in the camps of Ṣabrā and Shātīlā (September 16-18, 1982). The Pope reacted by saying that there were

---

[580]   See: G. E. I r a n i, *The Papacy and the Middle East...*, p. 98-153.

[581]   Quoted by G. E. Irani (*The Papacy and the Middle East...*, p. 141) from *L'Osservatore Romano* (June 7-8, 1982).

[582]   As Cardinal S. Dziwisz recalled: "One day in the summer of 1982, she [Mother Teresa] unexpectedly showed up at Castel Gandolfo to ask for John Paul II's blessing before leaving for Lebanon. I brought her to see the Holy Father, who was just then receiving a group of young people. He asked her to sit next to him and explained to the kids that she was going to a country torn by a civil war. Mother Teresa went carrying a candle with an image of Our Lady on top. When she arrived in Beirut, she obtained a ceasefire for as long as the candle remained lit. This gave her the chance to get about seventy handicapped children, most of them Muslim, to safety." (S. D z i w i s z, *A Life with Karol...*, p. 175).

[583]   About the role of Italian politicians in organizing the meeting with 'Arafāt, see: J. Moskwa, *Prorok...*, p. 200-201.

[584]   M. P a r k e r, *Priest of the World's Destiny: John Paul II*, Milford, OH: Faith Publishing Company, 1995, p. 66.

[585]   J. Kwinty recalls the issue in his book: *Man of the Century...*, p. 456-457.

[586]   About the conflicts see: G. E. I r a n i, *The Papacy and the Middle East...*, p. 141-145.

"no sufficient words to condemn such crimes, which are repulsive to the human and Christian conscience."[587]

Following the Israeli invasion of 1982, for most of the decade, the situation in Lebanon was characterized by armed violence and the inability of the government to restore order.[588] Between 1983 and 1984, there were continuous misunderstandings between the Holy See and the Maronite leadership in Lebanon which resulted from the pro-Israeli attitude adopted by some Christians in Lebanon and Christian disobedience to the religious authority.[589] That, in turn, caused deepening of "the Lebanese crisis." In order to ease the rising tensions, in the spring of 1984, John Paul II issued three important messages.[590] The first was addressed to the Maronite patriarch, the second to the Lebanese people and the third to the Bishops of the Catholic Church. In these messages, the Pope spoke about his concerns about the fate of Lebanon and the need to preserve its unique role as an example of harmonious Christian-Muslim coexistence. He also emphasized the fact that the fate of Eastern Christian communities was directly linked to the lot of the Lebanese Christians. Therefore, the Pontiff called upon them not only to narrow their differences but to engage anew in a dialogue of life with their non-Christian brothers in Lebanon. The focal point of these messages was to let the Lebanese Christians know that they had a very important place in papal priorities. Although, as Irani observed, the messages "did not have the expected impact," the Maronite leaders became less critical about the Holy See and its representatives and "Christians in Lebanon understood finally that Rome had become their last beacon of hope in that area."[591]

As for the Palestinian question, in subsequent years John Paul II addressed the issue on many occasions. During his visit to Austria in June 1988, the Pope again called for the recognition of equality in dignity for the Israeli Jews and the Palestinians, pointing out that the Palestinians had a right to a homeland "like every other nation, according to international law."[592] His active engagement in the Middle

---

[587] Ibid., p. 144.

[588] Muslim and Christian militia groups continued their fighting, the armed PLO aimed at reestablishing their presence in the country, and the Shi'a community rallied behind two militant organizations, i.e., Amal and Hizballah, to realize their political and religious aspirations. The involved outside forces, namely Israel which occupied a "security zone" in the South, Syria with its forty thousands troops located in the Central and Eastern region ready to enforce suitable decisions, and the Shi'a groups supported financially by Iran and calling for the establishment of an Islamic state in Lebanon, they were significantly contributing to rising tensions, the paralysis of the already unstable government and hostility.

[589] For a further discussion, see: Ibid., p. 145-148. For an analysis of the threefold relationship between the patriarchate, the papacy, and the monastic orders during the 1975-1990 Lebanese Civil War, see: A. D. M. Henley, "Politics of a Church at War: Maronite Catholicism in the Lebanese Civil War," *Mediterranean Politics*, vol. 13/3 (November 2008), p. 353-369.

[590] See: *L'Osservatore Romano*, weekly edition, (May 14, 1984), p. 10-11.

[591] G. E. Irani, *The Papacy and the Middle East...*, p. 149.

[592] Quoted by A. Kreutz (*Vatican and the Palestinian-Israeli Conflict...*, p. 164) from *Globe and Mail* (June 25, 1988), p. 14.

Eastern conflicts was followed by his increasing contact with Egypt, Jordan, Morocco, Tunisia, Algeria, Iraq, Kuwait, Lebanon, Syria and Sudan.

In the years of the *First Intifāda*, the mass resistance to Israeli occupation in the West Bank and the Gaza Strip,[593] the Pope expressed his wish for the violence to end despite the fact that he well understood the frustrations of the Palestinian people. In his efforts towards a Middle East settlement and the protection of Palestinian rights, the Pope met in 1988 with King Ḥusayn of Jordan (February 1) and President Mubārak of Egypt (February 5). Furthermore, on February 4, Monsignor Achille Silvestrini, a key member of the Vatican's policy staff, held talks with Fārūq Khaddūmī, regarded as the Foreign Minister of the PLO. Moreover, in January 1988, in a symbolic gesture of support and recognition for the Palestinian people in general and a small Christian community in the Holy Land in particular, John Paul II appointed a Palestinian priest, Rev. Mīshīl Ṣabbāḥ, as Latin Patriarch of Jerusalem.[594] After the PLO's decision to explicitly accept Israel's right to exist and reject all forms of terrorism, the Pope received Yāsir 'Arafāt in audience on December 24, 1988.[595] On that occasion, John Paul II once again expressed the hope that "both people would soon see to beginning [*sic*] of understanding and peace, which would put an end finally to their suffering and their fears."[596]

In the subsequent months, the situation in Lebanon remained one of John Paul II's priorities. On September 7, 1989, the Pope published his *Apostolic Letter on the Situation in Lebanon*.[597] While referring to his preoccupation with the situation in Lebanon and the attention given to that country by his predecessors, i.e., Paul VI and John Paul I, the Holy Father spoke of the "unique value of Lebanon and its human and spiritual motherland" and expressed his conviction that "Lebanon cannot be left to its solicitude."[598] In the letter, the Holy Father called upon Christians in the Middle

---

[593] *Intifāda* (ar. term for uprising) – two recent Palestinian campaigns directed at ending of the Israeli military occupation. The *First Intifāda* began in 1987, violence declined in 1991 and it came to an end with the signing of the Oslo accords (August 1993) and the creation of the Palestinian National Authority. The *Al-Aqṣā Intifāda*, also known as the *Second Intifāda*, was a violent Palestinian-Israeli conflict that began in September 2000 and lasted until June 2004. For a thorough discussion on related issues see: N. A t e e k, M. H. E l l i s, R. R. R u e t h e r (eds.), *The Faith and Intifada: Palestinian Christian Voices*, New York: Orbis Books, 1992.

[594] A. Kreutz (*Vatican and the Palestinian-Israeli Conflict...*, p. 162.)

[595] John Paul II's subsequent meetings with 'Arafāt: April 6, 1990, September 2, 1995, December 12, 1998. During his pilgrimage to the Holy Land the Pope was received by 'Arafāt in the Palestinian Autonomy (March 22, 2000).

[596] J o h n P a u l II and J.-L. T a u r a n, *The Holy See at the Service of Peace: Pope John Paul II's Addresses to the Diplomatic Corps (October 1978 – September 1988)*, ed. M. K e e n a n, Vatican: Pontifical Council for Justice and Peace, 1988, p. 71.

[597] J e a n - P a u l II, "Lettre apostolique à tous les évêques de l'Eglise Catholique sur la situation du Liban" (Septembre 3, 1989), online: http://www.vatican.va/holy_father/john_paul_ii/apost_letters/documents/hf_jp-ii_apl_07091989_situation-lebanon_fr.html, access: March 29, 2011.

[598] Ibid., no. 5. (D. Rudnicka-Kassem: own translation)

East, and in particular Catholics, to remember and appreciate the Lebanese tradition of Christian-Muslim cooperation. Moreover, he expressed his conviction that despite many misunderstanding and arising problems, religious pluralism, as observed in Lebanon, should remain essential for assuring and preserving freedom, peace and dignity of man.[599]

As mentioned previously, almost a decade after the Israeli invasion in 1982, the situation in Lebanon was critical. At the outbreak of the civil war in 1975, in Lebanon the population was sixty percent Muslim and forty percent Christian. The Shi'as, who had the least representation in the political system, had become the largest single religious community, and by the end of the 1980s they made up at least one-third of the total population. Therefore, the restoration of the government required reworking the constitution and the National Pact so as to reflect the Muslim majority. In the view that any such reform would diminish the political power of the Maronites, their leadership preferred the partition of Lebanon and the establishment of a separate Maronite homeland. The Lebanese crisis continued and following the failure of different compromise proposals during the 1980s, finally in October 1989, due to an initiative of the Arab League, Lebanese politicians were invited to Ṭā'if in Saudi Arabia. Despite their differences, they managed to work out an agreement that gave the Muslims a greater role in Lebanon's political system and clearly affirmed religious identity as the core of Lebanese politics while preserving confessionalism.[600] The Ṭā'if Accord, signed on October 22, 1989, also declared the intention of extending Lebanese government sovereignty over southern Lebanon.[601] Furthermore, the agreement also acknowledged a special relationship with Syria.

---

[599] Ibid.

[600] In 1989, Rafīq al-Ḥarīrī (1944-2005) was the power behind the Ṭā'if Agreement ("National Reconciliation Accord," or "Document of National Accord"), which succeeded in ending the war, and the drafting of a new constitution for Lebanon. This agreement was the political contract that laid down the principles of national reconciliation that governs political life in Lebanon today; it was negotiated in Ṭā'if, Saudi Arabia, in September 1989, and approved by the Lebanese parliament on November 4, 1989. The agreement recognized the changed composition of the population and reduced the authority: some of the powers of the presidency (Maronite) was transferred to the prime minister (Muslim) and the cabinet (divided equally between Muslims and Christians) and the religious representation in parliament was changed from the existing six-to-five ratio in favor of Christians to an equal number of seats for Muslims and Christians. See the complete text of the document: "The Ta'if Accord," online: http://www.al-bab.com/arab/docs/lebanon/taif.htm, access: March 29, 2011.

[601] Though Israel withdrew from southern Lebanon in 2000, armed Hizballah militia remained in control of the area.

John Paul II's diplomatic efforts to prevent the Persian Gulf War of 1991

The political developments of the early 1990s, such as the failure of the Palestinian *intifāḍa* to bring about a change in Israel's relentless settlement policy, impending migration of hundreds of thousands of Soviet Jews to Israel following the collapse of the Soviet Union, as well as a new world order with the emergence of the United States as the ally of Israel and the sole superpower, created an atmosphere of frustration and uncertainty in the Arab World.

In consequence, the already difficult political conditions in the Middle East became more complicated as existing tensions intensified. Under such unfavorable circumstances, aggressive propaganda launched against Israel and the United States by Ṣaddām Ḥusayn, the only national leader who unequivocally championed the Palestinian cause, found a receptive Arab audience.[602] On August 2, 1990, the Iraqi army invaded Kuwait, and six days later the Iraqi government announced that Kuwait had been annexed and became the nineteenth province of Iraq.[603] With the prospects of Ṣaddām Ḥusayn exercising control over the oil-producing Gulf, the Americans decided on military intervention to protect Saudi Arabia from possible Iraqi aggression. In the meantime, the Bush administration set about building an international coalition against Iraq, i.e., to commit forces to Operation Desert Shield, and while working through the UN Security Council, pushed through resolutions demanding Iraq's withdrawal from Kuwait and imposing a trade embargo on all goods to and from Iraq and Kuwait. In early November, President Bush, who had already made the decision to go to war, announced the need for the coalition to develop an offensive military action.

The outbreak of the Gulf crisis mobilized the Pope to do everything in his power to avoid military conflict. Using each and every occasion to address the problem, John Paul II tried to explain that war could never be regarded as an appropriate and just means used in resolving international disputes, and putting forth examples of cases, such as Vietnam, Lebanon and Afghanistan, he argued that ultimately the military interventions proved to be futile and senseless. As for the particular reference to Iraq, according to the Holy Father, the war could not be considered "just," since its aim was "to rectify a violation of international law, but the refusal to

---

[602] Ṣaddām Ḥusayn justified Iraq's ongoing military buildup with the argument that the only way to force Israel to recognize Palestinian rights was for the Arab states to achieve military parity with Israel. He also warned Israel that Iraq would retaliate against any Israeli attack on an Arab state.

[603] W. L. Cleveland, *A History...*, p. 428-436. About the history of Iraq see: C. Hunt, *The History of Iraq*, Westport, CY: Greenwood Press, 2005; W. R. Polk, *Understanding Iraq: The Whole Sweep of Iraqi History, from Genghis Khan's Mongols to the Ottoman Turks to the British Mandate to the American Occupation*, New York: HarperCollins, 2005; M. M. Dziekan, *Historia Iraku*, Warszawa: Dialog, 2002.

explore the available diplomatic avenues of dialogue, mediation, and negotiation itself amounted to another betrayal of the same international law."[604]

On November 18, 1990, during his *Angelus* appeal for peace and for "an end of injustice in the Middle East," John Paul II expressed his concerns about the possibility of a war in Iraq:

> The situation in the Persian Gulf continues to be the cause for serious concern and anguish. May the merciful God give light and strength to those who are called to respect the ethical principles which must serve as the basis for relations among States and may He grant all humanity the grace of not experiencing the horror of another conflict.[605]

In the same month, the UN Security Council passed Resolution no. 678, setting January 15, 1991, as the deadline for the complete withdrawal of Iraqi forces from Kuwait and authorizing the "use of all necessary means" to enforce Iraq's pullout after January 15.[606]

At that point, John Paul II further engaged himself in the matter by undertaking efforts to prevent military action. With persistency and determination, he appealed for dialogue and negotiations, so an adequate solution for resolving the conflict could be found. On January 12, 1991, John Paul II received the diplomats accredited to the Holy See for the traditional exchange of good wishes for the New Year. In his speech, the Pope put a special emphasis on the Middle East, and in particular on the dangerous developments in the Persian Gulf area. While referring to his telegram, sent to the Secretary General of the United Nations, the Holy Father condemned the Iraqi armed invasion of Kuwait and the "brutal violation of international law as defined by the UN and by moral law." However, his concerns related to the conflict went further. The Pope strongly opposed the military intervention that had been already planned by the United States and allied forces. He explained that:

> while the massive concentration of men and arms which has followed it has been aimed at putting an end to what must be clearly defined as aggression, there is no doubt that, should it even in limited military action, the operations would be particularly costly in human life, to say nothing of the ecological, political, economic and strategic consequences, whose full gravity and impact we have perhaps not yet completely assessed.[607]

Furthermore, his warning against reverting to arms in an attempt to resolve political and religious conflicts confirmed the Pope's deep conviction that such a measure

---

[604] S. Dziwisz, *A Life with Karol...*, p. 207.
[605] "Pope John Paul II's *Angelus* Message for Sunday" (November 18, 1990), *Islamochristiana*, vol. 17 (1991), p. 273.
[606] "Resolution 678 (1990) Adopted by the Security Council at its 2963rd meeting" (November 29, 1990), online: http://www.casi.org.uk/info/undocs/gopher/s90/32, access: March, 29, 2011.
[607] "The Holy Father's address to the Diplomatic Corps...," p. 276.

would prove futile because "without entering into the profound causes of violence in this part of the world, a peace obtained by arms could only prepare new acts of violence."[608] John Paul II always fully supported the activity of the United Nations, which was established "to preserve the future generations from the scourge of war" and "to check every act of aggression." While convinced that with its engagement, the crisis would be overcome and the danger of war in the Persian Gulf eliminated, he reminded people that:

> true friends of peace know that now more than ever is the time for dialogue, for negotiation, and for affirming the primacy of international law. *Yes, peace is still possible; war would be a decline for all humanity.*[609]

As the UN deadline for a resolution of the Gulf crisis was approaching, the Pope intensified his fervent appeals for last-minute dialogue and negotiations. Moreover, he called upon Catholics throughout the world to observe a Day of Prayer for Peace in the Middle East on January 13. On that day, when an impressive crowd gathered on St. Peter's Square for the noontime recitation of the *Angelus*, John Paul II used the occasion to appeal, once again, to world leaders to refrain from the military option, and instead to agree on a conference where they could negotiate a feasible solution to the Gulf crisis. He said:

> From the very beginning of this crisis, and with greater insistence in recent days, I have felt the need to invite those who are responsible for the fate of the people to reflect on the extreme necessity of making dialogue and reason prevail and of preserving justice and international order without recourse to armed conflict...It is an appeal which I, for my part, feel the need to address to all interested parties in this hour which is so decisive for the destiny of individuals and nations.[610]

The Pope's struggle continued despite rising tensions. As observed, throughout the history of his pontificate, John Paul II never hesitated to address heads of states with appeals to reassess their policy and to change their decisions. Therefore, on January 15, in an effort to prevent the war in the Persian Gulf, the Holy Father sent letters to President George Bush and President Ṣaddām Ḥusayn.

In his message to President Bush, while "voicing the thoughts and concerns of millions of people," the Pope stressed "the tragic consequences which a war in that area could have" and restated his firm belief that:

> War is not likely to bring an adequate solution to international problems and that, even though an unjust situation might be momentarily met, the consequences that would possibly derive from war would be devastating and tragic...that the use of arms, and

---

[608]   Ibid.
[609]   Ibid.
[610]   Ibid., p. 279.

especially of today's highly sophisticated weaponry, would give rise, in addition to suffering and destruction, to new and perhaps worse injustices.[611]

Following his address, John Paul II went on with a straightforward appeal to the President to "not spare further efforts to avoid decisions which would be irreversible and bring suffering to thousands of families." Furthermore, "with lively faith to the Lord," that "peace can still be saved" the Holy Father called for "a last minute effort at dialogue," so "sovereignty may be restored to the people of Kuwait and that international order which is the basis for a coexistence between peoples truly worthy of mankind may be re-established in the Gulf area and in the entire Middle East." In addition, while making the President aware of his responsibility "before history," the Pope appealed for careful consideration and wisdom "to make decisions which will truly serve the good of your fellow-citizens and of the entire international community."[612]

In his letter to President Ṣaddām Ḥusayn, John Paul II also spoke firmly about his conviction that "no international problem can be adequately and worthily solved by recourse to arms," and explained that such an experience should teach "all humanity that war, besides causing many victims, creates situations of grave injustice which, in their turn, constitute a powerful temptation to further recourse to violence."[613] While expressing his hopes that for all the parties involved in the conflict, there was still time for dialogue leading to "the path for avoiding such a catastrophe," the Pope appealed to President Ḥusayn for good will and readiness "to make a generous gesture which will avoid war." Such a gesture, John Paul II believed, would be "a great step before history, for it would mark a victory of international justice and the triumph of that peace to which all people of good will aspire."[614]

Unfortunately, the Pope's letters did not bring the expected results and the hopes for avoiding the military option practically vanished. On January 16, 1991, during a general audience, the Holy Father's appeal for peace was very dramatic. The Pope, joined by thousands of people, was still trying to convince the world that war would not be a just or effective means for resolving international problems and that war was "a journey of no return."[615] Despite all the Pontiff's efforts, the military intervention in Iraq began.[616] On January 17, 1991, during an audience for the officials of the Ro-

---

[611] "Pope John Paul II's Appeal to Both President George Bush and President Saddam Hussein" (January 15, 1991), *Islamochristiana*, vol. 17 (1991), p. 280.

[612] Ibid.

[613] Ibid.

[614] Ibid., p. 281.

[615] Ibid.

[616] In his book *A Life with Karol...*, Cardinal Dziwisz recalls the Pope's efforts to avoid the war in Iraq saying: "Some people were shocked that John Paul II would speak so insistently about peace at a time like that. Some thought he was 'neutral,' or embraced 'moral equivalence,' or even a pro-Arab, Third World radical. On the other hand, though, there were others who tried to enlist him in the ranks of pacifists – in another words, to slap him with an ideological or po-

man Vicariate, John Paul II expressed his deep regrets over the outbreak of the Gulf War and while repeating his appeal for peace once again asserted:

> War is not the answer... I pray that the experience of this first day of conflict will be enough to make people understand the need for the rights of all peoples in the region to be made the subject of a particular commitment on the part of the international community. It is a question of problems the solution of which can only be sought in an international meeting at which all the interested parties are present and cooperate frankly and calmly.[617]

During the air war of January-February 1991 and the brief ground war of February 24 to 28, John Paul II made twenty-five more appeals for just peace in the Persian Gulf, addressing both leaders and the international community.[618] In his plea for peace on January 27, the Holy Father made reference to the principles of *Nostra Aetate*, saying:

> Let us pray again for and with all believers belonging to the three religions which have their historical roots in the Middle East: Jews, Christians and Muslims. Faith in the same God must not be the cause for conflict and rivalry, but a commitment to overcome the existing contrasts by dialogue and negotiations.[619]

The Pope tried "all that was humanly possible" to avoid the war, and following its commencement he continued his mission of peace and "did not stop with recriminations over what hadn't been done."[620] As Cardinal Dziwisz recalled, John Paul II had decided (in consultation with the members of the Secretariat of the State) on both humanitarian aid and further diplomatic measures.[621] The first major diplomatic initiative was a summit meeting in Rome.[622]

The Persian Gulf War was terminated on April 11, 1991, with a cease-fire negotiated between the United States, its allies and Iraq. The UN Security Council, the United States and its allies imposed on Iraq numerous economic sanctions, enforced

---

litical label. If I may say so, this was a genuine insult to a fundamentally meek, peace-loving man who followed the way of nonviolence, as we would say today. The insult was even worse considering his background as a Pole who had personally experienced two totalitarisms. Most of all, though, it was a slap in the face for a Pope who was a witness to the God of peace and the spokesman of humanity's yearning for Peace."(S. Dziwisz, *A Life with Karol...*, p. 207-208).

[617] *"War is not an answer*: Pope John II's Audience for the Officials of the Roman Vicariate" (January 17, 1991), *Islamochristiana*, vol. 17 (1991), p. 281-282.

[618] G. Weigel, *Witness to Hope...*, p. 621.

[619] "Pope John Paul II's *Angelus* Appeal for an End to the War" (January 27, 1991), *Islamochristiana*, vol. 17 (1991), p. 283.

[620] S. Dziwisz, *A Life with Karol...*, p. 208.

[621] Ibid.

[622] On March 4-5, 1991, representatives of the episcopates from the countries directly implicated in the Gulf War met in the Vatican. See: G. Weigel, *Witness to Hope...*, p. 621.

Iraqi-no-fly zones to protect Kurds in northern Iraq and Shi'as in the south, and on-going inspections to prevent Iraqi development of chemical, biological, and nuclear weapons.[623]

In the aftermath of the war, when, due to the initiative of the United States, Israel, Jordan and the Palestine Liberation Organization decided to participate, for the first time, in Middle East peace process negotiations, John Paul II became an even more active participant in the diplomacy of the region. The Vatican's vision of establishing mutually acceptable peaceful accommodations between Israelis and Palestinians, including fulfilling the criteria of justice, became the priority in the Pope's diplomatic efforts. Therefore, with pragmatism and determination, he set in motion the process leading to the Holy See's diplomatic recognition of Israel and subsequently relations with the PLO.

The Pope's task of establishing official Vatican relations with Israel and representatives of the Palestinian people

In the Middle East, Christian minorities live in a society that is predominantly Muslim. Therefore, according to the Pope, it was his duty to encourage and promote a dialogue of life between the Christians and the Muslims. However, when it came to the question of peace in the Middle East, that dialogue had to include a third party, namely the followers of Judaism. All the diplomatic efforts of the Pope were directed to promoting peaceful coexistence and ensuring the observance of the human rights of Jews, Christian and Muslims.[624] In 1991, while addressing the participants of an interreligious meeting in Rome, the Pope said:

> Jews, Christians and Muslims, as we know, come from different religious traditions,but have many ties to each other. In fact, all the believers of these three religions refer back to Abraham, *pater omnium credentium*, for whom they have a profound respect, although in different ways. Peace among these religions constitutes such a great good and such an important contribution to all of human society. If there is not an amiable peace among these religions how can harmony in society be found?[625]

---

[623] For a comprehensive account of the Persian Gulf war, see: L. Freedman and E. Karsh, *The Gulf Conflict, 1990-1991: Diplomacy and War in the New World Order*, Princeton, NJ: Princeton University Press, 1993; L. C. Hillstrom, *War in the Persian Gulf Primary Sources: From Operation Desert Storm to Operation Iraqi Freedom* Detroit: UXL, 2004; O. Schwab, *The Gulf Wars and the United States: Shaping the Twenty-First Century* Westport, CT: Praeger Security International, 2009.

[624] See: M. Arkoun, "New Perspectives for a Jewish-Christian-Muslim Dialogue," *Journal of Ecumenical Studies*, vol. 26 (1989), p. 345-352.

[625] "The Holy See's Address to Christians, Jews and Muslims during an Interreligious Meeting in Rome," *Islamochristiana*, vol. 17 (1991), p. 291-292.

Consistency, pragmatism and a view of long-standing goals shaped papal diplomacy in the Middle East. Therefore, the Vatican's support for Palestinians had always been balanced with concern for Israel and the world's Jewish community, relations with which were regarded by Church leaders as vitally important. John Paul II was well aware that apart from religious traditions and the actual control of Christian and Muslim Holy Places, Israel possessed two other strong advantages: its indisputable position as the strongest military power in the area, and its special religious and cultural ties with Christians in the West. By contrast, the divided Arab states had comparatively little bargaining power against the Israelis.

Since the beginning of his pontificate, John Paul II frequently displayed his sympathies towards the Jews and their cause.[626] As the head of the Roman Catholic Church, fully committed to dialogue with Judaism, the Pope initiated official and unofficial contact on many occasions with both Jewish spiritual leaders and Israeli politicians.[627] Moreover, in a symbolic gesture of this recognition, sympathy and support for the Jews and their cause, on April 12, 1986, he became the first Pope ever to visit the synagogue in Rome. While the distance between the Vatican and the synagogue was only a few kilometers, as Chief Rabbi Elio Toaff remarked, it had taken "two thousand years" to be acknowledged by a Roman Pope.[628]

Informal negotiations with the Israelis began in November 1991, with the help of the Israeli ambassador to Italy.[629] In July 1992, a special Holy See-Israel Bilateral Commission was formed to negotiate the establishment of diplomatic relations. The process progressed relatively slowly. There were many unsettled, difficult issues, such as the status of Jerusalem and the situation of the Palestinians. However, little by little, progress was made. The Labor Party had won the June elections in Israel and Yitzhak Rabin became the Prime Minister. On October 23, 1992, during his audience with John Paul II, the new Foreign Minister Shimon Peres formally invited the Pope to visit Israel. However, a year elapsed before an agreement was reached on establishing diplomatic relations.

Meanwhile, on September 12, 1993, Israeli Prime Minister Rabin and PLO Chairman 'Arafāt signed an agreement at the White House in Washington on partial Palestinian self-rule in the Occupied Territories. This fact gave a new impulse to the Holy See-Israeli negotiations. On September 23, John Paul II received the chief Ashkenazi Rabbi of Israel, Meyer Lau, in Castel Gandolfo. During the audience, the Pope rejoiced, "Today my visit to Jerusalem is nearer than ever."[630] Finally, on December 30, 1993, Israel and the Holy See signed an agreement in Jerusalem

---

[626] See: E. J. Fisher and L. Klenicki (eds.), *Pope John Paul II on Jews and Judaism: 1979-1986*, Washington: United States Catholic Conference, 1987.

[627] T. Szulc, *Pope John Paul II...*, p. 450.

[628] Ibid., p. 451.

[629] Tad Szulc recalls the process of establishing diplomatic relations between the Holy See and Israel in his book: *Pope John Paul II...*, p. 449-154.

[630] Ibid., p. 453.

establishing full diplomatic relations. Afterwards, John Paul II explained his decision. He said:

> It must be understood that Jews, who for two thousand years were dispersed among the nations of the world, had decided to return to the land of their ancestors. This is their right. And even those who look upon the nation of Israel with an unsympathetic eye recognize this right. The Holy See also recognized this right from the outset, and the act of establishing diplomatic relations with Israel is simply an international affirmation of this relationship.[631]

In his book *Crossing the Threshold of Hope*, published in 1994, John Paul II once again displayed his satisfaction about establishing full diplomatic relations between the Holy See and Israel. The Pope wrote:

> I am pleased that as a result of the peace process currently taking place, despite setbacks and obstacles in the Middle East, and thanks also to the initiative of the state of Israel, it became possible to establish diplomatic relations between the Apostolic See and Israel. As for the recognition of the state of Israel, it is important to reaffirm that I myself never had any doubts in this regard.[632]

As pointed out previously, in all his statements related to the Palestinian-Israeli dispute, John Paul II always clearly affirmed his recognition of the political rights of both the Jews and the Palestinians. Therefore, the establishment of diplomatic relations with Israel was followed by the Pope's efforts to give official recognition to the Palestine Liberation Organization, in its capacity as an official representative of the Palestinian people. During the 1980s, the Vatican had already made contact several times with the Palestinian authorities.[633] In the early 1990s there was a series of talks, with the principal purpose of strengthening mutual cooperation between the Holy See and the PLO. Finally, on October 25, 1994, according to the *communiqué* agreed upon by the Holy See and the PLO, "it was decided to give the already long-existing and fruitful working contacts a permanent and official character."[634] Subsequently, the PLO opened an office of representation at the Holy See. The Apostolic Nuncio in Tunisia was appointed as liaison of the leaders of the PLO. Furthermore, as stated in the *communiqué*:

> The two parties have also committed themselves to cooperate, each with its own means and according to its own characteristics and responsibilities, in preserving the religious and cultural values which mark the people of the region, and which properly belong to the Holy Land and especially to the Holy City of Jerusalem.[635]

---

[631] Ibid.
[632] John Paul II, *Crossing the Threshold...*, p. 100.
[633] A. Kreutz, "The Vatican and the Palestinians...," p. 124.
[634] T. Szulc, Pope *John Paul II...*, p. 457.
[635] Ibid., p. 458.

The Vatican's task to establish diplomatic ties with both the Jews and the Palestinians was accomplished. In January 1996, on the occasion of the exchange of greetings with the Ambassadors accredited to the Holy See, the Pope concluded his difficult diplomatic efforts in a very simple way. He stated:

> Today we cannot but rejoice to see here, for the first time, the representative of the Palestinian people. For more than a year, the Holy See has enjoyed diplomatic relations with the state of Israel…It is the eloquent sign that the Middle East has resolutely taken the path of peace proclaimed to mankind by the Child born in Bethlehem.[636]

John Paul II's attempts to ease the Palestinian-Israeli conflict and to settle the Palestinian question

The peace process that began after the signing of the agreement between Israel and the Palestinian Liberation Organization in Washington on September 13, 1993, was expected to end in May 1999, with the establishment of the Palestinian state. It was also planned that within a few years of that continuous process, the most difficult questions, such as the problem of Palestinian refugees and the status of Jerusalem, would be resolved.

Meanwhile, John Paul II was following the peace process attentively and his numerous efforts to appease the Palestinian-Israeli conflict continued. In the course of preparations for the Grand Jubilee of 2000 and the Pope's pilgrimage to the Holy Land, the Holy See pursued the task of "cleaning memories" concerning Christian-Jewish relations.[637] In October/November 1997, the Vatican organized the International Symposium *The Roots of Anti-Judaism in the Christian Environment.*[638] On March 16, 1998, the Vatican Commission for Relations with Judaism published an important, related document, i.e., *We Remember: A Reflection on Shoah.*[639] The publication caused a number of discussions and controversies.[640] Nevertheless, it had

---

[636] John Paul II, "Address of the Holy Father on the Occasion of the Exchange of Greetings…", no. 2.

[637] J. Moskwa, *Prorok…*, p. 207. During his pontificate, John Paul II made about one hundred apologies for the Church's past wrongdoings. He apologized to Jews for the inactivity and silence of many Catholics during the Holocaust and to Muslims for the sins of the Crusaders. Refer to: L. Accattoli, *When a Pope Asks Forgiveness: The Mea Culpa's of John Paul II*, trans. J. Aumann, Boston: Pauline Books, 2000. Also see: "Homily of the Holy Father *Day of Pardon*," (March 12, 2000), online: http://www.vatican.va/holy_father/john_paul_ii/homilies/documents/hf_jp-ii_hom_20000312_pardon_en.html, access: March 29, 2011.

[638] Ibid., p. 207-208.

[639] See: Commission for Religious Relations with Jews, "*We Remember: A Reflection on the Shoah*" (March 16, 1998), online: http://www.vatican.va/roman_curia/pontifical_councils/chrstuni/documents/rc_pc_chrstuni_doc_16031998_shoah_en.html, access: March 29, 2011.

[640] See: G. Weigel, *Witness to Hope…*, p. 824-826.

opened the way for the most important events of the Grand Jubilee – the request for forgiveness and the Pope's pilgrimage to the Holy Land.[641] The Government of Israel officially invited John Paul II there.

The Palestinian question never ceased to be one of the Holy Father's priorities as he firmly continued his support for the legitimate rights of the Palestinian people. On June 12, 1998, the Pope again received Yāsir 'Arafāt.[642] At that time, the PLO leader visited the Vatican as the President of the Palestinian National Authority. He invited John Paul II to Bethlehem, most likely seeking the Holy See's help to ease relations with Israel and pursue peace talks.

The year 2000 brought new developments to the Vatican policy concerning the Palestinian question. On February 15, 2000 the Holy See, the Sovereign Authority of the Catholic Church, and the Palestine Liberation Organization, the representative of the Palestinian people working for the benefit and on behalf of the Palestinian Authority, signed an agreement regulating the status of the Catholic Church on the territory of the Palestinian Autonomy. The preamble of this document contained a decisive call for a just solution to the Palestinian-Israeli conflict. It was stated that the two parties were:

> Calling for a peaceful solution of the Palestinian-Israeli conflict, which would realize the inalienable national legitimate rights and aspirations of the Palestinian people, to be reached through negotiation and agreement, in order to ensure peace and security for all the peoples of the region on the basis of international law, relevant United Nations and its Security Council resolutions, justice and equity.[643]

The two parties were also declaring that an equitable solution for the issue of Jerusalem, based on international resolutions, was fundamental for peace in the entire region of the Middle East and, therefore, they were:

> Calling for a special statute of Jerusalem, internationally guaranteed, which should safeguard the following:
> a) Freedom of religion and conscience for all;
> b) The equality before the law of the three monotheistic religions and their institutions and the followers in the City;
> c) The proper identity and sacred character of the City and its universally significant religious and cultural heritage;
> d) The Holy Places, the freedom of access to them and of worship in them;
> e) The Regime of "Status Quo" in the Holy Places, where it applies.[644]

Israel protested against the agreement, calling it "interference in negotiations between the Israelis and the Palestinians." The fact that the Preamble contained

---

[641] Ibid., p. 876.
[642] John Paul II met with Yāsir 'Arafāt several times.
[643] "The PLO – Vatican Agreement" (February 15, 2000), online: http://www.jewishvirtualli-brary.org/jsource/Peace/plovatican.html, access: March 29, 2011.
[644] Ibid.

an appeal for the international status of Jerusalem, and that the document included a statement saying that "unilateral decisions and actions altering the specific character and status of Jerusalem are morally and legally unacceptable,"[645] met with strong criticism from Israeli politicians.[646]

Meanwhile, the efforts of the international community to foster the peace talks between the Israelis and the Palestinians continued. However, despite numerous attempts to negotiate, a compromising solution that could be acceptable for both sides was not found. In the summer of 2000, Israel and the PLO decided to resume talks. The summit in Camp David (July 12-15, 2000), under the auspices of the United States' President Bill Clinton and with the presence of the Israeli Prime Minister Ehud Barak and the PLO representative Yāsir 'Arafāt, did not move the matters any further. The second round of the Camp David negotiations (December 19-23, 2000) as well as the subsequent attempts in Ṭāba, Egypt (July 2001) also ended with no results. Therefore, at that point the peace process was frozen. The total dissatisfaction of the Palestinians with the peace negotiations led to the eruption of the *Second Intifāḍa*.[647] The already difficult situation became even more complicated and the tensions between the Israelis and the Palestinians rose again.

The escalation of Palestinian terrorist actions and the Israeli military responses culminated in March 2002. Finally, during the night from March 28 to 29, Israeli Prime Minister Ariel Sharon sent his army to the territory of the Palestinian Autonomy. The reaction of the international community uncovered deep divisions. John Paul II addressed the matter on March 3 (one day after the Israeli army took over Ramallah, the seat of the Palestinian government), during his Easter message *Urbi et Orbi*. Well aware of the gravity of the situation, the Pope remained neutral and addressed the matter in general terms. He spoke about his concerns with "the tragic sequence of atrocities and killings that bloody the Holy Land, plunged again in these very days into horror and despair," and the fact that again in this precious place "war has been declared on peace!"[648] Then, once again, he expressed his conviction that "nothing is resolved by war" or "through reprisal and retaliation." Furthermore, in the face of this "truly great tragedy" in the Holy Land, the Pope concluded:

> No one can remain silent and inactive,
> no political or religious leader!
> Denunciation must be followed by practical acts of solidarity
> that will help everyone to rediscover mutual respect
> and return to frank negotiation.[649]

---

[645] Ibid.

[646] J. Moskwa, *Prorok...*, p. 251.

[647] Refer to the footnote no. 593, p. 167.

[648] "*Urbi et Orbi* Message of His Holiness John Paul II" (March 31, 2002), online: http://www. vatican.va/holy_father/john_paul_ii/messages/urbi/documents/hf_jp-ii_mes_20020331_ easter-urbi_en.html, access: March 29, 2011.

[649] Ibid.

Although the carefully chosen words while addressing the issue of the Holy Land crisis could be taken to indicate John Paul II's impartiality and neutrality, his position with regard to the Palestinian-Israeli conflict was clear. His disapproval of the Israeli action was accompanied by a condemnation of Palestinian terrorism.[650] Therefore, the Pope supported UN Resolution no. 1402 calling for the withdrawal of the Israeli army from the Palestinian territories and referring to the danger of the Palestinian terrorist actions.[651]

However, tensions and reciprocal attacks continued. On April 2, 2002, a group of armed Palestinian Arab terrorists forced their way into the Church of the Nativity in Bethlehem, one of Christianity's most sacred sites, the birthplace of Christ. They sought refuge from the Israel Defense Forces action against suicide bombing activity originating from West Bank locations.[652] For 38 days, until May 10, 2002, the world watched as the nuns and priests became "voluntary hostages" between the two conflicting sides, namely the Palestinians inside and the Israelis outside the church. The situation was extremely difficult and at any minute could have resulted in the exchange of fire and the eventual desecration and destruction of the church. Under the circumstances, the Holy See decided to intervene, directing strong diplomatic protests to both sides of the conflict. One may say that the uncompromising and impartial stand of John Paul II and the Vatican diplomacy prevented both the Israelis and the Palestinians from the attacks and resulted in negotiations leading to resolving this crisis in the Holy place.[653]

As the tensions between the Israelis and the Palestinians continued, the Pope kept reminding the world about the urgent need to remain on the path of dialogue and negotiations. On August 11, 2002, John Paul II once again addressed the issue of the Palestinian-Israeli conflict, devoting almost the entire *Angelus* message to it. Expressing his concerns about the "victims of a deadly unending spiral of retaliation," the Pope explained that "neither attacks, nor walls that separate, nor even retaliation that will ever lead to a just solution of the continuing conflict."[654] Furthermore, he

---

[650] A. Gianelli and A. Tornielli, *Papi e Guerra: Il ruolo dei Pontefici dal primo conflitto mondiale all'attaco in Iraq*, Milano: In Giornale, 2003. Polish edition: iidem, *Papieże a wojna: Od pierwszego światowego konfliktu do ataku na Irak*, trans. L. Rodziewicz, Kraków: Wydawnictwo M, 2006, p. 294.

[651] "UN Resolution 1402," online: http://www.palestinehistory.com/history/documents/doc07. htm#UN1402, access: March 29, 2011.

[652] On March 28, 2002 after a series of terrorist attacks within Israeli cities that cost many over 125 civilian lives, Israel launched Operation Defensive Shield. The goal was to dismantle the terrorist infrastructure. The operation consisted of moving Israeli forces into Judea and Samaria (the West Bank) and Gaza for the purpose of arresting terrorists, finding and confiscating weapons and destroying facilities for the manufacture of explosives.

[653] A. Gianelli and A Tornielli, *Papieże a wojna...*, p. 297.

[654] John Paul II, "*Angelus*" (August 11, 2002), no.1, online: http://www.vatican.va/holy_father/john_paul_ii/angelus/2002/documents/hf_jp-ii_ang_20020811_en.html, access: March 29, 2011.

assured the Christians living in the conflicted area about his sentiments of profound solidarity and spiritual closeness, saying:

> Faced with this humanitarian tragedy, which does not seem to show any signs of hope, *no one can remain indifferent.* That is why, once again, I appeal to the Israeli and Palestinian political leadership *to set out anew on the path of sincere negotiation…*
> I call on Christians of every part of the world to join in my fervent and trusting prayer. Mary, Queen of Peace, grant that the cries of those who suffer and die in the Holy Land will finally be heard.[655]

Despite the fact that the Pope's words did not stop the frequent outbreak of reciprocal hostility and violence between the Palestinians and the Israelis, he continued his tireless effort to convince both sides of the conflict that "the shattered order cannot be fully restored except by a response that combines justice with forgiveness."[656]

The Jubilee Pilgrimage to the Holy Land

In his apostolic letter *Tertio Millenio Adveniente,*[657] published on November 10, 1994, as well as in the *Letter Concerning the Pilgrimage to the Places Linked to the History of Salvation,*[658] published on June 29, 1999, John Paul II emphasized the exclusively religious character of the Jubilee pilgrimage to the Holy Land planned for the year 2000. The Pope's intention was to walk in the footsteps of Abraham, Moses, Jesus and Paul; to revisit the origins of the history of salvation. As he had imagined, the first stop was supposed to be Ur of the Chaldees in Iraq but he was refused the necessary permission. So, ultimately, he had to initiate his pilgrimage with a solemn commemoration of Abraham in the Vatican.[659]

---

[655] Ibid., no. 3.
[656] "Message of His Holiness John Paul for the Celebration of the World Day of Peace: *No Peace without Justice, No Justice without Forgiveness*" (January 1, 2002), no. 2, online: http://www.vatican.va/holy_father/john_paul_ii/messages/peace/documents/hf_jp-ii_mes_20011211_xxxv-world-day-for-peace_en.html, access: March 29, 2011.
[657] "Apostolic Letter *Tertio Millennio Adveniente* of His Holiness Pope John Paul II to the Bishops, Clergy and Lay Faithful on Preparation for the Jubilee of the Year 2000" (November 10, 1994), online: http://www.vatican.va/holy_father/john_paul_ii/apost_letters/documents/hf_jp-ii_apl_10111994_tertio-millennio-adveniente_en.html, access: March 29, 2011.
[658] "Letter of the Supreme Pontiff John Paul II Concerning Pilgrimage to the Places Linked to the History of Salvation" (June 29, 1999), online: http://www.vatican.va/holy_father/john_paul_ii/letters/documents/hf_jp-ii_let_30061999_pilgrimage_en.html, access: March 29, 2011.
[659] As Cardinal Dziwisz recalled: "He wasn't happy about the negative answer, obviously. The thing that bothered him even more was that they hadn't understood his intention, which was to follow in the footsteps of Abraham, the man whom both Christians and Muslims look up to as their father of faith." (S. Dziwisz, *A Life with Karol…*, p. 241).

Although, as Cardinal Dziwisz pointed out, the multinational peacekeepers did not hesitate to guarantee security, Ṣaddām Ḥusayn "courteously" refused, claiming that the Pope's safety there was at risk.[660]

As it was expected, John Paul II also wanted his journey "to the roots of the faith" to be an occasion to promote his dialogue with the followers of Judaism and Islam, thus an occasion to get involved with politics and contribute to building the peace process in the Middle East. Therefore, as Moskwa wrote:

> The political scenario of the journey that had been precisely planned by the Vatican diplomacy anticipated that the pilgrimage would include three countries: Jordan, Israel and the Palestine Autonomy. The emphasis on the sovereign character of that "temporary political structure" strenghtened the position of its president Yāsir ʿArafāt giving the boost to the hopes of Palestinian people. However, at the same time it intensified the feeling of insecurity in the Israeli nationalistic circles.[661]

It should be pointed out that the speeches given by the Pope during his Jubilee pilgrimage to the Holy Land included references to the Middle Eastern problems and in particular to the question of the Palestinian-Israeli conflict.

On March 20, 2000, in his address during the welcome ceremony at the airport in Amman, while referring to the harmonious coexistence of Christians and Muslims in the Hashemite Kingdom of Jordan, John Paul II pointed out that the peace process in the Middle Eastern area had to continue despite the mounting difficulties and obstacles. A lasting peace, according to the Pope, required understanding and cooperation among people "who acknowledge the one true, indivisible God, the Creator of all that exists."[662] Therefore, developing an interreligious dialogue between the Jews, the Christians and the Muslims, the Pope insisted, should become the priority. As the Holy Father explained:

> The three historical monotheistic religions count peace, goodness and respect for the human person among the highest values. I earnestly hope that my visit will strengthen the already fruitful Christian–Muslim dialogue which is being conducted in Jordan, particularly through the Royal Interfaith Institute.[663]

The following day, on March 21, 2000, John Paul II went to Israel. Addressing the Israeli officials and people gathered at the Tel Aviv Airport, the Pope recalled his visit to the Synagogue in Rome in 1986 and expressed his satisfaction with the progress of Christian-Jewish relations at the historical, theological and political levels.

---

[660]   Ibid.

[661]   J. Moskwa, *Prorok...*, p. 243-244 (D. Rudnicka-Kassem: own translation).

[662]   "Jubilee Pilgrimage of His Holiness John Paul II to the Holy Land (March 20-26, 2000): Speech of the Holy Father John Paul II at the Welcome Ceremony in Jordan," no. 2.

[663]   Ibid.

He also referred to the issue of interreligious dialogue in the Holy Land involving the followers of the three monotheistic religions and said:

> I pray that my visit will serve to encourage an increase of interreligious dialogue that will lead Jews, Christians and Muslims to seek in their respective beliefs, and in the universal brotherhood that unites all the members of the human family, the motivation and the perseverance to work for the peace and justice which the peoples of the Holy Land do not yet have, and for which they yearn so deeply.[664]

March 22, 2000, was an important day for the Palestinian people. John Paul II visited the Palestinian Autonomy. His speech at the Presidential Palace in Bethlehem once again confirmed the Pope's decisive stand with regard to the Palestinian question. He stated:

> Peace for the Palestinian people! Peace for all the peoples of the region! No one can ignore how much the Palestinian people have had to suffer in recent decades. Your torment is before the eyes of the world. And it has gone for too long. The Holy See has always recognized that the Palestinian peoples have the natural right to a homeland… In the international forum, my predecessors and I have repeatedly proclaimed that there would be no end to the sad conflict in the Holy Land without stable guarantees for the rights of all the peoples involved, on the basis of international law and the relevant United Nations resolutions and declarations.[665]

As a sign of the Pope's solidarity with the Palestinian people, his pilgrimage to the birthplace of Jesus included a visit to the Deheisheh Refugee Camp located not far from Bethlehem. His speech in defense of the rights of Palestinian refugees was quite emotional. John Paul II said firmly:

> You have been deprived of many things, which represent basic needs of the human person: proper housing, health care, education and work. Above all you bear the sad memory of what you were forced to leave behind, not just your material possessions, but your freedom, the closeness of relatives, and the familiar surroundings and cultural traditions which nourished your personal and family life…The degrading conditions in which refuges often have to live…the fact that displaced persons are obligated to

---

[664] "Jubilee Pilgrimage of His Holiness John Paul II to the Holy Land (March 20-26, 2000): Speech of the Holy Father John Paul II: Welcome Ceremony in Israel" (Tel Aviv, March 21, 2000), no. 4, online: http://www.vatican.va/holy_father/john_paul_ii/travels/documents/hf_jp-ii_spe_20000321_israel-arrival_en.html, access: March 29, 2011.

[665] "Jubilee Pilgrimage of His Holiness John Paul II to the Holy Land (March 20-26, 2000): Speech of John Paul II: Welcome Ceremony in the Palestinian Autonomous Territories" (Bethlehem, March 22, 2000), no. 2, online: http://www.vatican.va/holy_father/john_paul_ii/travels/documents/hf_jp-ii_spe_20000322_bethlehem-arrival_en.html, access March 29, 2011.

remain for years in settlements camps: these are the measure of the urgent need for a just solution to the underlying causes of the problem.[666]

March 23, 2000 brought significant events concerning Christian-Jewish relations. First, the Pope met with Ashkenazi and Sephardic rabbis, then he was received by the Israeli President Ezer Weizman, and, finally, he visited the Holocaust memorial at Yad Vashem. In the Hall of Remembrance, the Holy Father walked slowly towards the eternal flame and bent his head in a silent prayer. John Paul II began his address with the Psalm 31,[667] and then continued by saying:

In this place of memories, the mind and hearts and soul feel an extreme need for silence. Silence in which to remember. Silence in which to try to make some of the memories, which come flooding back. Silence because there're no words enough to deplore the terrible tragedy of the Shoah…I have come to Yad Vashem to pay homage to the millions of Jewish people who, stripped of everything, especially of their human dignity were murdered in the Holocaust…We wish to remember…to ensure that never again will evil prevail.[668]

Then the Pope went to greet seven Holocaust survivors. As Weigel recalled: "the Pope was not receiving the survivors, he was honoring their experience and their memories by walking with difficulty, to meet them."[669]

Despite all the Pontiff's efforts to ease the religious and political tensions in the Holy Land, unfortunately they rose again during the tripartite interreligious meeting at the Notre Dame Pontifical Institute in Jerusalem.[670] John Paul II waited, and then ignoring all the misunderstandings, went on with his address, explaining that "a religion is the enemy of exclusion and discrimination, of hatred and rivalry" and that it "must not become an excuse for violence and conflict, particularly when religious identity coincides with cultural and ethnic identity."[671] Furthermore, the Pope once

---

[666] "Jubilee Pilgrimage of His Holiness John Paul II to Mount Sinai: Speech of the Holy Father John Paul II: Visit to the Refugee Camp of Dheisheh" (March 22, 2000), no. 1-2, online: http://www.vatican.va/holy_father/john_paul_ii/travels/documents/hf_jp-ii_spe_20000322_deheisheh-refugees_en.html, access: March 29, 2011.

[667] "I have become like a broken vessel.
I hear the whispering of many – terror on every side! –
as they scheme together against me, as they plot to take my life.
But I trust in you, O lord; I say, 'You are my God'." (Ps 31: 13-15).

[668] "Jubilee Pilgrimage of His Holiness John Paul II to the Holy Land (March 20-26, 2000): Speech of John Paul II: Visit to the Yad Vashem Museum" (Jerusalem, March 23, 2000), no. 1, online: http://www.vatican.va/holy_father/john_paul_ii/travels/documents/hf_jp-ii_spe_20000323_yad-vashem-mausoleum_en.html, access: March 29, 2011.

[669] G. Weigel, *Witness to Hope…*, p. 873.

[670] Ibid., p. 874.

[671] "Jubilee Pilgrimage of His Holiness John Paul II to the Holy Land (March 20-26, 2000: Address of John Paul II: Interreligious Meeting…," no. 4.

again assured the world of the Church's commitment to developing an interreligious dialogue with the members of Jewish faith and the followers of Islam. He pointed out that:

> Such a dialogue is not an attempt to impose our views upon others. What it demands of all of us is that, holding to what we believe, we listen respectfully to one another, seek to discern all that is good and holy in each other's teachings and cooperate in supporting everything that flavors mutual understanding and peace.[672]

One may say that John Paul II's long-awaited Jubilee pilgrimage to the Holy Land was a significant event for the history of Christianity, and despite some embarrassing moments had considerable impact on the development of interreligious dialogue and understanding among the followers of the three great monotheistic religions.

"No to war": the Pope's offensive of peace and his protest against the military intervention in Iraq

The first year of the twenty-first century, and in particular the events of September 11, 2001, brought about the rise of political tensions in the world. The news about the terrorist attack on the World Trade Center in New York reached the Pope in Castel Gandolfo.[673] The day after was for the Holy Father a day of mourning. After celebrating Mass, he held a special general audience in Saint Peter's Square. John Paul II was terribly worried because he knew that as a result of September 11, the violence could dangerously increase. Moreover, as Cardinal Dziwisz pointed out, the Pontiff was aware of the fact that "if we were going to defeat terrorism, we also needed to eliminate the huge social and economic inequalities between the First World and the Third."[674] During the audience, the Holy Father said:

> Yesterday was a dark day in the history of humanity, a terrible affront to human dignity. After receiving the news, I followed with intense concern for the developing situation, with heartfelt prayers to the Lord. How is it possible to commit acts of such savage cruelty? The human heart has depths from which schemes of unheard-of ferocity some-

---

[672] Ibid.
[673] As Cardinal Dziwisz recalled: "The telephone rang. It was Cardinal Sodano, the secretary of state, and he sounded frightened. The Pope indicated that the television should be turned on, and then he saw the dramatic images of the Twin Towers collapsing, with thousands of victims trapped inside. Filled with suffering, he spent the rest of the afternoon going back and forth between the chapel and the television." (S. Dziwisz, *A Life with Karol...*, p. 243.)
[674] Ibid., p. 244.

times emerge, capable of destroying in a moment the normal daily life of a people. But faith comes to our aid at these times when words seem to fail. Christ's word is the only one that can give a response to the questions which trouble our spirit. Even if the forces of darkness appear to prevail, those who believe in God know that evil and death do not have the final say. Christian hope is based on this truth; at this time our prayerful trust draws strength from it.[675]

With UN Resolution no. 1368 from September 12, 2001[676] and the American plans to fight terrorism, beginning with the military intervention in Afghanistan, the political and religious tensions in the Middle East had risen again. John Paul II, appalled by those dangerous developments, engaged himself again, urging the international community on many occasions to undertake common initiatives for the cause of justice and peace in the region. It should be pointed out that with the rapidly increasing rise of anti-Islamic sentiments, it was important for the Pope that the people around the world did not follow these negative emotions.[677] Moreover, according to him, it was essential for them to be constantly aware of the clear distinction between Islamic terrorism and the true Islamic religion. John Paul II wanted to assure Muslims that despite the circumstances, the principles of *Nostra Aetate*, along with the Catholic Church's commitment to a sincere dialogue with them, remained valid. Therefore, on September 22, 2001, the Holy Father went on a pilgrimage to Kazakhstan, a Muslim majority country. On September 23, during his meeting with the Ordinaries of Central Asia in Astana, the Pope said that "[r]espect and dialogue should also be fostered in relation to the *Muslim community*."[678] The day after, while addressing representatives of the Kazakhs world of culture, John Paul referred to the issue of love and justice as the origin of humanity. He said:

In this context, and precisely here in this Land of encounter and dialogue, and before this distinguished audience, I wish to reaffirm the Catholic Church's respect for Islam, for authentic Islam: the Islam that prays, that is concerned for those in need. Recalling the errors of the past, including the most recent past, all believers ought to unite their

---

675 John Paul II, "General Audience" (September 12, 2001), online: http://www.vatican.va/holy_father/john_paul_ii/audiences/2001/documents/hf_jp-ii_aud_20010912_en.html, access: March 29, 2011.

676 "Security Council Condemns, 'In Strongest Terms', Terrorists Attack on United States: Unanimously Adopting Resolution 1368 (2001), Council Calls on All States to Bring Perpetrators to Justice," online: http://www.un.org/News/Press/docs/2001/SC7143.doc.htm, access: March 29, 2011.

677 Some Muslim authorities and Muslim scholars shared the Pope's concerns. For a reflection on related issues see: M. Sammak, "The Arab Muslim World after September the 11th," *Islamochristiana*, vol. 28 (2002), p. 1-11.

678 "Pastoral Visit in Kazakhstan, Meeting with the Ordinaries of Central Asia: Address of the Holy Father" (Astana, September 23, 2001), no. 7, online: http://www.vatican.va/holy_father/john_paul_ii/speeches/2001/september/documents/hf_jp-ii_spe_20010923_kazakhstan-astana-ordinaries_en.html, access: March 29, 2011.

efforts to ensure that God is never made the hostage of human ambitions. Hatred, fanaticism and terrorism profane the name of God and disfigure the true image of man.[679]

As the Taliban did not comply with the points of the UN Resolution no. 1368, on November 7, 2001, the Anglo-American bombardment of Kabul began. The entire international community, including the Vatican, supported the right of the United States to respond to the attack on September 11, 2001. However, John Paul II, convinced of the inefficacy of military solutions, continued to "confront" the ongoing "offensive of war" with his persistent "offensive of peace." On November 18, 2001, during the *Angelus* prayer, while sharing with people his concerns about the world predicament, the Pope said:

> In a situation made dramatic by the ever present threat of terrorism, we feel the need to cry out to God. The more insurmountable the difficulties and obscure the prospects, the more insistent must our prayer be, to beg of God the gift of mutual understanding, harmony and peace.[680]

The Pope subsequently proposed making December 14, 2001, a day of fasting "to pray fervently to God to grant to the world stable peace based on justice, and make it possible to find adequate solutions to the many conflicts that trouble the world."[681] Furthermore, the Holy Father also announced his intention to "invite the representatives of the world religions to come to Assisi on 24 January 2002, to pray for the overcoming of opposition and the promotion of authentic peace." John Paul II was especially concerned about Muslims. He explained:

> In particular, we wish to bring Christians and Muslims together to proclaim to the world that religion must never be a reason for conflict, hatred and violence. In this historic moment, humanity needs to see gestures of peace and to hear words of hope.[682]

The military intervention in Afghanistan terminated on December 6, 2001. However, with the escape of Bin Lādin, the danger of possible al-Qaeda terrorist actions was not eliminated.

---

[679] "Pastoral Visit in Kazakhstan, Meeting with Represantatives of the World of Culture: Address of John Paul II" (Astana, September 24, 2001), no. 5, online: http://www.vatican.va/holy_father/john_paul_ii/speeches/2001/september/documents/hf_jp-ii_spe_20010924_kazakhstan-astana-culture_en.html, access: March 29, 2011.

[680] John Paul II, *"Angelus"* (November 18, 2001), no. 1, online: http://www.vatican.va/holy_father/john_paul_ii/angelus/2001/documents/hf_jp-ii_ang_20011118_en.html, access: March 29, 2011.

[681] Ibid., no. 2. December 14 was the last day of Ramadan (the month of fasting for Muslims) and it coincided with Advent for Christians. Therefore, the Pope asked Catholics to fast on the same day.

[682] Ibid.

Meanwhile, the implementation of the American plans to fight terrorism contin-ued. The next target was Iraq.

As previously mentioned, John Paul II always rejected the use of military means in resolving political conflicts. Therefore, the American plans to fight terrorism with Iraq were strongly opposed by the Pope.[683] The Holy Father's action to prevent this second military conflict was "timely and insistent."[684] Day by day he followed the development of the situation.

On January 13, 2003, in his address to the Diplomatic Corps accredited to the Holy See for the traditional exchange of New Year greetings, John Paul II, while re-ferring to the developments in the Middle East, namely the preparations for military intervention in Iraq, once again articulated his protest with persistency and determi-nation by saying "NO TO WAR!" For him war always meant "a defeat for human-ity." The Pope emphasized that there were other "methods worthy of individuals and nations in resolving their differences" such as "international law, honest dialogue, and solidarity between States, the noble exercise of diplomacy."[685] His views con-cerning the situation were already known to the diplomats. Therefore, he approached them as follows:

> Without needing to repeat what I said to you last year on this occasion, I will simply add today, faced with the constant degeneration of the crisis in the Middle East, that the solution will never be imposed by recourse to terrorism or armed conflict, as if military victories could be the solution. And what are we to say of the threat of a war which could strike the people of Iraq, the land of the Prophets; a people already sorely tried by more than twelve years of embargo?[686]

Then, the Pope went on with a firm, straightforward explanation saying that:

> War is never just another means that one can choose to employ for settling differences between nations. As the Charter of the United Nations Organization and international law itself remind us, war cannot be decided upon, even when it is a matter of ensur-ing the common good, except as the very last option and in accordance with very strict conditions, without ignoring the consequences for the civilian population both during and after the military operations.[687]

In his diplomatic struggle to avoid the war, the Pontiff met with the German Minister of Foreign Affairs Yoshka Fisher (February 7), the Iraqi Minister of For-

---

[683] For a thorough account of John Paul II's diplomatic efforts to prevent the American interven-tion in Iraq, see: J. Moskwa, *Prorok...*, p. 347-395.

[684] "Intervention by Cardinal Angelo Sodano: A 25-Year Pontificate At The Service Of Peace," no. 11, online: http://www.vatican.va/roman_curia/secretariat_state/2003/documents/rc_seg-st_20031018_sodano-xxv-pontificate_en.html, access: March 29, 2011.

[685] "Address of His holiness John Paul II to the Diplomatic Corps" (January 13, 2003), no. 4.

[686] Ibid.

[687] Ibid.

eign Affairs Ṭāriq 'Azīz (February 14), the Secretary General of the United Nations Kofi Anan (February 18), the British Prime Minister Tony Blair (February 22), the Prime Minister of Spain Jose Maria Aznar and the Representative of the Iranian Government of Mohammed Reza Khatami (February 27). Moreover, he also tried direct mediation and sent his special envoys, Cardinal Roger Etchegaray (to Baghdad) and Cardinal Pio Laghi (to Washington) with letters to both presidents, i.e., Ṣaddām Ḥusayn and George W. Bush, "inviting them to reflect before God and before their own conscience on the possible ways of resolving the dispute in order to protect the primary good of peace, founded on justice and international law."[688]

It should be pointed out that the peace offensive of John Paul II was characterized by his independent opinion, his avocation to avoid the diplomatic divisions and support for the United Nations as the only guarantor of the correct application of the international law. The Pope was convinced that the war, not justified by a UN resolution, was unlawful. Therefore, he continued with his persistent call for dialogue, so the war with all its tragic consequences could be avoided.

The issue of *L'Osservatore Romano*, the official Vatican daily newspaper from the 24th-25th of February 2003, had an unusual front page. Three big letters composing the word *mai* (never) covered the biggest part of it. Above the title was written "Never one against the other," and under the title "Never terrorism and logic of war." The rest of the page was taken up by the text of the Sunday morning *Angelus* prayer, in which the Pope expressed his sorrows that at the beginning of the third millennium "the international community has been living in great apprehension on account of the *danger of a war* that might upset the whole Middle East region and aggravate the tensions." Addressing the people of the whole world, he also reminded them that "we can never be happy if we are *against one another*, the future of humanity can never be assured by terrorism and the logic of war."[689] Moreover, with the conviction that Christians "were called to be *sentinels of peace* wherever we live and work," he invited all Catholics to "dedicate with special intensity next March 5, Ash Wednesday, *to prayer and fasting for the cause of peace*, especially in the Middle East."[690] The word *mai,* that the Pontiff repeated four times, became the slogan of anti-war demonstrations.[691]

On Ash Wednesday (March 5, 2003), during the general audience, while appealing to the peoples' consciousness and hearts, John Paul II said:

> There is also a close link between fasting and prayer. Prayer means listening to God; fasting favors this openness of heart…It is necessary that everyone consciously assume responsibility and engage in a common effort to spare humanity another tragic conflict.

---

[688] Ibid.

[689] John Paul II, *"Angelus"* (February 23, 2003), no. 1, online: http://www.vatican.va/holy_father/john_paul_ii/angelus/2003/documents/hf_jp-ii_ang_20030223_en.html, access: March 29, 2011.

[690] Ibid., no. 2.

[691] J. Moskwa, *Prorok…*, p. 387.

This is why I wanted this Ash Wednesday to be a *Day of Prayer and Fasting* to implore peace for the world. We must ask God, first of all, for conversion of heart, for it is in the heart that every form of evil, every impulse to sin is rooted; we must pray and fast for the peaceful coexistence of peoples and nations.[692]

On March 16, the Pope reminded the member countries of the United Nations, and particularly those in the Security Council, that "the use of force represents the last recourse, after having exhausted every other peaceful solution, in keeping with the well-known principles of the UN Charter."[693] In view of "the *tremendous consequences* that an international military operation would have for the population of Iraq and for the balance of the Middle East region" and taking into account "the extremisms that could stem from it,"[694] the Holy Father went on with his straightforward call for last minute dialogue and negotiations:

I say to all: There is still time to negotiate; there is still room for peace, it is never too late to come to an understanding and to continue discussions.
To reflect on one's duties, to engage in energetic negotiations does not mean to be humiliated, but *to work with responsibility for peace*.[695]

On the night of March 20, the war against Ṣaddām Ḥusayn began. In the days that followed, as Cardinal Dziwisz recalled, the Pope was overcome by grief:

He felt the enormity of this new tragedy. At the same time, though, I thought he had a certain inward serenity. At no point, not even to the end, did he ever resign himself even to the mere idea of the war. And he was convinced that it was his duty to do everything to stop it. He defended peace, as he had always done…He had tried to do his duty before God, Church, and man. And he had done it as a free man who was not controlled either by the West or by the East – the same as always. Perhaps this is why he was able to use his moral authority and his credibility to keep Islamic-Christian relations from becoming a bone of contention in the war.[696]

Despite the fact that President Bush decided not to take into consideration the Pope's firm stand against the American military intervention in Iraq, the Holy See's diplomatic efforts to prevent it continued until the last days before the invasion and after it.[697] As the Pope predicted, once again the military solution proved to be rather

---

[692] "General Audience of John Paul II" (March 5, 2003), no. 3, online: http://www.vatican.va/holy_father/john_paul_ii/audiences/2003/documents/hf_jp-ii_aud_20030305_en.html, access: March 29, 2011.

[693] John Paul II, "*Angelus*" (March 16, 2003), no. 2, online: http://www.vatican.va/holy_father/john_paul_ii/angelus/2003/documents/hf_jp-ii_ang_20030316_en.html, access: March 29, 2011.

[694] Ibid.

[695] Ibid.

[696] S. Dziwisz, *A Life with Karol…*, p. 246.

[697] On April 20, 2003, in his Message "Urbi et Orbi" the Pope said: "Peace in Iraq! With the support of the international community, may the Iraqi people become the protagonists of the

inadequate. Iraq is still today overcome by internal religious and political conflicts, spreading violence and terrorist attacks. However, the Pope's firm, persistent and tireless protest against the war in Iraq did have international impact, because as Cardinal Sodano pointed out:

> There remains, however, one fact worthy of mention, one which very attentive observers of international politics have highlighted: the repeated, pondered and passionate Speeches of the Holy Father against the war in Iraq have made it so that, even among the Arabic peoples or adherents of Islam, this war has not been perceived as a "Christian war" against Muslims, and it has nothing at all to do with a religious war of the West against the Muslim world.[698]

The Pope's Annual Message to the diplomats and the international community in the year 2004 once again confirmed his determination for the cause of peace and his protest against war. John Paul II appealed to the international community to strengthen their efforts in pursuing the task of removing threats to peace. As for the problem of Iraq, he referred to his own tireless struggle to "avoid the grievous war" and pointed out that under the circumstances, the crucial matter was to help the newly-freed Iraqis build their future. Once again, the Pope referred to the urgent need to resolve the Palestinian-Israeli conflict:

> The failure to solve the Palestinian-Israeli issue remains a permanent factor of destabilization for the whole region, not to speak of the indescribable sufferings; it has caused both the Israeli and the Palestinian peoples. I will never tire of repeating to the leaders of these two peoples: the choice of weapons, the recourse to terrorism, on one side and, on the other, the reprisals, humiliation of the adversary and propaganda loaded with hate, lead nowhere. Respect for the legitimate aspirations of both parties, a return to the negotiating table and the concrete commitment of the International Community alone can be the first step towards a solution. True and lasting peace cannot be merely reduced to keeping a balance between the forces in question; it is the result of moral and juridical action.[699]

John Paul II's efforts to ease the religious and political tensions in the Middle East continued, despite some setbacks and controversy, until the end of his pontificate. Why was the Pope's involvement in Middle Eastern affairs that important?

---

collective rebuilding of their country." (*"Urbi et Orbi* Message of His Holiness John Paul II" (April 20, 2003), no. 5, online: http://www.vatican.va/holy_father/john_paul_ii/messages/urbi/documents/hf_jp-ii_mes_20030420_easter-urbi_en.html, access: March 29, 2011.

[698] "Intervention by Cardinal Angelo Sodano…," no. 11.

[699] "Address of His Holiness Pope John Paul II to the Diplomatic Corps Accredited to the Holy See for the Traditional Exchange of New Year Greetings" (January 12, 2004), online: http://www.vatican.va/holy_father/john_paul_ii/speeches/2004/january/documents/hf_jp-ii_spe_20040112_diplomatic-corps_en.html, access: March 29, 2011.

We all know that the situation in the Middle East is extremely difficult. We are also well aware that military solutions are short-lived and may only result in further conflict and violence. In light of the policy that was adopted by John Paul II, the importance of the Holy See's voice in the international community has significantly increased. The Holy See intervened in world affairs as a religious institution, relying on the impact of the moral prestige of the Pontiff.[700] John Paul II did not threaten anybody but spoke, addressing both political leaders and the common people. His words had great symbolic value. As Cardinal Dziwisz pointed out, "whenever some trial was in the offing, he never worried beforehand about whether or not he would be defeated."[701] Therefore, he was able to awaken people's consciousness and alert their moral sensitivity, forcing them to re-think and re-assess their ideas and their actions, and eventually make them seriously consider his opinion and apply it in resolving the complex issues of the Middle Eastern reality.

Summary

John Paul II's involvement in Middle Eastern political problems, characterized by the path of religious reconciliation between the followers of Christianity, Islam and Judaism, focused on three major issues: Palestinian-Israeli conflict, war in Lebanon and military interventions in Iraq.

With regard to the Palestinian-Israeli conflict, John Paul II fully supported the position of his predecessor, Paul VI. However, while recognizing the political rights of both the Jews and the Palestinians, the Pope was convinced – and this was the fundament of the Holy See's official position for the years to come – that the security of one nation, namely the Israelis, could not be established at the expense of the rights of the other side, i.e., the Palestinians.

Since the outbreak of the war in Lebanon in 1975, John Paul II focused on continued efforts to save the territorial integrity of the country. When following the Israeli invasion of 1982 and the increased engagement of Syria, Lebanon was overcome by armed violence and became a center of confrontations between the Arabs and the Israelis and in consequence between the East and the West, the Pope did not spare his diplomatic efforts and appeals to reach a Middle East settlement, assuring the protection of the Palestinian rights.

John Paul II always rejected the use of military means in resolving political problems. Therefore, in 1990, with the outbreak of the Gulf crisis, he did everything in his power to avoid military conflict. In the aftermath of the war, it was due to the initiative of the United States that Israel, Jordan and the Palestine Liberation

---

[700] See: G. E. Irani, *The Papacy and the Middle East...*, p. 4-5, 159-160.
[701] S. Dziwisz, *A Life with Karol...*, p. 246.

Organization decided to participate, for the first time, in Middle East peace process negotiations. The Pope's vision of the establishment of some kind of a peaceful accommodation between Israelis and Palestinians, that would fulfill the criteria of justice, became the priority while he set in motion the diplomatic process leading to the Holy See's diplomatic recognition of Israel and relations with the PLO.

For John Paul II, the military option was never the right one. Therefore, the American plans for the terrorism-preventing war with Iraq were also met with timely and insistent opposition from the Pope. Moreover, as he predicted, the second war in Iraq in 2003 only brought a short-lived, temporary solution and resulted in people's sufferings and further conflict.

John Paul II's efforts to appease the religious and political tensions in the Middle East continued, despite some setbacks and controversy, until the end of his pontificate. The Pontiff addressed both political leaders and common people with words that carried a great symbolic weight, hoping to awaken people's consciousness and to encourage implementing his opinion in resolving the complex issues of the Middle Eastern reality.

Conclusion

During the past two decades, an impressive number of interpretations of the international world order have been formulated. The authors of all these complex reflections offered a variety of possible visions from one of "the end of history," through the theory of "the clash of civilizations" and up to the concepts of "the universal global order." All these visions were based primarily on the appearance of political and economic foundations and realities. One may say that some of these theories increased our awareness about important matters. However, they also may have multiplied our anxieties and evoked fears concerning the future.

Parallel to these often pessimistic visions, there was another one, quite positive and which could be certainly considered insightful. This was John Paul II's vision, characterized by the idea of building a global moral community of humanity, explained to us step by step and over and over again during the time of his long pontificate.[702] In his reflection about the international world order, John Paul II viewed the international reality from a different perspective. This was the perspective of a witness to human dignity and a witness to hope for a better future despite all the negative apocalyptic visions and predictions. John Paul II proposed to the world a positive vision of a long-term, accessible, feasible and phased program for peace.

The key concept of that vision is the guiding value of the superior benefit of peace. It was based on the Pope's deep conviction that history should be perceived through the prism of ethics and morality, and not through the short lenses of economic gains and growing political powers. Therefore, peace as a gift from God constitutes the essential good for each and every person and for the entire human family. One may agree with Weigel that this vision originated from the Holy Father's "different

---

[702] In recent years, some political theorists of international relations have emphasized the moral aspect of such relations. See: D. Boucher, *Political Theories of International Relation: From Thucydides to the Present*, New York: Oxford University Press, 1998, p. 395-405.

idea of history."[703] The fact that John Paul II came from the Polish nation, namely one that was for more than one hundred years deprived of its political autonomy and survived as a nation through its language, literature, music and religion, definitely strengthened his conviction that neither politics nor economy should be a driving force in history. In other words, the Pontiff strongly believed that culture, which has a spiritual power, over time was always more effective in history than brute force. Furthermore, it was also sustainable.

In his numerous speeches, addresses and documents the Pope explained over and over that peace, as outlined by John XXIII in *Pacem in Terris*, required four conditions, namely truth, justice, love and freedom. Only the fulfillment of the above conditions, the Holy Father believed, would guarantee the respect for the human rights. In 1981, in his Message for the celebration of the World Day of Peace, John Paul II reminded people that "peace must be realized in truth; it must be built upon justice; it must be animated by love; it must be brought to being in freedom (cf. *Pacem in Terris*)."[704] He urged everyone to give the issue of peace deeper thought. Twenty-two years later, in his Message for the World Day of Peace, entitled "*Pacem in Terris*: a Permanent Commitment," he concluded his own reflection stating:

> *Truth* will build peace if every individual sincerely acknowledges not only his rights, also his own duties towards others. *Justice* will build peace if in practice everyone respects the rights of others and actually fulfils his duties towards them. *Love* will build peace if people feel the needs of others as their own and share what they have with others, especially the values of mind and spirit which they possess. *Freedom* will build peace and make it thrive if, in the choice of the means to that end, people act according to reason and assume responsibility for their own actions.[705]

As pointed out previously, since the beginning of his pontificate, John Paul II was committed and determined to implement in his teaching and actions both the essence of the social teaching of the Church with its crucial document *Pacem in Terris* by John XXIII, and the conclusions of the Second Vatican Council, and in particular, its newly-developed attitude towards non-Christian religions. All of these factors, according to the Pope, reconfirmed the need to defend human rights and required a new approach of the Catholic Church to world society, which is undertaking the task already initiated by Paul VI of developing dialogue with non-Christians.

John Paul II exerted a historical influence on intercultural dialoguing and as a dialogue builder was capable of evoking people's own responses and their will-

---

[703]   G. Weigel, *Witness to Hope...*, p. 22.

[704]   "Message of His Holiness John Paul II For the Celebration of the Day of Peace: *To Serve Peace, Respect Freedom*" (January 1, 1981), no. 2.

[705]   "Message of His Holiness John Paul II for the Celebration of the World Day of Peace: *Pacem in Terris*, A Permanent Commitment" (January 1, 2003), no. 3, online: http://www.vatican.va/holy_father/john_paul_ii/messages/peace/documents/hf_jp-ii_mes_20021217_xxxvi-world-day-for-peace_en.html, access: March 30, 2011.

ingness to create and engage in a dialogue with others. It is important to note that John Paul II's global footprint includes providing people with inspirational energy and encouragement to change their attitudes, laying the groundwork for unforgettable grand gestures, such as admitting mistakes and wrongdoings. The Pope was convinced that in the modern, changing world, his teaching should be directed towards encouraging people to apply whatever they could learn from the individual discovery of personal and environmental realities into collective meaning making. His re-definitions of coexistence and mutual engagement will continue to bring fruit as more and more analysis is done to understand the importance and the mechanisms of dialoguing. All in all, the core sense and the subject of John Paul II's dialogical teaching were to create a worldly dialogue.

Dialogue, both with religious and lay people, as well as solidarity were, according to the Pope, the only way that could lead the world to peace. Furthermore, in the view of the Holy Father, dialogue, characterized by sincerity, patience and loyalty, was the only appropriate strategy in international relations. Only through a sincere dialogue could people and nations resolve their problems, starting from simple misunderstandings and up to global conflicts. Furthermore, the Pope believed that once this skill was learned it would continue giving, and thus offer an alternative conflict-resolution approach linked with prevention.

On October 5, 1995, in his address to the United Nations Assembly, the Pope explained:

> *We do not live in an irrational or meaningless world.* On the contrary, there is a *moral logic* which is built into human life and which makes possible dialogue between individuals and peoples. If we want a *century of violent coercion* to be succeeded by a *century of persuasion*, we must find a way to discuss the human future intelligibly. The universal moral law written on the human heart is precisely that kind of "grammar" which is needed if the world is to engage this discussion of its future.[706]

"That kind of grammar," a moral code, the Pope believed, was particularly important in the Middle East, where conflicting political, social and religious interests were coming to the fore and the efforts of attaining peace seemed at times to be ephemeral. Therefore, in John Paul II's strategy for peace in this region, the development of a sincere interreligious dialogue with the Muslim *umma* played the most important role. Drawing extensively on all the positive moments extracted from the thirteen centuries of history of Christian-Muslim relations, such as the inspiring examples of the activity of the forerunners of interreligious dialogue, the essence of the Second Vatican Council's related conclusions and the dialogical teaching of Paul VI, the Pontiff established and developed in an unprecedented way his own path of dialogical encounter with the Muslim world.

---

[706] "Apostolic Journey of His Holiness John Paul II to the United States of America: The Fiftieth General Assembly…," no. 3.

There is no doubt that John Paul II should be credited with opening a new, positive and promising chapter in the history of Christian-Muslim relations based on his sincere dialogical commitment. Moreover, one may also say that the Pope's dialogue with the followers of Islam, despite diverse opinions, became the most effective tool in easing the existing Middle Eastern tensions and resulted in the observable fact that the road for peace in this conflicting and troubled area was and still remains open.

On the second Sunday in December 1978, less than two months after his election, while addressing the people gathered on St. Peter's Square, John Paul II expressed, in a very emotional way, his wish to go to the Holy Land:

> Oh! How I wish I could repeat his words, at this moment! How I wish I could go to the land of my Lord and Redeemer! How I wish I could find myself in those very streets in which the People of God used to walk at that time, climb to the top of Sinai, where the Ten Commandments were given to us! How I wish I could pass along all the roads between Jerusalem, Bethlehem and the Sea of Galilee! How I wish I could stop on the mount of the Transfiguration, from where the massif of Lebanon appears: „Tabor and Hermon joyously praise thy name" (Psalm 89:12).
> This was and is my greatest desire, ever since the beginning of my pontificate.[707]

These sentiments were natural and human. For the Bishop of Rome, the pilgrimage to Jerusalem was the most important one. People waited in expectation of John Paul II's announcement of the date on which he would fulfill his dream. Having built the emotions of the crowd on St. Peter's Square to great heights, the Pope said:

> But, regretfully, I must at least for the present, forget this pilgrimage![708]

"At least for the present"? More than twenty years passed. In the meantime, John Paul II went on ninety pilgrimages to many places around the world. As for the Holy Land, he did not go there until March (20-26) of the year 2000. Why did he postpone this pilgrimage for such a long time?

For many years, the Middle East has been an area of the highest political and religious tensions resulting in so-far unresolved conflicts. The news from this inflamed part of the world more and more dominate our media and the Middle Eastern events begin to have not only a global but a more and more local impact, influencing various aspects of our daily life.

It appears as though John Paul II inspired and fostered the movement leading to the fall of communism in Central and Eastern Europe. However, as has already been pointed out in the introduction, we are not sufficiently aware that many of the positive changes that we observed in the Middle East in the past three decades, especially the road to the peace process, which has been many times abruptly interrupted

---

[707] John Paul II, *"Angelus"* (December 10, 1978).
[708] Ibid.

and blocked, are attributable to the enormous efforts of the very same person, John Paul II.

Concern for each and every person, respect for inalienable human rights despite religion, ethnic and racial origin, or sexual orientation, initiating dialogue and striving for reconciliation and understanding no matter how difficult the problems and how complicated the circumstances: these were the issues that the Holy Father addressed consistently throughout his pontificate.

Since the beginning of his pontificate, the voice of John Paul II was always present in Middle Eastern affairs. While realizing that the Middle Eastern political, social and religious tensions, together with the Western involvement and interventions in the area, could easily result in an outbreak of violence leading to a serious global war, the Pontiff deliberately postponed his pilgrimage to the Holy Land and undertook the difficult and almost impossible task of building bridges between the conflicting sides, so the situation could stabilize and the road to peace could open. With patience and determination, John Paul II engaged himself in developing a sincere interreligious dialogue and used it as the most effective tool for easing the religious and political tensions and promoting a peaceful coexistence in the region, thus preparing a better climate for his most important pilgrimage. His diplomatic efforts concerning the Middle East focused on two crucial issues, namely the Palestinian-Israeli conflict and the status of Jerusalem and the Holy Land. Moreover, the Pope was also concerned with the protection of Christian minorities living in these regions.

Determination, objectivism and pragmatism, but most of all one clearly outlined far-reaching goal: peace and security in the Middle East – this is how one could describe all the related diplomatic efforts observed during the pontificate of John Paul II.

"Peace [in the Middle East] based on equitable recognition of the rights of all, cannot fail to include the consideration and just settlement of the Palestinian question,"[709] the Pope stated on October 2, 1979, while addressing the United Nations General Assembly. One year later in his famous homily in Otranto, he once again strongly confirmed the equal rights of both nations: the Jews and the Palestinians.

In the 1980s, during the war in Lebanon, John Paul II demonstrated, on a number of occasions, his solidarity with the victims of the Israeli bomb attacks. In 1982, during a meeting with Yāsir 'Arafāt, he condemned the Israeli attacks and the Palestinian terrorism as well as retaliating actions, and appealed to both parties of the conflict for negotiations.

The Pope's persistent appeals for peace in the Middle East were accompanied by his focus both on the increasing diplomatic contacts of the Holy See with Muslim, and in particular Arab countries, such as Egypt, Jordan, Morocco, Tunisia, and Algeria, Iraq, Syria, Lebanon and Sudan, and on the continuous development of a sincere dialogue with Muslims in the spirit of *Nostra Aetate*. Moreover, in order to pursue

---

[709] "Apostolic Journey to the United States of America: Address of His Holiness John Paul II to the 34th General Assembly…," no. 10.

his strategy for peace, John Paul II did not hesitate to meet with the heads of the governments from the Arab, African and Western states.

In 1984, in his apostolic letter *Redemptionis Anno*, while referring to the question of Jerusalem, he confirmed the position of his predecessor Paul VI, stating that "the unique and universal" character of the city should be preserved. However, John Paul II gave the symbolic meaning of the Holy City an even wider dimension. It was the Pontiff's opinion that Jerusalem should become the fundament and a crucial point of reference in the process of finding an adequate solution to the Palestinian-Israeli conflict, and be a challenging opportunity, which despite many still-unresolved obstacles, would keep Christians, Jews and Muslims in peace. Moreover, the Holy Father called upon "all the people in the Middle East" to rediscover "the true essence of their history," in order to "overcome this tragic situation they lived in."[710]

It should be emphasized that since the beginning, the Pope's support for the Palestinians' demands was accompanied by sympathy for the Jews and support of Israel.

In the 1980s, John Paul II commented on a number of occasions on the difficulties of existing relations between Christianity and Judaism, and as the head of the Catholic Church he confirmed his commitment to interreligious dialogue. On April 12, 1986, in a symbolic gesture of his support for the Jews, he visited, as the first Pope in history, the synagogue in Rome.

In January 1988, the Pope once again supported the rights of the Palestinians and appointed Bishop Mīshīl Ṣabbāḥ the Latin patriarch of Jerusalem. In December of the same year, after the Palestinian Liberation Organization officially acknowledged the existence of the state of Israel and declared the withdrawal of terrorist actions, John Paul II met for the second time with Yāsir 'Arafāt and expressed his hope that both nations would soon enter the road of peace and reconciliation.

At the beginning of the 1990s, the whole world witnessed two major dramatic events: Iraq's invasion of Kuwait and the United States' military intervention. Moreover, the Persian Gulf War was strongly criticized by the Vatican. "Peace is still possible: war would be the defeat of humanity," John Paul II stated in August 1990, right before Operation Desert Storm began.[711] "War is not an answer,"[712] the Holy Father warned, directing his words to President Bush and appealing both to the parties of the conflict and to the entire international community for the exchange of military action for peace negotiations.

---

[710] "From the Apostolic Letter of John Paul II *Redemptionis Anno*".

[711] The Pope repeated these words on January 12, 1991. See: "John Paul II Address to the Diplomatic Corps Accredited to the Holy See" (January 12, 1991), *Islamochristiana*, vol. 17 (1991), p. 278.

[712] See: D. Rudnicka-Kassem, "Wojna nie jest rozwiązaniem: Dialog międzyreligijny Jana Pawła II jako program pokoju i stabilizacji na Bliskim Wschodzie," in: Magdalena Lewicka and Czesław Łapicz (ed.), Dialog chrześcijańsko-muzułmański: Historia i współczesność, zagrożenia i wyzwania, Toruń: Wydawnictwo Naukowe Uniwersytetu Mikołaja Kopernika, 2011, s. 47-59.

In the aftermath of the war, when, due to the initiative of the United States, Israel, Jordan and the PLO decided to participate, for the first time, in Middle East peace process negotiations, John Paul II became an even more active participant in the diplomacy of the region. The Vatican's vision of the establishment of some sort of a peaceful accommodation between Israelis and Palestinians, an accommodation which would be acceptable to both, fulfill the criteria of justice and, in consequence, contribute to peaceful settlements concerning other political and religious conflicts in the Middle East, became the priority in the Pope's diplomatic efforts. With pragmatism and determination, John Paul II set in motion the process leading to the Holy See's diplomatic recognition of Israel and subsequently, to relations with the PLO.

On September 12, 1993, the Prime minister of Israel, Yitzhak Rabin and the Leader of the PLO signed at the White House the official agreement about the establishment of the Palestinian Autonomy. This fact, despite many controversial opinions, gave an extra impulse to speed up the Vatican-Israeli negotiations, and soon afterwards, John Paul II's efforts brought long-awaited results. On December 30, 1993, in Jerusalem, the agreement about the establishment of official diplomatic relations between the Vatican and Israel was signed. As for the character of the Holy See's contact with the Palestinians, one should mention that on October 25, 1994, the Vatican's relations with the PLO as the representative of the Palestinian people acquired official diplomatic status.

In the mid-1990s, it seemed as if the first phase of his longest pilgrimage was slowly coming to its successful end. After a long period of tensions and conflicts, the political climate in the Middle East was visibly favoring initiating peace talks.

The world had entered the twenty-first century. In March 2000, John Paul II went to the Holy Land to complete the second phase of his longest pilgrimage. In May 2001, the Pontiff made his historic visit to the Umayyad Grand Mosque in Damascus, marking the beginning of a new stage in the relations between Christianity and Islam.

However, the first years of the twenty-first century have proven that the path for dialogue and peace in the Middle East was still uncertain and the bridges already built might be too shaky. With the events of September 11, 2001 and the subsequent military intervention in Afghanistan and Iraq, political and religious tension rose again. The situation at that time was critical and the Pope once again began his campaign against violence and the recourse to arms. Once again he strongly articulated his "No to War!" mantra.

Since the beginning of his pontificate, John Paul II emphasized on numerous occasions that "human affairs must be dealt humanely, not with violence" and that "it is not permissible to kill in order to impose a solution."[713] On January 1, 2003, less than three months before the military intervention in Iraq began, in his Message for the Celebration of the World Day of Peace, the Pope referred to the question of the Middle East, saying:

---

[713] "Message of His Holiness John Paul II for the Celebration of the Day of Peace: *To Reach Peace, Teach Peace*" (January 1, 1979), no. 1.

Perhaps nowhere today is there a more obvious need for the correct use of political authority than in *the dramatic situation of the Middle East and the Holy Land*. Day after day, year after year, the cumulative effect of bitter mutual rejection and an unending chain of violence and retaliation have shattered every effort so far to engage in serious dialogue on the real issues involved...The fratricidal struggle that daily convulses the Holy Land and brings into conflict the forces shaping the immediate future of the Middle East shows clearly the need for men and women who, out of conviction, will implement policies firmly based on the principle of respect for human dignity and human rights. Such policies are incomparably more advantageous to everyone than the continuation of conflict. A start can be made on the basis of this truth.[714]

The call for *dialogue* and *peace* in the Middle East had always been and remained fundamental for John Paul II's mission. It was always his great wish and conviction that something considered practically impossible would become possible. On October 5, 1980, in his homily delivered in Otranto the Holy Father said:

Towering high over all this world, like an ideal center, a precious jewel-case that keeps the treasures is the Holy City, Jerusalem, today the object of a dispute that seems without a solution, tomorrow – if people only want it! – tomorrow will be a crossroad of reconciliation and peace.[715]

As the world impatiently awaits the return of a conscious dialogical spirit, we might become witnesses of the "tomorrow" that might come sooner than we think. "If people only want it!"

---

[714] "Message of His Holiness John Paul II for the Celebration of the World Day of Peace: *Pacem in Terris, A Permanent Commitment*" (January 1, 2003), no. 7.

[715] N. Bakalar and R. Balkin (eds.), *The Wisdom of John Paul II...*, p. 121.

Bibliography

Primary sources:

Documents of the Catholic Church:

I) From the pre-Vatican II period:
"*De Motione Oecumenica*," *Acta Apostolicae Sedis*, annus 42 (1950), series 2, vol. 17, p. 142-157.

II) Documents of the Second Vatican Council with references to the issue of interreligious dialogue:

with indirect references:
"The Constitution on the Sacred Liturgy *Sacrosanctum Concilium* Solemnly Promulgated by His Holiness Pope Paul VI" (December 4, 1963), online: http://www.vatican.va/archive/hist_councils/ii_vatican_council/documents/vat-ii_const_19631204_sacrosanctum-concilium_en.html, access: March 10, 2011.
"Decree on Ecumenism *Unitatis Redintegratio*" (November 21, 1964), online: http://www.vatican.va/archive/hist_councils/ii_vatican_council/documents/vat-ii_decree_19641121_unitatis-redintegratio_en.html, access: March 10, 2011.
"Decree on Priestly Training *Optatam Totius* Proclaimed by His Holiness Pope Paul VI" (October 28, 1965), online: http://www.vatican.va/archive/hist_councils/ii_vatican_council/documents/vat-ii_decree_19651028_optatam-totius_en.html, access: March 10, 2011.
"Declaration on Christian Eduaction *Gravissimum Educationis* Proclaimed by His Holiness Pope Paul VI" (October 28, 1965), online: http://www.vatican.va/archive/hist_councils/ii_vatican_council/documents/vat-ii_decl_19651028_gravissimum-educationis_en.html, access: March 10, 2011.
"Decree on the Apostolate of the Laity *Apostolicam Actuositatem* Solemnly Promulgated by His Holiness, Pope Paul VI" (November 18, 1965), online: http://www.vatican.va/archive/hist_councils/ii_vatican_council/documents/vat-ii_decree_19651118_apostolicam-actuositatem_en.html, access: March 10, 2011.

with direct references:

"Dogmatic Constitution on Divine Revelation *Dei Verbum* Solemnly Promulgated by His Holiness Pope Paul VI" (November 18, 1965), online: http://www.vatican.va/archive/ hist_councils/ii_vatican_council/documents/vat-ii_const_19651118_dei-verbum_en.html, access: March 10, 2011.

"Decree *Ad Gentes* on the Mission Activity of the Church" (December 7, 1965), online: http://www.vatican.va/archive/hist_councils/ii_vatican_council/documents/vat-ii_de-cree_19651207_ad-gentes_en.html, access: March 10, 2011.

"Declaration on Religious Freedom *Dignitatis Humanae* on the Right of the Person and of Communities to Social and Civil Freedom in Matters Religious Promulgated by His Holiness Pope Paul VI" (December 7, 1965), online: http://www.vatican.va/archive/ hist_councils/ii_vatican_council/documents/vat-ii_decl_19651207_dignitatis-humanae_ en.html, access: March 10, 2011.

"Pastoral Constitution on the Church in the Modern World *Gaudium et Spes* Promulgated by His Holiness, Pope Paul VI" (December 7, 1965), online: http://www.vatican.va/ archive/hist_councils/ii_vatican_council/documents/vat-ii_cons_19651207_gaudium-et-spes_en.html, access: March 10, 2011.

with references to Islam:

"Dogmatic Constitution on the Church *Lumen Gentium* Solemnly Promulgated by His Holiness Pope Paul VI" (November 21, 1964), online: http://www.vatican.va/archive/ hist_councils/ii_vatican_council/documents/vat-ii_const_19641121_lumen-gentium_en. html, access: March 10, 2011.

"Declaration on the Relation of the Church to Non-Christian Religions *Nostra Aetate* Proclaimed by His Holiness Pope Paul VI" (October 28, 1965), online: http://www.vatican. va/archive/hist_councils/ii_vatican_council/documents/vat-ii_decl_19651028_nostra-aetate_en.html, access: March 10, 2011.

III) Papal documents:

Pius XII

encyclicals:

"*Auspicia Quaedam* Encyclical of Pope Pius XII on Public Prayers for World Peace and Solution of the Problem of Palestine to Patriarchs, Primates, Archbishops, Bishops, and Other Ordinaries *In Peace and Communion with the Holy See*" (May 1, 1948), online: http:// www.vatican.va/holy_father/pius_xii/encyclicals/documents/hf_p-xii_enc_01051948_ auspicia-quaedam_en.html, access: March 25, 2011.

"*In Multiplicibus Curis*: Encyclical of Pope Pius XII on Prayers for Peace in Palestine to the Venerable Brethren, the Patriarchs, Primates, Archbishops, Bishops, and Other Ordinaries in Peace and Communion with the Apostolic See" (October 24, 1948), online: http:// www.vatican.va/holy_father/pius_xii/encyclicals/documents/hf_p-xii_enc_24101948_ in-multiplicibus-curis_en.html, access: March 25, 2011.

"*Redemptoris Nostri Cruciatus*: Encyclical of Pope Pius XII on the Holy Places in Palestine to the Venerable Brethren the Patriarchs, Primates, Archbishops, Bishops, and Other Ordinaries in Peace and Communion with the Apostolic See" (April 15, 1949), online: http:// www.vatican.va/holy_father/pius_xii/encyclicals/documents/hf_p-xii_enc_15041949_ redemptoris-nostri-cruciatus_en.html, access: March 25, 2011.

"*Laetamur Admodum:* Encyclical of Pope Pius XII Renewing Exhortation for Prayers for Peace for Poland, Hungary, and the Middle East to the Venerable Brethren, the Patriarchs, Primates, Archbishops, Bishops, and Other Local Ordinaries in Peace and Communion with the Apostolic See" (November 1, 1956), online: http://www.vatican.va/holy_father/ pius_xii/encyclicals/documents/hf_p-xii_enc_01111956_laetamur-admodum_en.html, access: March 25, 2011.

John XXIII

encyclical:
"*Pacem in Terris*: Encyclical of Pope John XXIII on Establishing Universal Peace in Truth, Justice, Charity, and Liberty" (April 11, 1963), online: http://www.vatican.va/holy_father/john_xxiii/encyclicals/documents/hf_j-xxiii_enc_11041963_pacem_en.html, access: March 10, 2011

Paul VI

encyclicals:
"*Ecclesiam Suam*, Encyclical of Pope Paul VI on the Church" (August 6, 1964), online: http://www.vatican.va/holy_father/paul_vi/encyclicals/documents/hf_p-vi_enc_06081964_ecclesiam_en.html, access: March 10, 2011.
"*Populorum Progressio*: Encyclical of Pope Paul VI on the Development of Peoples" (March 26, 1967), online: http://www.vatican.va/holy_father/paul_vi/encyclicals/documents/ hf_p-vi_enc_26031967_populorum_en.html, access: March 10, 2011.

apostolic exhortations:
"*Evangelii Nuntiandi*: Apostolic Exhortation of His Holiness Pope Paul VI to the Episcopate, to the Clergy and to All the Faithful of the Entire World" (December 8, 1975), online: http://www.vatican.va/holy_father/paul_vi/apost_exhortations/documents/hf_ p-vi_exh_19751208_evangelii-nuntiandi_en.html, access: March 10, 2011.
"*Nobis in Animo*: Esortazione apostolica di sua santità Paolo pp. VI all'episcopato, al clero ed ai fedeli di tutto il mondo sulle accresciute necessità della Chiesa in terra santa" (March 25, 1974), online: http://www.vatican.va/holy_father/paul_ii/apost_exhortations/documents/hf_p-vi_exh_19740325_nobis-in-animo_if.html, access: March 27, 2011.

speeches and other documents:
"Address of the Holy Father Paul VI to King Hussein Ibn Talal of Jordan" (April 29, 1978), online: http://www.vatican.va/holy_father/paul_vi/speeches/1978/april/documents/ hf_p-vi_spe_19780429_re-hussein-giordania_en.html, access: March 29, 2011.
"Address of Paul VI to the Ambassador of the Republic of Pakistan to the Holy See" (September 18, 1969), online: http://www.vatican.va/holy_father/paul_vi/speeches/1969/ september/documents/hf_p-vi_spe_19690918_ambasciatore-pakistan_en.html, access: March 10, 2011.
"Address of the Holy Father Paul VI to the Egyptian President Visiting for the First Time the Apostolic See" (April 8, 1976), online: http://www.vatican.va/holy_father/paul_vi/ speeches/1976/documents/hf_p-vi_spe_19760408_presidente-egitto_en.html, access: March 10, 2011.
"Address of the Holy Father Paul VI to the New Ambassador of the Syrian Arab Republic to the Holy See" (December 15, 1977), online: http://www.vatican.va/holy_father/paul_vi/

speeches/1977/december/documents/hf_p-vi_spe_19771215_ambasciatore-rep-araba_
en.html, access: March 29, 2011.
"Pilgrimage to the Holy Land Address of Paul VI to the King of Jordan" (January 4, 1964),
online: http://www.vatican.va/holy_father/paul_vi/speeches/1964/documents/hf_p-vi_
spe_19640104_jordania_en.html, access: March 10, 2011.
"To the Faithful at the *Angelus Domini*, Rome" (October 17, 1965), in: F. Gioia (ed.), *Interreligious Dialogue: The Official Teaching of the Catholic Church (1963-1995)*, Boston:
Pauline Books & Media, 1997, p. 140.
"Voyage Apostolique à Istanbul, Ephèse et Izmir: Discours du Pape Paul VI au Chef des Musulmans" (Istanbul, Juillet 25, 1967), online: http://www.vatican.va/holy_father/paul_vi/
speeches/1967/july/documents/hf_p-vi_spe_19670725_comunita-musulmana_fr.html,
access: March 27, 2011.

John Paul I

"Radio Message *Urbi et Orbi*" in: F. Gioia (ed.), *Interreligious Dialogue: The Official Teaching of the Catholic Church (1963-1995)*, Boston: Pauline Books & Media, 1997, p. 211.

John Paul II

encyclicals:
"*Redemptor Hominis* to his Venerable Brothers in the Episcopate the Priests the Religious Families, the Sons and Daughters of the Church and to All Men and Women of Good Will at the
Beginning of his Papal Ministry" (March 4, 1979), online: http://www.vatican.va/holy_
father/john_paul_ii/encyclicals/documents/hf_jp-ii_enc_04031979_redemptor-hominis
_en.html, access: March 15, 2011.
"*Dominum et Vivificantem*: On the Holy Spirit in the Life of the Church and the World"
(May 18, 1986), online: http://www.vatican.va/holy_father/john_paul_ii/encyclicals/
documents/hf_jp-ii_enc_18051986_dominum-et-vivificantem_en.html, access: March
15, 2011.
"*Sollicitudo Rei Socialis*: To the Bishops, Priests, Religious Families, Sons and Daughters
of the Church and all People of Good Will for the Twentieth Anniversary of *Populorum Progressio*" (December 30, 1987), online: http://www.vatican.va/holy_father/john_
paul_ii/encyclicals/documents/hf_jp-ii_enc_30121987_sollicitudo-rei-socialis_en.html,
access : March 15, 2011.
"*Redemptoris Missio*: On the Permanent Validity of the Church's Missionary Mandate" (December 7, 1990), online: http://www.vatican.va/holy_father/john_paul_ii/encyclicals/
documents/hf_jp-ii_enc_07121990_redemptoris-missio_en.html, access: March 15, 2011.

apostolic exhortations:
"Apostolic Exhortation *Familiaris Consortio* of Pope John Paul II to the Episcopate to the
Clergy and to the Faithful of the Whole Catholic Church on the Role of the Christian
Family in the Modern World" (November 22, 1981), online: http://www.vatican.va/
holy_father/john_paul_ii/apost_exhortations/documents/hf_jp-ii_exh_19811122_famil-
iaris-consortio_en.html, access: March 10, 2011.
"Exhortation apostolique post-synodale: une espérance nouvelle pour le Liban de sa sain-
teté Jean-Paul II aux patriarches, aux évêques, au clergé, aux religieux, aux religieuses

et à tous les fidèles du Liban," online: http://www.vatican.va/holy_father/john_paul_ii/
apost_exhortations/documents/hf_jp-ii_exh_19970510_lebanon_fr.html, access: March
27, 2011.

"Post-Synodal Apostolic Exhortation *Christifideles Laici* of His Holiness John Paul II on the
Vocation and the Mission of the Lay Faithful in the Church and in the World" (December 30, 1988), online: http://www.vatican.va/holy_father/john_paul_ii/apost_exhorta-
tions/documents/hf_jp-ii_exh_30121988_christifideles-laici_en.html, access: March 15,
2011.

"Post-Synodal Appostolic Exhortation *Ecclesia in Africa of the Holy Father John Paul II to
the Bishops, Priests and Deacons, Men and Women Religious and All the Lay Faithful
on the Church in Africa and its Evangelizing Mission towards the Year 2000*" (September
14, 1995), online: http://www.vatican.va/holy_father/john_paul_ii/apost_exhortations/
documents/hf_jp-ii_exh_14091995_ecclesia-in-africa_en.html, access: March 15, 2011.

"Post-Synodal Apostolic Exhortation *Ecclesia in Asia* of the Holy Father John Paul II to
the Bishops, Priests and Deacons, Men and Women in the Consecrated Life and All the
Lay Faithful on Jesus Christ the Saviour and his Mission of Love and Service in Asia:
'...That They May Have Life, and Have it Abundantly' (Jn 10:10)" (November 6, 1999),
online: http://www.vatican.va/holy_father/john_paul_ii/apost_exhortations/documents/
hf_jp-ii_exh_06111999_ecclesia-in-asia_en.html, access: March 15, 2011.

"Post-Synodal Apostolic Exhortation *Ecclesia in Oceania* of His Holiness Pope John Paul
II to the Bishops Priests And Deacons Men and Women in the Consecrated Life and All
the Lay Faithful on Jesus Christ and the Peoples of Oceania: Walking His Way, Telling
His Truth, Living His Life" (November 22, 2001), online: http://www.vatican.va/holy_
father/john_paul_ii/apost_exhortations/documents/hf_jp-ii_exh_20011122_ecclesia-in-
oceania_en.html, access: March 15, 2011.

"Post-Synodal Apostolic Exhortation *Ecclesia in Europa* of His Holiness Pope John Paul II
to the Bishops Men and Women in the Consecrated Life and All the Lay Faithful on Jesus Christ Alive in His Church the Source of Hope for Europe" (June 28, 2003), online:
http://www.vatican.va/holy_father/john_paul_ii/apost_exhortations/documents/hf_jp-ii_
exh_20030628_ecclesia-in-europa_en.html, access: March 15, 2011.

apostolic letters:

"From the Apostolic Letter of John Paul II *Redemptionis Anno*" (April 20, 1984), online:
http://www.biblebelievers.org.au/redempti.htm, access: March 27, 2011.

"Lettre apostolique à tous les évêques de l'Eglise Catholique sur la situation du Liban" (Septembre 3, 1989), online: http://www.vatican.va/holy_father/john_paul_ii/apost_letters/
documents/hf_jp-ii_apl_07091989_situation-lebanon_fr.html, access: March 29, 2011.

"Apostolic Letter *Tertio Millenio Adveniente* of His Holiness Pope John Paul II to the Bishops, Clergy and Lay Faithful on Preparation for the Jubilee of the Year 2000" (November
10, 1994), online: http://www.vatican.va/holy_father/john_paul_ii/apost_letters/docu-
ments/hf_jp-ii_apl_10111994_tertio-millennio-adveniente_en.html, access: March 15,
2011.

"Apostolic Letter the Rapid Development of the Holy Father John Paul II to those Responsible for Communications" (January 24, 2005), online: http://www.vatican.va/holy_fa-
ther/john_paul_ii/apost_letters/ documents/hf_jp-ii_apl_20050124_il-rapido-sviluppo_
en.html, access: March 15, 2011.

apostolic constitution:
"Apostolic Constitution *Pastor Bonus*" (June 28, 1988), online: http://www.vatican.va/holy_
    father/john_paul_ii/apost_constitutions/documents/hf_jp-ii_apc_19880628_pastor-bonus
    -index_en.html, access: March 15, 2011.

speeches, messages and other documents:
"Address of His Holiness John Paul II to the Diplomatic Corps" (January 13, 2003), online:
    http://www.vatican.va/holy_father/john_paul_ii/speeches/2003/january/documents/hf_
    jp-ii_spe_20030113_diplomatic-corps_en.html, access: March 20, 2011.
"Address of His Holiness Pope John Paul II to the Diplomatic Corps" (January 10, 2002),
    online: http://www.vatican.va/holy_father/john_paul_ii/speeches/2002/january/
    documents/hf_jp-ii_spe_20020110_diplomatic-corps_en.html, access: March 27,
    2011.
"Address of His Holiness Pope John Paul II to the Diplomatic Corps Accredited to the Holy
    See for the Traditional Exchange of New Year Greetings" (January 12, 2004), online:
    http://www.vatican.va/holy_father/john_paul_ii/speeches/2004/january/documents/hf_
    jp-ii_spe_20040112_diplomatic-corps_en.html, access: March 29, 2011.
"Address of John Paul II at the Conclusion of the Concert Dedicated to the Theme of Rec-
    onciliation among Jews, Christians and Muslims" (January 17, 2004), online: http://
    www.vatican.va/holy_father/john_paul_ii/speeches/2004/january/documents/hf_jp-ii_
    spe_20040117_concerto-riconciliazione_en.html, access: March 15, 2011.
"Address of John Paul II to the Members of the Secretariat for Non-Christians" (April 27,
    1979), online: http://www.vatican.va/holy_father/john_paul_ii/speeches/1979/april/doc-
    uments/hf_jp-ii_spe_19790427_segret-non-cristiani_en.html, access: March 15, 2011.
"Address of the Holy Father on the Occasion of the Exchange of Greetings with the Diplo-
    matic Corps Accredited to the Holy See" (January 13, 1996), online: http://www.vatican.
    va/holy_father/john_paul_ii/speeches/1996/documents/hf_jp-ii_spe_13011996_diploma-
    tic-corps_en.html, access: March 27, 2011.
"Address of the Pope at the Conclusion of the Plenary Assembly of the Secretariat," (March
    3, 1984), in: *The Attitude of the Church towards the Followers of Other Religions: Reflec-
    tions and Orientations on Dialogue and Mission*, Vatican: Polyglot Press, 1984, p. 3-6.
"*Angelus*" (December 10, 1978), online: http://www.vatican.va/holy_father/john_paul_ii/an-
    gelus/1978/documents/hf_jp-ii_ang_19781210_en.html, access: March 15, 2011.
"*Angelus*" (November 18, 2001), online: http://www.vatican.va/holy_father/john_paul_ii/
    angelus/2001/documents/hf_jp-ii_ang_20011118_en.html, access: March 29, 2011.
"*Angelus*" (August 11, 2002), online: http://www.vatican.va/holy_father/john_paul_ii/ange-
    lus/2002/documents/hf_jp-ii_ang_20020811_en.html, access: March 29, 2011.
"*Angelus*" (February 23, 2003), online: http://www.vatican.va/holy_father/john_paul_ii/an-
    gelus/2003/documents/hf_jp-ii_ang_20030223_en.html, access: March 29, 2011.
"*Angelus*" (March 16, 2003), online: http://www.vatican.va/holy_father/john_paul_ii/ange-
    lus/2003/documents/hf_jp-ii_ang_20030316_en.html, access: March 29, 2011.
"Apostolic Journey of His Holiness John Paul II to Lebanon (May 10-11, 1997): Arrival
    Ceremony at Beirut International Airport, Speech of Pope John Paul II" (May 10, 1997),
    online: http://www.vatican.va/holy_father/john_paul_ii/travels/documents/hf_jp-ii_spe_
    10051997_lebanon-arrival_en.html, access March 27, 2011.
"Apostolic Journey of His Holiness John Paul II to Lebanon (May 10-11, 1997): Homily
    during Mass at a Naval Base in Beirut" (May 11, 1997), online: http://www.vatican.

va/holy_father/john_paul_ii/travels/documents/hf_jp-ii_hom_11051997_en.html, access: March, 27, 2011.

"Apostolic Journey of His Holiness John Paul II to the United States of America: The Fiftieth General Assembly of the United Nations Organization: Address of His Holiness John Paul II" (New York, October 5, 1995), online: http://www.vatican.va/holy_father/john _paul_ii/speeches/1995/october/documents/hf_jp-ii_spe_05101995_address-to-uno_en. html, access: March 27, 2011.

"Apostolic Journey to Benin, Uganda and Khartoum (Sudan): Eucharistic Concelebration in Honor of Blessed Josephine Bakhita: Homily of His Holiness John Paul II" (Khartoum, February 10, 1993), online: (http://www.vatican.va/holy_father/john_paul_ii/ homilies/1993/documents/hf_jp-ii_hom_19930210_khartoum_en.html, access: March 27, 2011.

"Apostolic Journey to the United States of America: Address of His Holiness John Paul II to the 34th General Assembly of the United Nations" (New York, October 2, 1979), online: http://www.vatican.va/holy_father/john_paul_ii/speeches/1979/october/documents/hf_ jp-ii_spe_19791002_general-assembly-onu_en.html, access March 27, 2011.

"Apostolic Pilgrimage to Nigeria, Benin, Gabon and Equatorial Guinea: Address of John Paul II to the Muslim Religious Leaders: Kaduna (Nigeria)" (February 14, 1982), online: www.vatican.va/holy_father/john_paul_ii/speeches/1982/february/documents/hf_jp-ii_ spe_19820214_musulmani-nigeria_en.html, access March 15, 2011.

"General Audience" (September 12, 2001), online: http://www.vatican.va/holy_father/john_ paul_ii/audiences/2001/documents/hf_jp-ii_aud_20010912_en.html, access: March 29, 2011.

"General Audience of John Paul II" (March 5, 2003), online: http://www.vatican.va/holy_fa-ther/john_paul_ii/audiences/2003/documents/hf_jp-ii_aud_20030305_en.html, access: March 29, 2011.

"Homily of the Holy Father *Day of Pardon*," (March 12, 2000), online: http://www.vati-can.va/holy_father/john_paul_ii/homilies/documents/hf_jp-ii_hom_20000312_pardon_ en.html, access: March 29, 2011.

"John Paul II's Address at the Audience with the Officials of the Pontifical Council for Inter-religious Dialogue and the Representatives of the World Islamic Call Society" (February 15, 1990), *Islamochristiana*, vol. 16 (1990), p. 294-295.

"John Paul II's Address during the Meeting with Muslims in Accra (Ghana)" (May 8, 1980), *Islamochristiana*, vol. 6 (1980), p. 212.

"John Paul II's Address during the Meeting with Muslims in Nairobi (Kenya)" (May 7, 1980), *Islamochristiana*, vol. 6 (1980), p. 211-212.

"John Paul II's Address to the Diplomatic Corps accredited to the Holy See"(January 12, 1991), *Islamochristiana*, vol. 17 (1991), p. 278.

"John Paul II's Speech during the Welcome Ceremony at Uganda's Entebbe Airport" (February 5, 1993), *Islamochristiana*, vol. 19 (1993), p. 300-303.

"Joint Declaration of Pope John Paul II and the Ecumenical Patriarch Dimitrios I" (November 30, 1979), online: http://www.vatican.va/roman_curia/pontifical_councils/ chrstuni/ch_orthodox_docs/rc_pc_chrstuni_doc_19791130_jp-ii-dimitrios-i_en.html, access: March 27, 2011.

"Jubilee Pilgrimage of His Holiness John Paul II to Mount Sinai: Celebration of the Word at the Mount Sinai, Homily of the Holy Father John Paul II" (February 26, 2000), online:http://www.vatican.va/holy_father/john_paul_ii/travels/documents/hf_jp-ii_hom_ 20000226_sinai_en.html, access: March 27, 2011.

"Jubilee Pilgrimage of His Holiness John Paul II to Mount Sinai: Ecumenical Meeting at the New Cathedral of Our Lady of Egypt, Speech of the Holy Father John Paul II" (Cairo, February 25, 2000), online: http://www.vatican.va/holy_father/john_paul_ii/travels/documents/hf_jp-ii_spe_20000225_egypt-ecumen_en.html, access: March 27, 2011.

"Jubilee Pilgrimage of His Holiness John Paul II to Mount Sinai: Mass in the Indoor Stadium of Cairo, Homily of the Holy Father John Paul II" (February 25, 2000), online: http://www.vatican.va/holy_father/john_paul_ii/travels/documents/hf_jp-ii_hom_20000225_cairo_en.html, access: March 27, 2011.

"Jubilee Pilgrimage of His Holiness John Paul II to Mount Sinai: Speech of the Holy Father John Paul II at the Arrival Ceremony" (Cairo, February 24, 2000), online: http://www.vatican.va/holy_father/john_paul_ii/travels/documents/hf_jp-ii_spe_20000224_egypt-arrival_en.html, access: March 27, 2011.

"Jubilee Pilgrimage of His Holiness John Paul II to the Holy Land (March 20-26, 2000: Address of John Paul II: Interreligious Meeting at the Notre Dame Pontifical Institute" (Jerusalem, March 23, 2000), online: http://www.vatican.va/holy_father/john_paul_ii/travels/documents/hf_jp-ii_spe_20000323_jerusalem-notre-dame_en.html, access: March 27, 2011.

"Jubilee Pilgrimage of His Holiness John Paul II to the Holy Land (March 20-26, 2000): Homily of the Holy Father, Jordan –Amman Stadium" (Amman, March, 21, 2000), online: http://www.vatican.va/holy_father/john_paul_ii/travels/documents/hf_jp-ii_hom_20000321_amman_en.html, access: March 27, 2011.

"Jubilee Pilgrimage of His Holiness John Paul II to the Holy Land (March 20-26, 2000): Speech of the Holy Father John Paul II at the Welcome ceremony in Jordan" (Amman, March 20, 2000), online: http://www.vatican.va/holy_father/john_paul_ii/travels/documents/hf_jp-ii_spe_20000320_jordan-arrival_en.html, access: March 27, 2011.

"Jubilee Pilgrimage of His Holiness John Paul II to the Holy Land (March 20-26, 2000): Speech of the Holy Father John Paul II: Welcome Ceremony in Israel" (Tel Aviv, March 21, 2000), online: http://www.vatican.va/holy_father/john_paul_ii/travels/documents/hf_jp-ii_spe_20000321_israel-arrival_en.html, access: March 29, 2011.

"Jubilee Pilgrimage of His Holiness John Paul II to the Holy Land (March 20-26, 2000): Speech of John Paul II: Welcome Ceremony in the Palestinian Autonomous Territories" (Bethlehem, March 22, 2000), online: http://www.vatican.va/holy_father/john_paul_ii/travels/documents/hf_jp-ii_spe_20000322_bethlehem-arrival_en.html, access March 29, 2011.

"Jubilee Pilgrimage of His Holiness John Paul II to Mount Sinai: Speech of the Holy Father John Paul II: Visit to the Refugee Camp of Dheisheh" (March 22, 2000), online: http://www.vatican.va/holy_father/john_paul_ii/travels/documents/hf_jp-ii_spe_20000322_deheisheh-refugees_en.html, access: March 29, 2011.

"Jubilee Pilgrimage of His Holiness John Paul II to the Holy Land (March 20-26, 2000): Speech of John Paul II: Visit to the Yad Vashem Museum" (Jerusalem, March 23, 2000), online: http://www.vatican.va/holy_father/john_paul_ii/travels/documents/hf_jp-ii_spe_20000323_yad-vashem-mausoleum_en.html, access: March 29, 2011.

"Letter of His Holiness Pope John Paul II to Artists" (April 23, 1999), online: http://www.vatican.va/holy_father/john_paul_ii/letters/documents/hf_jp-ii_let_23041999_artists_en.html, access: March 15, 2011.

"Letter of the Supreme Pontiff John Paul II Concerning Pilgrimage to the Places Linked to the History of Salvation" (June 29, 1999), online: http://www.vatican.va/holy_father/

john_paul_ii/letters/documents/hf_jp-ii_let_30061999_pilgrimage_en.html, access: March 29, 2011.

"Message of His Holiness Pope John Paul II for the Celebration of the Day of Peace: *To Reach Peace, Teach Peace*" (January 1, 1979), online: http://www.vatican.va/holy_father/john_paul_ii/messages/peace/documents/hf_jp-ii_mes_19781221_xii-world-day-for-peace_en.html, access: March 27, 2011.

"Message of His Holiness John Paul II For the Celebration of the Day of Peace: *To Serve Peace, Respect Freedom*" (January 1, 1981), online: http://www.vatican.va/holy_father/john_paul_ii/messages/peace/documents/hf_jp-ii_mes_19801208_xiv-world-day-for-peace_en.html, access: March 25, 2001.

"Message of His Holiness Pope John Paul II for the Celebration of the Day of Peace. *Dialogue for Peace, A Challenge for our Times*" (January 1, 1983), online: http://www.vatican.va/holy_father/john_paul_ii/messages/peace/documents/hf_jp-ii_mes_19821208_xvi-world-day-for-peace_en.html, access: March 15, 2011.

"Message of His Holiness John Paul II for the Celebration of the World Day of Peace: *Pacem in Terris, A Permanent Commitment*" (January 1, 2003), online: http://www.vatican.va/holy_father/john_paul_ii/messages/peace/documents/hf_jp-ii_mes_20021217_xxxvi-world-day-for-peace_en.html, access: March 30, 2011.

"Message of His Holiness John Paul II for the Celebration of the World Day of Peace: *Religious Freedom: Condition for Peace*" (January 1, 1988), online: http://www.vatican.va/holy_father/john_paul_ii/messages/peace/documents/hf_jp-ii_mes_19871208_xxi-world-day-for-peace_en.html, access: March 25, 2001.

"Message of His Holiness Pope John Paul II for the Celebration of the World Day of Peace: *To Build Peace, Respect Minorities*" (January 1, 1989), online: http://www.vatican.va/holy_father/john_paul_ii/messages/peace/documents/hf_jp-ii_mes_19881208_xxii-world-day-for-peace_en.html, access: March 15, 2011.

"Message of His Holiness John Paul for the Celebration of the World Day of Peace: *No Peace without Justice, No Justice without Forgiveness*" (January 1, 2002), online: http://www.vatican.va/holy_father/john_paul_ii/messages/peace/documents/hf_jp-ii_mes_20011211_xxxv-world-day-for-peace_en.html, access: March 29, 2011.

"Meeting with the Muslim Leaders, Omayyad Great Mosque, Damascus: Address of the Holy Father" (May 6, 2001), online: http://www.vatican.va/holy_father/john_paul_ii/speeches/2001/documents/hf_jp-ii_spe_20010506_omayyadi_en.html, access: March 27, 2011.

"Pastoral Journey to Benin, Uganda and Khartoum (Sudan): Meeting with General Omar Hassan Ahmed Al-Bashir, President of the Republic of the Sudan: Address of His Holiness John Paul II" (Khartoum, February 10, 1993), online: http://www.vatican.va/holy_father/john_paul_ii/speeches/1993/february/documents/hf_jp-ii_spe_19930210_presidente-sudan_en.html, access: March 27, 2011.

"Pastoral Visit in Kazakhstan, Meeting with Representatives of the World of Culture: Address of John Paul II" (Astana, September 24, 2001), online: http://www.vatican.va/holy_father/john_paul_ii/speeches/2001/september/documents/hf_jp-ii_spe_20010924_kazakhstan-astana-culture_en.html, access: March 29, 2011.

"Pastoral Visit in Kazakhstan, Meeting with the Ordinaries of Central Asia: Address of the Holy Father" (Astana, September 23, 2001), online: http://www.vatican.va/holy_father/john_paul_ii/speeches/2001/september/documents/hf_jp-ii_spe_20010923_kazakhstan-astana-ordinaries_en.html, access: March 29, 2011.

"Pope John Paul II's Address to the Muslim Population of Kaduna" (February 14, 1982), *Islamochristiana*, vol. 8 (1982), p. 240-241.

"Pope John Paul II's *Angelus* Appeal for an End to the War" (January 27, 1991), *Islamochristiana*, vol. 17 (1991), p. 283.

"Pope John Paul II's *Angelus* Message for Sunday" (November 18, 1990), *Islamochristiana*, vol. 17 (1991), p. 273.

"Pope John Paul II's Appeal to Both President George Bush and President Saddam Hussein" (January 15, 1991), *Islamochristiana*, vol. 17 (1991), p. 280-281.

"Prayer for Peace at the Greek-Orthodox Church in Quneitra: Address of John Paul II" (Golan Heights, May 7, 2001), online: http://www.vatican.va/holy_father/john_paul_ii/speeches/2001/documents/hf_jp-ii_spe_20010507_prayer-peace_en.html, access: March 27, 2011.

"The Address of the Holy See to the Members of the Plenaria of the Pontifical Council for Interreligious Dialogue" (April 26, 1990), *Islamochristiana*, vol. 16 (1990), p. 295-297.

"The Holy Father's Address to the Diplomatic Corps Accredited to the Holy See" (January 12, 1991), *Islamochristiana*, vol. 17 (1991), p. 277-279.

"The Holy Father's Homily during the Ecumenical Prayer Vigil," Islamochristiana, vol. 19 (1993), p. 250-252.

"The Holy See's Address to Christians, Jews and Muslims during an Interreligious Meeting in Rome," *Islamochristiana*, vol. 17 (1991), p. 290-291.

"The Speech of the Holy Father John Paul II to Young Muslims during his Meeting with Them in Casablanca" (Morocco, August 19, 1985), *Encounter: Documents for Muslim-Christian Understanding*, vol. 128 (August 1986), p. 2-10.

"To Bishops from Indonesia on Their *ad limina* Visit" (Rome, May 20, 1989), in: F. Gioia (ed.), *Interreligious Dialogue: The Official Teaching of the Catholic Church (1963--1995)*, Boston: Pauline Books & Media, 1997, p. 406-407.

"To Muslims and Hindu Representatives of Kenya" (Nairobi, August 18, 1985), in: F. Gioia (ed.), *Interreligious Dialogue: The Official Teaching of the Catholic Church (1963-1995)*, Boston: Pauline Books & Media, 1997, p. 295-297.

"To the Bishops of Mali on Their *ad limina* Visit" (Rome, November 26, 1981), in: F. Gioia (ed.), *Interreligious Dialogue: The Official Teaching of the Catholic Church (1963--1995)*, Boston: Pauline Books & Media, 1997, p. 248-249.

"To the Catholic Community of Ankara" (Ankara, November 29, 1979), in: F. Gioia (ed.), *Interreligious Dialogue: The Official Teaching of the Catholic Church (1963-1995)*, Boston: Pauline Books & Media, 1997, p. 219-223.

"To the Participants in the Sixth Assembly of the World Conference on Religion and Peace (WCRP) at the Synod Hall" (Rome, November 3, 1994), in: F. Gioia (ed.), *Interreligious Dialogue: The Official Teaching of the Catholic Church (1963-1995)*, Boston: Pauline Books & Media, 1997, p. 529-532.

"To the People of Pakistan" (Karachi, February 16, 1981), in: F. Gioia (ed.), *Interreligious Dialogue: The Official Teaching of the Catholic Church (1963-1995)*, Boston: Pauline Books & Media, 1997, p. 234-235.

"To the Representatives of the Muslim Community in France" (Paris, May 31, 1980), in: F. Gioia (ed.), *Interreligious Dialogue: The Official Teaching of the Catholic Church (1963-1995)*, Boston: Pauline Books & Media, 1997, p. 233-234.

"To Representatives of the Muslims of Cameroon" (Yaoundé, August 12, 1985), in: F. Gioia (ed.), *Interreligious Dialogue: The Official Teaching of the Catholic Church (1963-1995)*, Boston: Pauline Books & Media, 1997, p. 290-291.

"To the Representatives of Muslims of the Philippines" (Darao, February 20, 1981), in: F. Gioia (ed.), *Interreligious Dialogue: The Official Teaching of the Catholic Church (1963-1995)*, Boston: Pauline Books & Media, 1997, p. 235-237.

"To the Secretariat for Non-Christians" (Rome, April 27, 1979), in: F. Gioia (ed.), *Interreligious Dialogue: The Official Teaching of the Catholic Church (1963-1995)*, Boston: Pauline Books & Media, 1997, p. 215-218.

"*Urbi et Orbi* Message of His Holiness John Paul II" (March 31, 2002), online: http://www.vatican.va/holy_father/john_paul_ii/messages/urbi/documents/hf_jp-ii_mes_20020331_easter-urbi_en.html, access: March 29, 2011.

"*Urbi et Orbi* Message of His Holiness John Paul II" (April 20, 2003), online: http://www.vatican.va/holy_father/john_paul_ii/messages/urbi/documents/hf_jp-ii_mes_20030420_easter-urbi_en.html, access: March 29, 2011.

"Visita pastorale ad Otranto: Omelia di Giovanni Paolo II" (October 5, 1980), online: http://www.vatican.va/holy_father/john_paul_ii/homilies/1980/documents/hf_jp-ii_hom_19801005_otranto_it.html, access March 29, 2011.

"Voyage Apostolique au Togo, en Côte D'Ivoire, au Cameroun i, en République Centrafricaine, au Zaïre, au Kenya, au Maroc: Messe à L'Institut 'Charles de Foucauld': Homélie du Pape Jean-Paul II" (Casablanca, Août 19, 1985), online: http://www.vatican.va/holy_father/john_paul_ii/homilies/1985/documents/hf_jp-ii_hom_19850819_casablanca_fr.html, access: March 27, 2011.

"Voyage Apostolique en Tunisie: Rencontre avec les représentants du monde politique, culturel et religieux: Discours du Saint-Père Jean-Paul II" (Avril 14, 1996), online: http://www.vatican.va/holy_father/john_paul_ii/speeches/1996/april/documents/hf_jp-ii_spe_19960414_world-culture_fr.html, access: March 27, 2011.

"*War is not an answer*: Pope John II's Audience for the Officials of the Roman Vicariate" (January 17, 1991), *Islamochristiana*, vol. 17 (1991), p. 281-282.

"Welcome Ceremony in Damascus: Address of John Paul II" (May 5, 2001), online: http://www.vatican.va/holy_father/john_paul_ii/speeches/2001/documents/hf_jp-ii_spe_20010505_president-syria_en.html, access: March 27, 2011.

"Youth Meeting at the Greek-Catholic Cathedral – Damascus: Address of John Paul II" (May 7, 2001), online: http://www.vatican.va/holy_father/john_paul_ii/speeches/2001/documents/hf_jp-ii_spe_20010507_youth_en.html, access March 27, 2011.

IV) Commission for Religious Relations with Jews:
"*We Remember: A Reflection on the Shoah*" (March 16, 1998), online: http://www.vatican.va/roman_curia/pontifical_councils/chrstuni/documents/rc_pc_chrstuni_doc_16031998_shoah_en.html, access: March 29, 2011.

V) 25ᵗʰ Anniversary of the Pontificate of John Paul II, Symposium Organized by the College of Cardinals:
"Intervention by Cardinal Angelo Sodano: A 25-Year Pontificate At The Service Of Peace," online: http://www.vatican.va/roman_curia/secretariat_state/2003/documents/rc_seg-st_20031018_sodano-xxv-pontificate_en.html, access: March 29, 2011.

Works of Karol Wojtyła (John Paul II):

John Paul II, *Crossing the Threshold of Hope*, Toronto: Alfred A. Knopf Canada, 1994.

_____, *Love and Responsibility*, New York: Farrar, Straus, Giroux, 1981.

_____, *Memory and Identity: Conversations at the Dawn of a Millennium*, New York: Rizzoli, 2005

_____, *Poezje – Poems*, trans. Jerzy Peterkiewicz, afterward Krzysztof Dybciak, Kraków: Wydawnictwo Literackie, 1998.

_____, *The Place Within: The Poetry of John Paul II*, trans. Jerzy Peterkiewicz, London: Hutchinson, 1994.

_____, *Tryptyk rzymski: Medytacje – Roman Triptych: Meditations*, trans. Jerzy Peterkiewicz, Kraków: Wydawnictwo Literackie, 2003.

_____ and Jean-Louis Tauran, *The Holy See at the Service of Peace: Pope John Paul II's Addresses to the Diplomatic Corps (October 1978 – September 1988)*, ed. Marjorie Keenan, Vatican: Pontifical Council for Justice and Peace, 1988.

Wojtyła, Karol, *Sources of Renewal: The Implementation of the Second Vatican Council*, trans. P. S. Falla, San Francisco: Harper and Row, 1980.

_____, *The Acting Person*, trans. Andrzej Potocki, Dordrecht and London: D. Reidel Publishing Company, 1979.

_____, *The Collected Plays and Writings on Theater*, trans. and introduction Boleslaw Taborski, Berkeley: University of California Press, 1987.

_____, John Paul II, *Poezje, dramaty, szkice. Tryptyk rzymski*, foreword Marek Skwarnicki, Kraków: Wydawnictwo Znak, 2004.

_____, *U podstaw odnowy: Studium o realizacji Vaticanum II*, Kraków: Polskie Towarzystwo Teologiczne, 1972.

Other Documents:

"2253 (ES-V): Measures Taken by Israel to Change the Status of the City of Jerusalem" (July 4, 1967), online: http://unispal.un.org/UNISPAL.NSF/0/A39A906C89D-3E98685256C29006D4014, access: March 27, 2011.

"Basic Law: Jerusalem" (July 30, 1980), online: http://zionism-israel.com/hdoc/Basic_Law_Jerusalem.html, access: March 27, 2011.

"Egypt," online: https://www.cia.gov/library/publications/the-world-factbook/geos/eg.html, access: October 30, 2011.

"Jordan," online: https://www.cia.gov/library/publications/the-world-factbook/geos/jo.html, access: October 30, 2011.

"Lebanon," online: https://www.cia.gov/library/publications/the-world-factbook/geos/le.html, access: October 30, 2011.

"Morocco," online: https://www.cia.gov/library/publications/the-world-factbook/geos/mo.html, access: October 30, 2011.

"Pakistan," online: https://www.cia.gov/library/publications/the-world-factbook/geos/pk.html, access: October 30, 2011.

"Syria," online: https://www.cia.gov/library/publications/the-world-factbook/geos/sy.html, access: October 30, 2011.

"Tunisia," online: https://www.cia.gov/library/publications/the-world-factbook/geos/ts.html, access: October 30, 2011.

"Turkey," online: https://www.cia.gov/library/publications/the-world-factbook/geos/tu.html, access: October 30, 2011.

"Resolution 678 (1990) Adopted by the Security Council at its 2963rd meeting" (November 29, 1990), online: http://www.casi.org.uk/info/undocs/gopher/s90/32, access: March, 29, 2011.

"Security Council Condemns, 'In Strongest Terms', Terrorists Attack on United States: Unanimously Adopting Resolution 1368 (2001), Council Calls on All States to Bring Perpetrators to Justice," online: http://www.un.org/News/Press/docs/2001/SC7143.doc.htm, access: March 29, 2011.

"The PLO – Vatican Agreement" (February 15, 2000), online: http://www.jewishvirtuallibrary.org/jsource/Peace/plovatican.html, access: March 29, 2011.

"The Ta'if Accord," online: http://www.al-bab.com/arab/docs/lebanon/taif.htm, access: March 29, 2011.

"UN Resolution 1402," online: http://www.palestinehistory.com/history/documents/doc07.htm#UN1402, access: March 29, 2011.

Secondary sources:

Periodicals:
Globe and Mail (1988).
L'Osservatore Romano (1967, 1973, 1979, 1980, 1982, 1984, 1988, 2004).
Proche-Orient Chrétien (1964, 1974, 1976).
The Middle East Quarterly, vol. 8 (2001), no. 1: *Disappearing Christians in the Middle East.*

Books and articles:
Abu Tabak, Nidal, "Pytania muzułmanina do chrześcijanina – odpowiedzi chrześcijanina na pytania muzułmanina," *Ateneum Kapłańskie*, vol. 151 (2008), no. 2 (597), p. 267-279.

Aburish, Said K., *Arafat: From Defender to Dictator*, New York & London: Bloomsbury Press, 1998.

Adams, Charles J., "Islam and Christianity: The Opposition and Similarities," in: Roger M. Savory and Dionisius A. Agius (eds.), *Logos Islamicos: Studia Islamica in Honorem Georgii Michaelis Wickens*, Toronto: Pontifical Institute for Medieval Studies, 1984, p. 287-306.

Accattoli, Luigi, *When a Pope Asks Forgiveness: The Mea Culpa's of John Paul II*, trans. Jordan Aumann, Boston: Pauline Books, 2000.

Allen-Shore, Lena, *Building Bridges: Pope John Paul II and the Horizon of Life*, foreword Stanislaw Dziwisz, Ottawa: Novalis Press and Saint Paul University, 2004.

Anawati, Georges C., "An Assessment of the Christian-Islamic Dialogue," in: Kail C. Ellis (ed.), *The Vatican, Islam and the Middle East*, Syracuse, NY: Syracuse University Press, 1987, p. 51-68.

_____, *Polémique, apologie et dialogue islamo-chrétiens: Positions classiques médiévales et positions contemporaines*, Roma: Pontificia Universita Urbaniana, 1969.

Arendt, Hannah, *The Life of the Mind*, vol. 1, New York: Harcourt Brace Jovanovich, 1978.

Arinze, Francis, "The Place of Dialogue in the Church's Mission: Reflections on *Redemptoris Missio*," *Bulletin*, vol. 26 (1991), no. 1, p. 20-23.

Arkoun, Mohammed, "New Perspectives for a Jewish-Christian-Muslim Dialogue," *Journal of Ecumenical Studies*, vol. 26 (1989), p. 345-352.

_____, "The Notion of Revelation: From *Ahl al-Kitab* to the Societies of the Book," *Die Welt des Islams*, vol. 28 (1988), p. 62-89.

Armour, Rollin, *Islam, Christianity and the West: A Troubled History*, Maryknoll, NY: Orbis Books, 2002.

Armstrong, Karen, *Jerusalem: One City, Three Faiths*, New York: Alfred A. Knopf, 1996.

Ateek, Naim, Marc H. Ellis and Rosemary Radford Ruether (eds.), *The Faith and Intifada: Palestinian Christian Voices*, New York: Orbis Books, 1992.

Bakalar, Nick and Richard Balkin (eds.), *The Wisdom of John Paul II: The Pope on Life's Most Vital Questions*, introduction John W. White, San Francisco: HarperSanFrancisco, 1995.

Balwierz, Marian, "Katolickie podstawy dialogu z religiami niechrześcijańskimi," in: Wacław Hryniewicz, Jan Sergiusz Gajek and Stanisław Józef Koza (eds.), *Ku chrześcijaństwu jutra: Wprowadzenie do ekumenizmu*, Lublin: Towarzystwo Naukowe Katolickiego Uniwersytetu Lubelskiego, 1996, p. 676-701.

Basetti-Sani, Giulio, "A Catholic Islamist Louis Massignon (1883-1983)," *Bulletin*, vol. 18 (1983), no. 3, 258-265.

Bat, Yeor, *The Dhimmi: Jews and Christians under Islam*, preface Jacques Ellul, trans. David Maisel, Paul Fenton and David Littman, Rutherford, CA: Fairleigh Dickinson University Press, London: Associated University Presses, 1985.

Belmekki, Belkacem, *Sir Sayyid* Ahmad Khan and the Muslim Cause in British India, Berlin: Klaus Schwarz, 2010.

Benvenisti, Meron, *Jerusalem: The Torn City*, Minneapolis: University of Minnesota Press, 1976.

Biechler, James E. and H. Lawrence Bond (eds.), *Nicholas of Cusa on Interreligious Harmony: Text, Concordance, and Translation of De Pace Fidei*, Lewiston: Edwin Mellen Press, 1990.

Borrmans, Maurice, *Guidelines for Dialogue between Christians and Muslims*, trans. R. Marston Speight, New York: Paulist Press, 1990.

_____, "Jérusalem dans la tradition religieuse musulmane," *Islamochristiana*, vol. 7 (1981), p. 1-18.

_____, "Le séminaire du dialogue Islamo-Chrétien de Tripoli (Libye, février 1-6, 1976)," *Islamochristiana*, vol. 2 (1976), p. 135-170.

_____, "Le Pape Paul VI et les Musulmans," *Islamochristiana*, vol. 4 (1978), p. 1-10.

_____, "Ludovico Marracci et sa traduction latine du Coran," *Islamochristiana*, vol. 28 (2002), p. 73-86.

Boucher, David, *Political Theories of International Relation: From Thucydides to the Present*, New York: Oxford University Press, 1998.

Boullata, Issa J., "*Fa-stabiqū 'l-khayrāt*: A Qur'anic Principle of Interfaith Relations," in: Yvonne Yazbeck Haddad and Wadi Zaydan Haddaad (eds.), *Christian-Muslim Encounters*, Gainesville: University Press of Florida, 1995, p. 43-53.

Breiner, Bert F. and Christian W. Troll, "Christianity and Islam," in: John Esposito (ed.), *The Oxford Encyclopedia of Modern Islamic World*, vol. 1, New York: Oxford University Press, 1995, p. 280-286.

Bull, Marcus Graham and Norman Housley (eds.), *The Experience of Crusading*, Cambridge and New York: Cambridge University Press, 2003.

Bunson, Matthew, *The Pope Encyclopedia: An A to Z of the Holy See*, New York: Crown Trade Paperback, 1995.

Burman, Thomas E., *Reading the Qur'ān in Latin Christendom, 1140-1560*, Philadelphia: University of Pennsylvania Press, 2007.

_____, *Religious Polemic and the Intellectual History of the Mozarabs, c. 1050-1200*, Leiden and New York: E. J. Brill, 1994.

_____, "*Tathlîth al-waḥdanîyâh* and the Twelfth-Century Andalusia Christian Approach to Islam," in: John Victor Tolan (ed.), *Medieval Christian Perceptions to Islam: A Book of Essays*, New York: Garland Pub., 1994, p. 109-128.

Capponi, Niccolò, *Victory of the West: The Story of the Battle of Lepanto*, London: Macmillan, 2006.

Carlyle, Thomas, *The Best Known Works of Thomas Carlyle: Including Sartor Resartus, Heroes and Hero Worship and Characteristics*, New York: Book League of America, 1942.

Caspar, Robert, "Islam According to Vatican II: On the Tenth Anniversary of *Nostra Aetate*," *Encounter*, vol. 21 (January 1976), p. 1-7.

Cassidy, Edward Idris, *Ecumenism and Interreligious Dialogue: Unitatis Redintegratio, Nostra Aetate*, New York: Paulist Press, 2005.

Cattan, Henry, "The Status of Jerusalem under International Law and United Nations Resolutions," *Journal of Palestine Studies*, vol. 10/3 (1981), p. 3-4.

Chenu, Marie-Dominique, *Introduction à l'étude de Saint Thomas d'Aquin*, Montréal: Institut d'études médiévales de l'université de Montréal, 1950.

_____, *Toward Understanding St. Thomas*, trans. Albert M. Landry and Dominic Hughes, Chicago: H. Regnery Publishing, 1964.

Cleveland, William L., *A History of the Modern Middle East*, Boulder: Westview Press, 1994.

Colbert, Edward P., *The Martyrs of Córdoba (850-859): A Study of the Sources*, Washington, DC: Catholic University of America Press, 1962.

Collin, Bernardin, *Recueil de documents concernant Jérusalem et les lieux saints*, Jérusalem: Franciscan Printing Press, 1982.

Cutler, Allan, "The Ninth-Century Spanish Martyrs' Movement and the Origins of Western Christian Missions to Muslims," *Muslim World*, vol. 55 (1965), p. 321-339.

Daniel, Norman, "Christian-Muslim Polemics," in: Mircea Eliade [et al.] (ed.), *The Encyclopedia of Religion*, vol. 11, New York: Macmillan, 1987, p. 402-404.

_____, *Islam and the West: The Making of an Image*, Oxford: Oneworld Publications, 1993.

Dreyfus, Paul, *Jean XXIII*, Paris: Artheme Fayard, 1979.

Dupuis, Jacques, "Dialogue and Proclamation in Two Recent Documents," *Bulletin*, vol. 27 (1992), no. 2, p. 165-172.

Dziekan, Marek M., *Historia Iraku*, Warszawa: Dialog, 2007.

Dziwisz, Stanisław, *A Life with Karol: My Forty-Year Friendship with the Man Who Became Pope: Cardinal Stanislaw Dziwisz in Conversation with Gian Franco Svidercoschi*, New York: Doubleday, 2008.

Ebied, Riffat Y. and David Thomas (eds.), *Muslim-Christian Polemics during the Crusades: The Letter from the People of Cyprus and Ibn Abī Ṭālib al-Dimashqī's Response*, Leiden and Boston: E. J. Brill, 2005.

Eckardt, Jo-Jacqueline, *Lessing's Nathan the Wise and the Critics, 1779-1991*, Columbia, SC: Camden House, 1993.

Ehrenkreutz, Andrew S., *Saladin*, Albany: State University of New York Press, 1972.

Eliade, Mircea [et al.] (ed.), *The Encyclopedia of Religion*, vol. 11, New York: Macmillan, 1987.

Ellis, Kail C. (ed.), *The Vatican, Islam and the Middle East*, Syracuse, NY: Syracuse University Press, 1987.

Encyclopaedia of Islam, vol. 5, Leiden: E. J. Brill, 1960.

Esposito, John L., *The Islamic Threat: Myth or Reality?*, New York: Oxford University Press, 1995.

_____ (ed.), *The Oxford Encyclopedia of Modern Islamic World*, vol. 1, New York: Oxford University Press, 1995.

Ferrari, Silvio, "The Vatican, Israel and the Jerusalem Question (1943-1984)," *The Middle East Journal*, vol. 39 (1985), no. 2, p. 316-331.

Fisher, Eugene J. and Leon Klenicki (eds.), *Pope John Paul II on Jews and Judaism: 1979-1986*, Washington: United States Catholic Conference, 1987.

Fitzgerald, Michael L., "The Secretariat for Non-Christians is Ten Years Old," *Islamochristiana*, vol. 1 (1975), p. 87-96.

Francisco, Adam S., *Martin Luther and Islam: A Study in Sixteenth-Century Polemics and Apologetics*, Leiden and Boston: E. J. Brill, 2007.

Freedman, Lawrence and Efraim Karsh, *The Gulf Conflict, 1990-1991: Diplomacy and War in the New World Order*, Princeton, NJ: Princeton University Press, 1993.

Friedman, Isaiah, *The Question of Palestine, 1914-1918: British-Jewish-Arab Relations*, London: Routledge & K. Paul, 1973.

Gacek, Adam, *Arabic Manuscripts: A Vademecum for Readers*, Leiden and Boston, E. J. Brill, 2009.

_____, *The Arabic Manuscript Tradition: A Glossary of Technical Terms and Bibliography*. Leiden and Boston, E. J. Brill, 2001.

_____, *The Arabic Manuscript Tradition: A Glossary of Technical Terms and Bibliography – Supplement*, Leiden and Boston, E. J. Brill, 2008.

Gianelli, Andrea and Andrea Tornielli, *Papi e Guerra: Il ruolo dei Pontefici dal primo conflitto mondiale all'attaco in Iraq*, Milano: Il Giornale 2003, Polish Edition: *Papieże a wojna: Od pierwszego światowego konfliktu do ataku na Irak*, trans. Lucyna Rodziewicz, Kraków: Wydawnictwo M, 2006.

Gioia, Francesco (ed.), *Interreligious Dialogue: The Official Teaching of the Catholic Church (1963-1995)*, Boston: Pauline Books & Media, 1997.

Goddard, Hugh, *A History of Christian-Muslim Relations*, Edinburgh: Edinburgh University Press, 2000.

Goitein, S. D. "al-Ḳuds: Part A. History," in: *Encyclopaedia of Islam*, vol. 5, Leiden: E. J. Brill, 1960, p. 322-339.

Goldhill, Simon, *The Temple of Jerusalem*, Cambridge, MA: Harvard University Press, 2005.

Grabar, Oleg, "al-Ḳuds: Part B. The Monuments," in: *Encyclopaedia of Islam*, vol. 5, Leiden: E. J. Brill, 1960, p. 339-344.

Groblicki, Julian and Eugeniusz Florkowski (eds.), *Sobór Watykański II: Konstytucje, dekrety, deklaracje: Tekst polski*, Poznań: Wydawnictwo Pallottinum, 1968.

Guerriero, Elio and Marco Impagliazzo (eds.), *Storia delle Chiesa I cattolici e le Ciese cristiane durante il pontificato di giovanni Paolo II (1978-2005)*, Polish edition: *Najnowsza historia kościoła: Katolicy i kościoły chrześcijańskie w czasie pontyfikatu Jana Pawła II (1978-2005)*, trans. Jacek Partyka, Kraków: Wydawnictwo M, 2006.

Haddad, Yvonne Yazbeck, and Wadi Zaydan Haddad (eds.), *Christian-Muslim Encounters*, Gainesville: University Press of Florida, 1995.

Haj, Samira, *Reconfiguring Islamic Tradition: Reform, Rationality, and Modernity*, Stanford, CA: Stanford University Press, 2009.

Hammond, Robert, *The Philosophy of Alfarabi and its Influence on Medieval Thought*, New York: Hobson Book Press, 1947.

Hebblethwaite, Peter, *John XXIII: Pope of the Council*, London: Geoffrey Chapman, 1984.

_____, *Paul VI: The First Modern Pope*, New York: Paulist Press, 1993.

Henley, Alexander D. M., "Politics of a Church at War: Maronite Catholicism in the Lebanese Civil War," *Mediterranean Politics*, vol. 13/3 (November 2008), p. 353-369.

Hillstrom, Laurie Collier, *War in the Persian Gulf Primary Sources: From Operation Desert Storm to Operation Iraqi Freedom*, Detroit: UXL, 2004.

Hinze, Bradford E. and Irfan A. Omar, *Heirs of Abraham: The Future of Muslim, Jewish and Christian Relations*, Maryknoll, NY: Orbis Books, 2005.

Hodgson, Marshall G. S., *The Venture of Islam: Conscience and History in a World Civilization*, vol. 3: *The Gunpowder Empires and Modern Times*, Chicago and London: University of Chicago Press, 1974.

Hoeberichts, Jan, *Francis and Islam*, Quincy, IL: Franciscan Press, 1997.

Hopkins, Jasper, (trans. & analysis) *Nicholas of Cusa's "De pace fidei" and "Cribratio Alcorani,"* Minneapolis: Arthur J. Banning Press, 1994.

_____, *A Concise Introduction to the Philosophy of Nicholas of Cusa*, Minneapolis: University of Minnesota Press, 1978.

Hourani, Albert, *Europe and the Middle East*, Berkeley: University of California Press, 1980.

_____, *Islam in European Thought*, Cambridge: Cambridge University Press, 1995.

Housley, Norman, *Contesting the Crusade*, Malden, MA: Blackwell Publishing, 2006.

Hoyland, Robert (ed.), *Muslims and Others in Early Islamic Society*, Aldershot and Burlington, VT : Ashgate Variorum, 2004.

Hryniewicz, Wacław, Jan Sergiusz Gajek and Stanisław Józef Koza (eds.), *Ku chrześcijaństwu jutra: Wprowadzenie do ekumenizmu*, Lublin: Towarzystwo Naukowe Katolickiego Uniwersytetu Lubelskiego, 1996.

Hunt, Courtney, *The History of Iraq*, Westport, CY: Greenwood Press, 2005.

Ibn Hishām, 'Abd al-Malik *The Life of Muḥammad: A Translation of Ibn "Isḥāq's Sīrat Rasūl Allāh,"* trans. A. Guillaume, London: Oxford University Press, 1955.

Imber, Colin, *The Ottoman Empire, 1300-1650: The Structure of Power*, New York: Palgrave, 2002.

Irani, George Emile, "The Israeli-Palestinian Conflict," in: K. C. Ellis (ed.), *The Vatican, Islam and the Middle East*, Syracuse, NY: Syracuse University Press, 1987, p. 125-142.

_____, *The Papacy and the Middle East: The Role of the Holy See in the Arab-Israeli Conflict, 1962-1984*, Notre Dame, IN: University of Notre Dame Press, 1986.

Judycka, Joanna, *Wiara i rozum w filozofii Rajmunda Lulla*, Lublin: Wydawnictwo Katolickiego Uniwersytetu Lubelskiego, 2005.

Kafel, Salezy (ed.), *Antologia mistyków franciszkańskich*, vol. 2: *Wiek XIII-XIV*, Warszawa: Akademia Teologii Katolickiej, 1986.

Kasimow, Harold and Byron L. Sherwin (eds.), *No Religion is an Island: Abraham Joshua Heschel and Interreligious Dialogue*, Maryknoll, NY: Orbis Books, 1991.

Kedar, Benjamin Z., *Crusade and Mission: European Approaches towards the Muslims*, Princeton, NJ: Princeton University Press, 1984.

Keddie, Nikki R. and Hamir Algar, *An Islamic Response to Imperialism: Political and Religious Writings of Sayyid Jamāl ad-Dīn "al-Afghānī,"* Berkeley: University of California Press, 1983.

Kennedy, Arthur, "The Declaration on the Relationship of the Church to Non-Christian Religions, *Nostra* Aetate," in: Matthew L. Lamb and Matthew Levering (eds.), *Vatican II: Renewal within Tradition*, Oxford and New York: Oxford University Press, 2008, p. 396-409.

Khalidi, Tarif, *The Muslim Jesus: Sayings and Stories in Islamic Literature*, Cambridge, MA: Harvard University Press, 2001.

Khouri, Fred J., *The Arab-Israeli Dilemma*, Syracuse: Syracuse University Press, 1985.

_____, "The Jerusalem Question and the Vatican," in: Kail C. Ellis, (ed.), *The Vatican, Islam and the Middle East*, Syracuse, NY: Syracuse University Press, 1987, p. 143-162.

Khoury, Adel Theodore, *Les théologiens byzantins et l'Islam: Textes et auteurs (VIIIᵉ-XIIIᵉ s.)*, Louvain and Paris: Éditions Nauwelaerts and Beatrice-Nauwelaerts, 1969.

_____, *Polémique byzantine et l'Islam (VIIIᵉ-XIIIᵉ s.)*, Leiden: E. J. Brill, 1972.

Koenig, Franziskus, "Le monothéisme dans le monde contemporain," *MIDEO*, vol. 8 (1964--1966), p. 407-422.

Kościelniak, Krzysztof, *Grecy i Arabowie: Historia Kościoła melkickiego (katolickiego) na ziemiach zdobytych przez muzułmanów (634-1516)*, Kraków: Wydawnictwo UNUM, 2004.

Kreutz, Andrej, "The Vatican and the Palestinians: A Historical Overview," *Islamochristiana*, vol. 18 (1992), p. 109-125.

_____, *Vatican and the Palestinian-Israeli Conflict: The Struggle for the Holy Land*, New York: Greenwood Press, 1990.

Kritzek, James, *Peter the Venerable and Islam*, Princeton, NJ: Princeton University Press, 1964.

Küng, Hans [et al.], *Christianity and the World Religions: Paths of Dialogue with Islam, Hinduism, and Buddhism*, trans. Peter Heinegg, Garden City, NY: Doubleday, 1986.

Kwinty, Jonathan, *Man of the Century: The Life and Times of Pope John Paul II*, New York: Henry Holt and Company Inc., 1997.

Lamb, Matthew L., "The Challenges of Reform and Renewal within Catholic Tradition," in: Matthew L. Lamb and Matthew Levering (eds.), *Vatican II: Renewal within Tradition*, Oxford and New York: Oxford University Press, 2008, p. 439-442.

Lamb, Matthew L. and Matthew Levering (eds.), *Vatican II: Renewal within Tradition*, Oxford and New York: Oxford University Press, 2008.

Lamoreaux, John C., "Early Christian Responses to Islam," in: John Victor Tolan (ed.), *Medieval Christian Perceptions of Islam: A Book of Essays*, Garland Medieval Case Books 10, Garland Reference Library of Humanities 1786, New York & London: Garland, 1994, p. 3-28.

"Le dialogue vu par les musulmans," *Etudes Arabes*, 1995, no. 88-89.

Leasing, Gotthold Ephraim, *Nathan the Wise*, trans. and introduction Walter Frank Charles Ade, Woodbury, NY: Barron's Educational Series, Inc., 1972.

Lelong, Michel, *Jean-Paul II et l'islam*, Paris: François-Xavier de Guilbert, 2003.

_____, *L'Eglise catholique et l'islam*, Paris: Maisonneuve & Larose, 1993.

Lewis, Bernard, *Islam and the West*, New York: Oxford University Press, 1993.

_____, *The Arabs in History*, Oxford and New York: Oxford University Press, 1993.

_____, *The Middle East: 2,000 Years of History from the Rise of Christianity to the Present Day*, London: Weidenfeld & Nicolson, 1995.

Little, Donald P., *History and Historiography of the Mamlūks*, London: Variorum Reprints, 1986.

Llull, Ramon, *Llibre del gentil e dels tres savis*, Catala: Publicacions de l'Abadia de Montserrat, 2001.

Lomax, John Phillip, "Frederic II, His Saracens and the Papacy," in: John Victor Tolan (ed.), *Medieval Christian Perceptions to Islam: A Book of Essays*, New York: Garland Pub., 1994, p. 175-197.

Machniak, Jan, *Bóg i człowiek w poezjach i dramatach Karola Wojtyły – Jana Pawła II*, Kraków: Wydawnictwo Św. Stanisława BM Archidiecezji Krakowskiej, 2007.

Madges, William (ed.), *Vatican II: Forty Years Later*, Maryknoll, NY: Orbis Books, 2006.

Mansfield, Peter, *A History of the Middle East*, Toronto: Penguin Books, 1992.

Mari, Arturo, *Do zobaczenia w raju*, in conversation with Jarosław Mikołajewski, foreword Stanisław Dziwisz, Poznań: TVP Promotion Design, 2005.

Massignon, Louis, "Les trois prières d'Abraham," in: Youakim Moubarac (ed.), *Opera Minora*, vol. 3: *Arts et archéologie, la science de la compassion*, Beyrut: Dar al-Maaref, 1963, p. 804-816.

Mastnak, Tomaž, *Crusading Peace: Christendom, the Muslim World, and Western Political Order*, Berkeley, CA and London: University of California Press, 2002.

Maurice, Frederick Denison, *The Religions of the World and their Relations to Christianity Considered in Eight Lectures Founded by Robert Boyle*, London: John W. Parker, 1848.

McCurry, Don M. (ed.), *World Christianity, Middle East*, Monrovia, CA: MARC,1979.

McDonough, Sheila, *The Flame of Sinai: Hope and Vision in Iqbal*, Lahore: Iqbal Academy Pakistan, 2002.

Melville, Charles Peter (ed.), *Safavid Persia: The History and Politics of an Islamic Society*, London: I. B. Tauris, 1996.

Menocal, Maria Rosa, *The Ornament of the World: How Muslims, Jews, and Christians Created a Culture of Tolerance in Medieval Spain*, Boston: Little, Brown and Company (Inc.), 2002.

Merad, Ali, *Christian Hermit in an Islamic World: A Muslim's View of Charles de Foucauld*, trans., foreword and afterword Zoe Hersov, New York: Paulist Press, 1999.

Meyendorf, John, "Byzantine Views of Islam," *Dumbarton Oak Papers*, vol. 18 (1964), p. 113-132.

Moskwa, Jacek, *Prorok i polityk*, Warszawa: Świat Książki, 2003.

Müller, F. Max, *Introduction to the Science of Religion: Four Lectures Delivered at the Royal Institution in February and May 1870*, Varanasi: Bharata Manisha, 1972.

_____, *The Essential Max Müller: On Language, Mythology, and Religion*, ed. Jon R. Stone, New York: Palgrave MacMillan, 2002.

Murphy, Francis X., *The Papacy Today*, New York: McMillan Publishing Co., Inc., 1981.

Nagy, Stanisław, "Wprowadzenie do Deklaracji o stosunku Kościoła do religii niechrześcijańskich," in: Julian Groblicki and Eugeniusz Florkowski (eds.), *Sobór Watykański II: Konstytucje, dekrety, deklaracje: Tekst polski*, Poznań: Wydawnictwo Pallottinum, 1968.

Newman, Andrew J., *Safavid Iran: Rebirth of a Persian Empire*, London: I. B. Tauris, 2006.

O'Connor, Garry, *Universal Father: A Life of Pope John Paul II*, London: Bloomsbury Publishing Plc., 2006.

Parker, Michael, *Priest of the World's Destiny: John Paul II*, Milford, OH: Faith Publishing Company, 1995.

Penn, Michael, "Syriac Sources for the Study of Early Christian-Muslim Relations," *Islamochristiana*, vol. 29 (2003), p. 59-78.

Peters, E. F., *Jerusalem: The Holy City in the Eyes of Chroniclers, Visitors, Pilgrims, and Prophets from the Days of Abraham to the Beginnings of Modern Times*, Princeton, NJ: Princeton University Press, 1985.

Polk, William Roe, *Understanding Iraq: The Whole Sweep of Iraqi History, from Genghis Khan's Mongols to the Ottoman Turks to the British Mandate to the American Occupation*, New York: HarperCollins, 2005.

Prejs, Roland and Zdzisław Kijas (eds.), *Źródła Franciszkańskie: Pisma św. Franciszka, źródła biograficzne św. Franciszka, pisma świętej Klary i źródła biograficzne, teksty ustalające normy dla braci i sióstr od pokuty*, trans. Kajetan Ambrożbkiewicz, Bruno A. Gancarz [et al.], Kraków: Wydawnictwo OO. Franciszkanów "Bratni Zew," 2005.

Richards, John F., *The Mughal Empire*, Cambridge and New York: Cambridge University Press, 1992.

Riley-Smith, Jonathan, *The Oxford History of the Crusades*, New York: Oxford University Press, 2002.

Riyad, Umar, "Rashid Rida and a Danish Missionary: Alfred Nielsen and Three Fatwâs from *Al-Manâr*," *Islamochristiana*, vol. 28 (2002), p. 87-107.

Robinson, Neal, "Massignon, Vatican II and Islam as an Abrahamic Religion," *Islam and Christian-Muslim Relations*, vol. 2 (2) (December 1991), p. 182-205.

Rodinson, Maxime, *Muhammad*, trans. Anne Carter, New York: Pantheon Books, 1980.

Roggema, Barbara, *The Legend of Sergius Baḥīrā: Eastern Christian Apologetics and Apocalyptic in Response to Islam*, Leiden and Boston: E. J. Brill, 2009.

Ross, Alexander, *Pansebeia: or, a View of All Religions in the World with the Several Church-Governments from the Creation, till these Times: also, a Discovery of All Known Heresies, in all Ages and Places, and Choice Observations and Reflections throughout the Whole*, London: Printed for M. Gillyflower and W. Freeman, 1696.

Rossano, Pietro, "The Secretariat for Non-Christian Religions from the Beginnings to the Present Day: History, Ideas, Problems," *Bulletin*, vol. 14 (1979), no. 2-3, p. 88-109.

Rudnicka-Kassem, Dorota, "*Wojna nie jest rozwiązaniem: Dialog międzyreligijny Jana Pawła II jako program pokoju i stabilizacji na Bliskim Wschodzie*," in: Magdalena Lewicka and Czesław Łapicz (ed.), *Dialog chrześcijańsko-muzułmański: Historia i współczesność, zagrożenia i wyzwania*, Toruń: Wydawnictwo Naukowe Uniwersytetu Mikołaja Kopernika, 2011, s. 47-59.

Sage, Carleton M., *Paul Albar of Cordoba: Studies on His Life and Writings*, Washington, DC: Catholic University of America Press, 1943.

Sahas, Daniel J., *John of Damascus on Islam: The "Heresy of Ishmaelites,"* Leiden: E. J. Brill, 1972.

Sakowicz, Eugeniusz, *Dialog Kościoła z islamem według dokumentów soborowych i posoborowych (1963-1999)*, Warszawa: Wydawnictwo Uniwersytetu Kardynała Stefana Wyszyńskiego, 2000.

_____ (ed.), *Islam w dokumentach Kościoła i nauczaniu Jana Pawła II (1965-1996)*, Warszawa: Wydawnictwa Akademii Teologii Katolickiej, 1997.

_____, *Pryncypia dialogu Kościoła katolickiego z religiami Dalekiego Wschodu i Indii w świetle nauczania Soboru Watykańskiego II oraz dokumentów posoborowych*, Warszawa: Wydawnictwo Uniwersytetu Kardynała Stefana Wyszyńskiego, 2006.

_____ (ed.), *Jan Paweł II: Encyklopedia dialogu i ekumenizmu*, Radom: Polwen Polskie Wydawnictwo Encyklopedyczne, 2006.

_____, "Dialog międzyreligijny," in: Eugeniusz Sakowicz (ed.), *Jan Paweł II: Encyklopedia dialogu i ekumenizmu*, Radom: Polwen Polskie Wydawnictwo Encyklopedyczne, 2006, p. 129-161.

_____, "Islam and Christian-Muslim Relations in Poland," *Islamochristiana*, vol. 23 (1997), p. 139-146.

Sammak, M., "The Arab Muslim World after September the 11th," *Islamochristiana*, vol. 28 (2002), p. 1-11.

Savary, Claude (ed.), *Le Koran: Traduit de l'arabe, accompagné de notes: Précédé d'un Abrégé de la vie de Mahomet tiré des écrivains orientaux les plus estimés par M. Savary*, Paris: Garnier, 1951.

Savory, Roger M. and Dionisius A. Agius (eds.), *Logos Islamicos: Studia Islamica in Honorem Georgii Michaelis Wickens*, Toronto: Pontifical Institute for Medieval Studies, 1984.

Sawicka, Anna, *Drogi i bezdroża kultury katalońskiej*, Kraków: Księgarnia Akademicka, 2007.

Schimmel, Annemarie, *Islam: An Introduction*, Albany: State University of New York Press, 1992.

Schirmer, G., "John Harbison: Abraham," online: http://www.schirmer.com/default.aspx?TabId=2420&State_2874=2&workId_2874=24143, access: March 17, 2011.

Schwab, Orrin, *The Gulf Wars and the United States: Shaping the Twenty-First Century*, Westport, CT: Praeger Security International, 2009.

Serafian, Michael, *The Pilgrim: Pope Paul VI, The Council and The Church in a Time of Decision*, New York: Farrar and Straus, 1964.

Sfeir, Antoine, "Chrześcijanie na wschodzie," in: Elio Guerriero and Marco Impagliazzo (eds.), *Najnowsza historia Kościoła: katolicy i kościoły chrześcijańskie czasie pontyfikatu Jana Pawła II*, trans. Jacek Partyka, Kraków: Wydawnictwo M, 2006, p. 123-139.

Shahin, Emad Eldin, "Muḥammad Rashīd Riḍā's Perspectives on the West as Reflected in al-Manār," *Muslim World*, vol. 79 (April 1989), p. 113-132.

Shelledy, Robert B., "The Vatican's Role in Global Politics," *SAIS Review*, vol. 24 (Summer-Fall 2004), no. 2, p. 149-162.

Siddiqui, Ataullah, "Fifty Years of Christian-Muslim Relations: Exploring and Engaging in a New Relationship," *Islamochristiana*, vol. 26 (2000), p. 50-77.

Sherwin, Byron L. and Harold Kasimow (eds.), *John Paul II and Interreligious Dialogue*, Maryknoll, NY: Orbis Books, 1999.

Smith, Reginald Bosworth, *Mohammed and Mohammedanism: Lectures Delivered at the Royal Institution in Great Britain in February and March, 1874 by Reginald Bosworth Smith with an Appendix Containing Emanuel Deutsch's Article on "Islam,"* appendix Emanuel Deutsch, New York: Harper & Bross, 1875.

Southern, Richard William, *Western Views of Islam in the Middle Ages*, Cambridge: Harvard University Press, 1962.

Stein, Leonard, *The Balfour Declaration*, Jerusalem and London: Magnes Press, Hebrew University and Jewish Chronicle Publications, 1983.

Strathern, Paul, *Napoleon in Egypt: "The Greatest Glory,"* London: Jonathan Cape, 2007.

Streusand, Douglas E., *The Formation of the Mughal Empire*, Delhi and New York: Oxford University Press, 1989.

Swisher, Clayton E., *The Truth about Camp David: The Untold Story about the Collapse of the Middle East Peace Process*, New York: Nation Books, 2004.

Szulc, Tad, *Pope John Paul II: The Biography*, New York: Scribner, 1995.

Szymański, Wiesław Paweł, *Z mroku korzeni: O poezji Karola Wojtyły*, Kraków: Księgarnia Akademicka, 2005.

Tessier, Henri. "Chrétiens et Musulmans: Cinquante années pour approfondir leur relations," *Islamochristiana*, vol. 26 (2000), p. 33-50.

Tezcan, Baki, *The Second Ottoman Empire: Political and Social Transformation in the Early Modern World*, Cambridge and New York: Cambridge University Press, 2010.

The Attitude of the Church towards the Followers of Other Religions: Reflections and Orientations on Dialogue and Mission, Vatican: Polyglot Press, 1984.

The Meaning of the Holy Qur'ān, trans. and comment. 'Abdullah Yūsuf 'Alī, Beltsville, MD: Amana Publications, 1989.

"The Pope's Visit to the Sudan: A Survey through the Sudanese Press," *Encounter: Documents for Muslim-Christian Understanding*, no. 195-196 (1993), p. 3-27.

The Register of Pope Gregory VII 1073-1085: An English Translation, trans. H. E. J. Cowdrey, Oxford and, New York: Oxford University Press, 2002.

"The Synod for Lebanon, its Role and Importance for the Lebanese Society," online: http://www.opuslibani.org.lb/Lebanon/dos012.html, access: March, 27, 2011.

Tolan, John Victor (ed.), *Medieval Christian Perceptions of Islam: A Book of Essays*, New York: Garland Pub., 1994.

Tomko, Jozef. "Dialogue and Proclamation: Its Relation to the Encyclical *Redemptoris Missio*," *Bulletin*, vol. 26 (1991), no. 2, p. 204-209.

Troll, Christian W., "Mission and Dialogue: The Example of Islam," *Encounter: Documents for Muslim-Christian Understanding*, no. 189-190 (November-December 1992), p. 3-14.

_____, "Islam and Christianity Interacting in the Life of an Outstanding Christian Scholar of Islam: The Case of Louis Massignon (1883-1962)," *Islam and the Modern Age*, vol. 15 (August 1984), p. 157-166.

_____, "Christian-Muslim Relations in India: A Critical Survey," *Islamochristiana*, vol. 5 (1979), p. 119-149.

Urban, Józef, *Dialog międzyreligijny w posoborowych dokumentach Kościoła*, Opole: WT UO, 1999.

Urvoy, Dominique, "Ramon Lull et l'Islam," *Islamochristiana*, vol. 7 (1981), p. 127-146.

_____, "Soufisme et dialogue islamo-chretien," *Islamochristiana*, vol. 30 (2004), p. 55-64.

Vehlow, Katya, "The Swiss Reformers Zwingli, Bullinger and Bibliander and their Attitude to Islam (1520-1560)," *Islam and Christian-Muslim Relations*, vol. 6 (1995), p. 229-254.

Waardenburg, Jean Jacques (ed.), *Islam and Christianity: Mutual Perceptions since the Mid-20th Century*, Leuven: Peeters, 1998.

Warmińska, Katarzyna, *Tatarzy polscy: Tożsamość religijna i etniczna*, Kraków: Towarzystwo Autorów i Wydawców Prac Naukowych "Universitas", 1999.

Warrāq, Muḥammad ibn Hārūn, *Anti-Christian Polemic in Early Islam: Abū 'Īsá al-Warrāq's "Against the Trinity,"* ed. and trans. David Thomas, Cambridge and New York: Cambridge University Press, 1992.

Watt, William Montgomery, *The Influence of Islam on Medieval Europe*, Edinburgh: Edinburgh University Press, 1972.

Weigel, George, *Witness to Hope: The Biography of John Paul II (1920-2005)*, New York: Harper Perennial, 2005.

Wilde, Melissa J., *Vatican II: A Sociological Analysis of Religious Change*, Princeton, NJ: Princeton University Press, 2007.

Williams, George Hunston, *The Mind of John Paul II: Origins of His Thought and Action*, New York: The Seabury Press, 1981.

Waltz, James, "Muḥammad and the Muslims in St. Thomas Aquinas," *Muslim World*, vol. 66/2 (April 1976), p. 81-95.

_____, "The Significance of the Voluntary Martyrs of Ninth-Century Cordoba," *Muslim World*, vol. 60 (1970), p. 143-59.

Wolf, Kenneth Baxter, "Christian Views of Islam in Early Medieval Spain," in: John Victor Tolan (ed.), *Medieval Christian Perceptions to Islam: A Book of Essays*, New York: Garland Pub., 1994, p. 85-108.

Zapłata, Feliks, „Misyjny charakter Kościoła w konstytucji dogmatycznej *Lumen Gentium*," *Ateneum Kapłańskie*, vol. 58 (1966), no. 347, p. 326-336.

Zarębianka, Zofia and Jan Machniak (eds.), *Przestrzeń słowa: Twórczość literacka Karola Wojtyły – Jana Pawła II*, Kraków: Wydawnictwo św. Stanisława BM Archidiecezji Krakowskiej, 2006.

_____, *The Space of the Word: The Literary Activity of Karol Wojtyła – John Paul II*, Cracow: John Paul II Institute of Intercultural Dialogue, 2011.

Zebiri, Kate, *Muslims and Christians Face to Face*, Oxford and Rockport, MA: Oneworld Publications, 1997.

Zwemer, Samuel Marinus, *Raymund Lull: First Missionary to the Moslems*, Three Rivers: Diggory Press, 2006.

Żebrowski, Janusz, *Dzieje Syrii: Od czasów najdawniejszych do współczesności*, Warszawa: Dialog, 2006.

Additional literature:

Adler, Mortimer Jerome. *The Idea of Freedom: A Dialectical Examination of the Conception of Freedom,* Garden City, NY: Doubleday & Co., 1958.

Ajami, Fouad, *The Arab Predicament: Arab Political Thought and Practice Since 1967*, Cambridge: Cambridge University Press, 1992.

Anawati, Georges C., *Saint Thomas d'Aquin, Avicenne et le dialogue islamo-chrétien*, Cairo: Istituto italiano di cultura per la R.A.E., 1975.

Anees, Munawar Ahmad, Syed Z. Abedin and Ziauddin Sardar, *Christian-Muslim Relations: Yesterday, Today, Tomorrow*, London: Grey Seal Books, 1991.

Arinze, Francis, "Dialogue and Proclamation: Two Aspects of the Evangelizing Mission of the Church," *Bulletin*, vol. 26 (1991), no. 2, p. 201-203.

_____, "Christian-Muslim Relations in the 21st Century," *Pro Dialogo*, vol. 33 (1998), no. 1, p. 81-90.

_____, "The Way Ahead for Muslims and Christians," *Pro Dialogo*, vol. 31 (1996), no. 1, p. 26-32.

Arkoun, Mohammed, *Humanisme et islam: combats et propositions*, Paris: Vrin, 2005.
_____, "Réflexions d'un Musulman sur le 'Nouveau Catéchisme'," *Islamo-christiana*, vol. 19 (1993), p. 43-54.
Armstrong, Karen, *A History of God: The 4000-Year Quest of Judaism, Christianity and Islam*, New York: Ballantine Books, 1993.
_____, *Muhammad: A Western Attempt to Understand Islam*, London: Victor Gollancz, 1991.
_____, *The Battle for God*, New York: Alfred A. Knopf, 2000.
Barber, Benjamin R., *Fear's Empire: War, Terrorism, and Democracy*, New York and London: W.W. Norton & Co., 2003.
_____, *Jihad vs. McWorld*. New York: Ballantine Books, 1996.
Baron, Arkadiusz and Henryk Pietras (eds.), *Dokumenty soborów powszechnych: Tekst łaciński, grecki, arabski, ormiański, polski*, vol. 3: *1414-1445: Konstancja, Bazylea–Ferrara–Florencja–Rzym*, Kraków: Wydawnictwo WAM, 2003.
Bartoś, Tadeusz, *Jan Paweł II: Analiza krytyczna*, Warszawa: Wydawnictwo „Sic!", 2008.
Baum, Gregory, "The Impact of John Paul's Social Teaching," *Ecumenism* 79 (September 1985), p. 23-24.
Bejze, Bohdan (ed.), *W nurcie zagadnień posoborowych*, vol. 3, Warszawa: Wydawnictwo SS. Loretanek-Benedyktynek, 1969.
Benestad, J. Brian, "The Political Vision of John Paul II: Justice through Faith and Culture," *Communio*, vol. 8 (Spring 1981), p. 3-19.
Bernstein, Carl and Marco Politi, *His Holiness: John Paul II and the Hidden History of Our Time*, New York: Doubleday, 1996.
Bin Talal, El Hassan, *Christianity in the Arab World*, London: Arabesque Int., 1995.
Böckenförde, Ernst W., "Nowy sposób politycznego zaangażowania Kościoła. O 'teologii politycznej' Jana Pawła II," *Znak*, vol. 37 (1985), no. 3, p. 3-24.
Boisard, Marcel A., "Le Saint-Siège et la Palestine," *Relations Internationales*, vol. 28 (1981), p. 443-455.
Borutka Tadeusz, "Problematyka pokoju w nauczaniu Jana Pawła II," *Polonia Sacra*, vol. 4 (2000), no. 6, p. 35-48.
Boullata, Issa J., *Trends and Issues in Contemporary Arab Thought*, Albany, NY: State University of New York Press, 1990.
Buchała, Rudolf, "Stolica Apostolska a pokój międzynarodowy," *Chrześcijanin w Świecie*, vol. 10 (1978), no. 9, p. 1-18.
Burke, Jeffrey C., "Cooperation Between Christians and Muslims." *Encounter: Documents for Muslim-Christian Understanding*, no. 213 (March 1995), p. 3-28.
_____., "Christian-Muslim Encounters: Beyond Mere Recognition of Commonalities and Differences,"*Critical Review of Books in Religion*,vol. 9 (1996), p. 1-18.
Buttiglione, Rocco, *Karol Wojtyła: The Thought of the Man Who Became Pope John Paul II*, trans. Paolo Guietti and Francesca Murphy, foreword Michael Novak, Grand Rapids, MI: William B. Eerdmans Publishing Company, 1997.
Calvert, John, *Sayyid Qutb and the Origins of Radical Islamism*, New York: Columbia University Press, 2010.
Cardini, Franco., *Europa a Islam: Historia nieporozumienia*, trans. Bogumiła Bielańska, Kraków: Wydawnictwo Uniwersytetu Jagiellońskiego, 2006.
Carroll, B. Jill, *A Dialogue of Civilizations. Gülen's Islamic Ideals and Humanistic Discourse*, Somerset, NJ: the Light, Inc. and The Güllen Institute, 2007.

Casaroli, Agostino, "Stolica Apostolska i wspólnota międzynarodowa," *Chrześcijanin w Świecie*, vol. 7 (1975), no. 4, p. 30-45.

Chrostowski, Waldemar, *Rozmowy o dialogu*, Warszawa: Oficyna Wydawnicza „Vocatio", 1996.

Coleman, John A. (ed.), *One Hundred Years of Catholic Social Thought: Celebration and Challenge*, Maryknoll, NY: Orbis Books, 1991.

Cragg, Kenneth, *Christianity in World Perspective*, New York: Oxford University Press, 1968.

_____, *Christian-Muslim Inter-Text Now: From Anathemata to Theme*, London: Melisende, 2008,

Craig, M., *Man From a Far Country: A Portrait of Pope John Paul II*, London: Hodder and Stoughton, 1979.

Danecki, Janusz, *Arabowie*, Warszawa: Państwowy Instytut Wydawniczy, 2001.

_____, "Social and Political Functions of Islam," *Studies on the Developing Countries*, vol. 1 (1988), p.7-19.

Czarnecki Radosław S., "Czterdziestolecie encykliki 'Pacem in terris'," *Dziś*, vol. 14 (2003), no. 10, p. 132-134.

_____, "Projekcja osoby ludzkiej w encyklice Jana XXIII 'Pacem in terris'," *Przegląd Religioznawczy*, (2003), no. 1, p. 17-24.

Donohue, John J. and Christian W. Troll (eds.), *Faith, Power, and Violence: Muslims and Christians in a Plural Society, Past and Present*, Roma: Pontificio Istituto Orientale, 1998.

Dulles, Avery, *The Splendour of Faith: The Theological Vision of Pope John Paul II*, New York: The Crossroad Publishing Company, 2003.

Dupuis, Jacques, "Forms of Inter-religious Dialogue," *Bulletin*, vol. 20 (1985), no. 2, p. 164-171.

Dziedzic, Jan (ed.), *Religia we współczesnej Europie*, Kraków: Wydawnictwo Papieskiej Akademii Teologicznej w Krakowie, 2008.

Dziekan, Marek M. and Izabela Kończak (ed.), *Arabowie, islam, świat*, Łódź: Ibidem, 2007.

El-Hage, Youssef Kamal, "The Importance of Self-Criticism and Fighting the Other's Stereotyping in Christian-Muslim Relations: A Catholic Perspective," *Islamochristiana*, vol. 30 (2004), p. 97-110.

Esposito, John L. and Dalia Mogahed, *Who Speaks for Islam? What a Billion Muslims Really Think*, New York: Gallup Press, 2007.

_____ and John Obert Voll, *Islam and Democracy*, New York: Oxford University Press, 1996.

Evans, Graham and Jeffrey Newnham, *The Penguin Dictionary of International Relations*, London: Penguin Books, 1998.

Fallaci, Oriana, *Wywiad z sobą samą: Apokalipsa*, trans. Joanna Wajs, Warszawa: Wydawnictwo Cyklady, 2005.

Fitzgerald, Michael L., "Mission and Dialogue: Reflections in the Light of Assisi 1986," *Bulletin*, vol. 23 (1988), no. 2, p. 113-120.

_____, "Other Religions in the Catechism of the Catholic Church," *Pro Dialogo*, vol. 29 (1994), no. 1, p. 165-177.

Frossard, André, *Portrait of John Paul II*, San Francisco: Ignatius Press, 1990.

_____ and Pope John Paul II, *"Be Not Afraid!" John Paul II Speaks Out on His Life, His Beliefs, and His Inspiring Vision for Humanity*, New York: St. Martin's Press, 1984.

Gellner, Ernest, *Postmodernizm, Rozum i Religia*, trans. Maciej Kowalczuk, Warszawa: Państwowy Instytut Wydawniczy, 1992.

Górska, Elżbieta, "Bulla unii z Koptami – przekład i krytyczne opracowanie tekstów Soboru Florenckiego," in: Arkadiusz Baron and Henryk Pietras (eds.), *Dokumenty soborów powszechnych: Tekst łaciński, grecki, arabski, ormiański, polski*, vol. 3: *1414-1445: Konstancja, Bazylea–Ferrara–Florencja–Rzym*, Kraków: Wydawnictwo WAM, 2003, p. 571-619.

Gorgoń, Katarzyna, "Św. Franciszek z Asyżu prekursorem dialogu chrześcijan z islamem," *W nurcie franciszkańskim*, vol. 16 (2007), p. 137-149.

Griffiths, Martin (ed.), *Encyclopedia of International Relations and Global Politics*, London: Routledge, 2005.

_____ (ed.), *International Relations Theory for the Twenty-First Century: An Introduction*, London and New York: Routledge, 2007.

Haddad, Yvonne Yazbeck, *Contemporary Islam and the Challenge of History*, Albany: State University of New York Press, 1982.

Hallaq, Wael B., *An Introduction to Islamic Law*, Cambridge and New York: Cambridge University Press, 2009.

Halliday, Fred, *Islam and the Myth of Confrontation: Religion and Politics in the Middle East*, London and New York: I. B. Tauris & Co. Ltd., 1996.

Hanson, Eric O., *Religion and Politics in the International System Today*, Cambridge and New York: Cambridge University Press, 2006.

Hawkins, David R., *Power versus Force: An Anatomy of Consciousness, the Hidden Determinants of Human Behavior*, West Sedona, AZ: Veritas Publishing, 2004.

Hélou, Nelly, "Le pèlerinage de réconciliation," *La Revue du Liban*, no. 3792 (May 12-19, 2001), p. 12-18.

Herrmann, Horst, *Jan Paweł II złapany za słowo: Krytyczna odpowiedź na książkę Papieża*, trans. Robert Stiller, Gdańsk: Uraeus, 1995.

Höffner, Józef, "Problem pokoju w świetle wiary chrześcijańskiej," *Chrześcijanin w Świecie*, vol. 16 (1984), no. 1, p. 62-77.

Huntington, Samuel P., *The Clash of Civilizations and the Remaking of World Order*, New York: Simon & Schuster, 1996.

Jackowski, Antoni and Izabela Sołjan (ed.), *Leksykon Pielgrzymek Jana Pawła II*, Kraków: Wydawnictwo WAM, 2005.

Jadot, Jean L., "The Growth in Roman Catholic Commitment to Interreligious Dialogue since Vatican II," *Bulletin*, vol. 18 (1983), no. 3, p. 205-220.

Jérusalem: Le Moniteur Diocésain du Patriarcat Latin de Jérusalem, vol. 1-2 (Janvier-Février 1964).

Jędraszewski, Marek, *Wybrać większą wolność: Karol Wojtyła o człowieku*, Poznań: Księgarnia św. Wojciecha, 2004.

Kelly, John Norman Davidson, *The Oxford Dictionary of Popes*, Oxford: Oxford University Press, 1996.

Khoury, Adel Theodore (ed.), *Leksykon podstawowych pojęć religijnych: judaizm, chrześcijaństwo, islam*, trans. Józef Marzęcki, Warszawa: Instytut Wydawniczy PAX, 1998.

Kłoczowski, Jan Andrzej, *Filozofia dialogu*, Poznań: Wydawnictwo Polskiej Prowincji Dominikanów „W drodze", 2005.

Kondziela, Joachim, *Badania nad pokojem. Teoria i jej zastosowanie*, Warszawa: Ośrodek Dokumentacji i Studiów Społecznych, 1974.

_____, *Pokój w nauce Kościoła: Pius XII – Jan Paweł II*, Lublin: Redakcja Wydawnictw KUL, 1992.

_____, "Prakseologia pokoju," *Chrześcijanin w Świecie*, vol. 5 (1973), no. 6, p. 16-26.

_____, "The Social Dimension of Preparation for Peace," *Dialectics and Humanism*, vol. 10 (1983), no. 4, p. 47-54.

_____, "Rozwój nauki społecznej Kościoła na temat pokoju od Piusa XII do Jana Pawła II," *Życie Katolickie*, vol. 4 (1985), no. 6, p. 13-36.

Korporowicz, Leszek, "Komunikacja międzykulturowa jako transgresja," in: Tadeusz Paleczny and Monika Banaś (ed.), *Dialog na pograniczach kultur i cywilizacji*, Kraków: Wydawnictwo Uniwersytetu Jagiellońskiego, 2009, p. 75-84.

_____, *Socjologia kulturowa. Kontynuacje i poszukiwania*. Kraków: Wydawnictwo Uniwersytetu Jagiellońskiego, 2011.

Kościelniak, Krzysztof, (ed.), *Change and Stability: State, Religion and Politics in the Middle East and North Africa*, Kraków: Wydawnictwo UNUM 2010.

_____, "Change of Coptic Identity," in: Krzysztof Kościelniak (ed.), *Change and Stability: State, Religion and Politics in the Middle East and North Africa*, Kraków: Wydawnictwo UNUM, 2010, p. 77-92.

_____, "Dialog chrześcijańsko-muzułmański w kontekście ONZ-owskiej 'Deklaracji Praw Człowieka'," in: Jan Dziedzic (ed.), *Religia we współczesnej Europie*, Kraków: Wydawnictwo Papieskiej Akademii Teologicznej w Krakowie, 2008, 97-124.

_____, *Dżihad: Święta wojna w islamie: Związek religii z państwem, islam a demokracja, chrześcijanie w krajach muzułmańskich*, Kraków: Wydawnictwo M, 2002.

_____, "Świadomość ograniczeń kulturowych wśród muzułmanów jako źródło akulturacji muzułmańsko-chrześcijańskiej," in: Andrzej Pankowicz and Stefan Bielański (ed.), *Dialog i akulturacja: Judaizm, chrześcijaństwo i islam*, Kraków: Wydawnictwo Uniwersytetu Jagiellońskiego, 2007, p. 75-88.

_____, *Tradycja muzułmańska na tle akulturacji chrześcijańsko-islamskiej od VII do X wieku. Geneza, historia i znaczenie zapożyczeń nowotestamentowych w hadisach*, Kraków: Wydawnictwo UNUM, 2001.

_____, *XX wieków chrześcijaństwa w kulturze arabskiej, t. 1: Arabia starożytna: Chrześcijaństwo w Arabii do Mahometa*, Kraków: Wydawnictwo UNUM, 2000.

Kowalczyk, Stanisław, "Prawda jako wartość w nauczaniu Jana Pawła II," *Ateneum Kapłańskie*, vol. 129 (1997), p. 55-65.

_____, "Wolność – naturą, powołaniem i prawem człowieka," *Chrześcijanin w Świecie*, vol. 10 (1978), no. 1, s. 47-62.

Krucina, Jan, "Współrzędne między dobrem wspólnym społeczności międzynarodowej a pokojem," *Chrześcijanin w Świecie*, vol. 11 (1979), no. 1, p. 30-45.

_____, "'Gaudium et spes' – dokument jeszcze do odczytania," *Ateneum Kapłańskie*, vol. 77 (1986), no. 1, p. 36-49.

Krys, Roman, "Collective Political Human Rights According to Pope John Paul II," *Revue Belge de Droit International*, vol. 1 (1981).

_____, "Individual Human Rights According to Pope John Paul II," *Revue de Droit International de Sciences Diplomatiques et Politiques*, vol. 3 (1984).

Kukułka, Józef, "Pojęcie i istota międzynarodowego ładu pokojowego," *Stosunki Międzynarodowe*, vol. 8 (1989), p. 13-30.

Lagarde, Michel, "La paternité de Dieu dans l'Islam," *Pro Dialogo*, vol. 34 (1999), no. 3, p. 326-331.

Laskowski, Jerzy, "Sprawiedliwość przejawem wolności," *Chrześcijanin w Świecie*, vol. 20 (1988), no. 1, p. 1-8.

Lebioda, Dariusz Tomasz, *Tajemica papieża*, Bydgoszcz: Instytut Wydawniczy „Świadectwo", 1997.

Lecomte, Bernard, *Jean-Paul II*, Paris: Editions Gallimard, 2003.

Lewandowski, Jerzy (ed.), *Problematyka pokoju u papieży Jana XXIII i Jana Pawła II: Sympozjum zorganizowane przez Katedrę Teologii Wydziału Teologicznego Uniwersytetu Kardynała Stefana Wyszyńskiego, Warszawa, 15 października 2003 r.*, Ząbki: Apostolicum, 2004.

Lewicka, Magdalena and Czesław Łapicz (ed.), *Dialog chrześcijańsko-muzułmański: Historia i współczesność, zagrożenia i wyzwania*, Toruń: Wydawnictwo Naukowe Uniwersytetu Mikołaja Kopernika, 2011.

Lewis, Bernard, *Cultures in Conflict: Christians, Muslims, and Jews in the Age of Discovery*, New York: Oxford University Press, 1995.

_____, *What Went Wrong?: Western Impact and Middle Eastern Response*, Oxford and New York: Oxford University Press, 2002.

Łoziński, Krzysztof, "Prawa człowieka a pokój w nauczaniu społecznym Kościoła," *Chrześcijanin w Świecie*, vol. 15 (1983), no. 4, p. 1-15.

Majka, Józef, "Zagadnienie wojny i pokoju w nauce Soboru Watykańskiego II," in: Bohdan Bejze (ed.) *W nurcie zagadnień posoborowych*, vol. 3, Warszawa: Wydawnictwo SS. Loretanek-Benedyktynek, 1969, p. 143-158.

Marchione, Margherita, *Pope Pius XII: Architect for Peace*, New York: Paulist Press, 2000.

Massaro, Thomas and Thomas A. Shannon, *Catholic Perspectives on Peace and War*, Lanham, MD: Rowman & Littlefield Publishers, 2003.

Michel, Thomas, "Islamo-Christian Dialogue: Reflections on the Recent Teaching of the Church," *Bulletin*, vol. 20 (1985), no. 2, p. 172-193.

_____, "Pope John Paul II's Teaching about Islam in his Addresses to Muslims," *Bulletin*, vol. 21 (1986), no. 2, p. 182-191.

_____, "25 Years of Letters to Muslims for *Id al-Fitr*," *Bulletin*, vol. 28 (1993), no. 3, p. 300-302.

Morawski, Dominik, "Sztuka współżycia, czyli edukacja do pokoju," *Więź*, vol. 45 (2003), no. 1, p. 67-69.

Mrozek-Dumanowska, Anna and Jerzy Zdanowski, *Islam a globalizacja*, Warszawa: Wydawnictwo Naukowe ASKON, 2005.

Myers, Eugene A., *Arabic Thought and the Western World in the Golden Age of Islam*, New York: Ungar, 1964.

Napiórkowski, Andrzej, "Wiara broniąca prawdy," *Homo Dei*, vol. 69 (1999), no. 2, p. 17-26.

Nasr, Seyyed Hossein, *The Heart of Islam: Enduring Values for Humanity*, San Francisco: Harper San Francisco, 2002.

Nisbett, Richard E., *The Geography of Thought: How Asians and Westerners Think Differently – and Why*, New York and London: Free Press, 2003.

Neuhaus, Richard John, "The Mind of the Most Powerful Man in the World: John Paul II: Philosopher and Pope," *Worldview*, no. 24 (September 1981), p. 11-13.

Paleczny, Tadeusz and Monika Banaś (ed.), *Dialog na pograniczach kultur i cywilizacji*, Kraków: Wydawnictwo Uniwersytetu Jagiellońskiego, 2009.

Pankowicz, Andrzej and Stefan Bielański (ed.), *Dialog i akulturacja: Judaizm, chrześcijaństwo i islam*, Kraków: Wydawnictwo Uniwersytetu Jagiellońskiego, 2007.

Pegis, Anton C. (ed.), *Basic Writings of Saint Thomas*, vol. 1, New York: Random House, 1944.

Poniewierski, Janusz, *Pontyfikat: 25 lat*, foreword Józef Tischner, Kraków: Wydawnictwo Znak, 2003.

Quade, Quentin L. (ed.), *The Pope and Revolution: John Paul II Confronts Liberation Theology*, Washington, DC: Ethics and Public Policy Center, 1982.

Rahman, Fazlur, *Islam and Modernity: Transformation of an Intellectual Tradition*, Chicago and London: The University of Chicago Press, 1982.

Rahner, Karl, "Christianity and the Non-Christian Religions," *Theological Investigations*, vol. 5 (1966), p. 115-134.

_____, *Visions and Prophecies*, London: Burns & Oates, 1966.

Ramadan, Tariq, *Islam, the West, and the Challenges of Modernity*, Leicester: The Islamic Foundation, 2001.

_____, *To Be a European Muslim*, Leicester: The Islamic Foundation, 1999.

Ratzinger, Joseph, *"L'Unique alliance" de Dieu et le pluralisme des religions*, Saint-Maur: Parole et Silence, 1999.

_____, *Truth and Tolerance: Christian Belief and World Religions*, San Francisco: Ignatius Press, 2004.

Rico, Herminio, *John Paul II and the Legacy of Dignitatis Humanae*, Washington, DC: Georgetown University Press, 2002.

Roberson, Ronald, *The Eastern Christian Churches: A Brief Survey*, Rome: Pontificio Instituto Orientale, 1999.

Rossano, Pietro, "The Major Documents of the Catholic Church Regarding the Muslims," *Bulletin*, vol. 16 (1981), no. 3, p. 204-215.

Rudnicka-Kassem, Dorota, "Chrześcijaństwo – islam: koegzystencja, polemika, dialog," *Politeja*, vol. 1 (2004), p. 45-57.

_____, "John Paul II and His Dialogue with the Followers of Islam," *Acta Asiatica Varsoviensia*, vol. 18 (2005), p. 79-90.

_____, "Striving for a Feasible Solution: The Holy See's Position on the Issue of Jerusalem and the Status of the Holy Places," *Hemispheres, Studies in Cultures and Societies*, vol. 22 (2007), p. 1-22.

_____, "*We travel on the same boat*: The Role of John Paul II in the Development of Christian-Muslim Dialogue," in: Krzysztof Kościelniak (ed.), *Change and Stability: State, Religion and Politics in the Contemporary Middle East and North Africa*, Kraków: Wydawnictwo UNUM, 2010, p. 152-162.

Sakowicz, Eugeniusz, "Chrześcijaństwo wobec islamu," *Homo Dei*, vol. 68 (1998), no. 1, p. 45-49.

_____, "Duch Święty tajemniczo obecny w religiach i kulturach niechrześcijańskich," *Collectanea Theologica*, vol. 66 (1996), no. 4, p. 184-189.

_____, *Rozmowy o islamie i dialogu*, foreword Jacek Salij, Lublin: Polihymnia, 2007.

_____, and Nidal Abu Tabak, "Pytania chrześcijanina do muzułmanina – odpowiedzi muzułmanina na pytania chrześcijanina," *Ateneum Kapłańskie*, vol. 151 (2008), no. 2 (597), p. 280-284.

Schimmel, Annemarie, *Mystical Dimensions of Islam*, Chapel Hill: The University of North Carolina Press, 1975.

Schmitz, Kenneth L., *At the Center of the Human Drama: The Philosophical Anthropology of Karol Wojtyla / Pope John Paul II*, Washington, DC: Catholic University of America Press, 1993.

Silvestrini, Agostino, "Stolica Apostolska a wolność religijna," *Chrześcijanin w Świecie*, vol. 10 (1978), no. 2, p. 93-99.

Smith, Wilfred Cantwell, *What is Scripture?: A Comparative Approach*, Minneapolis: Fortress Press, 1993.

Stachowski, Zbigniew, "Polityka pokoju Jana Pawła II," *Studia Religioznawcze*, vol. 17 (1983), p. 153-171.

_____, "Miejsce pokoju w encyklice *'Ecclesiam suam'*," *Człowiek i Światopogląd*, no. 3, (1985), p. 74-85.

Steigerwald, Diane, *L'Islâm: Les valeurs communes au judéo-christianisme*, Montréal: Médiaspaul, 1999.

_____, "La tolérance de l'islam face au polythéisme et aux autres religions motothéistes?," *Cahiers de Etudes anciennes*, vol. 33 (1997), p. 23-30.

Symonides, Janusz, "Koncepcja 'kultury pokoju'," *Stosunki Międzynarodowe*, vol. 23-24 (2001), no 1-2, p. 23-38.

Szlachta, Bogdan, "Jan Paweł II a prawo," *Politeja*, vol. 1 (2004), p. 315-330.

Taylor, Charles, *Varieties of Religion Today: William James Revisited*, Cambridge, MA and London: Harvard University Press, 2002.

_____, *A Secular Age*, Cambridge, Mass.: Belknap Press of Harvard University Press, 2007.

Tischner, Józef, *Myślenie według wartości*, Kraków: Wydawnictwo Znak, 1982.

_____, *O człowieku: Wybór pism filozoficznych*, Wrocław: Zakład Narodowy im. Ossolińskich, 2003.

_____, "W poszukiwaniu istoty wolności," *Znak*, vol. 22 (1970), no. 7-8, p. 821-838.

Tkaczuk, Wacław, "Jan Paweł II i sprawa pokoju," *Za i Przeciw*, vol. 24 (1980), no. 1, p. 4.

Tworuschka, Udo, *Religie świata w dialogu*, trans. Adam Wąs, Poznań: Wydawnictwo Świętego Wojciecha, 2010.

Turgay, A. Üner, Developing a Dialogue with Islamic Communities in South and Southeast Asia: *Monograph*, Ottawa: DFAIT, 2003.

Waardenburg, Jean Jacques (ed.), *Muslim Perceptions of Other Religions: A Historical Survey*, New York: Oxford University Press, 1999.

Watt, William Montgomery, "Muslim and Christians after the Gulf War," *Islamochristiana*, vol. 17 (1991), p. 35-51.

Wieczorek, Adam (ed.), *Apostoł pokoju: Podróże apostolskie Jana Pawła II*, Warszawa: PAX, 1987.

Wiliński, Kazimierz (ed.), *Pluralizm i tolerancja*, Lublin: Wydawnictwo Uniwersytetu Marii Curie Skłodowskiej, 1998.

Willey, David, *God's Politician: Pope John Paul II, the Catholic Church, and the New World Order*, New York: St. Martin's Press, 1992.

Zabkar, Giuseppe, "Stolica Apostolska a wolność religijna (Przemówienie wygłoszone 6 III 1973 r. w Helsinkach)," *Chrześcijanin w Świecie*, no. 5 (1973), p. 69-73.

Zapłata, Feliks „Dekret *Ad gentes* o działalności misyjnej Kościoła," *Homo Dei*, vol. 35 (1966), no. 4, p. 205-213.

Zdanowski, Jerzy, *Historia Arabii Wschodniej*, Wrocław: Zakład Narodowy im. Ossolińskich – Wydawnictwo, 2004,

_____, *Historia Bliskiego Wschodu w XX wieku*, Wrocław: Zakład Narodowy im. Ossolińskich – Wydawnictwo, 2010.

_____, *Współczesna muzułmańska myśl społeczno-polityczna: Nurt Braci Muzułmanów*, Warszawa: Wydawnictwo Naukowe ASKON, 2009.

Zięba, Maciej, *Niezwykły pontyfikat*, rozmawia Adam Pawłowicz, Kraków: Wydawnictwo Znak, 1997.

Zięba Ryszard, "Pojęcie i istota bezpieczeństwa państwa w stosunkach międzynarodowych," *Sprawy Międzynarodowe*, no. 10 (1989), p. 49-70.

Zimoń, Henryk (ed.), *Religia w świecie współczesnym: Zarys problematyki religiologicznej*, Lublin: Towarzystwo Naukowe KUL, 2000.

Zwoliński, Andrzej (ed.), *Jan Paweł II: Encyklopedia Nauczania Społecznego*, Radom: Polskie Wydawnictwo Encyklopedyczne, 2005.

Żeleźnik, Tadeusz, "Pokój na fundamentach etycznych," *Kultura-Oświata-Nauka*, no. 5-6 (1987), p. 51-57.

Żuk-Łapińska, Ludmiła, *Problem tolerancji*, Warszawa: Wydawnictwa Uniwersytetu Warszawskiego, 1991.

Index

Names

Index

Places

The books published in the *Societas* Series (Bogdan Szlachta, Editor) are:

1. Grzybek Dariusz, *Nauka czy ideologia. Biografia intelektualna Adama Krzyżanowskiego*, 2005.
2. Drzonek Maciej, *Między integracją a europeizacją. Kościół katolicki w Polsce wobec Unii Europejskiej w latach 1997-2003*, 2006.
3. Chmieliński Maciej, *Max Stirner. Jednostka, społeczeństwo, państwo*, 2006.
4. Nieć Mateusz, *Rozważania o pojęciu polityki w kręgu kultury attyckiej. Studium z historii polityki i myśli politycznej*, 2006.
5. Sokołów Florian, *Nahum Sokołów. Życie i legenda*, oprac. Andrzej A. Zięba, 2006.
6. Porębski Leszek, *Między przemocą a godnością. Teoria polityczna Harolda D. Laswella*, 2007.
7. Mazur Grzegorz, *Życie polityczne polskiego Lwowa 1918-1939*, 2007.
8. Węc Janusz Józef, *Spór o kształt instytucjonalny Wspólnot Europejskich i Unii Europejskiej 1950-2005. Między ideą ponadnarodowości a współpracą międzyrządową. Analiza politologiczna*, 2006.
9. Karas Marcin, *Integryzm Bractwa Kapłańskiego św. Piusa X. Historia i doktryna rzymskokatolickiego ruchu tradycjonalistycznego*, 2008.
10. *European Ideas on Tolerance*, red. Guido Naschert, Marcin Rebes, 2009.
11. Gacek Łukasz, *Chińskie elity polityczne w XX wieku*, 2009.
12. Zemanek Bogdan S., *Tajwańska tożsamość narodowa w publicystyce politycznej*, 2009.
13. Lencznarowicz Jan, *Jałta. W kręgu mitów założycielskich polskiej emigracji politycznej 1944-1956*, 2009.
14. Grabowski Andrzej, *Prawnicze pojęcie obowiązywania prawa stanowionego. Krytyka niepozytywistycznej koncepcji prawa*, 2009.
15. Kich-Masłej Olga, *Ukraina w opinii elit Krakowa końca XIX – pierwszej połowy XX wieku*, 2009.
16. Citkowska-Kimla Anna, *Romantyzm polityczny w Niemczech. Reprezentanci, idee, model*, 2010.
17. Mikuli Piotr, *Sądy a parlament w ustrojach Australii, Kanady i Nowej Zelandii (na tle rozwiązań brytyjskich)*, 2010.
18. Kubicki Paweł, *Miasto w sieci znaczeń. Kraków i jego tożsamości*, 2010.
19. Żurawski Jakub, *Internet jako współczesny środek elektronicznej komunikacji wyborczej i jego zastosowanie w polskich kampaniach parlamentarnych*, 2010.
20. *Polscy eurodeputowani 2004-2009. Uwarunkowania działania i ocena skuteczności*, red. K. Szczerski, 2010.
21. Bojko Krzysztof, *Stosunki dyplomatyczne Moskwy z Europą Zachodnią w czasach Iwana III*, 2010.
22. *Studia nad wielokulturowością*, red. Dorota Pietrzyk-Reeves, Małgorzata Kułakowska, Elżbieta Żak, 2010.
23. Bartnik Anna, *Emigracja latynoska w USA po II wojnie światowej na przykładzie Portorykańczyków, Meksykanów i Kubańczyków*, 2010.
24. *Transformacje w Ameryce Łacińskiej*, red. Adam Walaszek, Aleksandra Giera, 2011.
25. Praszałowicz Dorota, *Polacy w Berlinie. Strumienie migracyjne i społeczności imigrantów. Przegląd badań*, 2010.
26. Głogowski Aleksander, *Pakistan. Historia i współczesność*, 2011.

27. Brążkiewicz Bartłomiej, *Choroba psychiczna w literaturze i kulturze rosyjskiej*, 2011.
28. Bojenko-Izdebska Ewa, *Przemiany w Niemczech Wschodnich 1989-2010. Polityczne aspekty transformacji*, 2011.
29. Kołodziej Jacek, *Wartości polityczne. Rozpoznanie, rozumienie, komunikowanie*, 2011.
30. Jach Anna, *Rosja 1991-1993. Walka o kształt ustrojowy państwa*, 2011.
31. Matyasik Michał, *Realizacja wolności wypowiedzi na podstawie przepisów i praktyki w USA*, 2011.
32. Dariusz Grzybek, *Polityczne konsekwencje idei ekonomicznych w myśli polskiej 1869--1939*, 2012.
33. Rafał Woźnica, *Bułgarska polityka wewnętrzna a proces integracji z Unią Europejską*, 2012.
34. Ślufińska Monika, *Radykałowie francuscy. Koncepcje i działalność polityczna w XX wieku*, 2012.
35. Fyderek Łukasz, *Pretorianie i technokraci w reżimie politycznym Syrii*, 2012.
36. Węc Janusz Józef, *Traktat lizboński. Polityczne aspekty reformy ustrojowej Unii Europejskiej w latach 2007-2009*, 2011.